Your future is now...

Prepare the right way...

Advance your career...

Get **REA**dy for the ASVAB
with REA's all-new test prep.

The Best Test Preparation for the

ASVAB

Armed Services Vocational Aptitude Battery

6th EDITION

Staff of Research & Education Association

with new material by
Julian Paul Keenan, Ph.D.

Research & Education Association
Visit our website at
www.rea.com

Research & Education Association
61 Ethel Road West
Piscataway, New Jersey 08854
e-mail: info@rea.com

The Best Test Preparation for the
ASVAB – *Armed Services Vocational Aptitude Battery*

Printed in the United States of America

Library of Congress Control Number 2005927764

International Standard Book Number 0-7386-0063-6

CONTENTS

PRACTICE TESTS

ABOUT RESEARCH & EDUCATION ASSOCIATION

Founded in 1959, Research & Education Association (REA) is dedicated to publishing the finest and most effective educational materials—including software, study guides, and test preps—for students in middle school, high school, college, graduate school, and beyond.

REA's Test Preparation series includes test preps for all academic levels in almost all disciplines. Research & Education Association publishes test preps for students who have not yet entered high school, as well as high school students preparing to enter college.

For college students seeking advanced degrees, REA publishes test preps for many major graduate school admission examinations in a wide variety of disciplines, including engineering, law, and medicine. Students at every level, in every field, with every ambition can find what they are looking for among REA's publications.

We invite you to visit us at *www.rea.com* to find out how "REA is making the world smarter."

ACKNOWLEDGMENTS

Special gratitude is extended to W. Alan Nicewander, Ph.D., head of the U.S. Department of Defense Personnel Testing Division, for providing insight into the new facets of the ASVAB battery.

We would like to thank Larry B. Kling, Vice President, Editorial Services, for supervising development; Pam Weston, Vice President, Publishing, for setting the quality standards for production integrity and managing the publication to completion; Jeanne Audino, Senior Editor, for preflight editorial review; Diane Goldschmidt, Associate Editor, for post-production quality assurance; Stacey Farkas, Senior Editor, for editorial contributions; and Christine Saul, Senior Graphic Designer, for designing our cover. Our indexer was Terry Casey.

ASVAB

Armed Services Vocational Aptitude Battery

Study Schedule

STUDY SCHEDULE

The following study schedule will help you to become thoroughly prepared for the ASVAB. Although the schedule is designed for an eight-week study program, you may see it as a series of steps that you can tailor to fit your available study time. Be sure to set aside some time each day to study; make your study time as routine as possible. This will not only help you to focus on the material, it will also allow you to reinforce and master the concepts needed for the exam. Try to study for at least one hour a day, but aim for *three*. Keep in mind that the more you study for the ASVAB, the more prepared and confident you will be on the day of the test.

Week 1	Use the diagnostic test by taking each subtest separately. Then analyze your answers and scores for each individual section. Make sure to time yourself! Determine your weaknesses by calculating your score with our chart on page 91. Once you have determined the area(s) in which you are the weakest, plan on studying those areas first.
Week 2	Study your three weakest subjects this week. For example, if you had the most trouble on the Mathematics Knowledge subtest, you would study the corresponding review and take any drills contained within the review. After reviewing the section completely, proceed to the next subject you need to brush up. Be sure to complete three subjects this week so you will have time to study all ten of them. Each time you complete a review, take that diagnostic subtest again to see how your score has improved.
Week 3	Study the three subtests on which you had average scores according to our scoring chart. For example, you may have found that you did fairly well on the Paragraph Comprehension and Word Knowledge subtests. You would study these reviews and take any drills in the reviews. Afterwards, you can retake the diagnostic subtest for each to see if your score has improved.

Week 4	Study your four strongest areas this week. If you did the best, for example, on Auto and Shop, and General Science, you would review those subjects and take each diagnostic subtest again to increase your scores further.
Week 5	Take Test 2. This is not a diagnostic test, so you should try to simulate the testing conditions as much as possible, especially regarding time. Taking the test under time restrictions will allow you to focus on both your strengths and your weaknesses. Make sure you take this test straight through in one sitting as a dry run. See if your scores have improved since you took your diagnostic test.
Week 6	Review any subject(s) in which brush-up is still in order.
Week 7	Take Test 3 under the same simulated conditions as the previously taken test. Notice any improvement in the amount of time you needed to complete a section. If you can maintain a brisk, even pace, you will have a better chance of completing all the items on the day of the test.
Week 8	Continue to review any items that remain unclear to you. Network with friends and acquaintances or seek help from a teacher if some items still stump you. You should now emerge with solid practice-test scores that are achieved within the timeframe of the actual test. This means you're ready to take the ASVAB with confidence and ease. Good luck!

ASVAB

*Armed Services Vocational
Aptitude Battery*

Succeeding on the ASVAB

SUCCEEDING ON THE ASVAB

PREPARING FOR THE ASVAB

By reviewing and studying this book, you can achieve a top score on the Armed Services Vocational Aptitude Battery, or ASVAB. The ASVAB assesses knowledge that you have gained throughout your high school career. Most of the knowledge tested on the ASVAB is covered in your high school classes, although you may find some unfamiliar or less studied subjects. Don't panic! We provide carefully constructed reviews and drills so that you can learn the information you will need to do well on the ASVAB.

The purpose of our book is to properly prepare you for the ASVAB by providing three full-length exams that accurately reflect the test in both types of questions and degree of difficulty. The practice exams include every type of question that can be expected, and detailed explanations are provided for every answer. Designed specifically to clarify the exam material, the explanations not only provide the correct answers, but also explain to the student why a particular answer to a question is more acceptable than any other response. By completing all three exams and studying the explanations, you can discover your strengths and weaknesses. This knowledge will allow you to concentrate on the sections of the exam you find most difficult.

ABOUT THE ASVAB

The most widely used multiple-aptitude test battery in the world, the ASVAB is required by the Armed Forces for new recruits joining one of the branches of the military following high school. The scores aid in the placement of new recruits into military occupations. The scores are also helpful, but not a requirement, in choosing an academic or vocational plan to be followed after high school graduation.

Once you take the test, you and your guidance counselor will receive a written report that analyzes your test scores and explains in what fields you might excel based not only on the test scores but on the type of interests and lifestyle you wish to pursue.

If you have a question about the test, you can call your local military recruiting office, or speak to your guidance counselor.

ASVAB TEST FORMAT

The exam contains eight "subtests," each of which is individually scored. The following chart shows you the eight subtests you will be encountering on the exam and gives a brief description of each as well as the time allowed and the number of questions.

Subtest and Description	Number of Questions	Minutes
General Science tests knowledge of physical, biological, and earth sciences	25	11
Arithmetic Reasoning measures ability to solve arithmetic problems	30	36
Word Knowledge tests ability to understand the meaning of words in context and through synonyms	35	11
Paragraph Comprehension tests ability to use reading skills to obtain information from written material	15	13
Auto and Shop Information measures knowledge of automobile mechanics, tools, and shop terminology and practices	25	11
Mathematics Knowledge tests knowledge of mathematical concepts and applications	25	24
Mechanical Comprehension measures knowledge of physical and mechanical principles and visualization of how objects work	25	19
Electronics Information measures knowledge of electricity and electronics	20	9

Each ASVAB subtest is timed, and the entire test takes about three hours to complete.

THE COMPUTERIZED ASVAB

The computerized ASVAB administration has been featuring a ninth subtest, Assembling Objects, which is designed to measure your strengths and weaknesses in spatial ability. This subtest gauges one's ability to visualize three-dimensional puzzle pieces and put them back together after being taken apart. Your score on this subtest has no affect on whether you will be accepted into the United States Armed Services. The results, however, can help you determine your career path. We have provided a review and full-length drill of the Assembling Objects subtest for practice. The drill is included *only* in our Diagnostic Test. You will have 9 minutes to complete these questions on the computerized test. Please check with your recruiter or guidance counselor for the most up-to-date information about the ASVAB computerized exam.

ABOUT THE DIAGNOSTIC TEST

Our Diagnostic Test is a full-length simulation designed to help you pinpoint your strengths and weaknesses on the ASVAB. For maximum benefit, it is best to replicate actual testing conditions by timing yourself and taking the test in a quiet place free from interruption.

Take and score each section separately. Then review the detailed explanations of answers to determine where to brush up your studies. This will allow you to get the most out of your precious study time. You'll know which reviews to study most carefully, which ones you can simply skim, and, crucially, the subject areas that will require extra help from a teacher or tutor. Once you've completed the Diagnostic Test and discoverd the areas where you will need to focus your study efforts, our study schedule on page xi will help block out your time.

ABOUT THE REVIEW SECTIONS

This book offers subject reviews that correspond to each of the subtests for which you will be studying, including: General Science, Arithmetic Reasoning, Word Knowledge, Paragraph Comprehension, Auto and Shop Information, Mathematics Knowledge, Mechanical Comprehension, and Electronics Information. Each review targets the very information you will find most handy to do well on the subtests.

Some of the reviews contain a "Plan of Attack" that will help you to learn a pattern for attacking certain types of problems or questions. Many of the reviews offer practice questions and charts or drawings for easy memorization. Every review contains all the information you will need to do well on the ASVAB.

ASVAB TEST-TAKING STRATEGIES

How to Beat the Clock

Every second counts and you will want to use the available test time for each section in the most efficient manner. Here's how:

1. Memorize the test directions for each section of the test. You do not want to waste valuable time reading directions on the day of the exam. Your time should be spent on answering questions.

2. Bring a watch and pace yourself. Work steadily and quickly. Do not get stuck on or spend too much time on any one question. If, after reading the question, you cannot answer it, make a note of it and continue. You can go back to it after you have completed the easier questions first.

3. As you work on the test, be sure that your answers correspond with the proper numbers and letters on the answer sheet.

Guessing Strategy

1. If you are uncertain about a question, guess. You will not be penalized for answering incorrectly, since wrong answers are not counted toward your final score. This means that you should never leave a blank space on your answer sheet. Even if you do not have time to narrow down the choices, be sure to fill in every space on the answer sheet. You will not be penalized for a wrong answer, but you will receive credit for any questions answered correctly by guessing.

2. You can improve your guessing strategy by eliminating any choices recognized as incorrect. As you eliminate incorrect choices, cross them out. Remember that writing in your test booklet is allowed and that by crossing out incorrect choices, you will be better able to focus on the remaining choices.

ABOUT THE SCORING

There is no "right" score on the ASVAB, since this is a test to help you choose a possible career. However, a high score will give you more fields from which to choose in the Armed Forces. The scores enable military personnel to determine the fields in which you will do well and the fields that may cause you trouble. Your guidance counselor is trained to interpret your score and give you career advice based on that score.

Each subtest is scored individually. Individual scores are also combined to yield composite scores that show your overall ability in verbal, math, and academic ability.

Your *raw score* is calculated using the following formula:

(Word Knowledge Score **x** 2) + (Paragraph Comprehension Score **x** 2) + (Arithmetic Reasoning Score) + (Mathematics Knowledge Score)

Three composite scores are calculated as follows:

Verbal Ability Composite = Word Knowledge Score + Paragraph Comprehension Score

Math Ability Composite = Arithmetic Reasoning Score + Mathematics Knowledge Score

Academic Ability Composite = Verbal Ability Composite + Math Ability Composite

The composite scores are provided to help students engage in career exploration. The composite scores, also known as Career Exploration Scores, help students get an idea of their verbal, math, and science and technical skills compared to other students in the same grade. These composite scores can be a valuable tool in helping you map out a career path.

The scores you receive in the General Science and Auto and Shop Information subtests are not used to calculate any of the composite scores. These scores are used by recruiters and guidance counselors to identify other careers that you may choose to pursue and be successful in.

Since it is helpful for you to know how well you are doing in the various subtests, we have developed scoring charts to help you pinpoint your strengths and weaknesses. Keep in mind that this is not the actual scoring on the official ASVAB, but that it is here to help guide you. Follow the directions carefully in the scoring section of this book to determine your strong and weak areas.

ABOUT OUR CAREER OPTIONS SECTION

This book also contains information on careers. This section, located in the back of the book, will allow you to learn about career options inside and outside the military. Take the career quiz after you complete and score your tests. By rating your interests for a variety of military and non-military occupations and comparing your test scores, you will be able to focus on career options in which you might excel.

IF YOU'D LIKE MORE INFORMATION...

Additional information on the ASVAB and opportunities in the United States Armed Forces is available at these websites:

http://www.asvabprogram.com

http://www.todaysmilitary.com

ASVAB

*Armed Services Vocational
Aptitude Battery*

Diagnostic
Test 1

GENERAL SCIENCE DIAGNOSTIC TEST 1

Time: 11 Minutes
25 Questions

(Answer sheets appear in the back of this book.)

DIRECTIONS: This is a test of 25 questions to find out how much you know about general science as usually covered in high school courses. Pick the best answer for each question, then blacken the space on your answer form which has the same number and letter as your choice.

1. Which of the following organisms contain chlorophyll?

   1–A   Viruses

   1–B   Fungi

   1–C   Bacteria

   1–D   Blue-green algae

2. Kangaroos are best classified as

   2–A   carnivores.

   2–B   primates.

   2–C   marsupials.

   2–D   ungulates.

3. Bryophytes

   3–A   make seeds.

   3–B   are nonvascular.

   3–C   produce wood.

   3–D   have roots.

4. The large intestine is part of the _____ system.

   4–A   digestive

   4–B   respiratory

   4–C   endocrine

   4–D   circulatory

5. Which of the following do not provide calories in your diet?

   5–A   Protein

   5–B   Carbohydrates

   5–C   Fiber

   5–D   Fats

6. The traditional chromosome representation for a human female is

   6–A   XX.   6–C   XY.

   6–B   YY.   6–D   XYX.

7. The study of the relationship between living things and their environment is called

   7–A   botany.   7–C   ecology.

   7–B   biology.   7–D   geology.

8. The storage areas in cells are called

   8–A   mitochondria.   8–C   nuclei.

   8–B   ribosomes.   8–D   vacuoles.

9. An example of a lever is a(n)

   9–A   doorknob.   9–C   screw.

   9–B   seesaw.   9–D   elevator.

10. The capacity to do work is called

   10–A energy.   10–C force.

   10–B power.   10–D efficiency.

11. Electric current in metals results from the flow of _____ from one place to another.

   11–A ions   11–C neutrons

   11–B protons   11–D electrons

12. When two simple magnets are brought together, the north pole of one will attract _____ of the other.

   12–A the north pole   12–C any part

   12–B the south pole   12–D no part

13. Mirages are caused by

   13–A reflection.   13–C refraction.

   13–B diffraction.   13–D diffusion.

14. When working with waves, frequency × _____ = speed.

   14–A hertz

   14–B amplitude

   14–C crest

   14–D wavelength

15. The periodic table lists elements according to

   15–A mass.

   15–B charge.

   15–C order of discovery.

   15–D atomic number.

16. Movement of molecules in matter ceases near

   16–A – 273°C

   16–B 0°C

   16–C 100°C

   16–D 212°C

17. A solution in which more solute can dissolve at a given pressure and temperature may best be called

   17–A concentrated.

   17–B saturated.

   17–C unsaturated.

   17–D supersaturated.

18. An example of a chemical change is

   18–A burning.

   18–B melting.

   18–C shredding.

   18–D denting.

19. Which of the following is not an agent of erosion?

   19–A Running water

   19–B Wind

   19–C Glaciers

   19–D Oxidation

20. Wind is most directly caused by differences in

   20–A air pressure.

   20–B humidity.

   20–C temperature.

   20–D pollution.

21. Seasons occur because earth's axis is tilted _____ from perpendicular to its plane of orbit.

   21–A $23^1/_2°$

   21–B 67°

   21–C 90°

   21–D 180°

22. Fiber's primary role in the diet is

    22–A providing energy.

    22–B growth and repair of body tissues.

    22–C metabolic functioning.

    22–D aiding in removal of body wastes.

23. Water freezes at

    23–A 0°C.   23–C 0°F.

    23–B 32°C.   23–D 212°F.

24. Broad, flat, low-hanging clouds are called

    24–A cirrus.   24–C stratus.

    24–B cumulus.   24–D altostratus.

25. A mixture of sugar and water is best called a

    25–A compound.   25–C suspension.

    25–B solution.   25–D colloid.

GENERAL SCIENCE DIAGNOSTIC TEST 1

ANSWER KEY

1. (D)	8. (D)	15. (D)	22. (D)
2. (C)	9. (B)	16. (A)	23. (A)
3. (B)	10. (A)	17. (C)	24. (C)
4. (A)	11. (D)	18. (A)	25. (B)
5. (C)	12. (B)	19. (D)	
6. (A)	13. (C)	20. (A)	
7. (C)	14. (D)	21. (A)	

Add up your correct answers and put the number here. _____

Now record your score on pages 91–92 and 451–452.

DETAILED EXPLANATIONS OF ANSWERS

1.   **(D)** Blue-green algae, green plants, and some euglenans contain chlorophyll. Other organisms do not contain chlorophyll.

2.   **(C)** Kangaroos are marsupials because they carry their young in a pouch in the mother's body.

3.   **(B)** Bryophytes are nonvascular plants represented by mosses, al-gae, and liverworts. Only Tracheophytes (vascular plants) fit answers (A), (C), and (D).

4.   **(A)** The large intestine retrieves water and minerals from waste matter. It is part of the digestive system, which breaks down food into usable components and absorbs them.

5.   **(C)** Fiber produces bulk to aid in the elimination of wastes. Protein (A), carbohydrates (B), and fats (D) all provide calories.

6.   **(A)** A genetic human female has two chromosomes, one X from the mother and one X from the father. Answer (C) represents a male, and answers (B) and (D) are not normally occurring.

7.   **(C)** The following scientific disciplines are matched with their areas of study: biology/living things (B), botany/plants (A), geology/land forms and structures (D), ecology/living things and their environment (C).

8.   **(D)** Vacuoles are storage areas. Ribosomes (B) form protein. Mito-chondria (A) release energy. Nuclei (C) control cell activity.

9.   **(B)** All choices are examples of simple machines: seesaw/lever (B), doorknob/wheel and axle (A), screw/inclined plane (C), elevator/pulley (D).

10. **(A)** Energy is the capacity to do work. Force is a push or pull on an object. Work = force × distance.

$$\text{Efficiency} = \frac{\text{output work}}{\text{input work}} \times 100.$$

11. **(D)** Electrons in metals are loosely connected to atoms and therefore can travel. Protons (B) and neutrons (C) are tightly held in the nuclei of atoms. Ions (A) are charged atoms, and can't flow easily through solid material.

12. **(B)** The north pole of one magnet will attract the south pole of another magnet while repelling the north pole of the other magnet.

13. **(C)** A mirage is caused when refraction occurs between air of different densities, such as cool autumn air and very hot air immediately above a sunny road.

14. **(D)** Frequency × wavelength = speed. Hertz (A) is the measurement for frequency. Amplitude (B) is the height of a wave. The crest (C) is the high point of the wave.

15. **(D)** The periodic table lists elements according to atomic number. Mass (A) and charge (B) are not used to arrange elements, because atoms of the same element may vary in mass (isotopes) or charge (ions).

16. **(A)** Molecules move almost constantly in proportion to their relative temperature. Molecules at lower temperatures move less, until they cease movement near absolute zero, which is –273°C.

17. **(C)** Unsaturated solutions are able to dissolve more solute, while saturated solutions (B) are not. Supersaturated solutions (D) are unstable and will readily form crystals due to an excess of solute.

18. **(A)** A chemical change results in the formation of new molecules. Choices (B), (C), and (D) represent physical changes. In burning, chemicals are broken down in the presence of oxygen to form new chemicals, including water and carbon dioxide.

19. **(D)** Erosion is the breaking down of rock and movement of soil by physical means. Oxidation is a chemical process.

20. **(A)** Wind is caused by differences in air pressure. The boundaries between areas of different pressure are called fronts. Fronts are where most winds are formed.

21. **(A)** The earth is tilted on its axis $23\frac{1}{2}°$. This causes the seasons as well as changes in day length to occur during the year.

22. **(D)** Fiber's main role is providing bulk to aid the large intestine in carrying away wastes.

23. **(A)** Water freezes at 0°C, which is equal to 32°F. 212°F (D) is the boiling point of water.

24. **(C)** All the answers are cloud types: cirrus/wispy (A); cumulus/fluffy (B); stratus/low, flat (C); altostratus/high, flat (D).

25. **(B)** All choices represent mixtures. Solutions are mixtures in liquid or gas phase, in which one material is dissolved in another.

ARITHMETIC REASONING DIAGNOSTIC TEST 1

Time: 36 Minutes
     30 Questions

(Answer sheets appear in the back of this book.)

DIRECTIONS: Each question has four multiple-choice answers, labeled by the number of the question and the letters A, B, C, or D. Select the single best answer.

---

1. A family wins $25,000 in the lottery. Of this money, half goes toward a new car, one-tenth goes into savings, and the rest is put into investments. How much did the family invest?

   1–A $25,000   1–C $10,000

   1–B $12,500   1–D $2,500

2. John can run six miles per hour and Bill can run four miles per hour. If they run in opposite directions for two hours, then how far apart will they be?

   2–A   20 miles   2–C   12 miles

   2–B   10 miles   2–D   8 miles

3. A stereo sells for $200, but it is on sale for 15% off. What is the sale price?

   3–A $170   3–C $160

   3–B $180   3–D $190

4. Sam had $10 and bought lunch for $4.99. How much did he have left?

   4–A $5.00   4–C $5.99

   4–B $4.99   4–D $5.01

5. Lisa wanted to visit her friend, who lived 90 miles away. She left at 8:00 and arrived at 10:00. How fast was she driving?

5–A   50 miles per hour   5–C   90 miles per hour

5–B   45 miles per hour   5–D   30 miles per hour

6. If a baseball player has 1,000 at bats in a season, and he receives no walks, how many hits would he need to have .300 batting percentage?

6–A   300   6–C   350

6–B   250   6–D   400

7. Susan deposits $5,000 in a bank at simple 6% interest annually. After one year how much money does she have?

7–A $5,030   7–C $5,300

7–B $5,060   7–D $5,600

8. Ralph walks from his home to the bank, which is two miles, from the bank to the pizza parlor, which is one mile, and then from the pizza parlor back home, which is two miles. What is the total length of Ralph's trip?

8–A   2 miles   8–C   4 miles

8–B   3 miles   8–D   5 miles

9. John wants to read a book, and the book has 244 pages. If he reads 20 pages per night, then how many days will it take him to finish the book?

9–A   12   9–C   14

9–B   13   9–D   15

10. A soccer team has 11 players and 33 oranges. How many oranges will each player receive?

10–A 3   10–C 4

10–B 2   10–D 1

11. A family consists of a father, a mother, a son, and a daughter. On a certain night the father makes no phone calls, the mother makes one, the daughter makes six, and the son makes eight. How many phone calls did the entire family make?

11–A 13   11–C 15

11–B 14   11–D 16

12. A football team scores 16, 21, and 10 points in their first three games. What is the point total for these three games?

    12–A 26   12–C 37

    12–B 31   12–D 47

13. Bob can bench press 400 pounds. Bill can bench press 300 pounds. How much more can Bob press than Bill?

    13–A 50 pounds   13–C 300 pounds

    13–B 100 pounds   13–D 400 pounds

14. A software program requires 3,700 bytes of memory. Each floppy disk has 800 bytes of memory. How many disks are required?

    14–A 5   14–C 3

    14–B 4   14–D 2

15. A healthy cholesterol level is no more than 200. If Jack had a cholesterol level of 237 before his diet, and his level dropped by 16 points since his diet, then how many more points must it drop to be healthy?

    15–A 19   15–C 21

    15–B 20   15–D 22

16. In football, 10 yards are required for a first down. If a yard is three feet and a foot is 12 inches, then how many inches are required for a first down?

    16–A 30   16–C 120

    16–B 60   16–D 360

17. George bikes at 20 miles per hour. He travels five miles. How many minutes will this take him?

    17–A 10   17–C 20

    17–B 15   17–D 30

18. A law firm has 25 employees, of which 20% are lawyers. How many lawyers are there?

18–A 5   18–C 7

18–B 6   18–D 8

19. A grocer buys milk for 49¢ per quart and sells it for 89¢ per quart. On a certain day he sold 26 quarts. What was his profit?

19–A $0.40   19–C $10.40

19–B $1.04   19–D $26.00

20. A school had twice as many male students as female students. There were 44 male students. How many total students were there?

20–A 66   20–C 22

20–B 44   20–D 88

21. An eyeglass manufacturer has 61 frames and 87 lenses. Each pair of glasses requires one frame and two lenses. How many pairs of glasses can be made?

21–A 44   21–C 43

21–B 148   21–D 61

22. A company orders 1,000 pens from a dealer. When the pens arrive, 50 are missing. Of those that did arrive, half go to the finance department. How many pens does the finance department receive?

22–A 525   22–C 950

22–B 450   22–D 475

23. Tapes usually costs $6.99, but they are on sale for one-third off. Sandra usually buys two tapes. With the same money, how many can she now buy?

23–A 2   23–C 4

23–B 3   23–D 5

24. Robert opened a savings account with $200. The account paid 6% interest after one year, and then Robert withdrew $6. How much did he have left?

24–A $206

24–C $212

24–B $200

24–D $218

25. John is six feet tall and Julie is five feet tall. If John's shadow is one foot, then how many inches is Julie's?

25–A 8

25–C 10

25–B 9

25–D 11

26. Jill, Susan, and Kelly go shopping for coats. Jill buys one, Kelly buys two, and Susan buys three. What is the average number of coats purchased?

26–A 1

26–C 6

26–B 3

26–D 2

27. Judy wants to dance for three hours. She has already danced for 155 minutes. How many more minutes does she need to dance to reach her goal?

27–A 5

27–C 25

27–B 15

27–D 35

28. To produce keys it costs $3.00 overhead and $0.50 per key. What does it cost to manufacture 12 keys?

28–A $9.00

28–C $15.00

28–B $12.00

28–D $6.00

29. Six oranges cost $3.00. What is the cost of each orange?

29–A $1.00

29–C $0.50

29–B $1.50

29–D $3.00

30. Jim and Doug run a six mile race. Doug finishes in 40 minutes and Jim runs at the rate of one mile per seven minutes. How much longer did it take Jim than Doug?

30–A 3 minutes

30–C 2 minutes

30–B 1 minute

30–D 4 minutes

ARITHMETIC REASONING DIAGNOSTIC TEST 1

ANSWER KEY

1. (C)	9. (B)	17. (B)	25. (C)
2. (A)	10. (A)	18. (A)	26. (D)
3. (A)	11. (C)	19. (C)	27. (C)
4. (D)	12. (D)	20. (A)	28. (A)
5. (B)	13. (B)	21. (C)	29. (C)
6. (A)	14. (A)	22. (D)	30. (C)
7. (C)	15. (C)	23. (B)	
8. (D)	16. (D)	24. (A)	

Add up your correct answers and put the number here. _____

Now record your score on pages 91–92 and 451-452.

DETAILED EXPLANATIONS OF ANSWERS

1.   **(C)**   The correct answer is (C). Half (or five-tenths) of the money goes to the car, and one-tenth goes to savings. That leaves four-tenths for investments, and four-tenths of $25,000 is $10,000. The other answers would be ten-tenths (A), five-tenths (B), and one-tenth (D).

2.   **(A)**   The answer is (A) because the rate at which they are moving away from each other is (4 + 6) miles per hour, or 10 miles per hour. In two hours this distance would be 20 miles. Choice (B) is the distance between the runners after one hour, choice (C) is the distance that John runs in two hours, and choice (D) is the distance that Bill runs in two hours.

3.   **(A)**   The answer is (A) because 15% of $200 is $30, so 15% off is $200 – $30 = $170. Choice (B) corresponds to 10% off, choice (C) to 20%, and choice (D) to 5%.

4.   **(D)**   The answer is (D) because $10 – $4.99 = $5.01. None of the other choices would, when added to $4.99, result in $10.

5.   **(B)**   The answer is (B) because it took two hours to cover 90 miles. Thus, the average speed was (90 miles)/(2 hours) = (90/2) miles per hour or 45 miles per hour. The other speeds would have taken either more or less than two hours to cover 90 miles.

6.   **(A)**   The answer is (A) because 300 hits out of 1,000 at bats would result in a .300 batting average. The other choices would result in either a higher or a lower batting average.

7.   **(C)**   The answer is (C) because 6% of $5,000 is $300. Thus, after one year Susan has $5,000 + $300 = $5,300.

8.   **(D)**   The answer is (D) because two miles plus one mile plus two miles is five miles.

9.   **(B)**   The answer is (B) because he can read 240 pages in the first 12 nights. Then he must read the last four pages on the thirteenth night.

10. **(A)** The answer is (A) because 33 divided by 11 is 3.

11. **(C)** The answer is (C) because $0 + 1 + 6 + 8 = 15$.

12. **(D)** The answer is (D) because $16 + 21 + 10 = 47$.

13. **(B)** The answer is (B) because $400 - 300 = 100$.

14. **(A)** The answer is (A) because the first four disks can hold $4 \times 800 = 3{,}200$ bytes. The fifth disk must hold the remaining 500 bytes.

15. **(C)** The answer is (C) because $237 - 16 = 221$, which is his current cholesterol level. He must reduce by $221 - 200 = 21$ points.

16. **(D)** The answer is (D) because one first down is $[(10 \text{ yards})] \times [(3 \text{ feet})/(1 \text{ yard})] \times [(12 \text{ inches})/(1 \text{ foot})] = (10 \times 3 \times 12)$ inches $= 360$ inches.

17. **(B)** The answer is (B) because five is a quarter of 20. Thus, it will take him a quarter of an hour, or 15 minutes.

18. **(A)** The answer is (A) because 20% of 25 is 5.

19. **(C)** The answer is (C) because the profit per quart is 40¢. He sells 26 quarts, so the total profit is (40×26)¢ $= 1040$¢ $= \$10.40$.

20. **(A)** The answer is (A) because there were half as many females as males. Thus, there were 22 females, so there were $44 + 22 = 66$ total students.

21. **(C)** The answer is (C) because there are enough frames to make 61 pairs, but only enough lenses for 43 pairs. To make 44 pairs would require 88 lenses.

22. **(D)** The answer is (D) because $(1000 - 50)/2 = 950/2 = 475$.

23. **(B)** The answer is (B) because Sandra has $2 \times (\$6.99) = \$13.98$. But today the tapes cost $\$6.99 \, (1^1/_3) = \$6.99 \, (^2/_3) = \$4.66$. But $\$13.98$ divided by $\$4.66$ is 3.

24. **(A)** The answer is (A) because after one year Robert had $\$200 + \$12 = \$212$. When he withdrew $6, he had $\$206$ left.

25. **(C)** The answer is (C) because six feet is to 12 inches as five feet is to Julie's shadow. That is, six feet/12 inches = five feet/Julie's shadow. Thus, Julie's shadow is $(12 \times 5)/6 = 10$ inches.

26. **(D)** The answer is (D) because the average of 1, 2, and 3 is $(1 + 2 + 3)/3 = 6/3 = 2$.

27. **(C)** The answer is (C) because an hour is 60 minutes. Thus, three hours is 180 minutes, so she still has $180 - 155 = 25$ minutes to go.

28. **(A)** The answer is (A) because it will cost $\$3.00 + 12(\$0.50) = \$3.00 + \$6.00 = \$9.00$.

29. **(C)** The answer is (C) because $\$3/6 = \$0.50$.

30. **(C)** The answer is (C) because it will take Jim seven miles per minute, or $6 \times 7 = 42$ minutes to finish the race. Thus, Doug will finish $42 - 40 = 2$ minutes earlier.

WORD KNOWLEDGE DIAGNOSTIC TEST 1

Time: 11 Minutes
     35 Questions

(Answer sheets appear in the back of this book.)

DIRECTIONS: The ASVAB Word Knowledge Test is a test of your vocabulary. The test consists of 35 questions, each containing an underlined word. Pick one word from the four choices that you believe is the best synonym for the underlined word. A synonym is a word that has the same or nearly the same meaning as, in this case, the underlined word. On your answer sheet, mark the space that matches your choice. Be sure you are marking your answer in the space that represents the proper question number.

Following are two sample questions.

S1. The best synonym for <u>conceal</u> is

    S1–A expose.   S1–C create.

    S1–B trick.   S1–D hide.

S1. **(D)** HIDE is the correct answer; to conceal means to keep from being discovered, or hide. (A) EXPOSE is synonymous with reveal, and is the opposite (antonym) of conceal; (B) TRICK means to deceive; (C) CREATE is synonymous with conceive.

S2. The parishioners <u>adorned</u> the statues each year at Easter.

    S2–A Decorated   S2–C Paid respects to

    S2–B Admired   S2–D Worshiped

S2. **(A)** DECORATED is the correct answer. To adorn means to decorate, especially with ornaments. (B) ADMIRED means regarded highly; (C) PAID RESPECTS TO means visited; (D) WORSHIPED is synonymous with adored.

1. The best synonym for <u>emit</u> is

   1–A   promise.   1–C   adorn.

   1–B   utter.   1–D   leave out.

2. The best synonym for <u>vegetate</u> is

   2–A   decay.   2–C   stagnate.

   2–B   stabilize.   2–D   smell.

3. The dog's <u>intermittent</u> barking annoyed her.

   3–A   periodic   3–C   obnoxious

   3–B   loud   3–D   shrill

4. The best synonym for <u>compensate</u> is

   4–A   motivate.   4–C   sponsor.

   4–B   protest.   4–D   repay.

5. The best synonym for <u>fortune</u> is

   5–A   patience.   5–C   habit.

   5–B   luck.   5–D   tendency.

6. Theresa <u>entreated</u> Jack to let her go with him.

   6–A   begged   6–C   asked

   6–B   tempted   6–D   paid

7. The best synonym for <u>atypical</u> is

   7–A   distinct.   7–C   usual.

   7–B   neutral.   7–D   abnormal.

8. The best synonym for <u>defect</u> is

   8–A   stain.   8–C   weakness.

   8–B   vice.   8–D   flaw.

9. Mr. Waters was well-known for his <u>miserly</u> ways.

    9–A spendthrift   9–C mean

    9–B ungenerous   9–D solemn

10. The best synonym for <u>arrogant</u> is

    10–A scornful.   10–C sarcastic.

    10–B critical.   10–D vain.

11. The best synonym for <u>persevere</u> is

    11–A harass.   11–C separate.

    11–B conserve.   11–D endure.

12. The mood of the vacation changed drastically when the children became <u>irritable</u>.

    12–A competitive   12–C stubborn

    12–B quarrelsome   12–D cooperative

13. The best synonym for <u>courteous</u> is

    13–A brave.   13–C inquisitive.

    13–B civil.   13–D impudent.

14. The best synonym for <u>endeavor</u> is

    14–A exertion.   14–C extremity.

    14–B recovery.   14–D preparation.

15. The youngster eyed his dinner with <u>dismay</u>.

    15–A loathing   15–C indifference

    15–B disappointment   15–D hunger

16. The best synonym for <u>malinger</u> is

    16–A discipline.   16–C shirk.

    16–B defame.   16–D grow.

17. The best synonym for <u>ponder</u> is

    17–A conclude.   17–C consider.

    17–B believe.   17–D exploit.

18. The food at the buffet was <u>abundant</u> and delicious.

    18–A rich   18–C colorful

    18–B desirable   18–D plentiful

19. The best synonym for <u>yield</u> is

    19–A resign.   19–C brandish.

    19–B merge.   19–D proceed.

20. The best synonym for <u>confirm</u> is

    20–A verify.   20–C imprison.

    20–B stand up to.   20–D baptize.

21. The young woman appeared <u>indignant</u> about the situation.

    21–A apologetic   21–C angry

    21–B flustered   21–D unconcerned

22. The best synonym for <u>discrete</u> is

    22–A tactful.   22–C unwise.

    22–B different.   22–D shrewd.

23. The mayor thought the <u>obstinate</u> man attended the meetings just to annoy him.

    23–A violent   23–C stubborn

    23–B vulgar   23–D smelly

24. The best synonym for <u>reform</u> is

    24–A abstain.   24–C improve.

    24–B agree.   24–D stop.

25. The old codger was reknowned for his <u>liberal</u> political views.

    25–A broad-minded   25–C exact

    25–B crazy   25–D slanderous

26. The best synonym for <u>occur</u> is

    26–A establish.   26–C exist.

    26–B reside.   26–D think.

27. The best synonym for <u>immoral</u> is

    27–A virtuous.   27–C indestructible.

    27–B loving.   27–D unethical.

28. The best synonym for <u>prudent</u> is

    28–A modest.   28–C nosy.

    28–B cautious.   28–D stingy.

29. The accountant determined that the project would be <u>profitable</u> for the company.

    29–A monetary   29–C expensive

    29–B commercial   29–D advantageous

30. The woman's question was so off target—it was simply <u>absurd</u>.

    30–A dumb   30–C foolish

    30–B extreme   30–D ignorant

31. The best synonym for <u>blatant</u> is

    31–A obvious.   31–C quiet.

    31–B angry.   31–D vain.

32. The best synonym for <u>idle</u> is

    32–A famous.   32–C inactive.

    32–B motivate.   32–D absorb.

33. The best synonym for <u>docile</u> is

    33–A obedient.   33–C youthful.

    33–B shy.   33–D charming.

34. The children often complained about being <u>bored</u> during their summer vacation.

    34–A impatient   34–C disappointed

    34–B uninterested   34–D frustrated

35. The best synonym for <u>gait</u> is

    35–A pace.   35–C barrier.

    35–B profit.   35–D entrance.

WORD KNOWLEDGE DIAGNOSTIC TEST 1

ANSWER KEY

1. (B)	10. (A)	19. (A)	28. (B)
2. (C)	11. (D)	20. (A)	29. (D)
3. (A)	12. (B)	21. (C)	30. (C)
4. (D)	13. (B)	22. (B)	31. (A)
5. (B)	14. (A)	23. (C)	32. (C)
6. (A)	15. (B)	24. (C)	33. (A)
7. (D)	16. (C)	25. (A)	34. (B)
8. (D)	17. (C)	26. (C)	35. (A)
9. (B)	18. (D)	27. (D)	

Add up your correct answers and put the number here. _____

Now record your score on pages 91–92 and 451-452.

DETAILED EXPLANATIONS
OF ANSWERS

1.   **(B)**   Emit means to utter. (A) PROMISE is a synonym for commit; (C) ADORN means to decorate; (D) LEAVE OUT is synonymous with omit.

2.   **(C)**   Vegetate means either to grow in the manner of a plant or to lead a passive existence; stagnate, which means to be inactive, motionless, or stale, is closer to these definitions than (A) DECAY, to decline in health; (B) STABILIZE, to make steady, or limit fluctuations; or (D) SMELL.

3.   **(A)**   Intermittent means periodic or occasionally. Barking may also be (B) LOUD, (C) OBNOXIOUS, or (D) SHRILL, but none of these words are synonyms for intermittent.

4.   **(D)**   Compensate most closely means repay. (A) MOTIVATE means to provide an incentive for action; (B) PROTEST means to speak against; (C) SPONSOR means to assume responsibility for.

5.   **(B)**   The words LUCK and fortune are so closely related in meaning that they are often used interchangeably. Fortune can also be defined as accident, success, fate, or wealth; (A) PATIENCE, (C) HABIT, and (D) TENDENCY are not synonymous with fortune.

6.   **(A)**   Entreated means begged. (B) TEMPTED is a synonym for entice; (C) ASKED doesn't convey the sense of desperation meant by the word entreat; and (D) PAID is a synonym for one meaning of the verb "treat."

7.   **(D)**   Atypical means irregular or unusual; abnormal is the word choice closest in meaning to this definition. (A) DISTINCT means separate or notable; (B) NEUTRAL means undecided or indifferent (not caring); (C) USUAL is the opposite of atypical.

8.   **(D)**   A defect is a flaw. The other choices—(A) STAIN, (B) VICE, and (C) WEAKNESS—can indicate a defect, but flaw is the most precise choice.

9. **(B)** Miserly means ungenerous, stingy. (A) SPENDTHRIFT is the opposite of miserly; (C) MEAN is a synonym for nasty; and (D) SOLEMN is closer in meaning to sedate or gloomy.

10. **(A)** An arrogant person assumes an air of superiority over others; a scornful person openly dislikes or rejects (a person or idea) as unworthy. (B) CRITICAL, meaning judgemental, is close—but the word critical implies more objectivity than the word arrogant. (C) a SARCASTIC person is bitter, especially in speech; (D) a VAIN person is boastful of his appearance or accomplishments.

11. **(D)** Persevere means to endure or continue in spite of adverse conditions. (A) HARASS is synonymous with persecute; (B) CONSERVE is synonymous with preserve; and (C) SEPARATE is synonymous with sever.

12. **(B)** Irritable means easily annoyed or angered; (B) QUARRELSOME best fits this definition. (A) COMPETITIVE means eager to compete or win; (C) a STUBBORN person is one who won't give in; (D) COOPERATIVE is an antonym of irritable.

13. **(B)** Courteous and (B) CIVIL both mean polite. (A) BRAVE is a synonym for courageous; (C) INQUISITIVE is a synonym for curious; (D) IMPUDENT means rude and is the opposite of courteous.

14. **(A)** An endeavor is an (A) EXERTION, an attempt, or an effort of some kind. (B) a RECOVERY means having regained something that had been lost; (C) an EXTREMITY is an outermost part; (D) a PREPARATION is a planning measure.

15. **(B)** Disappointment is one of the meanings of the word dismay. (A) LOATHING is synonymous with disdain; (C) INDIFFERENCE means not caring; (D) HUNGER is not related.

16. **(C)** To malinger is to fake that you're sick in order to avoid work—in other words, to shirk (avoid) your responsibilities. (A) DISCIPLINE means to teach or punish; (B) DEFAME is synonymous with malign; (D) GROW is not related.

17. **(C)** Ponder means to consider, meditate. (A) CONCLUDE means to decide or to end; (B) BELIEVE means to think or trust; (D) EXPLOIT is synonymous with pander.

18. **(D)** Abundant means plentiful. Food may also be (A) RICH in taste, (B) DESIRABLE, or (C) COLORFUL—but the definitions of these words are very different from the meaning of the word abundant.

19. **(A)** Yield means to resign or give in. (B) MERGE means to blend together without abrupt change (an important difference when driving!); (C) BRANDISH is synonymous with wield; (D) PROCEED means to continue or advance after an interruption.

20. **(A)** Confirm means to verify, remove doubt, or strengthen. (B) STAND UP TO is synonymous with confront; (C) IMPRISON is synonymous with confine. (D) BAPTIZE means to spiritually purify, to initiate, or to christen.

21. **(C)** Indignant means angry. (A) APOLOGETIC means sorry; (B) FLUSTERED means confused; (D) UNCONCERNED is synonymous with indifferent.

22. **(B)** Discrete and DIFFERENT are synonymous. (A) TACTFUL means thoughtful, as does the homophone of discrete, *discreet*; (C) UNWISE means foolish; and (D) SHREWD means sneaky or clever.

23. **(C)** Obstinate means STUBBORN. (A) VIOLENT (extreme, sudden, furious), (B) VULGAR (offensive), and (D) SMELLY do not have the same or a similar meaning.

24. **(C)** Reform means to IMPROVE, change for the better. (A) ABSTAIN is synonymous with refrain; (B) AGREE is synonymous with conform; (D) STOP, meaning to halt activity, is an opposite of reform, which requires action.

25. **(A)** Two meanings of the word liberal are "generous" and "open-minded" (BROAD-MINDED). (B) Liberal and CRAZY are not synonymous; (C) EXACT is synonymous with literal; (D) SLANDEROUS is synonymous with libelous.

26. **(C)** To occur means to happen or appear; of the choices given, the best synonym is EXIST, which also describes a state of being. (A) ESTABLISH means to introduce, settle, or cause; (B) RESIDE means to live; (D) THINK has many meanings, none of which comes close to the meanings of occur.

27. **(D)** Immoral means UNETHICAL, against accepted cultural values. (A) VIRTUOUS is the opposite of immoral; (B) LOVING can be synonymous with amorous; (C) INDESTRUCTIBLE is synonymous with immortal.

28. **(B)** Prudent means CAUTIOUS, wise, frugal. (A) To be MODEST is synonymous with prudishness; (C) NOSY and (D) STINGY aren't related.

29. **(D)** Profitable means ADVANTAGEOUS. Although "profitable" is often used when discussing money matters, it may apply to things other than financial matters. (A) MONETARY (of or relating to money), (B) COMMERCIAL (of or relating to commerce), and (C) EXPENSIVE (costing a lot of money) all pertain to money—but do not necessarily mean advantageous.

30. **(C)** The best synonym for absurd is FOOLISH. (A) DUMB means lacking intelligence; (B) EXTREME means exceeding the usual or expected; (D) IGNORANT means unknowing.

31. **(A)** Blatant and OBVIOUS are direct synonyms. (B) ANGRY, (C) QUIET, and (D) VAIN are not at all related.

32. **(C)** Idle can mean either INACTIVE, useless, or lazy. (A) FAMOUS people are sometimes *idols*; (B) MOTIVATE and (D) ABSORB are not related.

33. **(A)** Docile means OBEDIENT or easily taught or managed. (B) SHY, (C) YOUTHFUL, and (D) CHARMING have very different meanings.

34. **(B)** Bored means UNINTERESTED. When a person is bored, he may also feel (A) IMPATIENT (intolerant or anxious) or (D) FRUSTRATED, but these words aren't synonymous with bored. (C) DISAPPOINTED, meaning let down, also does not apply.

35. **(A)** One's gait is his manner of walking or a rate of progress; PACE is the best synonym of the choices given. (C) BARRIER and (D) ENTRANCE are synonymous with gate (a homonym); (B) PROFIT is synonymous with gain.

PARAGRAPH COMPREHENSION DIAGNOSTIC TEST 1

Time: 13 Minutes
       15 Questions

(Answer sheets appear in the back of this book.)

DIRECTIONS: This test consists of 15 paragraphs that test your ability to understand and retrieve information from passages you have read. Each paragraph is followed by an incomplete question or statement. You must read each of the paragraphs and select the one lettered choice that best completes the statement or question. Your score is based on the number of correct answers. Try to answer every question, but don't spend too much time on any single question.

Here is a sample paragraph.

S1. Concrete is one of the oldest known materials. A mixture of sand, cement, and gravel, concrete was invented by the Romans before Jesus Christ was born. The famous Roman roads were made of it, and many of those roads are still in use throughout Europe.

Based on this passage, you could say that

S1–A concrete does not last long.

S1–B concrete was invented by the Romans.

S1–C concrete is a mixture of sand, gravel, and dirt.

S1–D all the roads in Europe are made of concrete.

S1. **(B)** The correct answer is (B), concrete was invented by the Romans.

1. It is very important to find well-written books for your children. A story that will make them laugh or want to know what happens next will motivate them to read even though it's difficult. Your local public library is filled with such books, and the children's librarian is skilled at locating these treasures.

   According to the paragraph, children will read books because

   1–A   their parents force them to.

   1–B   they are difficult.

   1–C   they are not difficult.

   1–D   the stories will make them laugh or wonder.

2. By 1700, two colleges had been founded in the colonies: Harvard, and William and Mary. Other cultural activities before 1700 were limited. The few writings of the colonists, mostly historical narratives, journals, sermons, and some poetry, were printed in England.

   The colonists' attempts at creative writing

   2–A   were printed in New England.

   2–B   included novels and spy stories.

   2–C   were sometimes written by priests or ministers.

   2–D   were mostly written in colleges.

3. The true scientist does not thrive on truth. The true scientist thrives on doubt. Skepticism is the hallmark of the pioneer in the world of science. The scientist would rather spend a lifetime chasing doubt than spend it believing things that are not true.

   The main idea of this paragraph is

   3–A   scientists are negative thinkers.

   3–B   truth does not exist for the scientist.

   3–C   skepticism and scientific inquiry go together.

   3–D   truth is not important to scientists.

4. A cave is a natural opening in the ground extending beyond the zone of light and large enough to permit the entry of man. Occurring in a wide variety of rock types and caused by widely differing processes, caves range in size from single small rooms to interconnecting passages many miles long.

This paragraph implies from its definition of cave that

4–A   all caves do not have the same characteristics.

4–B   the opening must be large enough to admit man.

4–C   not all openings into the Earth are classified as caves.

4–D   must be a natural opening in the ground.

5. To the casual observer, large garden plots in Europe appear to be simply clusters of miniature gardens with scattered fruit trees. More observant travelers are impressed by the care taken with these plots. Gardens are free of weeds and carefully use every square foot. Many gardens have a festive air, with flags flying.

According to this paragraph, the reader might infer that

5–A   observant travelers are easily impressed.

5–B   Europeans take a great deal of time to care for their gardens.

5–C   many gardens are festive.

5–D   crops in the gardens are plentiful.

6. Married couples with no children often work two jobs for five or more years to purchase the American dream, a home of their own. They often find that after purchasing a home they must both continue working to meet their financial obligations. Their desire to have children, their careers, and their buying a home are often not compatible.

This paragraph implies

6–A   fewer married couples will be able to purchase a home and have children.

6–B   fewer couples will have children.

6–C   fewer couples will purchase a home.

6–D   fewer women will have careers.

7. The cost for inventions is often covered by large corporations, which may also provide research and development facilities. Corporations also help inventors contribute ideas without the inventors suffering the loss of income or security. Many good ideas, however, are never brought into the marketplace and the cost of products is high because of the cost of development.

   Which of the following is not a way in which corporations assist inventors?

   7–A   Corporations help cover the inventor's costs.

   7–B   Corporations help with research facilities.

   7–C   Corporations keep inventors secure.

   7–D   Corporations create the marketplace.

8. Research in leper colonies unveiled the fact that victims grew blind. A study discovered that the nerves that cause eyes to blink grew insensitive, so the eyes would not cleanse themselves naturally. The real cause of the blindness of lepers was actually not part of the disease at all. Now a simple operation to restore blinking saves many from a sightless life.

   The main point of this paragraph is

   8–A   scientists discovered that lepers go blind.

   8–B   nerves that cause eyes to blink are insensitive.

   8–C   eyes do not cleanse themselves naturally.

   8–D   scientists found a simple, treatable cause for blindness in lepers.

9. Strawberries are grown in Arkansas, Alabama, Mississippi, and Florida. Blueberries are grown in Nevada, Alabama, Mississippi, and Arizona. Boysenberries are grown in Arkansas, Nevada, Utah, Mississippi, and Florida. Blackberries are grown in Arizona, Nevada, Utah, and Colorado. Raspberries are grown in Arizona, Mississippi, Alabama, and Arkansas. Gooseberries are grown in Alabama, Mississippi, Florida, and Utah.

   If someone wanted to grow boysenberries, gooseberries, and blackberries, he or she should live in

   9–A   Alabama.   9–C   Nevada.

   9–B   Arizona.   9–D   Utah.

10. Cacti originate in areas where water is available only occasionally, and therefore are conditioned to deal with long periods of drought. They possess adaptations enabling them to store moisture for times of scarcity. Leaves may be eliminated altogether, or the moisture in the leaves may be protected by a leathery surface, thick spines, or even a powdery coating.

According to this paragraph, it can be assumed that cacti grow

10–A near deep rivers.

10–B in areas of high rainfall.

10–C only in captivity.

10–D where it rains occasionally.

11. A child who is constantly scolded and made to feel he does everything wrong may have a difficult time developing socially. He may be so afraid of displeasing the adults around him that he keeps to himself, or he may take the opposite route and go out of his way to create trouble.

The main idea in this passage is

11–A children develop only with parents.

11–B constantly scolded children may have trouble developing socially.

11–C social development depends upon pleasing adults.

11–D children always create trouble.

12. The body structure of birds is adapted to life in the air. Their wings, tails, hollow bones, and internal air sacs all contribute to this great faculty. These adaptations make it possible for birds to seek out environments most favorable to their needs at different times of the year.

In this paragraph, "adaptations" refers to

12–A coloration.

12–B size.

12–C physical properties of the bird.

12–D flying from one place to another.

13. Speech-language scientists generally define children as disordered if they lag significantly behind children the same age in speaking. But British studies show that the normal range for early language acquisition is wide. Most normal children speak their first word anywhere from six to 18 months, and combine words into phrases for the first time anywhere from ten to 24 months. It takes a skilled practitioner to distinguish between a slow child and one with a true disorder.

The basic implication of this passage is

13–A only a speech-language pathologist should be consulted about matters of speech and language.

13–B there is no difference between a slow child and a truly language-delayed child.

13–C ranges in language development are so wide only a skilled pathologist can see the differences.

13–D examinations do not necessarily show differences.

14. The most common worldwide diet deficiency caused by lack of protein is kwashiorkor. Kwashiorkor is now known to be rampant in most developing nations. Children with this disease suffer severe growth retardation, vulnerability to illness, swelling of the abdomen with water, and marked apathy. Victims' responses are so reduced that one who smiles is considered to be on the road to recovery.

The word "rampant" in this passage means

14–A widespread.

14–B not throughout any given population.

14–C just in children.

14–D just in adults.

15. The development of the brain's differences is part of the overall maturing of the nervous system that occurs before birth. Scientists believe that sometime in the middle of gestation, nerve cells migrate to the parts of the brain in which they will stay. This brain cell migration usually begins at about the sixteenth week and ends by the twenty-fourth week of gestation.

In this passage, "gestation" refers to

15–A   weeks 16–24 of the prenatal period.

15–B   the nine months of prenatal development.

15–C   the beginning of the prenatal period.

15–D   the end of the prenatal period.

PARAGRAPH COMPREHENSION DIAGNOSTIC TEST 1

ANSWER KEY

1. (D)	6. (A)	11. (B)
2. (C)	7. (D)	12. (C)
3. (C)	8. (D)	13. (C)
4. (C)	9. (D)	14. (A)
5. (B)	10. (D)	15. (B)

Add up your correct answers and put the number here. _____

Now record your score on pages 91–92 and 451-452.

DETAILED EXPLANATIONS OF ANSWERS

1. **(D)** Children are motivated to read stories that make them laugh (laughter is a form of amusement) or want to know what happens. "Wanting to know what happens" is another way of saying "wonder" what happens.

2. **(C)** Some of the products were sermons. Ministers and priests are people who write sermons. The answer must be (C).

3. **(C)** Skepticism is doubt. The writer of the paragraph says that "Skepticism is the hallmark of the . . . world of science." In other words, doubt is the hallmark (sign) of a true scientist. So, skepticism and scientific inquiry go hand in hand.

4. **(C)** All choices except (C) are stated as part of the definition of a cave. Only (C) is probably true, based on what the writer suggests, or implies.

5. **(B)** Gardeners put so much work into these gardens—pruning, weeding, and so on. The reader can logically infer that European gardeners must take a great deal of time to produce orderly gardens. After all, great gardens aren't grown in a day!

6. **(A)** The writer shows that having both a home and children don't work together. Consequently, the reader can assume that fewer couples will both purchase homes and have children. The writer doesn't say anything definite about having fewer children or any of the other choices.

7. **(D)** The passage says nothing about the corporations creating the marketplace, only that although corporations help, many good ideas do not reach the marketplace.

8. **(D)** When lepers failed to blink, their eyes could not cleanse themselves naturally. Doctors discovered a simple operation to restore blinking, which then kept the eyes clean, and kept the lepers from going blind. Doctors discovered that a lack of blinking, not leprosy itself, is what causes blindness.

9. **(D)** Utah is the only state that grows all three types of berries.

10. **(D)** Cacti grow where water is available only occasionally. So, they grow where it rains (water) occasionally.

11. **(B)** The first sentence says almost exactly the same thing. Nothing is said about the effect of pleasing adults.

12. **(C)** Since the body structure of birds includes a number of *physical properties,* and since there is more than one such property, (C) has to be the correct answer.

13. **(C)** The writer states that "it takes a skilled practitioner to distinguish between a slow child and one with a true disorder." So, only a practitioner such as a scientist can see the differences.

14. **(A)** "Rampant" means running wild, or widespread. Notice that the sentence before suggests this when it states that kwashiorkor is "the most common" deficiency.

15. **(B)** The paragraph discusses a period of development in human beings that is prenatal, which means before birth. Changes in the brain take place in the middle of that period—the sixteenth through twenty-fourth weeks (second through sixth months of pregnancy). Gestation must therefore be the nine-month period before humans are born.

AUTO & SHOP DIAGNOSTIC TEST 1

Time: 11 Minutes
25 Questions

(Answer sheets appear in the back of this book.)

> **DIRECTIONS:** For each question, read the four possible answers and select the one answer that you believe is correct. Fill in the corresponding letter on your answer sheet.

1. The piston moves up and down in the

   1–A   intake manifold.   1–C   cylinder.

   1–B   intake port.   1–D   transmission.

2. The cylinder head is

   2–A   above the block.   2–C   below the oil pan.

   2–B   below the block.   2–D   none of the above.

3. In regard to engines, TDC stands for

   3–A   transmission design center.

   3–B   transmission dead center.

   3–C   top dead center.

   3–D   traffic deceleration control.

4. The bumps on camshafts are called

   4–A   camshaft counterweights.

   4–B   camshaft bumps.

   4–C   cam dampers.

   4–D   cam lobes.

5. If a four-stroke cycle starts with the intake stroke, then the third stroke would be the

   5–A   intake stroke again.   5–C   compression stroke.

   5–B   power stroke.   5–D   exhaust stroke.

6. In regard to engines, ohv stands for

   6–A   overhead variation.   6–C   overhead valve.

   6–B   overhead vortex.   6–D   none of the above.

7. A push rod directly moves

   7–A   the valve stem.   7–C   the rocker arm.

   7–B   the valve head.   7–D   the camshaft.

8. In a two-stroke cycle engine, the fresh air-fuel mixture enters the crankcase through the

   8–A   inlet port.   8–C   intake port.

   8–B   exhaust port.   8–D   intake valve.

9. A common air-fuel ratio, by weight, is

   9–A   3:1.   9–C   1:1.

   9–B   10:1.   9–D   15:1.

10. One way to reduce NO_x is

   10–A   EGR.   10–C   ECS.

   10–B   air injection.   10–D   ohc.

11. The ratio for first gear in a five-speed manual transmission is approximately

   11–A   15:1.   11–C   1:1.

   11–B   10:1.   11–D   3:1.

12. An automatic transmission is essentially made up of

    12–A an axle housing and differential.

    12–B a cylinder and piston.

    12–C a torque converter and a planetary gearset.

    12–D a clutch and drive shaft.

13. The device that can be part of a suspension system is a

    13–A cylinder.   13–C differential.

    13–B spring.   13–D disc.

14. Ball-peen hammers are commonly used to work with

    14–A wood.   14–C metal.

    14–B plastic.   14–D none of the above.

15. Which of the following is a woodcutting handtool?

    15–A Open-end wrench   15–C Circle snips

    15–B Rawhide mallet   15–D None of the above

16. Which of the following is a type of noncalibrated caliper?

    16–A Spring   16–C Both (A) and (B)

    16–B Coil   16–D None of the above

17. Which of the following is a type of wood screw head?

    17–A Flat   17–C Oval

    17–B Round   17–D All of the above

18. What are the two classes of lubricants?

    18–A Gasoline and diesel   18–C Water and oil

    18–B Oils and greases   18–D Both (A) and (B)

19. The most important advantage of a vernier caliper is

    19–A light weight.

    19–B low price.

    19–C it provides accurate measurements.

    19–D none of the above.

20. Carpenter's hammers are commonly used to

    20–A bend steel.   20–C drive and draw nails.

    20–B break plastic.   20–D all of the above.

21. Which of the following is a type of washer?

    21–A Flat   21–C None of the above

    21–B Cylindrical   21–D Both (A) and (B)

22. Which of the following is a type of nut?

    22–A Wing   22–C Stop

    22–B Cap   22–D All of the above

23. With which of these heads does one use a Phillips head screwdriver?

    23–A   23–C

    23–B   23–D None of the above

24. The above tool is a(n)

    24–A screwdriver.   24–C expansion reamer.

    24–B countersink.   24–D hacksaw.

25. Which is a shake proof washer?

    25–A   25–C

    25–B   25–D None of the above

AUTO & SHOP
DIAGNOSTIC TEST 1

ANSWER KEY

1. (C)	8. (A)	15. (D)	22. (D)
2. (A)	9. (D)	16. (A)	23. (A)
3. (C)	10. (A)	17. (D)	24. (B)
4. (D)	11. (D)	18. (B)	25. (C)
5. (B)	12. (C)	19. (C)	
6. (C)	13. (B)	20. (C)	
7. (C)	14. (C)	21. (A)	

Add up your correct answers and put the number here. _____

Now record your score on pages 91–92 and 451-452.

DETAILED EXPLANATIONS OF ANSWERS

1.   **(C)**   The piston fits tightly within the cylinder and closes off the opening of the cylinder. The piston moves freely, up and down, within the cylinder despite fitting tightly. The intake manifold (A) and intake port (B) lead to the cylinder but are not in the cylinder like the piston. (D) is incorrect because the transmission is completely separate from the cylinder.

2.   **(A)**   The cylinder block has cylindrical holes going through it with both ends open. The cylinder head bolts to the top of the cylinder block to seal off one end and form the complete cylinder. Once again, a tight-fitting piston seals the cylinder at the bottom.

3.   **(C)**   TDC stands for "top dead center." TDC is the highest point a piston can travel during its stroke within the cylinder.

4.   **(D)**   The small bumps on the camshaft are called cam lobes. The cam lobes, because of their shape, push the valves open at the right time by either lifting the valve tappets which, in turn, open the valves, by lifting push rods which via a rocker arm opens the valves, or by opening the valves directly (overhead camshaft engine).

5.   **(B)**   The third stroke is the power stroke, where the mixture is ignited near TDC while under compression, which causes it to expand rapidly and push down on the piston. When the intake stroke is counted as the first stroke, the order for a four-stroke cycle is intake, compression, power, and exhaust strokes.

6.   **(C)**   The abbreviation ohv stands for overhead valve. The ohv arrangement is named "overhead" because the intake and exhaust valves reside in the cylinder head.

7.   **(C)**   As the cam lobe pushes up on a push rod, the push rod moves the rocker arm. It is the rocker arm which then pushes open the valve (made up of the valve head and valve stem). The valve spring pulls the valve shut again.

8. **(A)** In a two-stroke cycle engine fresh air-fuel mixture enters the crankcase through an inlet port and enters and leaves the combustion chamber through intake (C) and exhaust (B) ports (no valves (D) are used).

9. **(D)** A common air-fuel ratio, by weight, for most SI engines, is approximately 15:1. This means that if an engine uses 15 pounds of air, it needs one pound of fuel to mix with the air in order to run correctly. The carburetor is designed to keep this 15:1 ratio constant as more air is pulled through it. A 10:1 ratio (or lower) would not be a normal air-fuel ratio. It would be a rich air-fuel ratio.

10. **(A)** When high combustion temperatures (2,500–5,000° F) exist NO_x is formed. One way of reducing NO_x emission is through exhaust gas recirculation (EGR). An EGR system recirculates a portion of the hot exhaust gases back into the intake manifold which dilutes the incoming air-fuel mixture and ultimately lowers the combustion temperatures within the cylinders. This results in lower NO_x production. ECS (C) and air injection (B) are used for reduction of CO and HC. The abbreviation ohc (D) has nothing to do directly with emission control.

11. **(D)** The sizes of gears in a five-speed manual transmission result in a gear ratio of about 3:1 for first gear in most automobiles and make starting the automobile from rest a smooth and easy process because the transmission output shaft is receiving three times more torque than the transmission input shaft or crankshaft. Put another way, the engine crankshaft and transmission input shaft are turning three times faster than the transmission output shaft.

12. **(C)** An automatic transmission is essentially made up of a torque converter and a housing which holds the planetary gearset. The torque converter is a type of hydraulic drive system that transfers and multiplies engine torque from the crankshaft to the transmission (planetary gearset) input shaft. The planetary gearsets form the four forward gears and the reverse gear of the automatic transmission.

13. **(B)** Springs are used in suspension systems to allow the wheels of the automobile to move up and down over bumps while maintaining stability through turns.

14. **(C)** Ball-peen hammers are mostly used by people who work with metal or around machinery. These hammers are distinguished from car-

penter hammers by a variable-shaped peen, rather than a claw, at the opposite end of the face.

15. **(D)** An open-end wrench (A) is a type of wrench used to turn nuts and bolts. A rawhide mallet (B) is used for driving wooden-handled chisels, gouges, and wooden pins or for forming metal. Circle snips (C) are used for cutting sheet metal and steel. A woodcutting handtool would be, for example, a handsaw.

16. **(A)** Spring calipers are a type of simple, noncalibrated caliper used in conjunction with a scale to measure inside or outside diameters. Spring calipers have the legs joined by a strong spring hinge.

17. **(D)** Flat, round, and oval, in addition to Phillips and lag heads, are all types of wood screw heads. Wood screws are used to securely hold wood and have the advantage of being removable.

18. **(B)** Lubricants are of two general classes: oils and greases. Oils are fluids; greases are semisolid at ordinary temperatures. Oils are often used in oil baths or in a gear box. Greases are used to provide additional protection against corrosion. Gasoline and diesel (A) are types of fuels and water is not commonly classified as a lubricant.

19. **(C)** The most distinct advantage of a vernier caliper, over other types of calipers, is its ability to provide very accurate measurements over a large range. It can measure both internal and external surfaces and requires the ability to read the vernier scale.

20. **(C)** The primary use of the carpenter's hammer is to drive and draw (pull) nails. The carpenter's hammer has either a curved or straight claw and the face is either bell-faced or plain-faced.

21. **(A)** Flat washers are a type of washer used to back up bolt heads and nuts, and to provide larger bearing surfaces. They prevent damage to the surfaces of metal parts.

22. **(D)** Wing nuts, cap nuts, and stop nuts are all types of nuts. Another type of nut is a thumb nut. Wing nuts and thumb nuts are used to tighten things down by hand. Cap nuts are used when appearance is important. Stop nuts are used when permanent tightness is important.

23. **(A)** Phillips head screwdrivers are used with screw heads which have a cross shape in the head.

24. **(B)** Countersinks are used to bevel the mouth of a hole so the head of a screw or rivet can be set flush with the material it is holding.

25. **(C)** Shake proof lock washers are star-like in shape and have teeth or lugs that grip both the work and the nut.

MATHEMATICS KNOWLEDGE
DIAGNOSTIC TEST 1

Time: 24 Minutes
25 Questions

(Answer sheets appear in the back of this book.)

> **DIRECTIONS:** Each question has four multiple-choice answers, labeled by the number of the question and the letters A, B, C, or D. Select the single answer which is correct.

1. What percent of 40 is 20?

    1–A 30%   1–C 50%

    1–B 40%   1–D 60%

2. In a small company, 60% of the employees are women. A third of the women smoke. There are eight female smokers. How many employees are there?

    2–A 40   2–C 60

    2–B 50   2–D 70

3. If one angle of a right triangle is 50°, then how many degrees are there in the smallest angle?

    3–A 40°   3–C 50°

    3–B 45°   3–D 90°

4. If the length of one side of a rectangle is six inches, and its area is 24 inches, then what is the length of the shortest side (in inches)?

    4–A 1   4–C 3

    4–B 2   4–D 4

5. What is the square root of 144?

    5–A 11   5–C 13

    5–B 12   5–D 14

6. What is the product of $(x + 2)(x - 2)$?

   6–A $x^2 - 4$ 6–C $2x + 4$

   6–B $x - 4$ 6–D $x^2 + 4$

7. If one leg of a right triangle is five inches and the hypotenuse is one foot – one inch, what is the length of the other leg?

   7–A 6 inches   7–C 1 foot

   7–B 10 inches   7–D 1 foot – 2 inches

8. The radii of two circles have the ratio of 1:2, what is the ratio of the area of the larger circle to the smaller circle?

   8–A 8:1   8–C 1:4

   8–B 2:1   8–D 4:1

9. What is x if $10x + 36 = 2x + 4$?

   9–A -8 9–C 4

   9–B -4 9–D 8

10. If x is the length of a side of a square and its area and perimeter are equal, what is x?

    10–A 4   10–C 9

    10–B 8   10–D 16

11. If $3x > 9$, then which of the following must be true?

    11–A $x \geq 3$ 11–C $x \leq 3$

    11–B $x > 3$ 11–D $x < 3$

12. A salesman needs to sell 200 items in a week. If he sells 42 on Monday, 28 on Tuesday, 59 on Wednesday, and 61 on Thursday, then what percent of his mission has he completed?

    12–A 80%   12–C 90%

    12–B 85%   12–D 95%

13. If $-2x < 4$, then which of the following must be true?

    13–A $x < -2$ 13–C $x \le -2$

    13–B $x > -2$ 13–D $x \ge -2$

14. If one angle of an isosceles triangle is 60°, then how many more degrees are in the largest angle than in the smallest?

    14–A 0°

    14–B 5°

    14–C 10°

    14–D It cannot be determined from the given information.

15. If one angle of a right triangle is 30°, then how many more degrees are in the largest angle than in the smallest?

    15–A 30°   15–C 60°

    15–B 45°   15–D 90°

16. If $4x + 2 = 10$, then what is x?

    16–A 5   16–C 3

    16–B 4   16–D 2

17. If $18/x = 4.5$, then what is x?

    17–A 3   17–C 5

    17–B 4   17–D 6

18. If $x + y = 6$ and $y - 2 = 4$, then what is x?

    18–A 0   18–C 2

    18–B 1   18–D 3

19. The usual price of a car is $10,000. The dealer raises the price by 20%, and then takes off 20% with a sale. What is the new sale price?

    19–A $9,000   19–C $9,600

    19–B $9,200   19–D $10,000

20. In a small town 400 voters agree with a certain issue. This constitutes 20% of the voters. How many voters are there?

20–A 2,000   20–C 2,800

20–B 2,400   20–D 3,200

21. A farmer has 32 feet of fencing, and he wants to fence in the largest possible rectangular area. How long (in feet) should the sides of the rectangle be?

21–A 6 and 10   21–C 8 and 8

21–B 7 and 9   21–D 9 and 9

22. If a man walks 24 feet north, then 10 feet east, how far is he from his original location?

22–A 23 feet   22–C 25 feet

22–B 24 feet   22–D 26 feet

23. Jim reads one page of a 28 page book the first night, two the second night, three the third night, and so on. How many days will it take him to finish the book?

23–A 6   23–C 8

23–B 7   23–D 9

24. If a circle's circumference equals its area, what is its radius?

24–A 2   24–C 4

24–B 3   24–D 5

25. What is the square root of 225?

25–A 13   25–C 15

25–B 14   25–D 16

MATHEMATICS KNOWLEDGE DIAGNOSTIC TEST 1

ANSWER KEY

1. (C)	8. (D)	15. (C)	22. (D)
2. (A)	9. (B)	16. (D)	23. (B)
3. (A)	10. (A)	17. (B)	24. (A)
4. (D)	11. (B)	18. (A)	25. (C)
5. (B)	12. (D)	19. (C)	
6. (A)	13. (B)	20. (A)	
7. (C)	14. (A)	21. (C)	

Add up your correct answers and put the number here. _____

Now record your score on pages 91–92 and 451-452.

DETAILED EXPLANATIONS
OF ANSWERS

1.   **(C)**   The answer is (C) because 20 is half, or 50%, of 40.

2.   **(A)**   The answer is (A) because one third of the female population is eight. Thus, there are $3 \times 8 = 24$ women, so 24 is 60% of the employees. Dividing by 60%, $^{24}/_{.60} = 40$, so there are 40 employees.

3.   **(A)**   The answer is (A) because a right triangle has one angle of 90°, and the sum of the three angles of any triangle is 180°. So the three angles are 90°, 50°, and $180 - 90 - 50 = 40°$. The smallest is 40°.

4.   **(D)**   The answer is (D) because the area is $6x$, where x is the length of the other side. Then $6x = 24$, so $x = 4$.

5.   **(B)**   The answer is (B) because $12 \times 12 = 144$.

6.   **(A)**   The answer is (A) because $(x + 2)(x - 2) = x^2 - 2x + 2x - 4 = x^2 - 4$.

7.   **(C)**   The answer is (C) because, using the Pythagorean Theorem and letting x be the length of the other side, $5^2 + x^2 = 13^2$ (because one foot and one inch is 13 inches). Then $25 + x^2 = 169$, or $x^2 = 169 - 25 = 144$. Then x is 12 inches, or one foot.

8.   **(D)**   The answer is (D) because the area of a circle with radius r is πr^2, and the area of the larger circle is $\pi(2r)^2 = 4\pi r^2$. Thus, the ratio is 4:1.

9.   **(B)**   The answer is (B) because $10(-4) + 36 = 2(-4) + 4 = -4$.

10.   **(A)**   The answer is (A) because the area is x^2 and the perimeter is $4x$. Then $4x = x^2$, or x is 0 or 4. But x cannot be 0 (because then there would be no square), so $x = 4$.

11.   **(B)**   The answer is (B) because dividing by three gives $x > 3$.

12. **(D)** The answer is (D) because $42 + 28 + 59 + 61 = 190$, and $190/200 = 95/100 = 95\%$.

13. **(B)** The answer is (B) because dividing by -2 (and reversing the direction of the inequality) results in $x > -2$.

14. **(A)** The answer is (A) because the triangle must be equilateral, so all angles are equal. Each angle is $60°$.

15. **(C)** The answer is (C) because the third angle must be $60°$, so the largest minus the smallest is $90 - 30 = 60°$.

16. **(D)** The answer is (D) because $(4 \times 2) + 2 = 10$.

17. **(B)** The answer is (B) because $18/4 = 4.5$.

18. **(A)** The answer is (A) because $y = 6$ from the second equation, therefore after substituting y into the first equation we get $x = 0$.

19. **(C)** The answer is (C) because after the mark-up the price is ($10,000) (20\%) = $12,000. After the sale, the price is ($12,000) (80\%) = $9,600.

20. **(A)** The answer is (A) because 20\% of 2,000 is 400.

21. **(C)** The answer is (C) because the first three choices would make a 32 foot perimeter but the fourth would not, and thus is ruled out. The first three choices would yield areas of 60, 63, and 64 square feet, so choice (C) results in the largest area.

22. **(D)** The answer is (D) by the Pythagorean Theorem. Using $x^2 = 10^2 + 24^2 = 100 + 576 = 676$. Then $x = 26$.

23. **(B)** The answer is (B) because $1 + 2 + 3 + 4 + 5 + 6 + 7 = 28$.

24. **(A)** The answer is (A) because $2\pi r = \pi r^2$, or $2r = r^2$. Since r cannot be 0, $r = 2$.

25. **(C)** The answer is (C) because $15 \times 15 = 225$.

MECHANICAL COMPREHENSION DIAGNOSTIC TEST 1

Time: 19 Minutes
25 Questions

(Answer sheets appear in the back of this book.)

DIRECTIONS: Choose the best answer to each question and then darken the oval on your answer sheet.

1. The effort *E* needed to lift the 300-pound crate off the deck is

   1–A   150 lb.

   1–B   100 lb.

   1–C   75 lb.

   1–D   900 lb.

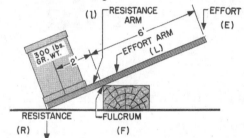

2. The mechanical advantage in this situation is

   2–A   2.

   2–B   4.

   2–C   5.

   2–D   3.

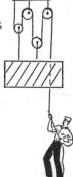

3. In the example shown, determine the force *P* needed to balance the two forces acting on the bell crank.

   3–A   160 lb

   3–B   62.5 lb

   3–C   80 lb

   3–D   112 lb

4. Determine the tension T that the 180-lb worker must exert on the rope in order to support himself in the bosun's chair.

    4–A   45 lb

    4–B   90 lb

    4–C   180 lb

    4–D   36 lb

5. A sailor is busy tearing a crate open. What must be the mechanical advantage in this situation?

    5–A   5

    5–B   0.42

    5–C   0.2

    5–D   6

6. The machine, shown in the figure below, is an example of

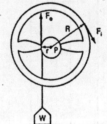

    6–A   a block and tackle.

    6–B   a Class III lever.

    6–C   a couple.

    6–D   a Class I lever.

7. The total twist or torque on the wheel applied by the officer on the gun pointer is

    7–A   10 ft-lb.

    7–B   20 ft-lb.

    7–C   40 ft-lb.

    7–D   120 ft-lb.

8. The true diameter of the half-inch drill bit as measured by the micrometer shown is

8–A   0.500 inch.

8–B   0.530 inch.

8–C   0.503 inch.

8–D   0.350 inch.

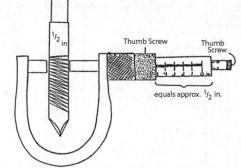

9. In the gear train below, when the leftmost gear turns in the direction shown, what direction does the gear on the far right turn?

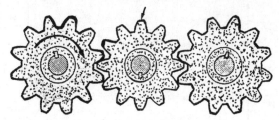

9–A   The center gear turns clockwise and the right gear turns counterclockwise.

9–B   The center gear turns counterclockwise and the right gear turns clockwise.

9–C   The center gear and the right gear both turn clockwise.

9–D   The center gear and the right gear both turn counterclockwise.

10. A tank for holding fresh water aboard a ship is 10 feet long, 6 feet wide, and 4 feet deep. Each cubic foot of water weighs about 62.5 pounds. What is the pressure on the bottom?

10–A 1.74 psi   10–C 2.61 psi

10–B 4.35 psi   10 D 20.88 psi

11. Assuming a $1^1/_2$-foot length of the lever arm, and a $^3/_8$-inch pitch for the thread, what is the theoretical mechanical advantage of the screw jack?

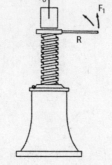

11–A 4.71

11–B 48

11–C 25.12

11–D 301.44

12. Which of the following statements is always true about the screw jack?

12–A The mechanical advantage is always less than one.

12–B The presence of friction is a big disadvantage.

12–C The presence of friction is a big advantage.

12–D The threads are cut so that the force used to overcome friction is always smaller than the force used to do useful work.

13. The turnbuckle is a device used to take all the slack out of a rope or cable attached between two fixed points. What must be true about the threads of such a device?

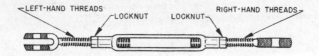

13–A Both bolts of the turnbuckle have left-hand threads.

13–B Both bolts of the turnbuckle have right-hand threads.

13–C The pitch of the thread on one side must be twice that on the other side.

13–D One bolt of the turnbuckle has left-hand threads, and the other bolt has right-hand threads. Thus by turning the turnbuckle, slack can be taken out or added to the cable.

14. What is the function of the idler in the gear train below?

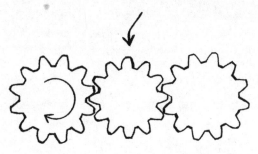

   14–A Double the speed of the right gear.

   14–B Reduce the speed of the left gear.

   14–C Reverse the direction of rotation of the right gear but keep the speed unchanged.

   14–D Transmit the rotation to the right gear, keeping both the direction and speed unchanged.

15. The theoretical mechanical advantage of any gear train is

   15–A the product of the number of teeth on the driven gears, divided by the product of the number of teeth on the driver gears.

   15–B the ratio of the number of teeth on the driven gears, divided by the ratio of the number of teeth on the driver gears.

   15–C the difference between the number of teeth on the driven gears and the number of teeth on the driver gears.

   15–D the sum of the number of teeth on the driver gears and the number of teeth on the driven gears.

16. To raise the 600-pound load 20 feet, the sailor needs to exert a pull of

   16–A 150 pounds.

   16–B 120 pounds.

   16–C 3000 pounds.

   16–D 100 pounds.

17. In the previous question, the length of tackle the sailor needs to pull in order to lift the block 20 ft is

17–A 20 ft.

17–C 100 ft.

17–B 4 ft.

17–D 80 ft.

18. A horsepower, which is the unit in which power is measured, is given by

18–A 33,000 ft-lb per minute.

18–B 550 ft-lb per minute.

18–C 33,000 ft-lb per second.

18–D 550 ft-lb per hour.

19. Which of the following statements applies to a torsion spring?

19–A It tends to shorten in action.

19–B It tends to lengthen in action.

19–C It is made to transmit a direct pull.

19–D It operates by coiling and uncoiling and is made to transmit a twist instead of a direct pull.

20. The serviceman must move the rear end of a machine one half-foot against a frictional resistance of 1,500 pounds. If the jack he's using has a $2^1/_2$-foot handle, how much effort must he exert? The pitch of the jack screw is $^1/_4$ in.

20–A 4 pounds

20–B 6.17 pounds

20–C 2 pounds

20–D 24 pounds

21. In reality, the force exerted on the handle as calculated in the previous problem wouldn't do the job, and a pull of at least 10 pounds would be required. What is the efficiency of the jack?

21–A 80%

21–C 0.66%

21–B 40%

21–D 20%

22. Which of the following is NOT a type of sliding motion bearing?

22–A Reciprocal motion bearing

22–B Thrust bearing

22–C Journal bearing

22–D Ball bearings

23. In order to add or subtract the revolutions of two shafts, which of the following machines is used?

23–A The gear differential

23–B The helical spring

23–C The Hooke-type universal joint

23–D The Bendix-Weiss universal joint

24. In the Prony brake set up shown here, the pulley turns in a clockwise direction. The friction between the belt and the pulley makes the belt try to move with the pulley. If Scale A reads 25 pounds and Scale B reads 5 pounds, what is the drag, or force against which the motor is working?

24–A 25 pounds

24–B 5 pounds

24–C 20 pounds

24–D 30 pounds

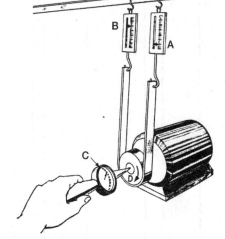

25. What power is supplied to a 12-hp motor, having an efficiency of 90%, when it is delivering its full rated power?

25–A 13.3 hp   25–C 12 hp

25–B 10.8 hp   25–D 11 hp

MECHANICAL COMPREHENSION DIAGNOSTIC TEST 1

ANSWER KEY

1. (B)	8. (C)	15. (A)	22. (D)
2. (B)	9. (B)	16. (B)	23. (A)
3. (D)	10. (A)	17. (C)	24. (C)
4. (D)	11. (D)	18. (A)	25. (A)
5. (A)	12. (C)	19. (D)	
6. (D)	13. (D)	20. (C)	
7. (B)	14. (D)	21. (D)	

Add up your correct answers and put the number here. _____

Now record your score on pages 91–92 and 451-452.

DETAILED EXPLANATIONS
OF ANSWERS

1. **(B)** (A) is incorrect. l is taken to be 3', $L = 6$'. (B) is correct.

$$\frac{L}{l} = \frac{R}{E};$$

$L = 6$, $l = 2$, $R = 300$. Cross multiply $\Rightarrow E = \frac{1}{3}(300) = 100$. (C) is incorrect. L is taken to be 8', $l = 2$'. (D) is incorrect. The wrong formula was used:

$$\frac{L}{l} = \frac{E}{R}.$$

2. **(B)** (A) is incorrect. This is the number of pulley hinges connected to the load, but each pulley is supported by two parts. (B) is correct. The load is lifted by four parts of the rope around the three left pulleys. (C) is incorrect. The fifth part of the rope (held by the man) does not lift the load but only serves to change the direction of the fourth part. (D) is incorrect. This is the number of pulley hinges connected to the top fixture, which serve to support the top three pulleys, not the load.

3. **(D)** (A) is incorrect, used

$$5P = (40 + 60) \times 8 = 800 \Rightarrow P = 160$$

(B) is incorrect, used

$$8P = (40 + 60) \times 5 = 500 \Rightarrow P = 62.5$$

(C) is incorrect, used

$$5P = (40 + 60) \times 4 = 400 \Rightarrow P = 80$$

(D) is correct.

$$5P = 40 \times 8 + 60 \times 4 = 560 \Rightarrow P = 112 \text{ lb}$$

4. **(D)** (A) is incorrect. This assumes only four parts of the rope support the load:

$$\frac{180}{4} = 45$$

(B) is incorrect. This assumes only two parts of the rope support the load. (C) is incorrect. This assumes the rope-pulley arrangement only serves to change the force's direction. (D) is correct. By holding the fifth part of the rope, the worker effectively divides his weight in five parts which then support the whole weight:

$$\frac{180\ lb}{5} = 36\ lb$$

5. **(A)** (A) is correct. $2^{1/2}' = 30''$.

$$M.A. = \frac{R}{E} = \frac{L}{l} = \frac{30''}{6''} = 5$$

(B) is incorrect, taken $L = 2^{1/2}''$. (C) is incorrect, used inverted formula:

$$M.A. = \frac{l}{L} = \frac{1}{5}$$

(D) is incorrect, used $L = 30'' + 6'' = 36''$.

6. **(D)** (A) is incorrect because, in the block and tackle, the effort is applied at the other end of the rope and at the same distance from the axle center. (B) This machine is actually a revolving Class I lever, because the fulcrum (axle center) is between the effort and the resistance. (C) This is not a couple because only one effort, F_1, is applied. (D) This is the proper answer, because the machine is a revolving Class I lever.

7. **(B)** (A) is incorrect because this is only the moment of the top or bottom force:

$$20\ lb \times {}^{1}/2\ ft = 10\ ft\text{-}lb.$$

(B) is correct, it is the sum of the torques of the top and bottom forces:

$$10\ ft\text{-}lb + 10\ ft\text{-}lb = 20\ ft\text{-}lb.$$

(C) is incorrect, the torque is computed wrong:

$$20\ lb \times 2\ ft = 40\ ft\text{-}lb$$

and the two torques are added as such. (D) is incorrect, the radius was mistakenly taken to be 6 ft instead of 6 inches:

$$20\ lb \times 6\ ft = 120\ lb\text{-}ft.$$

8.   **(C)**   (A) is incorrect. This is not what the micrometer measures, only the nominal value of the drill bit diameter. (B) is incorrect. This assumes one of the units on the thimble is $1/100$ of an inch. It is actually $1/25$ of $1/40$ inch, or $1/1000$ of an inch. (C) is correct. This assumes correctly that the units on the sleeve are in tenths of an inch, while those on the thimble are in thousandths of an inch. (D) is incorrect. This assumes the units on the sleeve in hundredths of an inch and those on the thimble in tenths of an inch.

9.   **(B)**   (A) is incorrect. The center gear must be turning counterclockwise if the left gear is turning clockwise. (B) is correct. The center gear turns opposite to the left gear, that is counterclockwise, while the right gear turns opposite to the center gear, which is clockwise. (C) and (D) are incorrect. Two gears in series never turn in the same direction.

10. **(A)**   (A) is correct.

$$\text{Force} = \text{Weight of water} = \text{weight per cubic foot} \times \text{volume}$$

$$= 62.5 \text{ pounds/ft}^3 \times 10 \text{ ft} \times 6 \text{ ft} \times 4 \text{ ft}$$

$$= 15,000 \text{ lb}$$

Bottom Area $= 10 \times 6 = 60 \text{ ft}^2 = 60 \times 144 = 8,640 \text{ in}^2$

so that

$$P = \frac{F}{A} = \frac{15,000 \text{ lb}}{8,640 \text{ in}^2} = 1.74 \text{ psi}$$

(B) is incorrect. Here, the area was taken to be

$4 \times 6 = 24 \text{ ft}^2 = 3,456 \text{ in}^2$

which is depth $\times$ length. (C) is incorrect. Here, the area was taken to be

$10 \times 4 = 40 \text{ ft}^2 = 5,760 \text{ in}^2$

which is depth $\times$ width. (D) is incorrect. Here, the area was taken to be

$10 \times 6 = 60 \text{ ft}^2$

which is width $\times$ length, but was converted to square inches using 12 in^2 per ft^2:

$60 \times 12 = 720 \text{ in}^2.$

11. **(D)** (A) is incorrect, algebraic error in the use of the formula:

$$M.A. = \frac{2\pi r}{p}$$

$$= \frac{2 \times 3.14 \times 18}{\dfrac{3}{8}}$$

was taken to be $2 \times 3.14 \times 18 / (3/8) = 4.71$. (B) is incorrect, wrong formula for the mechanical advantage:

$$M.A. = \frac{r}{p}$$

$$= \frac{18}{\dfrac{3}{8}} = 6 \times 8 = 48$$

(C) is incorrect, wrong units used in the correct formula (did not convert the radius to inches):

$$\frac{2 \times 3.14 \times 1.5}{\dfrac{3}{8}} = 25.12$$

(D) is correct.

$$M.A. = \frac{2\pi r}{p} = \frac{2 \times 3.14 \times 18}{\dfrac{3}{8}} = \frac{(2 \times 3.14 \times 18) \text{ in}}{.375 \text{ in}} = 301.44$$

12. **(C)** (A) is incorrect. This cannot be true because the screw jack would be useless. (B) is incorrect. The presence of friction is a big advantage as explained in (C). (C) is correct. The presence of friction happens to be an advantage in the case of the screw jack because it holds the load in place while no input force is being applied. It also prevents the jack from spinning right back down to the bottom as soon as the handle is released. (D) is incorrect. The threads are cut so that the force used to overcome friction is *greater* than the force used to do useful work.

13. **(D)** (A) and (B) are incorrect. The turnbuckle cannot turn with this arrangement. (C) is incorrect. The threads on the turnbuckle must have the

same pitch. (D) is correct. As can be guessed from the figure shown, this and the condition that the pitch on both threads be of the same size, are necessary and sufficient conditions for the proper operation of the turn-buckle.

14. **(D)** (A) is incorrect. This cannot be the case since the right gear and the left gear have the same number of teeth. (B) is incorrect for the same reason mentioned in (A). (C) is incorrect. The idler turns counterclock-wise, while the right gear turns clockwise, in the same direction as the left gear. (D) is correct. This is the correct function of the idler.

15. **(A)** The correct answer is (A). It is easy to see this in the case of one gear driving another: the mechanical efficiency is indeed the ratio of the number of teeth on the output (or driven) gear to the number of teeth on the input (or driver) gear. It is also obvious that if a third gear is driving these two gears, the mechanical advantage becomes equal to the product of the number of teeth on the two driving gears divided by the number of teeth on the driven gear.

16. **(B)** (A) is incorrect. This assumes a mechanical advantage of 4. It is actually 5. (B) is correct. The mechanical advantage is 5 = number of ropes in contact with the moving block

$$\Rightarrow \frac{600}{5} = 120 \text{ pounds.}$$

(C) is incorrect. The effort is obtained by dividing the resistance by the mechanical advantage, not multiplying it. (D) is incorrect. The mechanical advantage was incorrectly taken to be 6 in this case.

17. **(C)** (A) is incorrect. It should be obvious that the sailor has to pull the rope a greater distance than the load is lifted. (B) is incorrect. The length the rope has to be pulled is obtained by multiplying the 20 ft by the mechanical advantage 5, not dividing. (C) is correct. The correct length is obtained by multiplying 20 ft by the mechanical advantage 5:

20 × 50 = 100 ft.

(D) is incorrect. The mechanical advantage was taken to be 4. It is actually 5.

18. **(A)** A horsepower is the power required to lift a 330-pound load 100 ft in one minute, thus it is equivalent to 33,000 ft-lb per minute. It is also equivalent to

$$\frac{33,000}{60} = 550 \text{ ft-lb per second or } 33,000 \times 60 = 1,980,000 \text{ ft-lb per hour.}$$

19. **(D)** (A), (B), and (C) apply to helical compression and tension springs, while (D) applies to the torsion spring.

20. **(C)** (A) is incorrect because it assumes the effort is acting on a distance of $\pi \times R$ instead of $2\pi R$. (B) is incorrect because it assumes the effort is acting on a distance of $2R$ instead of $2\pi R$. (C) is correct.

$$F_1 \times S_1 = F_2 \times S_2$$

where

F_1 is the unknown force on the handle.

$S_1 = 2\pi R = 2 \times 3.14 \times 2.5 \text{ ft}$

$F_2 = 1,500 \text{ lb}$

$$S_2 = \frac{1}{4"} = \frac{1}{48} \text{ft}$$

so that

$$F_1 = \frac{1,500 \text{ lbs}}{48 \times 2 \times 3.14 \times 2.5} = 2 \text{ pounds}$$

(D) is incorrect because $S_2 = {}^1/_4"$ was not converted to feet and the result is 12-fold in error.

21. **(D)** (A) is incorrect. Only 2 of the 10 pounds is usefully employed to do the job. (B) is incorrect. This is based on the wrong result that the effort is 4 pounds. (C) is incorrect. This is obtained by taking the ratio

$$\frac{10}{1,500} \times 100\%$$

which is not the efficiency of the machine. (D) is correct.

$$\frac{2 \text{ lb}}{10 \text{ lb}} \times 100\% = 20\%$$

22. **(D)** While (A), (B), and (C) are examples of sliding motion bearings, (D) is an example of the antifrictional type.

23. **(A)** The gear differential is a mechanism capable of adding and subtracting the total revolutions of two shafts. The helical spring (B) is used for compression, tension or torsion, while the two universal joints (C), (D) are two types of couplings which are used to couple two shafts so as to turn as one shaft.

24. **(C)** The correct force is 20 pounds which is the difference between 25 and 5. It is not the sum of the two forces, nor is it any of the forces by itself.

25. **(A)** From the definition of efficiency,

$$\text{efficiency} = \frac{\text{power output}}{\text{power input}}$$

we invert the relation to get:

$$\text{power input} = \frac{\text{power output}}{\text{efficiency}}$$

$$= \frac{12}{0.9} = 13.33 \text{ hp}$$

Thus, the correct answer is (A).

ELECTRONICS INFORMATION DIAGNOSTIC TEST 1

Time: 9 Minutes
20 Questions

(Answer sheets appear in the back of this book.)

> **DIRECTIONS:** Choose the best answer to each question by darkening the oval on your answer sheet.

Following are two sample questions.

S1. What is the current at point C in the figure?

S1–A 0 A

S1–B 10 A

S1–C – 10 A

S1–D – 9.3 A

S1. **(A)** First we must recognize D_1 as a diode. Then by realizing the current is positive, we see that the current is trying to enter the diode in the anode end (the anode end only accepts negative current). If current cannot flow through D_1, the current at point C must be zero.

S2. What is the voltage across the load R?

S2–A 13 V

S2–B 7 V

S2–C – 13 V

S2–D – 7 V

S2. **(A)** Recalling the theory that voltages *add* in series, we have + 13 V at point A. Since point A′ is grounded as shown by the symbol, the voltage across the load is + 13 V.

72

1. What is the period of the voltage waveform out of a wall outlet?

   1–A   60 seconds   1–C $1/60$ second

   1–B   6 seconds   1–D $1/6$ second

2. A television is brought from Germany to the U.S. It worked with 220 volts and 1 amp in Europe. What current would be needed for it to work in the U.S. at 110 volts?

   2–A $1/2$ amp   2–C   1 amp

   2–B   2 amps   2–D   4 amps

3. A fuse keeps burning out in the basement every time the toaster is turned on. You change the fuse from 15 amps to 20 amps and solve the problem. What have you done?

   3–A   A smart thing! Now you can use your toaster in peace.

   3–B   A dumb thing! The rating of the wire may not be able to handle the extra current.

   3–C   Nothing was accomplished, since the fuses have nothing to do with the power needed to run the toaster.

   3–D   Nothing at all because you should have decreased the fuse rating to stop it from blowing.

4. A wire is loose in a damp piece of high voltage equipment. This wire is not touching anything, but it has a very high voltage on it and it is very close to a ground pipe. What *could* happen?

   4–A   Nothing — as long as the wire touches nothing.

   4–B   The voltage can arc across to the ground pipe.

   4–C   The charge on the wire will melt the wire.

   4–D   The current will flow back up the wire and out causing the voltage to drop to zero.

5. One of the lights in your Christmas light string has burned out. This causes all of the lights to go out. Why?

   5–A   The lights are wired up in a parallel configuration so the voltage is equal across all of the lights.

5–B The burned-out light is a short circuit so this burns all of the other lights out.

5–C The lights are wired up in a series configuration so the current path is broken when the light burns out.

5–D The lights are wired up in a parallel configuration so the current path is broken when the light burns out.

6. Which of these is the safest place to be during a lightning storm?

6–A An automobile

6–B A swimming pool

6–C A golf course

6–D In the house holding a metal faucet so you can be grounded.

7. What symbol is shown here?

7–A A resistor

7–B A diode

7–C A capacitor

7–D A transistor

8. What is the best way to connect electronic wires?

8–A Wire-wrap

8–B Twist the two wires together

8–C Tape the two wires together

8–D Solder the two wires together

9. Ohm's Law is defined by which equation?

9–A $V = RI$ 9–C $Q = CV$

9–B $V = R^2 I$ 9–D $I = RV$

10. What is the usual color for insulation on a ground wire?

10–A Black   10–C Blue

10–B White   10–D Red

11. For an electrical fire in the kitchen, what must be used to put it out?

    11–A Water extinguisher

    11–B CO_2 extinguisher

    11–C Non-conductive extinguisher

    11–D Flour

12. Contacts are usually gold as opposed to copper because

    12–A copper is not pure and gold is.

    12–B copper oxidizes.

    12–C gold is cheap.

    12–D gold increases value of equipment.

13. What does this symbol stand for?

    13–A A transistor

    13–B A resistor

    13–C A varactor

    13–D An inducer

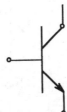

14. Fiber optics are preferred for phone lines over metal cables because

    14–A fiber is lighter so they can be carried easier up the telephone poles.

    14–B fiber lines are bigger so they can take more calls.

    14–C fiber lines can take more calls for the same size wire.

    14–D fiber lines can take less calls so there is a better quality.

15. A battery's voltage output is shown by which plot?

    15–A

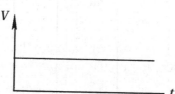

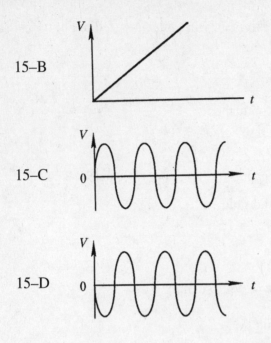

15–B

15–C

15–D

16. The Right Hand Rule (RHR) in electromagnetics is?

    16–A RHR is used to determine the direction of magnetic force lines.

    16–B RHR is used to determine the direction of electric field lines.

    16–C RHR is used to determine the direction of the flux capacitance.

    16–D RHR is used to determine North and South.

17. In a transformer

    17–A the primary has only a few turns, while the secondary has many turns to step up the voltage.

    17–B the primary has many turns, while the secondary has only a few turns to step up the voltage.

    17–C the primary and the secondary have an equal number of turns to step up the voltage.

    17–D the primary and the secondary do not have any turns, since that has nothing to do with stepping up the voltage.

18. The transformer shown has a step down ratio of

18–A 1:4.

18–B 1:2.

18–C 4:3.

18–D 4:1.

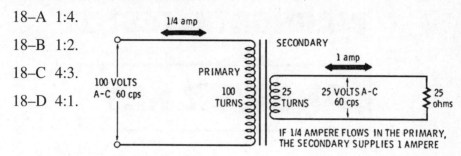

IF 1/4 AMPERE FLOWS IN THE PRIMARY,
THE SECONDARY SUPPLIES 1 AMPERE

19. How do you decrease line drop?

19–A Increase the overall impedance across the line.

19–B Increase the current and keep everything else equal.

19–C Line drop cannot be avoided; it's nature at work.

19–D Decrease the overall impedance in the line.

20. To discharge a capacitor safely, what must you do?

20–A Grab both terminals with your hands.

20–B Grab both terminals while wearing rubber gloves.

20–C Place a glass rod across the terminals.

20–D Place a screwdriver across the terminals.

ELECTRONICS INFORMATION DIAGNOSTIC TEST 1

ANSWER KEY

1. (C)	6. (A)	11. (C)	16. (A)
2. (B)	7. (C)	12. (B)	17. (A)
3. (B)	8. (D)	13. (A)	18. (D)
4. (B)	9. (A)	14. (C)	19. (D)
5. (C)	10. (B)	15. (A)	20. (D)

Add up your correct answers and put the number here. _____

Now record your score on pages 91–92 and 451-452.

DETAILED EXPLANATIONS
OF ANSWERS

1. **(C)** The period of something is equal to 1/frequency. We know that everything is operated at 110 volts and 60 Hz in our houses. A hertz (Hz) = 1/sec = sec^{-1}. So,

$$60 \text{ Hz} = 60 \text{ sec}^{-1} = \frac{1}{\text{period}} \Rightarrow \text{Period} = \frac{1}{60 \text{ sec}^{-1}} = \frac{1}{60} \text{ sec.}$$

2. **(B)** From the power equation,

$$P = VI$$

we have the TV from Europe:

$$P = (200)(1) = 220 \text{ Watts.}$$

To use this TV in the U.S., $V = 110$. So,

$$P = 220 \text{ W} = (110 \text{ V})(I)$$

$$2 \text{ amps} = I$$

3. **(B)** Fuses provide a safety limit for the protection of your household items. By putting a larger fuse in, we allow a greater amount of current to pass through. This could not only damage the other household items, but even more dangerously, could cause a problem with the house safety. Recall wiring is sized according to the amount of current expected to pass through. By allowing a larger current to pass through, we can cause the wire to burn up and start a fire.

4. **(B)** Normally air is a good insulator, but if enough charge is built-up on a wire's tip, it can "jump" or arc across to the ground pipe.

5. **(C)** Devices in series have a common current — if this current path is broken, the current cannot flow. Devices in parallel have a common voltage but not a common current.

6. **(A)** Only in an automobile with rubber tires are you not grounded and thus safe.

7.   **(C)**   The symbol is one of a capacitor. A capacitor is a device known for storing charge.

8.   **(D)**   Soldering is the best way to connect two wires. The solder provides stability mechanically and electrically.

9.   **(A)**   By definition Ohm's Law equals

$V = RI.$

10. **(B)**   Be very careful when checking wires — the white wire is usually the ground, not the black. The black and red are usually hot!

11. **(C)**   A fire extinguisher that puts out a foam that is non-conducting is needed. This will avoid any shocks.

12. **(B)**   Copper reacts with oxygen — oxidation. A film is produced called an oxide. This oxide is insulating. If an insulating film exists between contacts, the contact cannot be properly made.

13. **(A)**   This is the symbol for a transistor.

14. **(C)**   The capacity of fiber optic lines is much larger than that of metallic lines (wires).

15. **(A)**   A battery is a DC source. In other words, the output is constant over time.

16. **(A)**   By placing your right thumb in the direction of the current and curling your finger around the wire you can find the direction of the magnetic lines created.

17. **(A)**   The turns in the primary and the secondary of a transformer provide whether the voltage is increased or decreased. When the primary turns are less than the secondary, then the result is a step-down (a decrease). When the opposite is true, the effect is to step-up the voltage (increase).

18. **(D)**   From the relation:

$$\frac{N_{primary}}{N_{secondary}} = \frac{\text{\# of turns}}{\text{\# of turns}} = \text{Ratio}$$

$$\frac{100}{25} = \frac{4}{1}$$

19. **(D)** Line drop is caused by a decrease in voltage because of the resistance in the line. To avoid line drops make sure the resistance in the line is minimized.

20. **(D)** A screwdriver usually has a plastic or rubber handle — this keeps you from being grounded. By placing the metal part of the screwdriver across the terminals, the capacitor can be discharged without injury.

ASSEMBLING OBJECTS
DIAGNOSTIC TEST 1

Time: 9 Minutes
16 Questions

(Answer sheets appear in the back of this book.)

DIRECTIONS: Choose the answer that best shows the objects reassembled. Darken the corresponding oval on your answer sheet.

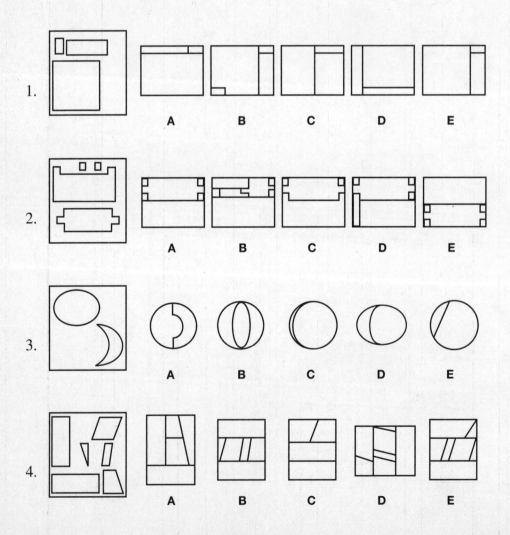

1.   A   B   C   D   E

2.   A   B   C   D   E

3.   A   B   C   D   E

4.   A   B   C   D   E

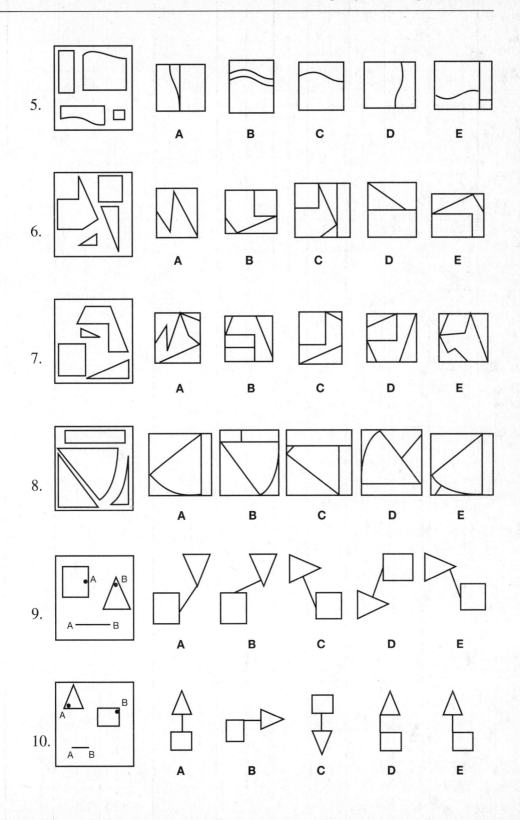

5.   A   B   C   D   E

6.   A   B   C   D   E

7.   A   B   C   D   E

8.   A   B   C   D   E

9.   A   B   C   D   E

10.   A   B   C   D   E

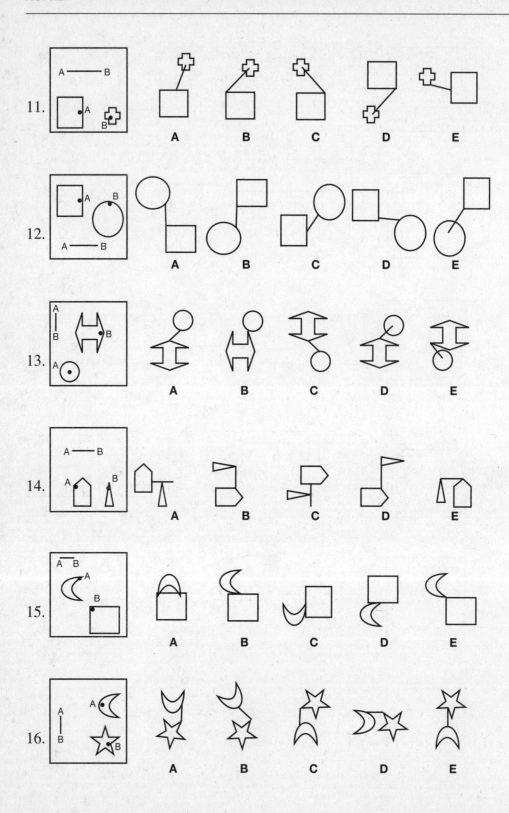

11.

12.

13.

14.

15.

16.

ASSEMBLING OBJECTS DIAGNOSTIC TEST 1

ANSWER KEY

1. (E)	7. (C)	12. (C)
2. (C)	8. (A)	13. (D)
3. (D)	9. (A)	14. (B)
4. (B)	10. (D)	15. (E)
5. (E)	11. (A)	16. (E)
6. (B)		

Add up your correct answers and put the number here. _____

Now record your score on pages 91–92 and 451-452.

DETAILED EXPLANATIONS
OF ANSWERS

1. **(E)** The first piece to mark is the square. This eliminates (B), (C), and (A). (D) does not have the small rectangle.

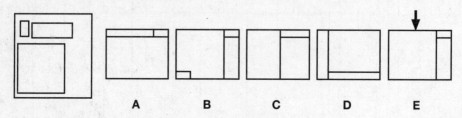

2. **(C)** (C) is the only shape with 4 pieces

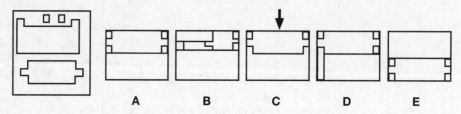

3. **(D)** The "moon shape" only appears in (D) and (B). (D) has 2 objects so it must be the right answer.

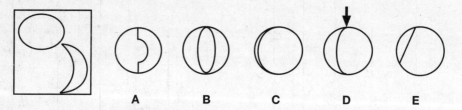

4. **(B)** (A) can be eliminated because it has 5 objects and (D) and (E) have 7. (B) is correct because it has the correct shapes.

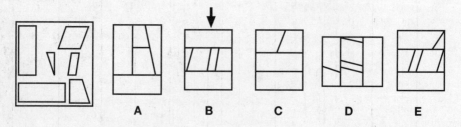

5. **(E)** Starting with the unique "wavy" shapes leaves (C), (D), and (E). (B) has 3 wavy shapes, not 2. (E) is correct because it has the 2 wavy objects and the 2 rectangles.

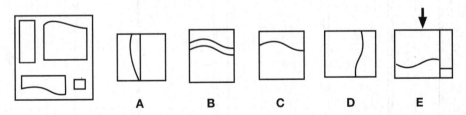

6. **(B)** Again, search for the unique shape first. This eliminates (A) and (D). The others are eliminated because the have rectangles, not a square.

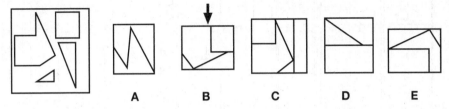

7. **(C)** (A) and (E) do not have the unique shape. (C) is the only one with the square.

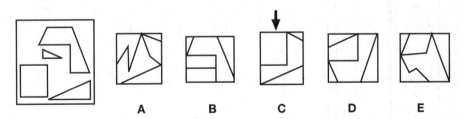

8. **(A)** The "pizza slice" eliminates (C). The large triangle eliminates (D). The large rectangle leaves only (A).

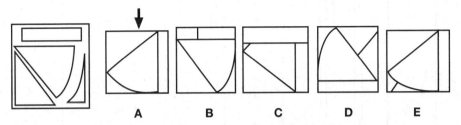

9. **(A)** The tip of the triangle must be used. This eliminates (C), (D) and (E). (A) is correct because it uses the middle of the square.

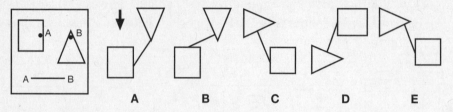

10. **(D)** The answer is (D) because it is the only object that uses the corner of both the square and the triangle.

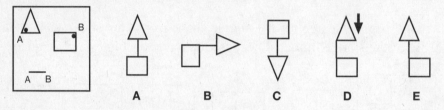

11. **(A)** The middle of the square leaves (A) and (E). The line must cross into the "cross" object. This leaves only (A).

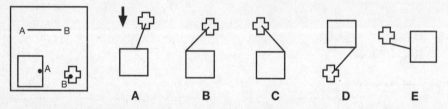

12. **(C)** The middle of the square leaves only (C).

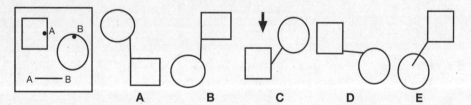

13. **(D)** The middle of the circle is used, leaving only (D) and (E). (D) is correct because it has the point of the arrow.

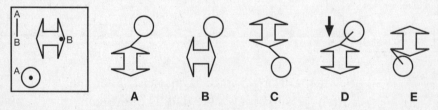

14. **(B)** The tip of the triangle leaves only (E) and (B). The side of the house object must be used, leaving (B) as the only right answer.

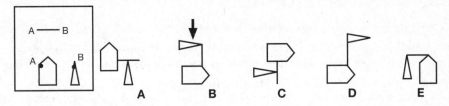

15. **(E)** The tip of the "moon" must connect to the corner of the square. This only occurs in (E).

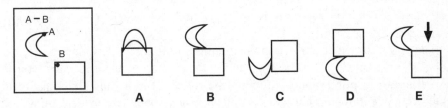

16. **(E)** The answer is (E). The middle of the moon must be used, which eliminates (A), (C) and (D). (E) is correct because it uses the middle of the star.

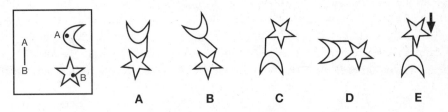

SELF-ASSESSMENT CHART

You have finished a complete ASVAB test. That wasn't so bad after all! You may find that you could answer more questions in the sections that interested you most. This may be because it is easier to concentrate on areas of greater interest, because you like them so much. For instance, if you have always been interested in how cars run, you may have done better on the Auto and Shop subsection. This theory also works in the reverse; sometimes you don't go out of your way to learn about the subjects that are of less interest to you. You should understand that a low score on a diagnostic subtest *does not necessarily mean* that you are "not good" at that section. You may have never been interested in it, or just never learned about it.

There is a study schedule at the beginning of this book designed to help you budget your study time wisely. It is important to keep your performance on the diagnostic test in mind while following the study schedule and studying for the ASVAB. The following self-assessment chart will help you to determine your performance level on the diagnostic test, and will also suggest some additional study hints that you can use along with the study schedule.

In order to find your performance level, refer to the individual answer sheet for each of the subtests in the Diagnostic Test. Take the number of questions you answered correctly on each subtest from the answer sheet and record it in the box immediately to the right of the name of that subtest on the chart below. For example, in General Science, you would look on p. 7 to find the number of questions you answered correctly, and place this number to the right of the words "General Science" in the chart on the next page.

The terms used on the self-assessment chart are straightforward: if you earned a rating of "Outstanding," consider this one of your strong subject areas. A rating of "Satisfactory" means that you would be considered proficient in this area. If your number of correct answers falls into the "Needs More Work" category, you should plan to focus on those subtests first. Start with the first hint in the "Rating" column for each test. Regardless of your score, you should follow the first hint. If your score is below "Outstanding," do the study hint under "Satisfactory," and so forth until you reach your skill level. So, if your score was "Satisfactory," you should follow the hint for "Outstanding" and then the hint for "Satisfactory." If your score indicates "Needs More Work," you should follow the "Outstanding" hint, then go to the "Satisfactory" hint, and, finally, the hint for "Needs More Work." For example, if you "Need More Work" on the General Science subtest, you should read the General Science Review, highlight scientific terms for quick reference, and then implement a flash-card system. These hints will help you to direct your study so that you can attack your points of weakness and develop them to boost your ASVAB score.

The review chapters are full of information that can help you raise your scores on each of the tests. If you did "Outstanding" on any subtest, *it is still important to read the review,* since you don't want the areas that are already strong to lag behind while you are working on your weaknesses.

SUBTEST	SCORE	RATING
1. General Science	More than 23 correct	**Outstanding**—Read the General Science Review.
25 Questions	20 – 23 correct	**Satisfactory**—As you read, highlight scientific terms for quick reference.
	Less than 20 correct	**Needs More Work**—Implement a flash-card system by placing each unknown term on one side of an index card and its definition on the other. Quiz yourself throughout the day.
2. Arithmetic Reasoning	More than 28 correct	**Outstanding**—Read the Arithmetic Reasoning Review.
30 Questions	25 – 28 correct	**Satisfactory**—Re-read the review before you take any practice tests.
	Less than 25 correct	**Needs More Work**—Try and re-try the problems you missed on the Diagnostic. If the same type of problem keeps giving you trouble, talk to your teacher.
3. Word Knowledge	More than 33 correct	**Outstanding**—Read the Word Knowledge Review.
35 Questions	30 – 33 correct	**Satisfactory**—Highlight any unfamiliar words, prefixes, and suffixes.
	Less than 30 correct	**Needs More Work**—Implement a flash-card system by placing each unknown word on one side of an index card, and the definition on the other side. Quiz yourself throughout the day.
4. Paragraph Comprehension	More than 13 correct	**Outstanding**—Read the Paragraph Comprehension Review.
15 Questions	11 – 13 correct	**Satisfactory**—Take notes on the review chapter. Re-take this subtest and apply the skills you learned from the review.
	Less than 11 correct	**Needs More Work**—Use your critical reading skills while doing outside reading in books and magazines throughout the day.
5. Auto and Shop Information	More than 23 correct	**Outstanding**—Read the Auto and Shop Information Review.
25 Questions	20 – 23 correct	**Satisfactory**—Highlight all unknown terms in the review chapter.
	Less than 20 correct	**Needs More Work**—Draw your own diagrams of all of the systems of cars, and make your own drawings of tools used in a shop.

SUBTEST	SCORE	RATING
6. Mathematics Knowledge	More than 23 correct	**Outstanding**—Read the Mathematics Knowledge Review.
25 Questions	20 – 23 correct	**Satisfactory**—After you read the review, go over the problems you answered incorrectly.
	Less than 20 correct	**Needs More Work**—Re-take the Diagnostic while referring back to the review. Consult a math teacher for any questions which continue to be a problem for you.
7. Mechanical Comprehension	More than 23 correct	**Outstanding**—Read the Mechanical Comprehension Review.
25 Questions	20 – 23 correct	**Satisfactory**—Refer to the review while correcting your test. Highlight and take notes on the concepts with which you had trouble.
	Less than 20 correct	**Needs More Work**—Sketch the machines, and make arrows to demonstrate the forces at work. For fun, and to more clearly understand the processes, you might try to build the more simple machines, like the pulley and the lever.
8. Electronics Information	More than 18 correct	**Outstanding**—Read the Electronics Information Review.
20 Questions	15 – 18 correct	**Satisfactory**—Highlight any material you don't recognize in the review, and sketch diagrams that demonstrate the concepts.
	Less than 15 correct	**Needs More Work**—On a piece of notebook paper, take notes on the chapter in your own words. Use this sheet (along with your own diagrams) to study throughout the day.
9. Assembling Objects	More than 14 correct	**Outstanding**—Read the Assembling Objects Review.
16 Questions	12 – 14 correct	**Satisfactory**—After you read the review, go over any problems you answered incorrectly.
	Less than 12 correct	**Needs More Work**—Re-take the Diagnostic while referring back to the review. For fun, and to more clearly understand the processes, you might try to build the objects with pieces of paper cut to size.

ASVAB
Armed Services Vocational Aptitude Battery

Subject Reviews

GENERAL SCIENCE REVIEW

General Science, as its name implies, is a broad survey of the most important concepts from the three basic fields of science: life science, physical science, and earth science. This review is not meant to serve as a textbook or comprehensive study of any given topic; rather, its purpose is to remind you of topics and concepts that are normally taught in junior and senior high school science classes.

Each of the basic science fields contain major specializations, as follows:

life science—biology, ecology, human health

physical science—measurement, chemistry, physics

earth science—astronomy, geology, meteorology, oceanography

LIFE SCIENCE

Biology

Biology is the study of living things. Living things are differentiated from nonliving things by the ability to perform all the following life activities at some point in a normal life span.

Life Activity	Function
food getting	procurement of food through eating, absorption, or photosynthesis
respiration	exchange of gases
excretion	elimination of wastes
growth and repair	increase in size over part or all of a life span, repair of damaged tissue
movement	willful movement of a portion of a living thing's body, or direction of growth in a particular direction
response	reaction to events or things in the environment
secretion	production and distribution of chemicals that aid digestion, growth, metabolism, etc.
reproduction	the making of new living things similar to the parent organism(s)

It is important to note that living things *must*, during a typical life span, be able to perform all these activities. It is quite common for nonliving things to perform one or more of these activities (for example: robots—movement, response, repair; crystals—growth).

Cells

Cells are the basic structure unit of living things. A cell is the smallest portion of a living thing that can, by itself, be considered living. Plant cells and animal cells, though generally similar, are distinctly different because of the unique plant structures, cell walls, and chloroplasts.

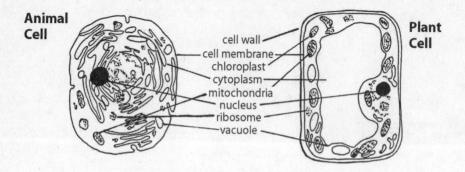

Animal Cell

cell wall
cell membrane
chloroplast
cytoplasm
mitochondria
nucleus
ribosome
vacuole

Plant Cell

Figure 1

Cells are made of several smaller structures, called organelles, which are surrounded by cell fluid, or cytoplasm. The function of several cell structures, including organelles, is listed below.

Cell Structure	Function
cell membrane	controls movement of materials into and out of cells
cell wall	gives rigid structure to plant cells
chloroplast	contains chlorophyll, which enables green plants to make their own food
cytoplasm	jellylike substance inside of a cell
mitochondria	liberate energy from glucose in cells for use in cellular activities
nucleus	directs cell activities; holds DNA (genetic material)
ribosome	makes proteins from amino acids
vacuole	stores materials in a cell

There are several processes cells perform to maintain essential life activities. Several of these processes, related to cell metabolism, are described below. Metabolism is the sum of chemical processes in living things.

Process	Organelle	Life Activity
diffusion	cell membrane	food getting, respiration, excretion
osmosis	cell membrane	food getting, excretion
phagocytosis	cell membrane	food getting
photosynthesis	chloroplasts	food getting
respiration (aerobic)	mitochondria	provides energy
fermentation	mitochondria	provides energy

Cells need to move materials into their structures to get energy and to grow. The cell membrane allows certain small molecules to flow freely across it. This flow of chemicals from areas of high concentration to areas of low concentration is called diffusion. Osmosis is diffusion of water across a semipermeable membrane. Particles too large to be passed through the cell membrane may be engulfed by the cell membrane and stored in vacuoles until they can be digested. This engulfing process is called phagocytosis.

All cells need energy to survive. Sunlight energy can be made biologically available by converting to chemical energy during photosynthesis. Photosynthesis is carried out in the chloroplasts of green cells. Chlorophyll, the pigment found in chloroplasts, catalyzes (causes or accelerates) the photosynthesis reaction that turns carbon dioxide and water into glucose (sugar) and oxygen.

$$6CO_2 + 6H_2O \xrightarrow[\text{chlorophyll}]{\text{sunlight}} C_6H_{12}O_6 + 6O_2$$

Sunlight and chlorophyll are needed for the reaction to occur. Chlorophyll, because it is a catalyst, is not consumed in the reaction and may be used repeatedly.

The term "respiration" has two distinct meanings in the field of biology. Respiration, the life activity, is the exchange of gases in living things. Respiration, the metabolic process, is the release of energy from sugars for use in life activities. Respiration, the metabolic process, occurs on the cellular level only. Respiration, the life activity, may occur at the cell, tissue, organ, or system level, depending on the complexity of the organism involved.

All living things get their energy from the digestion (respiration) of glucose (sugar). Respiration may occur with oxygen (aerobic respiration) or without oxygen (anaerobic respiration or fermentation). When respiration is referred to, it generally means aerobic respiration.

aerobic respiration: $C_6H_{12}O_6 + 6O_2 \longrightarrow 6CO_2 + 6H_2O + energy$

fermentation: $C_6H_{12}O_6 \longrightarrow CO_2 + alcohol + energy$

Aerobic respiration occurs in most plant and animal cells. Fermentation occurs in yeast cells and other cells in the absence of oxygen. Fermentation by yeast produces the alcohol in alcoholic beverages and the gases that make yeast-raised breads light and fluffy.

Classification

All known living things are grouped in categories according to shared physical traits. The process of grouping organisms is called classification. Carl Linné, also known as Linnaeus, devised the classification system used in biology today. In the Linnaeus system, all organisms are given a two-word name (binomial). The name given consists of a genus (e.g., Canis) and a species (e.g., lupus) designation. Genus designations are always capitalized and occur first in the binomial. Species designations usually start with a lowercase letter and occur second. Binomials are usually underlined or italicized, e.g., *Genus species,* or *Homo sapiens,* or *Canis lupus*.

There exists just one binomial for each organism throughout the scientific community. Similar genera of organisms are grouped into families. Families are grouped into orders, orders are grouped into classes, classes are grouped into phyla, and phyla are grouped into kingdoms. The seven basic levels of classification, listed from the largest groupings to the smallest, are: kingdom, phylum, class, order, family, genus, species.

Most biologists recognize five biological kingdoms today, the Animals, Plants, Fungi, Protists, and Monerans. Most living things are classified as plants or animals.

Monerans (e.g., bacteria, blue-green algae) are the simplest life forms known. They consist of single-celled organisms without a membrane bound cell nucleus. Blue-green algae make their own food by photosynthesis; bacteria are consumers or parasites.

Protists (e.g., protozoa, single-celled algae) are single-celled organisms having cell nuclei. Protozoa (e.g., amoeba, paramecia) are predators or decomposers. Algae (e.g., Euglena, diatoms) are producers and utilize photosynthesis.

Fungi (e.g., molds, mushrooms, yeast) are multicellular decomposers that reproduce through spores. (Yeast constitute an exception to the multicellular makeup of most fungi, in that they are single-celled and reproduce through budding.) Fungi are the only multicellular decomposers that are not mobile.

Plants

Plants are multicellular organisms that make their own food through photosynthesis. Plants are divided into two phyla, the Bryophyta and Tracheophyta. Bryophytes are nonvascular plants. They lack true roots and woody tissues. Bryophyta (e.g., moss, liverworts, and multicellular algae) live in water or in damp areas and reproduce by spores. Bryophytes do not grow very tall because they lack the structural support of vascular tissue.

Tracheophytes are vascular plants. They have woody tissues and roots. The woody tissues in vascular plants enable them to grow quite large. The roots of vascular plants enable them to find water even in soils that are dry at the surface.

Tracheophytes are divided into three classes, Filicinae, Gymnospermae, and Angiospermae. Filicinae are ferns. They reproduce by spores. Gymnosperms (e.g., spruce, pines) are plants whose seeds form in cones. The seeds are unprotected. Angiosperms (e.g., apple trees, grass) are plants whose seeds are protected by fruits or other structures. Angiosperms are further divided into monocots or dicots, based on seed structure. Cotyledons are food storage structures in seed embryos. Monocots (e.g., grasses, bananas) have one cotyledon per seed. Dicots (e.g., oak trees, pumpkins) have two cotyledons per seed.

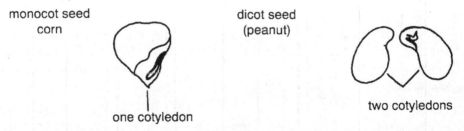

monocot seed
corn

one cotyledon

dicot seed
(peanut)

two cotyledons

Figure 2

Animals

Animals are multicellular organisms that cannot make their own food but can move themselves about. The animal kingdom is split into 26 phyla. Some of the phyla most important to humans are listed below.

Phyla	Examples	Traits
Porifera	sponges	no organs, pores in body let water flow through, bringing food and taking away wastes
Coelenterata (Cridaria)	jellyfish, corals, hydra	no organs, body sac-like, stinging cells to capture prey
Platyhelminthes	flatworms, flukes, tapeworms	single opening to body, true organs, often parasitic to humans
Aschelminthes (Nematoda)	roundworms	two openings to body, may be parasitic
Mollusca	snails, octopus, clams	gills, open circulatory system, produce shells (internal or external)
Annelida	earthworms, leeches	closed circulatory system
Arthropoda	spiders, insects, crabs	jointed exoskeletons, jointed legs
Echinodermata	starfish, sea urchins	plate-like internal skeleton, tube feet, spiny or knobby surface
Chordata	fish, birds, mammals, reptiles	notochord (primitive cartilaginous spine) and gills present at some point in development, hollow dorsal nerve cord

The arthropod and chordate phyla deserve special note. The arthropods include ten classes, three of which are very important to humans, the arachnidae, insecta, and crustaceae. Arachnids include spiders and ticks. These animals have two body regions and eight legs. Insects have three body regions and six legs. They include an incredible variety of animals; for example, grasshoppers, flies, beetles, and butterflies are typical insects. Crustaceans have two body regions and ten legs and live mostly in water. Crabs, crayfish, and lobsters are all crustaceans.

The chordate phylum has three subphyla, one of which is the vertebrata, or vertebrates. Vertebrates have an internal skeleton which includes a spine made up of vertebrae. The spine protects the dorsal nerve cord (spinal cord). Animals without spines (all phyla except Chordata) are called invertebrates.

Vertebrates

Eight classes of vertebrates exist, though four are often spoken of collectively as "fish."

	Class	Traits	Examples
F	Agnatha	jawless fish, no scales, cartilaginous skeleton	lampreys, hagfish
I	Placodermi	hinged jaws	extinct
S	Chondrichthyes	cartilaginous skeleton, no scales, jaws	sharks, skates, rays
H	Osteichthyes	bony skeleton, scales, jaws	bass, trout, goldfish
	Amphibia	aquatic eggs and larvae, terrestrial adults	frogs, toads, sala- manders
	Reptilia	terrestrial eggs and adults, cold-blooded	turtles, snakes, lizards
	Aves	feathers, warm-blooded, external egg development	eagles, ducks, pigeons
	Mammalia	fur, milk-producing, internal egg development, warm-blooded	rats, horses, humans

Most vertebrates are cold-blooded. Their bodies do not generate heat, so their body temperature is determined by their environment. Fish are cold-blooded animals with gills for respiration and fins for limbs. Reptiles are cold-blooded animals with lungs for respiration and legs for limbs (except for snakes). Amphibians are cold-blooded animals that start life with gills and fins, but then change. The change in form that amphibians undergo as they mature is called metamorphosis. Adult amphibians have lungs and legs.

Birds (Aves) and mammals are warm-blooded. Their bodies generate heat. Birds and mammals can also sweat to lower body temperature. Birds are covered with feathers and have eggs that develop outside the mother's body. Mammals are covered with fur and have eggs that develop within the mother's body.

Mammals are divided into seventeen orders, based on body structure. Some of the more familiar orders are listed on the following page.

Order	Examples	Traits
Marsupials	kangaroos, opossums	pouches in mothers for carrying young
Rodents	mice, rats, beavers, squirrels	gnawing teeth
Carnivores	dogs, bears, cats, skunks	meat eaters
Cetaceans	whales, dolphins, porpoises	aquatic, flippers for limbs
Primates	monkeys, apes, humans	opposable thumbs, erect posture, highly developed brains
Ungulates (2 orders)	horses, camels, buffaloes	grass chewers

Viruses

Viruses are organic particles that are capable of causing diseases in living things, such as smallpox, rabies, and influenza. Viruses are sometimes classified as living things because they contain genetic material and create offspring similar to themselves. Viruses are often not classified as living things because they have no ability to synthesize or process food, and cannot reproduce without the help of other organisms. Viruses are parasitic. Their basic structure is a protein shell surrounding a nucleic acid core.

ECOLOGY

Ecology is the study of the relationship between living things and their environment. An environment is all the living and nonliving things surrounding an organism.

Populations and Communities

A population is a group of similar organisms, like a herd of deer. A community is a group of populations that interact with one another. A pond community, for example, is made of all the plants and animals in the pond. An ecosystem is a group of populations which share a common pool of resources and a common physical/geographical area. A beech-oak-hickory forest ecosystem, for example, is made of populations in the forest canopy, on the forest floor, and in the forest soil.

Each population lives in a particular area and serves a special role in the community. This combination of defined role and living areas is the concept of niche. The niche of a pond snail, for example, is to decompose materials in ponds. The niche of a field mouse is to eat seeds in fields. When two populations try to fill the same niche, competition occurs. If one population replaces another in a niche, succession occurs. Succession is the orderly and predictable change of communities as a result of population replacement in niches.

A climax community is a community in which succession no longer occurs. Climax communities are stable until catastrophic changes, such as forest fires, hurricanes, or human clearing of land occurs. Each ecosystem type is defined by its climax communities, for example, beech-oak-hickory forests in the American Northeast or prairies in the American Midwest.

Food and Energy

Energy enters ecosystems through sunlight. Green plants turn this energy into food in the process of photosynthesis. Organisms that make their own food are called producers. Some animals get their food from eating plants or other animals. Animals that get their food energy from other living things are called consumers. Consumers that eat plants are herbivores; those that eat animals are carnivores; those that eat plants and animals are called omnivores. Animals that eat other organisms are called predators; the organisms that get eaten are called prey. Organisms that get their food energy from dead plants or animals are called decomposers.

As energy moves from one organism to another, it creates a pattern of energy transfer known as a food web.

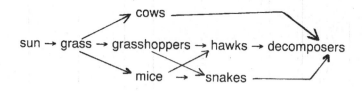

Figure 3

Arrows represent energy transfer in a food web. At each energy transfer (arrow) some energy is lost. Energy is lost because organisms use energy to grow, move, and live.

Many nutrients, such as nitrogen and phosphorous, are routinely cycled through the bodies of living things. These nutrient cycles are disrupted when humans remove parts of the ecosystem or add excess materials to an ecosystem.

Pollution is any material added to an ecosystem that disrupts its normal functioning. Typical pollutants are excess fertilizers and industrial emissions. Conservation is the practice of using natural areas without disrupting their ecosystems. Conservationists try to limit the amounts of pollution entering ecosystems.

Human Health

The Human Body

A human is a very complex organism. This complexity requires individual cells to become specialized at certain tasks. Groups of specialized cells form tissues, such as muscles, skin, or blood. Tissues are specialized to perform specific tasks. Groups of tissues form organs, such as the heart, kidney, or brain. Systems are groups of organs working together to perform the basic activities of life, such as excretion or reproduction. The human body has several systems in it.

The skeleton supports the body and gives it shape. The skeletal system is composed of bones, cartilage, and ligaments. The human body has 206 bones in it. The areas where two or more bones touch one another are called joints. Five types of joints exist in the human body; fixed joints (skull bones), hinge joints (elbow or knee), pivot joints (neck bones), sliding joints (wrist bones), and ball and socket joints (shoulder or hip). Bone surfaces in joints are often covered with cartilage, which reduces friction in the joint. Ligaments hold bones together in a joint.

The muscular system controls movement of the skeleton and movement within organs. Three types of muscle exist: striated (voluntary), smooth (involuntary), and cardiac. Cardiac muscle is found only in the heart and is involuntary. Smooth muscle is found in organs and cannot be consciously controlled (involuntary). Striated muscle is attached to a skeleton and its actions can be controlled at will, or voluntarily. Tendons attach muscles to bone. Muscles perform work by contracting. Skeletal muscles work in pairs. The alternate contraction of muscles within a pair causes movement in joints.

The digestive system receives and processes food. The digestive system includes the mouth, stomach, large intestine and small intestine. Food is physically broken down by mastication, or chewing. Food is chemically broken down in the stomach, where digestive enzymes break the food down into simple chemicals. The small intestine absorbs nutrients from food. The large intestine absorbs water from solid food waste.

The excretory system eliminates wastes from the body. Excretory organs include the lungs, kidneys, bladder, large intestine, rectum, and skin. The kidneys filter blood and excrete wastes, mostly in the form of urea. The bladder holds liquid wastes until they can be eliminated via the urethra. The large intestine absorbs water from solid food waste, and the rectum stores solid waste until it can be eliminated. The skin excretes waste through perspiration. The lungs excrete gaseous waste.

The circulatory system is responsible for internal transport in the body. It is composed of the heart, blood vessels, lymph vessels, blood, and lymph. The heart is a muscular four-chambered pump. The upper chambers are called atria and the lower chambers are called ventricles. Blood flows from the body to the (1) right atrium, to the (2) right ventricle, to the lungs, then to the (3) left atrium, to the (4) left ventricle, and back to the body.

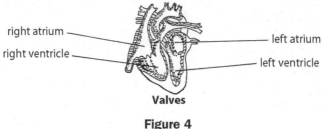

Figure 4

The heart chambers contract to expel the blood they contain. Blood flows in one direction through the heart because of valves within the heart and blood vessels. The closing of valves during heart contractions creates an audible heartbeat. An adult human heart normally contracts 60–80 times per minute.

There are three types of blood vessels: arteries, veins, and capillaries. Arteries have thick, muscular walls and carry oxygenated blood away from the heart. Veins have thin walls and carry de-oxygenated blood to the heart. Capillaries have extremely thin walls and connect arteries to veins.

Blood is always under pressure in the arteries. Blood pressure increases when the heart is contracting. Blood pressure during heart contractions is systolic pressure. Blood pressure during heart relaxation is diastolic pressure. Human blood pressure is always reported as a ratio of systolic pressure/diastolic pressure. Typical blood pressure for adults is 140 mm IIg/90 mm Hg. Pressures ranging far above or below these values indicate illness.

The fluid portion of blood is called plasma. The solid material in blood includes red blood cells, white blood cells, and platelets. Red blood cells carry oxygen to cells and carry carbon dioxide away from cells. White blood cells fight infections and produce antibodies. Platelets cause the formation of clots.

The lymphatic system drains fluid from tissues. Lymph nodes filter impurities in the lymph fluid, and often become swollen during infections.

The respiratory system exchanges oxygen for carbon dioxide. The respiratory system is composed of the nose, trachea, bronchi, lungs, and diaphragm. Air travels from the nose through the trachea and bronchi into the lungs. The air is drawn in by the contraction of the diaphragm, a muscle running across the body below the lungs. Gas exchange occurs in the lungs across air sacks called alveoli. Air is then pushed back toward the nose by relaxation of the diaphragm.

The nervous system controls the actions and processes of the body. The nervous system includes the brain, spinal cord, and nerves. Electrical impulses carry messages to and from the brain across the spinal cord and nerves. Nerves extend to every portion of the body. The spinal cord is protected by the back bone.

The three principal regions of the brain are the cerebrum, cerebellum, and brain stem. The cerebrum occupies 80% of the brain's volume and is responsible for intelligence, memory, and thought. The cerebellum is located at the lower rear portion of the brain, and it controls balance and coordination. The brain stem connects the brain to the spinal cord and is found at the lower central portion of the brain. The brain stem controls autonomic (involuntary) body functions and regulates hormones.

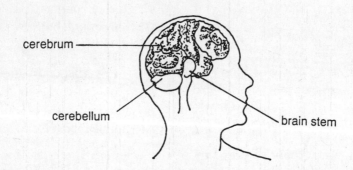

Figure 5

The endocrine system controls activities in the body through chemical agents called hormones. Hormones are produced in glands throughout the body and are excreted into the bloodstream. The brain controls production and release of hormones.

Listed below are several major endocrine glands and the most important hormones they produce.

Gland	Hormone	Action
hypothalamus	oxytocin	stimulates labor in childbirth and production of milk in females
pituitary	growth hormone	stimulates growth
thyroid	thyroxin	controls rate of cellular respiration
parathyroid	parathormone	controls amount of calcium in the blood
thymus	thymosin	helps to fight infections
adrenals	adrenalin	helps during stress and shock, activates flight-or-fight response
pancreas	insulin	regulates blood sugar
ovaries (female)	estrogen; progesterone	controls female maturing process; maintains pregnancy
testes (male)	testosterone	controls male maturing process

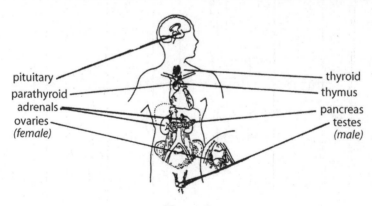

Figure 6

The reproductive system produces eggs and sperm which can combine to create an embryo. The female reproductive system includes the ovaries, fallopian tubes, uterus, and vagina. One egg each month is released from one of the ovaries and then travels down one of the fallopian tubes. If it is fertilized, it then becomes implanted in the lining of the uterus, where a baby begins to form. When sufficiently grown, the baby leaves the uterus and its mother's body through the vagina, or birth canal.

The male reproductive system consists of the testicles, vas deferens, urethra, and penis. Sperm are produced in the testicles. They move through the vas deferens from the testicles to the urethra. During intercourse, sperm pass through the penis (via the urethra) and into a woman's body. In a woman's body, sperm pass through the cervix into the uterus and up the fallopian tubes, where fertilization of an egg may take place.

Nutrition

Nutrition is the study of how living things utilize food substances. Food provides energy and raw materials for growth, repair, and metabolism. Energy (calories) is derived chiefly from carbohydrates, but also from fats and proteins. Raw materials for life processes come chiefly from protein, but also from carbohydrates (starches and sugars), fats, minerals, and vitamins. Fiber in the diet helps in elimination of wastes.

Listed below are several vitamins important to human health.

Vitamin	Principal Source	Deficiency Symptom(s)
A	green and yellow vegetables	night blindness, dry, brittle skin
B_1	cereals, yeast	beriberi (muscular atrophy and paralysis)
B_2	dairy products, eggs	eye problems
B_{12}	liver and meat	anemia
C	citrus fruits, tomatoes	scurvy
D	fortified milk, eggs	rickets (malformed bones)
E	meat, oils, vegetables	male sterility, muscular problems
K	green vegetables	impaired blood clotting

Foods can be placed in one of four basic food groups. A healthy diet is one which includes food from each of these groups daily, as shown below.

Food Group	Importance	Examples
Meat, Fish, and Eggs	protein	steak, trout
Dairy	fats, calcium, protein	milk, cheese
Fruits and Vegetables	fiber, minerals, vitamins	apples, carrots
Grains and Cereals	starch (for energy), protein, fiber	bread, pasta

Human Genetics

Each of the cells in a living thing has a specific structure and role in the organism. The structure of a cell and its function are determined, to a large degree, by the genes within a cell. Genes are code units of chromosomes within the nucleus of a cell. Genes give information about the structure and function of a cell.

Cells age and die. Organisms continue to live despite the death of individual cells because cells reproduce. Mitosis is the process of cell reproduction through cell division; one cell divides to become two new cells. During mitosis, the genetic material (genes) in the parent cell is copied so each of the offspring gets the same instructions (genes). The passing of genetic material from one generation to the next is called inheritance. The study of genetic material and inheritance is called genetics.

Most cells in the human body have 46 chromosomes. Some special cells, called eggs and sperm, have only 23 chromosomes. Egg and sperm cells get 23 chromosomes through meiosis, a process of cell division that reduces the number of chromosomes in a cell. Most cells in the human body reproduce quite often. Egg and sperm cells (sex cells) cannot reproduce until they join with another sex cell. The process of an egg and sperm cell joining is called fertilization.

A fertilized human sex cell has 46 chromosomes, 23 from the mother and 23 from the father. This fertilized sex cell will multiply to form a new organism. The genes of the new organism are a mixture of genes from both parents, so the new organism will be unique from each parent. The process of combining genetic materials from two parent organisms to form a unique offspring is called sexual reproduction.

During sexual reproduction an organism receives two genes for each trait, one from each parent. Sometimes one trait will mask another, as is the case with eye color. If a person has one gene for brown eyes and one gene for blue eyes, the person will always have brown eyes. A genetic trait that masks another, like the gene for brown eyes, is called a dominant trait. A gene that can be masked, like the gene for blue eyes, is called a recessive trait.

Understanding dominance helps us to figure out the genetic configuration of an individual. An individual with blue eyes must have two genes for blue eyes, since it is a recessive trait. Recessive traits are shown by lowercase letters, so the genetic symbol for blue eyes is "bb." An individual with brown eyes must have at least one gene for brown eyes, which is dominant. Dominant genes are shown by uppercase letters, so the genetic symbol for brown eyes could be "Bb" or "BB."

An individual with two different genes (e.g., Bb) for a trait is called heterozygous for that trait. An individual with two similar genes (e.g., BB or bb) for a trait is called homozygous for that trait.

When the genetic type of parents is known, the probability of the offspring showing particular traits can be predicted using the Punnett Square. A Punnett Square is a large square divided into four small boxes. The genetic symbol of each parent for a particular trait is written alongside the square, one parent along the top and one parent along the left side.

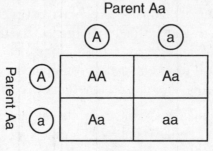

Figure 7

Each gene symbol is written in both boxes below or to the right of it. This results in each box having two gene symbols in it. The genetic symbols in the boxes are all the possible genetic combinations for a particular trait of the offspring of these parents. Each box has a 25% probability of being the actual genetic representation for a given child.

The genetic symbol "AA" in the example has a 25% probability of occurring. If a genetic symbol occurs in more than one box, the genetic probabilities are added. The genetic code "Aa" in the example has a 50% probability of occurring because it is shown in two boxes of the Punnett Square.

The Punnett Square shows how two parents can have a child with traits different from either parent. Two parents heterozygous for brown eyes (Bb), have a 25% probability of producing a child homozygous for blue eyes (bb), as shown in the example.

Human sex type is determined by genetic material in sperm. The genetic sex code for human females is XX. The genetic sex code for human males is XY. Eggs carry only X genes. Sperm carry X or Y genes. The probability of a fertilized human egg being male, or XY, is 50%.

Human blood type is determined genetically. Genes for blood type may be one of three kinds, i, I^A, or I^B. The i gene is recessive. Blood type O is caused by ii genetic code. The I^A and I^B genes are dominant. They may be represented by $I^A i$ or $I^A I^A$ and $I^B i$ or $I^B I^B$, respectively. Blood type AB has genetic code $I^A I^B$. Blood types fit the Punnett Square model.

PHYSICAL SCIENCE

Measurement

The physical characteristics of an object are determined by measurements. Measured characteristics include mass, volume, length, temperature, time, and area. There are two common measurement systems, English and metric.

Characteristic	English System	Metric System
mass/weight	pound (weight)	kilogram (mass)
volume	quart	liter
length	foot	meter
temperature	°Fahrenheit	°Celsius
time	second	second

The English system, used most often in the United States, does not have a consistent system of conversion factors between units.

EXAMPLE

1 yard = 3 feet, 1 foot = 12 inches, 1 yard = 36 inches

The metric system, used most often in science, has conversion factors between units based on multiples of 10.

EXAMPLE

1 kilometer = 1000 meters,
1 meter = 100 centimeters = 1000 millimeters

Prefixes in the metric system indicate the number of multiples of the base units, so it is simple to determine the conversion factors between units.

Prefix	Multiplication Factor	Unit Symbols
kilo	× 1000	km, kg, kl
no prefix (base unit)	× 1	m, g, l
deci	× 0.1	dm, dg, dl
centi	× 0.01	cm, cg, cl
milli	× 0.001	mm, mg, ml

A third measurement system, the International System of Units, is based on the metric system. The International System of Units differs from the metric system by using the Kelvin temperature scale. The size of a degree in the Celsius and Kelvin scale are the same, but "0°" is different. 0 Kelvin = –273° Celsius. 0 Kelvin, also known as absolute zero, is the temperature at which, theoretically, all molecular movement ceases.

To convert from °Celsius to °Fahrenheit, use the following equation:

$$°C = {}^5/_9 \, (°F - 32).$$

To convert from °Celsius to Kelvin, use the following equation:

$$°C + 273 = K.$$

CHEMISTRY

Matter is everything that has volume and mass. Water is matter because it takes up space, light is not matter because it does not take up space.

States of Matter

Matter exists in three states, as follows:

State	Properties	Example
solid	definite volume, definite shape	ice
liquid	definite volume, no definite shape	water
gas	no definite volume, no definite shape	water vapor or steam

Thermal energy causes molecules or atoms to vibrate. As vibration of particles increases, a material may change to a different state; it may melt or boil. Decreasing energy in a material may cause condensation or freezing. Another name for thermal energy is heat. Temperature is a measure of the average kinetic energy, or vibration, of the particles of a material. For most materials, the boiling point and freezing point are important. The boiling point of water is 100°C, and its freezing point is 0°C.

State Change	Process Name	Heat Change
solid ⟶ liquid	melting	heat added
liquid ⟶ gas	evaporation or boiling	heat added
gas ⟶ liquid	condensation	heat removed
liquid ⟶ solid	freezing	heat removed

Structure of Matter

Atoms are the basic building blocks of matter. Atoms are made of three types of subatomic particles, which have mass and charge. Protons and neutrons are found in the nucleus, or solid center of an atom. Electrons are found in the outer portion of an atom. This outer portion is mostly made of empty space. Under most conditions, atoms are indivisible. Atoms may be split or combined to form new atoms during atomic reactions. Atomic reactions occur deep inside the sun, in nuclear power reactors and nuclear bombs, and in radioactive decay.

Subatomic Particle	Mass	Charge	Location
proton	1 amu	+1	nucleus
neutron	1 amu	0	nucleus
electron	0 amu	−1	outside nucleus

Most atoms have equal numbers of protons and electrons, and therefore no net charge. Atoms with unequal numbers of protons and electrons have net positive or negative charges. Charged atoms are called ions. Atomic mass is determined by the number of protons and neutrons in an atom. The way to express atomic mass is in atomic mass units (amu).

A material made of just one type of atom is called an element. Atoms of an element are represented by symbols of one or two letters, such as C or Na. Two or more atoms may combine to form molecules.

Atoms of the same element have the same number of protons in their nucleus. An atom is the smallest particle of an element that retains the characteristics of that element. Each element is assigned an atomic number, which is equal to the number of protons in an atom of that element. The Periodic Table is a chart listing all the elements in order according to their atomic number. The elements are grouped vertically in the Periodic Table according to their chemical properties. The Periodic Table is a reference tool used to summarize the atomic structure, mass, and reactive tendencies of elements.

Molecules are clusters of atoms. Molecules form, decompose, or recombine during chemical reactions. Materials made of one type of molecule are called compounds. Compounds may be represented by formulae using atomic symbols and numbers. The numbers show how many atoms of each type are in the molecules. For example, the symbol for water, H_2O, shows that a molecule of water contains two hydrogen atoms and one oxygen atom. Atomic symbols without subscript numbers represent just one atom in a molecule.

Chemical compounds containing carbon are called organic, because these materials are often made by living things. The chemistry of organic compounds is complex and distinct from that of other compounds. Therefore, organic chemistry is a large and distinct discipline. Compounds without carbon are called inorganic.

Mixtures are materials made of two or more compounds or elements. They can be separated by physical means, such as sifting or evaporation. Liquid or gas mixtures are called suspensions, colloids, or solutions. Suspensions have particles that settle out unless the mixture is stirred. Dust in air is a suspension. Colloids have particles large enough to scatter light, but small enough to remain suspended without stirring. Milk is a colloid; it is opaque because its particles scatter light. Solutions have particles so small they do not scatter light. They are transparent to light and particles do not settle out.

A substance that dissolves another to form a solution is a solvent. Chemicals that are dissolved in solutions are called solutes. In a salt water solution, water is the solvent. Not all chemicals can function as solvents. Some solvents (like gasoline) are able to dissolve only certain solids. Water is sometimes called the "universal solvent" because it is able to dissolve so many chemicals.

Concentration is a measure of how much solute is in a solution. A given amount of solvent is able to dissolve only a limited amount of solute. This amount may be increased if the solution is heated or pressure on the solution is increased. Dilute solutions have relatively little solute in solution. Concentrated solutions have a lot of solute in solution.

Solutions that are able to dissolve more solute are called unsaturated. Solutions that cannot dissolve more solute are called saturated. Solutions that are saturated at high temperature or high pressure may become supersaturated at lower temperatures or pressures. Supersaturated solutions contain more dissolved solute than normally is present in a saturated solution. These solutions are unstable, and solute may crystallize out of the solution easily.

Chemical Reactions

Matter may undergo chemical and physical changes. A physical change affects the size, form, or appearance of a material. These changes can include melting, bending, or cracking. Physical changes do not alter the molecular structure of a material. Chemical changes do alter the molecular structure of matter. Examples of chemical changes are burning, rusting, and digestion.

Under the right conditions, compounds may break apart, combine, or recombine to form new compounds. This process is called a chemical reaction. Chemical reactions are described by chemical equations, such as $NaOH + HCl \longrightarrow NaCl + H_2O$. In a chemical equation, materials to the left of the arrow are called reactants and materials to the right of the arrow are called products. In a balanced chemical equation, the number of each type of atom is the same on both sides of the arrow.

unbalanced: $H_2 + O_2 \longrightarrow H_2O$

balanced: $2H_2 + O_2 \longrightarrow 2H_2O$

There are four basic types of chemical reactions: synthesis, decomposition, single replacement, and double replacement. A synthesis reaction is one in which two or more chemicals combine to form a new chemical.

EXAMPLE

$A + B \longrightarrow AB$, or $2H_2 + O_2 \longrightarrow 2H_2O$

A decomposition reaction is one in which one chemical breaks down to release two or more chemicals.

EXAMPLE

$AB \longrightarrow A + B$, or $2H_2O \longrightarrow 2H_2 + O_2$

A single replacement reaction involves a compound decomposing and one of its constituent chemicals joining another chemical to make a new compound.

EXAMPLE

$AB + C \longrightarrow A + BC$, or $Fe + CuCl_2 \longrightarrow FeCl_2 + Cu$

A double replacement reaction is one in which two compounds decompose and their constituents recombine to form two new compounds.

EXAMPLE

$AB + CD \longrightarrow AC + BD$, or $NaOH + HCl \longrightarrow NaCl + H_2O$

Acids and Bases

Acid and base are terms used to describe solutions of differing pH. The concentration of hydrogen ions in a solution determines its pH, which is based on a logarithmic scale.

Solutions having pH 0–7 are called acids and have hydrogen ions (H+) present. Common acids include lemon juice, vinegar, and battery acid.

Acids are corrosive, and taste sour. Solutions pH 7–14 are called bases (or alkaline), and have hydroxide ions (OH⁻) present. Bases are caustic and feel slippery in solution. Common bases include baking soda and lye. Solutions of pH 7 are called neutral and have both ions present in equal but small amounts.

The reaction created when an acid and base combine is a double replacement reaction known as a neutralization reaction. In a neutralization reaction, acid + base ⟶ water + salt.

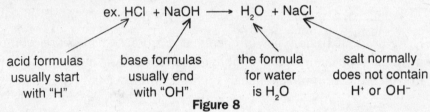

ex. $HCl + NaOH \longrightarrow H_2O + NaCl$

| acid formulas usually start with "H" | base formulas usually end with "OH" | the formula for water is H_2O | salt normally does not contain H⁺ or OH⁻ |

Figure 8

PHYSICS

Motion

Moving objects can be measured for speed or momentum. Speed is the distance an object travels per unit of time. Cars measure speed in miles or kilometers per hour.

$$\text{Speed} = \frac{\text{distance}}{\text{time}}$$

If a car travels 3.5 km in 7 minutes, it has a speed of 3.5 km/7 min, or 0.5 km/min.

Momentum is the tendency of an object to continue in its direction of motion.

Momentum = mass × speed

The heavier a moving object is, or the faster it is moving, the harder it is to stop the object or change its direction.

Energy and Work

Energy is the ability to do work. Energy comes in many different forms; examples include heat, light, and sound. All energy can be described as potential or kinetic. Potential energy is stored through chemical structure, position, or physical configuration. Kinetic energy is energy of motion. Light, sound, and heat are kinetic energy, as is the energy possessed by a moving object.

Energy can be transformed from one type to another, but it never is created or destroyed. The potential chemical energy in a peanut butter sandwich is transformed through digestion and metabolism into the kinetic energy of heat and motion. The potential energy of a book sitting on a shelf is turned into the kinetic energy of motion, sound, and heat as the book falls and hits the floor.

Heat is an important type of energy. Heat may travel through three paths: conduction, convection, and radiation. Conduction occurs when a hot material comes in contact with a cold one. Heat moves from a hot material into a cold material until the temperature of both is equal. An example of conduction is the heating of a metal spoon when it is used to stir a cup of hot tea.

Convection is based on a density change caused by heating. As materials, especially gases and liquids, are heated, they become less dense. Warm air, which is less dense, rises, while cold air, which is more dense, sinks. In a room or other enclosed space, this rising and falling of materials of different density creates a current of air (or other heated material). As heat is added to the space, from a source like a stove or sunny window, the current carries the heat through the space.

Radiation is heat that spreads out from a very hot source into the surrounding material. Radiant heat energy is carried by electromagnetic waves, just like the light given off by a hot light bulb filament. Radiant heat energy travels in straight lines in all directions from its source. Sources of radiant heat include wood stoves and light bulbs in homes.

Insulators are materials that slow down or prevent the movement of heat. Air is a good insulator. Most commercial insulation consists of a material with many pockets of air. Conductors are materials which transmit heat well. Metals are excellent heat conductors.

Work occurs when a force (push or pull) is applied to an object, resulting in movement.

Work = force × distance

The greater the force applied, or the longer the distance traveled, the greater the work done. Work is measured in newton-meters or foot-pounds. One newton-meter equals one joule.

Mass is a measure of the amount of matter in an object. Weight is the gravitational force on an object. Mass is a constant; it never changes with location. Weight varies with the pull of gravity. Objects weigh less on the moon than on Earth. In space, where there is no gravity, objects are weightless (but they still have mass).

Power is work done per unit time.

$$\text{Power} = \frac{\text{work done}}{\text{time interval}}$$

If someone moves an object weighing 5 newtons over a distance of 10 meters in 30 seconds, they use the power of 1.7 watts.

$$\frac{5n \times 10m}{30 \text{ sec}} = 1.7 \text{ n-m/sec, or } 1.7 \text{ watts}$$

1 watt = 1n-m/sec

Machines change the direction or strength of a force. Simple machines are used throughout our lives.

Simple Machine	Examples
inclined plane	ramp, wedge, chisel
screw	threads on bolts, cork screws, jar lids
lever	seesaw, crowbar, automobile jack
wheel and axle	doorknob, bicycle
pulley	fan belt, elevator

In designing machines, 100% efficiency is the goal.

$$\% \text{ efficiency} = \frac{\text{work done}}{\text{energy used}} \times 100.$$

100% efficiency can never be achieved, because some energy is always lost through friction or heat production.

Wave Phenomena

Sound and light are wave phenomena. Waves are characterized by wavelength, speed, and frequency. Wavelength is the distance between crests or troughs of waves.

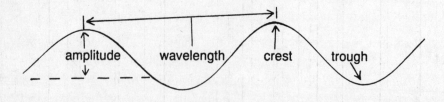

Figure 9

Speed is how fast a wave crest or trough moves. If a wave moves 4 meters in 2 seconds, its speed is 2 m/sec.

$$\text{speed} = \frac{\text{distance}}{\text{time}} = \frac{4\text{m}}{2\text{ sec}} = 2 \text{ m/sec}$$

Frequency is the number of crests or troughs that move past a point per second. Frequency is measured in Hertz. One wave moving past a point per second equals one Hertz.

$$\text{Frequency} = \frac{\text{speed}}{\text{wavelength}}.$$

Sound is caused by the vibration of objects. This vibration creates waves of disturbance that can travel through air and most other materials. If these sound waves hit your eardrum, you perceive sound.

Sound is characterized by its pitch, loudness, intensity, and speed. Pitch is related to frequency. High pitches (e.g., high music notes) have high frequencies. Loudness is related to wave amplitude. Loud sounds have big amplitudes. Sound intensity is measured in decibels. Intensity is related to amplitude and frequency of sound waves. Loud, high-pitched music has a much greater intensity than quiet, low-pitched music.

The speed of sound waves is related to their medium. Sound travels more quickly through more dense materials (solids, liquids) than less dense materials (gases). Sound does not travel through a vacuum.

Light is a type of electromagnetic wave. The chief types of electromagnetic waves, listed according to their relative frequency and wavelength, are shown below.

Low frequency $\leftarrow - - - - - - - - - \rightarrow$ high frequency

| radio waves | micro waves | infrared light | visible light | ultraviolet light | x-rays | gamma rays |

long wavelength $\leftarrow - - - - - - - \rightarrow$ short wavelength

Figure 10

Light travels much more quickly (300,000 km/sec) than sound does (330 m/sec). It can pass through a vacuum. As light passes through a material, it travels in a straight path. When light moves from one material to another, it may be transmitted, absorbed, reflected, or refracted.

Transparent materials (e.g., water, glass) allow light to pass directly through them. This passing through is called transmission. Opaque objects (e.g., wood) absorb light. No light comes out of them. Mirrors reflect light. They re-emit light into the medium it came from. Light rays going into a mirror are called incident rays. Light rays going out of a mirror are called reflected rays.

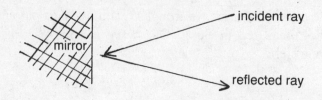

Figure 11

Refraction is the bending of light. Light may be refracted when it moves from one material to another (e.g., air ——→ water). Mirages are formed when light refracts while moving from cool air to warm air.

Sometimes, during refraction, sunlight is broken into the colors that form it, causing a spectrum. The colors in a spectrum are red, orange, yellow, green, blue, indigo, and violet. A rainbow is a spectrum caused when light passes from dry air into very humid air.

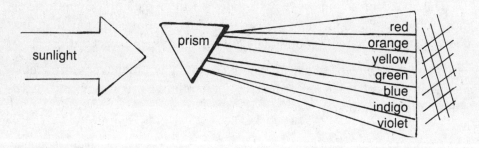

Figure 12

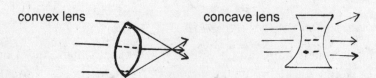

Figure 13

Lenses are transparent materials used to refract light. The shape of a lens determines how light passing through it will be bent.

Basic Electricity

All matter is made of atoms. All atoms contain positively charged particles, called protons, and negatively charged particles, called electrons. Protons are tightly bound to atoms and cannot move much. Electrons are loosely attached to atoms, and may leave one atom to join another.

Atoms may carry electrical charges. A neutral atom has equal numbers of protons and electrons in it. The charges of the protons and electrons cancel each other, so the atom has no net charge. If an atom has more electrons than protons, the extra electrons give the atom a negative charge. If an atom has fewer electrons than protons, the missing electrons leave the atom with a positive charge.

Electrons may not be destroyed. If two objects are rubbed together, however, electrons may move from one object to another, leaving both charged. Electrons may also flow through certain materials. The flow of electrons produces an electric current. Conductors are materials that let electrons flow freely (e.g., metals, water). Insulators are materials that do not let electrons flow freely (e.g., glass, rubber, air).

Electricity (electric current) flows from areas of many electrons to areas of few electrons. The path along which electrons flow is called a circuit. In a direct current (DC) circuit, electrons flow in one direction only. Alternating current (AC) is the type of current supplied over power lines. Alternating current changes direction many times per second.

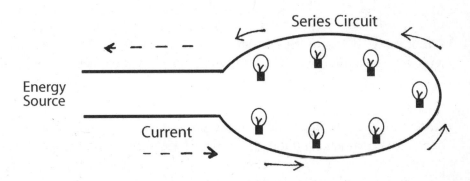

Figure 14

Circuits may be described as being in series or in parallel. Series circuits are made of a single pathway, through which all current must flow. If any part of a series circuit breaks, the circuit is "opened," and the flow of the current must stop. Some sets of Christmas tree lights are designed in series. If one bulb in the string of lights burns out, none of the lights in the string will work, because current is disrupted for the entire string.

Parallel circuits provide more than one pathway for current to flow. If one of the pathways is opened, so that current cannot flow in it, the current will continue to move through the other paths. Most circuits, for example those in our homes, are wired in parallel, so that burned out light bulbs and turned off television sets do not disrupt electricity used in other parts of our homes.

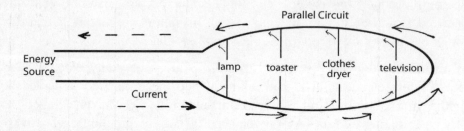

Figure 15

Fuses and circuit breakers are safety devices that limit the current flow in a circuit. Wires (lines) are limited in the amount of current they can safely carry. If too much current passes through them, they may heat up and melt or cause a fire. Current passing through lines increases with each appliance added to the circuit.

Fuses work by passing current through a thin metal ribbon. When the current exceeds the capacity of the fuse, the metal ribbon melts, leaving an open circuit, which cannot carry current. Circuit breakers use magnets and bimetallic strips to open circuits if the current becomes too great. Fuses must be replaced after they "blow," or melt. Circuit breakers may simply be reset to be used again.

Volts measure the work done as electrons move from one point to another within a circuit. Battery "strength," or ability to do work, is measured by volts. Amperes measure the current, or flow of charge through a circuit. Ohms measure the resistance to the flow of electrons.

Volts = amperes × ohms

Watts measure electrical power consumption. Electrical appliances and light bulbs are rated by their wattages so consumers can compare power consumption before purchasing these products. One watt equals one joule per second of power (one newton-meter per second). One watt of energy can lift an object weighing one newton over one meter in one second. A kilowatt-hour is the amount of energy used in one hour by one kilowatt of power.

Power = current × voltage, or 1 watt = 1 ampere × 1 volt

Magnetism

Magnets are solids that attract iron. Naturally occurring magnets are called lodestones. Magnetic forces make magnets attract or repel each other. Magnetic forces are created by regions in magnets called magnetic poles. All magnets have a north and a south pole. The north pole of one magnet will repel the north pole of another magnet; the same holds true for south poles. The south pole of one magnet will attract the north pole of another magnet.

A magnetic field is the area affected by magnetic force. A magnetic field surrounds both poles of a magnet. A magnetic field can be created by an electric current. Electromagnets create large magnetic fields with electric current. Similarly, if a wire is moved through a magnetic field, a current is produced. Electric generators make electricity by passing wires through a magnetic field.

The Earth has a magnetic field. Compasses are magnets that align themselves with the Earth's magnetic field.

EARTH SCIENCE

Earth science is the study of the Earth and its parts. Earth science has many subgroups, including, but not limited to, astronomy, geology, meteorology, and oceanography.

Astronomy

Astronomy is the study of celestial bodies and their movements.

The Earth is one of nine planets in our solar system. A solar system is composed of a star and the objects that move about it. The largest objects moving about a star are called planets. The planets in our solar system, beginning at the sun and moving away from it, are Mercury, Venus, Earth, Mars, Jupiter, Saturn, Uranus, Neptune, and Pluto.

Many objects smaller than planets exist in our solar system. If one of these smaller objects collides with Earth, it is called a meteor or "shooting star." The glow of a meteor is caused by its burning as it passes through our atmosphere. Meteors that reach the Earth's surface are called meteorites.

The Earth's path around the sun is called its orbit. The Earth's orbit around the sun, called a revolution, is completed in $365^1/_4$ days. An axis is an imaginary line passing through the poles of the Earth. The Earth spins on its axis, and each spin is called a rotation. One rotation takes 24 hours. Rotation causes the alternation of day and night on Earth.

The Earth revolves about the sun. Its axis is tilted $23^1/_2°$ from perpendicular to the plane of Earth's orbit. This tilt results in differing proportions of day and night on Earth throughout the year, and also causes the seasons. Day and night are of equal length only twice each year, at the autumnal equinox and vernal equinox (the first day of autumn and the first day of spring).

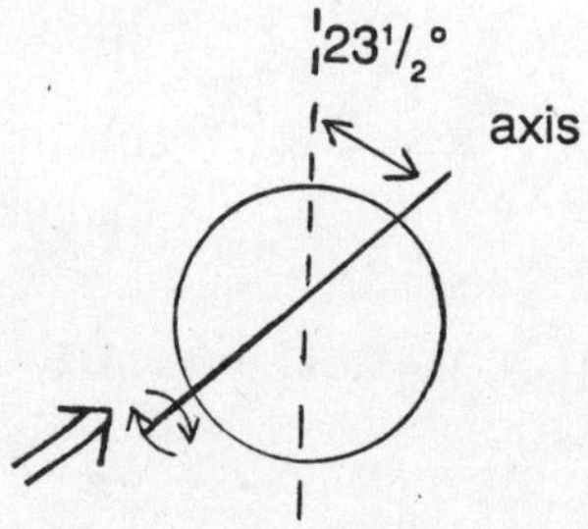

Figure 16

The moon is a satellite of Earth. It moves in orbit about Earth, and one revolution takes $27^1/_3$ days. The moon reflects sunlight, which causes it to glow. When the Earth blocks sunlight from reaching the moon, it creates a shadow on the moon's surface, known as a lunar eclipse. If the moon blocks sunlight from hitting the Earth, a solar eclipse is created. The moon has a gravitational pull on Earth which causes tides, or periodic changes in the depth of the ocean.

Geology

Geology is the study of the structure and composition of the Earth.

The Earth is composed of three layers, the crust, mantle, and core. The core is the center of the Earth, and is made of solid iron and nickel. It is about 7,000 km in diameter. The mantle is the semi-molten layer between the crust and core, and is about 3,000 km thick. The crust is the solid outermost layer of the Earth, ranging from 5–40 km thick. It is composed of bedrock overlaid with mineral and/or organic sediment (soil).

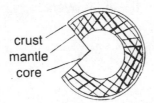

crust
mantle
core

Figure 17

Large sections of the Earth's crust, called plates, move at times, creating earthquakes, volcanoes, faults, and mountains. The study of these movements is called plate tectonics. Faults are cracks in the crust formed when plates move. Faults gape open when plates move apart and are closed when plates slide past one another. Earthquakes occur when plates slide past one another abruptly. Earthquakes may also be caused by volcanoes. Earthquakes are measured by a seismograph on the Richter scale.

Volcanoes form where plates move away from one another to let magma reach the crust's surface. Magma is molten rock beneath the Earth's crust. Lava is molten rock on the Earth's surface. Mountains are formed by volcanic activity or the collision of plates, which causes the crust to buckle upward.

Rocks are naturally occurring solids found on or below the surface of the Earth. Rocks are made of one or more minerals. Minerals are pure substances made of just one element or chemical compound. Rocks are divided into three groups, based on the way they are formed.

1. **Igneous**—rocks formed by cooling of magma or lava (e.g., granite, obsidian).

2. **Sedimentary**—rock formed from silt or deposited rock fragments by compaction at high pressures and/or cementation (e.g., shale, limestone).

3. **Metamorphic**—rocks formed from igneous or sedimentary rock after exposure to high heat and pressure (e.g., marble, slate).

Weathering is the breaking down of rock into small pieces. Rock is weathered by acid rain, freezing, wind abrasion, glacier scouring, and running water. Erosion is the transportation of rock or sediment to new areas. Agents of erosion include wind, running water, and glaciers.

Meteorology

Meteorology is the study of the atmosphere and its changes.

The atmosphere is a layer of air surrounding the Earth. Air is a mixture of gases, the most common being nitrogen and oxygen. The atmosphere is studied because 1) it protects (insulates) the Earth from extreme temperature changes, 2) it protects the Earth's surface from meteors, and 3) it is the origin of weather.

The atmosphere can be divided into several layers. The troposphere is the layer closest to Earth. Almost all life and most weather is found there. The stratosphere is the chief thermally insulating layer of the atmosphere. It contains the ozone layer and jet stream. The stratosphere is the region where ozone is produced. The thermosphere causes meteors to burn up by friction as they pass through. This layer reflects radio waves. The exosphere is the outer layer of the atmosphere. It eventually blends into the vast region we call "space."

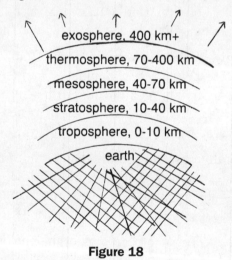

Figure 18

Weather is the local, short-term condition of the atmosphere. The two factors that affect weather most are the amounts of energy and water present. Most of the energy that affects weather comes from the sun. As solar (sun) energy hits the Earth, most of it is scattered or reflected by the atmosphere. The solar energy that gets through the atmosphere warms the Earth's crust, which in turn warms the atmosphere. The Earth does not absorb solar energy uniformly; the equator absorbs more than the poles do. This difference in energy (heat) absorption causes, in part, wind.

Water covers about 70 percent of the Earth's surface. As that water slowly evaporates, some of the vapor is held in the atmosphere. It is the water vapor in our atmosphere that causes humidity, fog, clouds, and precipitation.

An air mass is a huge area of air that has nearly uniform conditions of temperature and moisture. When two air masses meet, the boundary between them is called a front. Fronts are the location of most stormy weather.

Warm air is less dense than cold air. That means, a given volume of warm air weighs less than an equal volume of cold air. Air masses push down on the earth below them, causing air pressure. Warm air masses, because they are less dense, push down less and cause low pressure areas. Cold air masses, which are more dense, cause high air pressure. Air moves from high pressure to low pressure areas, causing wind.

Different aspects of the weather may be measured using special instruments.

Weather Aspect	Instrument
wind speed	anemometer
air pressure	barometer
humidity	hygrometer
temperature	thermometer

Clouds can be used to predict the weather.

Cloud Type	Appearance	Weather
stratus	flat, broad	light colored—stable weather conditions dark colored—rain expected soon
cumulus	fluffy, solid-looking	light colored—good weather dark colored—heavy rains, perhaps thunderstorms
cirrus	thin, wispy	changes in weather

Climate is the general atmospheric condition of a region over a long period of time.

Oceanography

Oceanography is the study of the ocean.

Sea water differs from fresh water in its salinity, or saltiness. Fresh water, the water we drink, has relatively few dissolved solids in it and has low salinity. Ocean water has a lot of dissolved material in it and therefore has a high salinity. Many materials are dissolved in sea water, but the most abundant dissolved material is common salt, sodium chloride.

Ocean waters move through tides, waves, and currents. Tides are periodic changes in ocean depth. They are caused by the gravitational pull of the moon on Earth. Most waves are caused by winds. Some ocean currents are caused by density differences in sea water. Currents are like rivers within the ocean. The swift-moving water in currents can transport material over large distances very quickly.

ARITHMETIC REASONING REVIEW

Arithmetic reasoning involves basic mathematical operations, such as addition, subtraction, multiplication, and division, of real numbers. Below is the real number system.

THE REAL NUMBER SYSTEM

All of the numbers used in arithmetic reasoning belong to a set called the **real numbers** or **reals**. This set can be represented graphically by the real number line.

Given the number line below, we arbitrarily fix a point and label it with the number 0. In a similar manner, we can label any point on the line with one of the real numbers, depending on its position relative to 0. Numbers to the right of 0 are positive, while those to the left are negative. Value increases from left to right, so that if a is to the right of b, it is said to be greater than b.

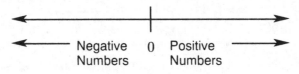

If we now divide the number line into equal segments, we can label the points on this line with real numbers. For example, the point 2 lengths to the left of 0 is -2, while the point 3 lengths to the right of 0 is $+3$ (the $+$ sign is usually assumed, so $+3$ is written simply as 3). The number line now looks like this:

These boundary points represent the subset of the reals known as the **integers**. The set of integers is made up of both the positive and negative whole numbers: $\{\ldots, -4, -3, -2, -1, 0, 1, 2, 3, 4, \ldots\}$. Some subsets of integers are:

Natural Numbers or Positive Numbers—the set of integers starting with 1 and increasing:

$\mathcal{N} = \{1, 2, 3, 4, \dots\}$.

Whole Numbers—the set of integers starting with 0 and increasing:

$\mathcal{W} = \{0, 1, 2, 3, \dots\}$.

Negative Numbers—the set of integers starting with -1 and decreasing:

$\mathcal{Z} = \{-1, -2, -3, \dots\}$.

Although there are several other important subsets of integers, those listed above are the only ones that we will need to be concerned about in our review.

Whole Numbers

The whole numbers, as defined above, are the set of all integers greater than or equal to 0. The operations of addition, subtraction, multiplication, and division of whole numbers will now be reviewed.

Addition of Whole Numbers

Addition is indicated by the plus (+) sign. The numbers being added are the addends, and the result of their addition together is the sum.

The numbers to be added are placed in a vertical column, with the last digit of each whole number being in the right most column. In this way, similar units are placed under each other: ones under ones, tens under tens, hundreds under hundreds, etc. For example, to add $102 + 8 + 91$, the addends would be aligned as follows:

$$\begin{array}{r} 102 \\ 8 \\ +\ 91 \\ \hline 201 \end{array}$$

    102   addend
      8   addend
  + 91   addend
    201   sum

Subtraction of Whole Numbers

Subtraction is indicated by the minus (–) sign, or often by the words "find the difference between." When setting up a problem, the number being subtracted from, the minuend, is placed above the number being subtracted, called the subtrahend. Similar units are arranged under each other, just as in addition. The result of the subtraction is called the difference or remainder. For example:

```
  522      minuend
 –101      subtrahend
  421      difference or remainder
```

Multiplication of Whole Numbers

Multiplication is indicated by the multiplication (×) sign. When setting up a multiplication problem, the number being multiplied, the multiplicand, is placed above the number which you are multiplying by, which is called the multiplier. The answer that is computed by multiplying the multiplicand by the multiplier is the product.

```
   13      multiplicand
 ×  4      multiplier
   52      product
```

If the multiplier is a single digit, then the computation is carried out as above. If the multiplier has more than one digit, then the multiplicand must be multiplied by each digit of the multiplier, beginning with the right digit, and moving to the left, from units, to tens, to hundreds, and so on. Each product obtained in this matter, called a partial product, is added together to form the final product.

```
   239      multiplicand
 ×  48      multiplier
  1912      partial product of 8 × 239
   956      partial product of 4 × 239
 11472
```

A very important part of this process is that the right digit of each partial product is vertically below the digit used in the multiplier to form that particular partial product. In the example above, the 2 in 1912 is below the 8 in the multiplier; likewise, the right digit of 956 is below the 4 in the multiplier.

Division of Whole Numbers

Division is indicated by the division (÷) sign, or the fraction (– or /) sign. The words "divided by" are also often used. Symbolically, two different representations are used. If the number you are dividing by is a single digit, the short division symbol)‾‾‾‾ is used. The long division symbol)‾‾‾‾ may be used for any division problem.

The number being divided into is the dividend; it is placed to the right of the vertical bar in the division symbols. To the left of the vertical bar, the number by which you are dividing, the divisor, is placed. The answer to the division is called the quotient; in short division, it is written below the horizontal bar, but in long division it is placed above the bar. Every division is not exact; the number left over is the remainder.

The following is an example of short division:

$$\text{divisor} \quad 7 \overline{)847} \quad \text{dividend}$$
$$121 \quad \text{quotient}$$

The problem is solved in this manner:

- 7 divided into 8 is 1, which is placed below the 8 in the quotient.

- The remainder is 1, changing the 4 to 14.

- 7 divided into 14 is 2, which is placed below the 4.

- There is no remainder.

- 7 divided into 7 is 1, which is placed below the 7.

- Again, there is no remainder.

Thus, $847 \div 7 = 121$.

As a quick means to double-check your answer, you may multiply the divisor by the quotient. If this product, plus any remainder, equals the dividend, then the answer is correct.

To check the problem above:

$$\begin{array}{r} 121 \\ \times \quad 7 \\ \hline 847 \end{array}$$

    quotient from problem
    multiplier from problem
    dividend from problem

The answer is correct.

For long division, the concept is similar, with the main difference being that each digit placed in the quotient will first be an estimate that will have to be checked for correctness.

Look at the following problem:

$$\begin{array}{r} 31 \\ \text{divisor} \quad 32 \overline{)\ 992} \\ -96 \\ \hline 32 \\ -32 \\ \hline 0 \end{array}$$

quotient
dividend

- First, estimate how many times 32 divides into 99.

- If you estimate 3, place 3 in the quotient and multiply the divisor, 32, by 3.

- Record this product, 96, below 99 and subtract.

One of two errors would have occurred if you had a different estimate:

- If the product you calculated was larger than 99, then you overestimated. Lower your estimate and try again.

- If, after subtracting your product from 99, your remainder is larger than the divisor, 32, then you underestimated. Try a larger estimate.

After successfully estimating 3, and subtracting the product, we have a remainder of 3.

- Bring down the next digit of the dividend, a 2.

- Estimate how many times 32 divides into 32, which is 1.

- Place 1 in the quotient.

- Multiplying 32 by 1, and subtracting this product from our previous remainder of 32, we are left with 0.

Thus, $992 \div 32 = 31$, with no remainder.

Verifying our answer:

$$
\begin{array}{r}
31 \\
\times\ 32 \\
\hline
62 \\
93 \\
\hline
992
\end{array}
$$

     31   quotient from problem
× 32   multiplier from problem
992   dividend from problem

FRACTIONS

The fraction, a/b, where the **numerator** is a and the **denominator** is b, implies that a is being divided by b. The denominator of a fraction can never be 0 since a number divided by 0 is not defined. If the numerator is greater than the denominator, the fraction is called an **improper fraction**. A **mixed number** is the sum of a whole number and a fraction, i.e., $4^3/_8 = 4 + {}^3/_8$.

To change an improper fraction to a mixed number, simply divide the numerator by the denominator. The remainder becomes the numerator of the fractional part of the mixed number, and the denominator remains the same, e.g.,

$$^{35}/_4 = 35 \div 4 = 8^3/_4$$

To check your work, change your result back to an improper fraction to see if it matches the original fraction.

DECIMALS

When we divide the denominator of a fraction into its numerator, the result is a **decimal**. The decimal is based upon a fraction with a denominator of 10, 100, 1000, ... and is written with a **decimal point**. Whole numbers are placed to the left of the decimal point where the first place to the left is the units place; the second to the left is the tens; the third to the left is the hundreds, etc. The fractions are placed on the right where the first place to the right is the tenths; the second to the right is the hundredths, etc.

Some examples of decimals:

$$12^3/_{10} = 12.3 \quad 4^{17}/_{100} = 4.17 \quad ^3/_{100} = .03$$

Addition and Subtraction of Decimals

To add numbers containing decimals, write the numbers in a column making sure the decimal points are lined up, one beneath the other. Add the numbers as usual, placing the decimal point in the sum so that it is still in line with the others. It is important not to mix the digits in the tenths place with the digits in the hundredths place, and so on.

Some examples of addition and subtraction of decimals:

2.558 + 6.391	57.51 + 6.2
2.558	57.51
+ 6.391	+ 6.20
8.949	63.71

Similarly with subtraction,

78.54 − 21.33	7.11 − 4.2
78.54	7.11
− 21.33	− 4.20
57.21	2.91

Note that if two numbers differ according to the number of digits to the right of the decimal point, zeros must be added.

$$.63 - .214 \qquad\qquad 15.224 - 3.6891$$

$$
\begin{array}{r}
.630 \\
- .214 \\
\hline
.416
\end{array}
\qquad\qquad
\begin{array}{r}
15.2240 \\
- 3.6891 \\
\hline
11.5349
\end{array}
$$

Multiplication of Decimals

To multiply numbers with decimals, simply multiply as usual. Then, to figure out the number of decimal places that belong in the product, find the total number of decimal places in the numbers being multiplied.

Some examples of multiplication of decimals:

6.555	(3 decimal places)	5.32	(2 decimal places)
× 4.5	(1 decimal place)	× .04	(2 decimal places)
32775		2128	
26220		000	
294975		2128	
29.4975	(4 decimal places)	.2128	(4 decimal places)

Division of Decimals

To divide numbers with decimals, you must first make the divisor a whole number by moving the decimal point the appropriate number of places to the right. The decimal point of the dividend should also be moved the same number of places. Place a decimal point in the quotient, directly in line with the decimal point in the dividend.

Some examples of division of decimals:

$$12.92 \div 3.4 \qquad\qquad 40.376 \div 7.21$$

$$
\begin{array}{r}
3.8 \\
3.4.\overline{)12.9.2} \\
-102 \\
\hline
272 \\
-272 \\
\hline
0
\end{array}
\qquad\qquad
\begin{array}{r}
5.6 \\
7.21.\overline{)40.37.6} \\
-3605 \\
\hline
4326 \\
-4326 \\
\hline
0
\end{array}
$$

PERCENTAGES

A **percent** is a way of expressing the relationship between part and whole, where whole is defined as 100%. A percent can be defined by a fraction with a denominator of 100. Decimals can also represent a percent. For instance,

$$56\% = 0.56 = {}^{56}/_{100}$$

$$48^1/_2\% = {}^{48.5}/_{100} = {}^{485}/_{1000} = .485$$

Though the vast majority of problems that you will face on the ASVAB test will be very similar to the examples that were covered, a brief review of some basic geometric concepts will also be needed.

GEOMETRY

Our study of geometry focuses on several different measurements. For flat, two-dimensional figures in a plane, we may measure the area and perimeter of a shape. The area is the space a figure encloses, while the perimeter is the measurement of the distance around a shape's outside boundary. Volume pertains to the space within a figure which has three dimensions: length and width as in a two-dimensional shape, and an added dimension, depth, or height. We will now examine some basic shapes.

Rectangle

A rectangle is a plane figure with four right angles. Opposite sides have equal lengths and are parallel. The area of a rectangle is the product of its length and width and is expressed in square units; the perimeter is the sum of the lengths of its sides.

4 ft

$A = lw = 4$ ft $\times$ 12 ft = 48 sq. ft.

$P = l + l + w + w = 12$ ft + 12 ft + 4 ft + 4 ft = 32 ft.

A square is a rectangle with four equal sides. Remember that a square is a rectangle, but a rectangle is not a square. The area is found by multiplying a side of the square by itself. The perimeter is the product of four and the length of a side.

8 ft

$A = l \times l = 8$ ft $\times$ 8 ft = 64 sq. ft.

$P = 4 \times l = 4 \times 8$ ft = 32 ft.

8 ft

Triangle

A triangle has three sides. The area of a triangle is found by multiplying its length, or base, by its height, and dividing this product by 2.

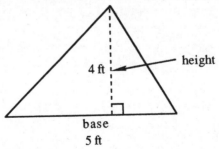

$A = (b \times h)/2$

$A = (5 \text{ ft} \times 4 \text{ ft})/2 = 20 \text{ sq. ft}/2 = 10 \text{ sq. ft}$

The perimeter is just the sum of the three sides.

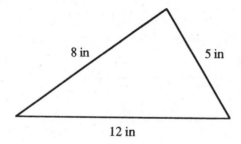

$P = 8 \text{ in} + 5 \text{ in} + 12 \text{ in} = 25 \text{ in}$

Circle

A circle is a perfectly round figure in a plane. The radius of a circle is the distance from the center of the circle to any point on the circle. The diameter of a circle is a straight line that runs from one point on the circle to another, and passes through the center of the circle.

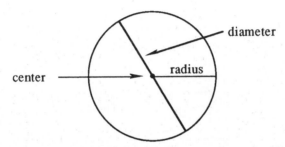

A mathematical constant used in several applications concerning circles is pi, which is represented by π. Pi has the value 3.14 when represented in decimal form and $\frac{22}{7}$ when represented as a fraction. Unless the problem states otherwise, the answer is usually left in terms of pi.

The area of a circle is obtained by squaring the radius and multiplying by pi. The perimeter of a circle, known as the circumference, is the product of 2 and the radius, multiplied by π. Therefore,

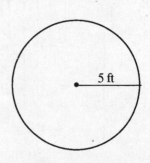

$A = \pi r^2$

$A = \pi \times 5 \text{ ft} \times 5 \text{ ft} = 25\pi \text{ sq. ft.}$

$P = 2\pi r$

$P = 2 \times \pi \times 5 \text{ ft} = 10\pi \text{ ft.}$

Rectangular Solid

The volume of any solid is the space within that solid. For a rectangular solid, the volume is the length × width × height, and is measured in cubic units.

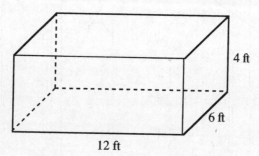

$V = l \times w \times h$

$V = 12 \text{ ft} \times 6 \text{ ft} \times 4 \text{ ft} = 288 \text{ cu. ft.}$

A cube is a rectangular solid which has sides of equal length. If we denote each side as having length s, then the volume of a cube is $s \times s \times s$, or s^3.

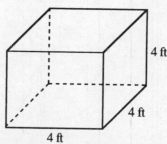

$V = s \times s \times s = s^3$

$V = 4 \text{ ft} \times 4 \text{ ft} \times 4 \text{ ft} = (4 \text{ ft})^3 = 64 \text{ cu. ft.}$

Cylinder

A cylinder is a circular solid. Its top and bottom are circles. The distance separating the circles is the cylinder's height. Its volume is the area of either of the circles, which is πr^2, multiplied by the height.

$V = \pi r^2 h$

$V = \pi \times (3 \text{ ft} \times 3 \text{ ft}) \times 6 \text{ ft} = 54\pi \text{ cu. ft.}$

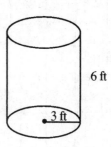

6 ft

3 ft

WORD KNOWLEDGE REVIEW

Communication is a valuable tool used in every aspect of daily life. When a person fails to communicate clearly, understanding is made more difficult—even impossible. Having a good vocabulary doesn't mean knowing a lot of words with many syllables. Rather, it means having knowledge of many words, and knowing how and where to use them. There's a time and place for both long and short words, and using words inappropriately is a sign of a poor communicator. As Mark Twain once said, "There is as much difference between a right word and an almost right word as there is between lightning and a lightning bug." Everyone—writer, speaker, reader, listener—benefits when a communicator is able to use the exact words needed to clearly express his or her thoughts.

Vocabulary tests are tools often used to determine the aptitude of job seekers, students, and applicants in training programs and the military. In testing your knowledge of words and their definitions, we can also make a general assessment of your ability to learn and to reason—two very important skills required in all occupations.

The ASVAB Word Knowledge Test measures communication skills by testing one's knowledge of synonyms. Two words are synonyms if they mean the same or nearly the same thing.

It's nearly impossible for two words to have the exact meaning, even though they may be synonyms. For instance, although "thin" and "skinny" are synonymous words, they convey a different "feeling," or connotation. Both words describe the condition of being somewhat underweight, but "thin" can be used in a positive sense, whereas "skinny" almost always has a negative feeling about it. When trying to choose a synonym for a word, you are looking for a word *close* in meaning, but not necessarily a word with the *exact* same definition.

The ASVAB Word Knowledge Test contains words commonly used by people with a high school-level education. Some words, of course, are encountered more frequently than others; careful reading of the word in question and the answer choices will frequently enable you to choose the correct answer, or at least narrow down the number of appropriate responses.

PLAN OF ATTACK

1. Know how much time you have to complete the test, and be aware of the time as you are taking it. Try to be at least half-way finished when your time is half up.

2. Read the questions and answers carefully. Read all answers before choosing one.

3. Work quickly but carefully. Answer the questions you know first, and skip questions that give you difficulty. When you've completed the easier questions, spend any remaining time on the harder ones.

4. Be sure you are marking your answer choice in the correct space on the answer sheet. Check at least every fifth question to be certain you are in the right spot.

5. When going back to the more difficult questions, stop and try to think of an answer. Check the answer choices to see if one of them is similar to your answer.

6. Eliminate all the answers you know are incorrect, and narrow down your field of possible answers. Be careful: sometimes an answer choice will be a synonym for a word that *sounds* like the word in question, but means something very different. Be sure that your answer is a synonym for the exact word in question—and that it's not a synonym for a word that just sounds like it.

7. Think of times when you might have heard the word in question used. If you can think of a phrase with the word in it, that may be especially helpful. Try to determine the "gist" of the word's meaning as it was used when you heard it, and see if an answer choice has a similar meaning.

8. Since there is no penalty for incorrect answers, make sure you answer all questions, even if you have to guess.

9. Check your answers if you have time at the end of the exam. However, change an answer only if you have a strong reason for doing so; usually your first instinct is the best choice. If you change an answer, be sure to erase your first choice completely.

The following words frequently appear on standardized vocabulary tests. The words are listed with brief definitions and their parts of speech to help you learn them. These are not the only words you need to know to take the ASVAB test—they are provided only to give you an idea of the kinds of words and the level of vocabulary on which you will be tested.

VOCABULARY WORD LIST

alleviate – (*v.*) – to relieve or lessen (discomfort); to decrease

altruism – (*n.*) – concern for the well-being of others; unselfishness

ambiguous – (*adj.*) – vague; not clear; having more than one meaning

amble – (*v.*) – to walk at a slow and easy pace

apathy – (*n.*) – indifference; lack of emotion

arrogant – (*adj.*) – full of self-importance; conceited

articulate – (*adj.*) – able to communicate clearly; (*v.*) – to express distinctly

benefactor – (*n.*) – one who gives money or other assistance

benign – (*adj.*) – kind; not harmful

compensate – (*v.*) – to make up for; to repay for services

comply – (*v.*) – to obey; to give in

condone – (*v.*) – to forgive or overlook; to excuse

contempt – (*n.*) – the condition of being despised; reproachful disdain

crucial – (*adj.*) – very important; critical; severe

debris – (*n.*) – rubbish; bits and pieces of stones, etc.

deference – (*n.*) – courteous respect for the wishes of another

deplete – (*v.*) – to use up

deter – (*v.*) – to discourage someone from doing something

discriminate – (*v.*) – to distinguish or differentiate; to show bias

disparity – (*adj.*) – distinction or difference; inequality

disprove – (*v.*) – to prove to be wrong or false

dubious – (*adj.*) – causing or feeling doubt; uncertain; skeptical

emerge – (*v.*) – to come into view; to become known; to evolve

emit – (*v.*) – to utter; send out; discharge

endeavor – (*n.*) – a good effort, an earnest attempt; (*v.*) – to make an effort, to try

evade – (*v.*) – to escape or avoid, especially by deception; to avoid answering directly expel – (*v.*) – to force out; dismiss by authority

facilitate – (*v.*) – to make easier or quicker

fastidious – (*adj.*) – not easy to please; oversensitive

fluent – (*adj.*) – able to write or speak easily; smoothly flowing

foremost – (*adj.*) – first; most important

fortify – (*v.*) – to strengthen; build

frivolous – (*adj.*) – unimportant; trivial; lacking seriousness

futile – (*adj.*) – useless; unsuccessful

grave – (*adj.*) – important; serious; solemn; (*n.*) – an underground burial place

harass – (*v.*) – to tease; torment; disturb

hinder – (*v.*) – to hold back; to impede or thwart progress

hypocrite – (*n.*) – person who says or pretends to believe one thing but does something different

ignorant – (*adj.*) – uneducated; unaware; uninformed

illegible – (*adj.*) – difficult or impossible to read

inadvertent – (*adj.*) – unintentional; not attentive; due to oversight

incentive – (*n.*) – a motive; something that urges a person to take action

indifferent – (*adj.*) – having no strong feelings or opinions; neutral; unconcerned

indulgent – (*adj.*) – inclined to satisfy a desire; often excessively

infamous – (*adj.*) – notorious; well known for bad behavior

instigate – (*v.*) – to urge on to action; to provoke; incite

intermittent – (*adj.*) – periodic; coming and going or stopping and starting at intervals

lethargic – (*adj.*) – sluggish; apathetic; unusually unenergetic

lucrative – (*adj.*) – profitable; produces wealth or money

malevolent – (*adj.*) – evil; full of harmful intent; malicious

mediocre – (*adj.*) – average; ordinary; undistinguished

nocturnal – (*adj.*) – of or active in the night

oblivious – (*adj.*) – forgetful or unaware

obscure – (*adj.*) – vague; not easily seen; not well known

obsolete – (*adj.*) – out of date; no longer in use

obstinate – (*adj.*) – stubborn; determined; resisting

persevere – (*v.*) – to continue doing something in spite of difficulty

philanthropy – (*n.*) – goodwill to mankind; a desire or effort to promote the well-being of others; a charitable act or gift

ponder – (*v.*) – to carefully think about

pretentious – (*adj.*) – claiming to be or acting important; ostentatious

prudent – (*adj.*) – using common sense in decision making; practicing careful management

ravenous – (*adj.*) – extremely hungry; greedy

redundant – (*adj.*) – repetitive; unnecessary; excessive; wordy

relevant – (*adj.*) – connected or applies to the matter under consideration; pertinent

remorse – (*n.*) – regret for wrongdoing; distress from feeling or being guilty

retaliate – (*v.*) – to pay back an injury or wrong in the same manner, to get even

satire – (*n.*) – ridicule, sarcasm, biting wit, or irony used to expose folly

semblance – (*n.*) – outward appearance, likeness

superficial – (*adj.*) – surface understanding; concerned only with the obvious; not thorough; shallow

tedious – (*adj.*) – tiresome, boring, dull

temper – (*v.*) – to moderate; to toughen; (*n.*) – one's disposition; calmness of mind; anger

tentative – (*adj.*) – not definite

undaunted – (*adj.*) – not discouraged or afraid, fearless

unflinching – (*adj.*) – firm, showing no sign of fear

vehement – (*adj.*) – violent; sudden; full of intense emotion; very energetic

virtuoso – (*n.*) – a person who excels in the performance of a fine art, especially a musician

volatile – (*adj.*) – unstable; explosive; lighthearted

PARAGRAPH COMPREHENSION REVIEW

Reading for understanding and information is basic to success. You cannot hold a good job without this skill. Good readers make good employees. Neglect it at your peril. The more you read, the more you know, and the better you get at it.

In taking these tests, your job will be to:

1. Understand the main point or topic (**T**) of a given paragraph, whether it is stated or implied by the writer.

2. Identify all the sentences used as evidence for or examples (**E**) of the main point. These **E** sentences may take the form of facts, examples, statistics, or illustrations. For our purposes, we will call all such evidence **examples**.

3. Define or understand specific words in context, sometimes literally (denotation) and sometimes figuratively (connotation).

T→NS→E+E+E: PARAGRAPH ORGANIZATION AND WHAT TO LOOK FOR

Paragraphs are units of thought expressed in several sentences and organized under a single idea. The controlling idea may be either implied or stated. Paragraphs often consist of an idea (or "T" for topic) supported by three or more sentences of evidence, or examples (or "E"), for what the writer means.

> (**T**opic sentence) — + → (**N**arrowing **S**entence — not always included) — + → Example 1 — + → Example 2 — + → Example 3, → etc.

EXAMPLE

S1.　(**T**) Dogs truly are a man's best friend. (**NS**) Dogs are the most faithful and loyal of creatures. (**E**) Divorced men may lose the wife, the house, the car, and the kids—but their dogs will still be at their sides. (**E**) Soldiers and knights often would not go into battle unless their warrior dogs were with them, and many of those dogs died for their masters.

In the sample above, the writer starts out with a general idea (**T**) or topic. But that idea demands evidence. Just because somebody says something is so doesn't make it true. What is the evidence? Maybe it is not true. Each of the examples (**E**) that the writer uses following the **T** sentence offers evidence for what s/he claims in (**T**) is true. Notice that this writer limits, or narrows (**NS**), what s/he says. **T** is too broad, so the writer narrows it down a bit by stating that dogs are man's best friend by virtue of their demonstrated faithfulness and loyalty.

But watch out! Not all paragraphs begin with the **T** sentence. S1 above could be written with the **T** sentence in the middle or end, but it would still be the main point.

EXAMPLE

S2.   (**NS**) Dogs are the most faithful and loyal of creatures. (**E**) Divorced men may lose the wife, the house, the car, and the kids—but their dogs will still be at their sides. (**T**) Dogs truly are a man's best friend. (**E**) Soldiers and knights often would not go into battle unless their warrior dogs were with them, and many of those dogs died for their masters.

For practice, read the following example:

EXAMPLE

S3.   The best things in life are free. (**T**opic sentence) Things that cost money are not as valuable as things we can put no price on. (**N**arrowing of idea) For example, how much is the sunshine per minute of warmth? (**E**xample #1) You cannot put a price on love. (**E**#2) There is no bill of sale for fresh air. (**E**#3)

You may not agree with the writer, but that doesn't matter. What s/he says supports the "**T**" that "the best things in life are free."

Implications and Inferences

Not all paragraphs have a **T** or an **NS**. Sometimes the **T** or **NS** is *implied* in a paragraph. For example, read the following paragraph:

EXAMPLE

S4.　(**E**) I want a wife who will wash my clothes and iron my shirts. (**E**) I want a wife who will clean the house and do the dishes. (**E**) I want a wife who will change the babies' diapers and cook my meals. (**E**) I want a wife who will do the shopping and greet me with my favorite cocktail when I come home tired from work.

Well, it's clear this guy wants a wife. Now, whatever you may think of this guy (never let your emotions cloud your feelings and get in the way of what was said), he is making a point about *what kind* of wife he wants. Notice that the paragraph is nothing but "**E**'s" (**E**xamples) in the sense we are talking about them. All of the sentences show, or exemplify, characteristics of the "wife" this husband wants—but no one of them "sums it up."

This writer *implies* in the paragraph, *without actually stating*, the kind of wife he wants. Yet we still get a pretty clear picture or idea of her. Even though he doesn't say it, if we "put it in a nutshell," we can see that the writer wants a traditional housekeeper wife (**T**).

This would probably be close to the **T** sentence of this writer's paragraph if he had actually stated rather than implied it. Some of you may have been *feeling* that what he wants is a slave, not a wife—but *be careful*: that's what you may feel, not what the writer is saying. *Don't confuse your feelings with the writer's facts or illustrations.*

Writers sometimes imply things that would be a logical extension of what they actually say. For example, it would be unreasonable to suggest that this writer is implying he wants a liberated feminist career woman for his spouse. This deduction does not logically follow the examples he offers in his paragraph. The examples don't support that idea.

Paragraph tests will often ask you what the reader can *infer* from a paragraph s/he has read. Actually, implications and inferences are very similar; the only difference is who is making them: writers imply, readers infer. For example, in this case, the reader could **infer** that the writer is a male who wants a conventional wife. He probably likes football, too. Probably—that's an **inference**: a reader's probable and reasonable conclusion or interpretation of an idea based upon what the writer has written. For example, it would be unreasonable to assume the writer was a woman—women generally have husbands, not wives.

CONNOTATION AND DENOTATION

Sometimes, you will be asked to determine **the meaning of a word** in the context of the paragraph. You may not have seen the word before, but from your understanding of the writer's intent, you should be able to figure out what it is s/he's after.

For example, read the following paragraph:

S5. Paris is a beautiful city, perhaps the most beautiful on Earth. Long, broad avenues are lined with seventeenth- and eighteenth-century apartments, office buildings, and cafes. Flowers give the city a rich and varied look. The bridges and the river lend an air of lightness and grace to the whole urban landscape.

In this paragraph, "rich" most nearly means

S5–A stupid.

S5–B polluted.

S5–C colorful.

S5–D dull.

If you chose "colorful" you would be right. Although "rich" literally means "wealthy" (a word's **denotation** is its literal meaning), here the writer means more than the word's literal meaning, and seems to be highlighting the variety and color that the flowers add to the avenues, that is, richness in a figurative sense.

The writer is using a non-literal meaning, or **connotation,** to show what s/he means. When we think of something "rich," we usually also think of abundance and variety and color as well as just plain numbers. In a similar way, the denotation of the word "mother" is "the female parent of offspring, usually mammals."

But when we look at the feelings and impressions—the connotations—that go along with "mother," we think of someone who is loving, nurturing, kind, and so on, which conveys a much deeper impression than the denotation of "female parent of offspring."

Most of the time, however, you will just be asked to identify the literal meaning, or denotation, of the word in question.

For example, read this paragraph:

S6. Many soporifics are on the market to help people sleep. Take a glass of water and two *Slumberol* and you get the "zzzzz" you need. *Snooz-aways* supposedly helps you get the sleep you need so you can go on working.

From this paragraph, a "soporific" is probably

S6–A a drug that helps you to stay awake.

S6–B a kind of sleeping bag.

S6–C a kind of bed.

S6–D a drug that helps you sleep.

Oh yeah, I knew that!

What the heck is a soporific? Never saw that one before! But, look, you can figure out what it means by looking at what is said around it. People take these "soporifics" to go to sleep, not to wake up! You can't take two beds and a glass of water to go to sleep, either. Imagine trying to get a bed down your throat with a glass of water! So, it must be some sort of pill that you take to sleep. Well, pills are usually drugs of some kind. So, it must be (D)! Positively!

Good luck!

PLAN OF ATTACK

To give yourself the best chance of success in the paragraph comprehension test, your plan of attack should be as follows:

Pre-Reading/Pre-Testing

1. Read the "Paragraph Comprehension Review" in this book so you understand what the test requires of you before you even get near to taking the test.

2. You may want to bone up on your vocabulary by working with a programmed vocabulary book or the vocabulary section of this book.

3. Don't panic. Work naturally and quickly. The best you can do is the best you can do.

Taking the Test: The Reading Process

Time is short, so pace yourself.

Five minutes after the test has begun, you should be working on the fifth paragraph. If you are not, speed up.

Ten minutes into the test, you should be on paragraph 15. If not, speed up. If you are ahead of this pace, don't worry, keep going and do extra steps (see below) when you get to the end.

Thirteen minutes into the test you should be done.

The reading process is basically a four-step event:

1. Read the passage completely through once.

2. Read the questions and choices about the paragraph. Make a temporary choice among those listed.

3. Review (re-read) the paragraph again.

4. Make your final choice and move on.

Step 1. Read the passage completely through once.

Read each paragraph and determine its implied *or* stated "**T**," i.e., its **main point** or **general idea.**

Identify what sentences are the "**E**" sentences.

Step 2. Read the questions and choices about the paragraphs.

- Be sure you understand the words.

- Do the choices ask you about the **T** or the **E** sentences?

- Make a temporary choice—don't write it in the answer column yet.

Step 3. Review the paragraph again.

- Go back and read the paragraph again to see if your choice *is backed up* either by the "**T**" of the paragraph or its **E**'s (facts, statistics, examples, *evidence* of any sort).

- If your choice doesn't "fit," or match the choice, try again.

- After two attempts, move on to the next paragraph.

   — While looking for the right choice, look for words that appear in *both* the choice and the paragraph.

   — If you don't find the identical word, look for a *paraphrase* (a way of saying the same thing in other words) of the terms used in the paragraph. See p. 148, S6–D, where the word "drug" is a synonym for "soporific." Sometimes the key will be a phrase, not just a single word.

Step 4. Make your final choice and move on.

Don't dawdle or get frustrated by the really troubling ones. If you haven't gotten it after two attempts, chances are you won't. Move on.

Extra Steps:

If you have time at the end, go back to the paragraphs that were difficult and review them again.

Believe in yourself. The best that you can do is the best that you can do.

AUTO REVIEW

In the last hundred years, no industrial development has so captivated the American people as the automobile. Automobiles take us to the corner store, to the mountains, around a race track, or around the world. Most of us cannot imagine life without the automobile. It is interesting to note that even though automobiles have become luxury items, full of plush leather, stereos, special features, and safety advances, its basic design is unchanged since its inception.

An automobile is a movable platform with four wheels, big enough to carry several people from one location to another in comfort and safety. Obviously, our cars of today are much more than just movable platforms!

Let's look at the basic elements of today's automobile.

Figure 1

WHEELS

To begin, there are the **wheels**. The most common element of any bicycle, car, train, or truck is the wheel. Invented thousands of years ago, the wheel makes it possible for us to move a heavy or light object across the ground. Today's automobile wheels are made up of a hard, round rubber compound inflated with air, called the tire, which is mounted on a steel or composite material hub called the **rim**.

The rim holds the air inside the tire while allowing us to mount the whole assembly onto the axle of our automobile. One wheel at each corner of our automobile and we're ready to roll!

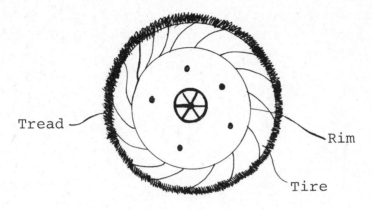

Tread

Rim

Tire

Figure 2

ENGINE

At one time, before the engine was invented, people used animals or themselves to push or pull something across the ground. We've all seen pictures of covered wagons going across the mountains or Roman chariots being pulled by horses or even people pushing or pulling carts along the streets. Now with the invention of the **engine**, we have created a source of power to move our platform across the ground.

Figure 3

Add some people to ride on our motorized platform with wheels and the automobile was born.

Cylinder and Piston

The power of the automobile engine comes from the burning of a small amount of gasoline and air in a small, enclosed space. As you can see in Figure 4, when this mixture is ignited it burns quickly (like an explosion) and pushes out in all directions. This pushing force can be used to move a part of the engine. The moving part then eventually can be used to drive the wheels of our automobile.

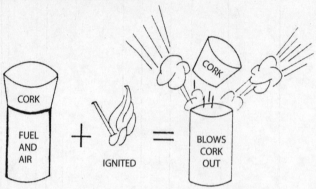

Figure 4 — When gasoline and air are burned in a confined area, heat and pressure are created (internal combustion). This is the chemical energy of the fuel and air converted into heat energy.

Engines always appear much more complicated than they really are. Without all the hoses and wires, engines have a few basic components. The first is the **cylinder**. Shaped like an empty can, open at one end, the cylinder holds the **piston**—which looks like a giant plug or plunger inside the cylinder. The close-fitting piston is the moving part of our engine which supplies the power to our automobile's wheels. It slides easily, up and down, inside the cylinder.

How do we change the up and down motion of the piston to the rotary motion needed to power our automobile? The same way we move a bicycle—by pumping our legs up and down. Look at Figure 5. First we attach a **connecting rod** to the piston. We attach the other end of the connecting rod to a **crankshaft**. The crankshaft is a long shaft with an off-set portion which moves in a circle. So while one end of the connecting rod moves up and down with the piston, the other end moves in a circle with the

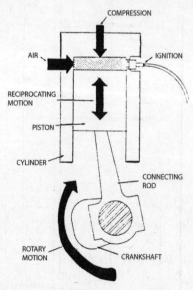

Figure 5

crankshaft. Think of our bicycle: Our knee is the piston, moving up and down. Our shin, calf, and foot is the connecting rod and the pedals and chain sprockets are the crank and crankshaft. As our knee moves up and down, our feet follow the pedals in a circle like the crankshaft! (See Figure 6.)

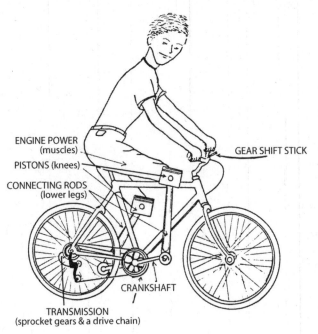

ENGINE POWER (muscles)

PISTONS (knees)

CONNECTING RODS (lower legs)

GEAR SHIFT STICK

CRANKSHAFT

TRANSMISSION (sprocket gears & a drive chain)

Figure 6

By the way, at the other end of the crankshaft there is a heavy flywheel like a grindstone to keep the crankshaft turning between power strokes of the piston. Otherwise, the piston would stop dead in the cylinder after the explosion. We want the piston to keep moving up and down so we can repeat the power stroke many times to keep our car moving.

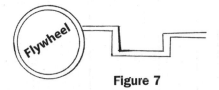

Figure 7

So far our engine has only one piston/cylinder arrangement attached to the crankshaft. But today's engines have between 4 and 8 cylinders. Engines with cylinders in a row are called **in-line engines** and engines with cylinders arranged at an angle off the crankshaft are called **V-type engines** (e.g., an in-line 6 cylinder or a V-8 cylinder). No matter how many cylinders we have, it's still the same basic piston arrangement.

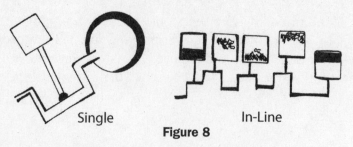

Single   In-Line

Figure 8

Now that we have our basic engine with moving pistons to supply power to the wheels, we need a way to get the air-fuel mixture into the cylinder and the burnt exhaust gases from the explosion out of the cylinder. So let's cut two holes in the top of the cylinder, like in Figure 10, above the piston. Over each hole, we'll put a tight fitting metal disc, like a stopper, which can be opened and closed. One disc will be opened to allow fresh air-fuel mixture into the cylinder then close and the other disc will open and close to allow the exhaust gases to leave the cylinder and make room for more fresh air-fuel mixture. These metal discs which open and close are called **valves**.

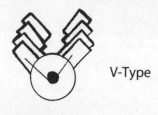

V-Type

Figure 9

The valves are controlled by a **camshaft, rocker arm**, and **rod assembly**. The whole assembly works like a fancy door opener. The camshaft is driven by the crankshaft (the same one which connects to our pistons), and it moves at one-half speed of the crankshaft to accurately open and close the valves at precisely the correct moment.

Air-Fuel System

In order to have an explosion in the cylinder, to move the piston downward, the air-fuel mixture must be supplied in the proper proportion. This feeding of the mixture in the proper amount is the job of the **carburetor**, as you can see in Figure 12. A fuel pump sends gasoline from the storage tank to an area of the carburetor called the **float bowl**. The float bowl is like a little pond with an open tube at one end. Air is sucked into the carburetor through the air filter, caused by the downward motion of the piston, and picks up speed as it passes through a reduced passageway in the carburetor, called the **venturi**. The speeding air passes by the opening to the float bowl and sucks a small amount of fuel with it. This air-fuel mixture, in mist form, then passes through the open valve in the cylinder

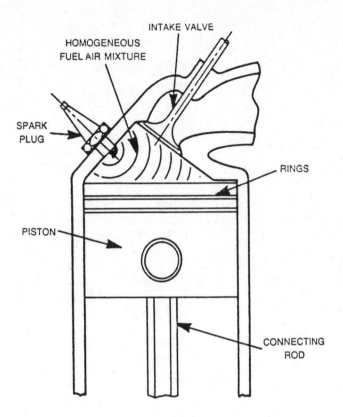

Figure 10 — This is where it all begins. Air and fuel mixture is admitted into the combustion chamber by the intake valve, compressed by the piston, and ignited. The explosion pushes the piston downward in the power stroke. Piston rings function as seals, containing the gas pressure to prevent power losses.

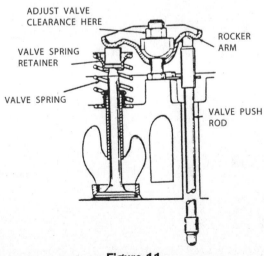

Figure 11

and into the chamber above the piston. This all happens at the exact, correct moment and with the exact amount of air-fuel mixture.

The accelerator pedal connects to the throttle valve at the base of the carburetor to determine just how much fuel-air mixture our engine needs. A ratio of 15 pounds of air to 1 pound of fuel is always needed to keep our mixture properly proportioned. Obviously, air plays just as important a role in our engine as gasoline.

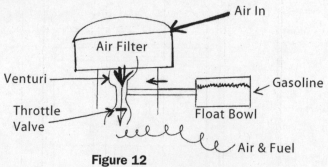

Figure 12

During the 1960s, in an effort to improve engine performance, achieve higher mileage ratings, and reduce emission pollutants, **electronic engine control** coupled with **fuel injectors** were developed.

The basic premise of electronic engine control (sometimes called electronic carburetion) is that by precisely controlling the amount of air-fuel mixture injected into the cylinder and varying its ratio depending upon engine needs then emission pollutants could be reduced and engine performance maximized.

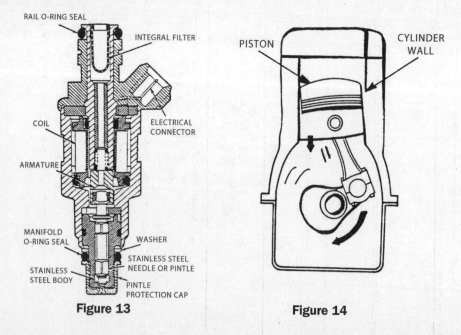

Figure 13   **Figure 14**

In an electronic engine control system, the carburetor is replaced by fuel injectors. (See Figure 13.) The system itself consists of a **small computer** or **microprocessor** to control the air-fuel mixture and an injector system. The microprocessor determines the needs of the engine based on its speed, whether it's pulling a heavy load like a trailer, and other outside factors, then it determines the required air-fuel ratio. The air-fuel mixture is then sent directly to the cylinders and made ready for the power stroke.

The injection system which sends the fuel into the cylinders is usually one of two arrangements. The first is called **single port injection (SPI).** Air-fuel mixture is sent to a throttle body on top of the engine. From the throttle body, the air-fuel travels through small steel tubes directly to the cylinder. In the second system, the throttle body is eliminated and the air-fuel travels directly from the fuel tank, through a manifold, and into each cylinder directly. In this manner, air-fuel mixture can be precisely controlled and unburned gases and emissions are kept to a minimum.

Now all that is needed is something to start the mixture in the cylinder burning, which will send the piston downward on its power stroke. So, we'll add a **spark plug**, which acts like a cigarette lighter, to create a spark. In the engine, we do this electronically by jumping electricity between the electrodes of the spark plug. This is called ignition because we are igniting the air-fuel mixture. As you can see in Figure 15, a **battery** furnishes the electricity for the spark plug but we need a few more items. A **coil** and **breaker** make a high voltage spark to ignite the mixture and the **distributor** makes sure the spark goes to the right spark plug at the right time.

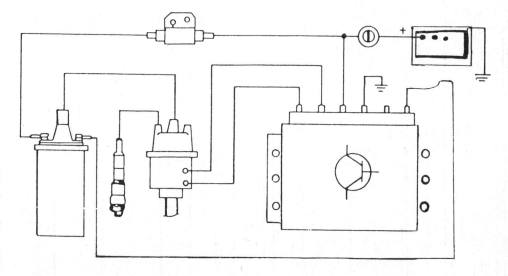

Figure 15

All of this happens very fast. In an eight-cylinder car going 55 miles an hour, the ignition system ignites 123 sparks each second! All this occurs at the precise, correct moment without a miss.

Remember our piston moving up and down in the cylinder? Well the reason the sparks have to be so precise and fast is that there are specific times when the piston needs the spark and specific times when it does not. There is no sense in causing a spark to occur if there's no fuel-air mixture in the cylinder ready to burn. Let's look at how the engine runs over a period of time without stopping.

How An Engine Works

Most engines are **four-stroke engines**. That means that it takes four strokes of the piston, "up-down-up-down," to complete one full cycle of events before repeating itself.

Look at Figure 16. First, the piston moves downward as the intake valve is opened. This downward action sucks in fresh air-fuel mixture from the carburetor into the cylinder. This first stroke is called the **intake stroke**.

Next, the intake valve closes and the piston moves up from its bottom-most position to the top of the stroke. As it moves upward, the air-fuel mixture in the cylinder is compressed or squeezed by the piston into a small space at the top of the cylinder. This action increases the pressure inside the cylinder. This is called the **compression stroke**.

Now, a spark from the spark plug ignites the mixture and causes it to explode or burn quickly. The explosion pushes out in all directions but the only thing that can move is the piston. So, the force in the cylinder pushes the piston back downward with tremendous force. This is called the **power stroke**.

Finally, the exhaust valve opens and the piston rises again and pushes the leftover burnt gases out of the cylinder to clear the way for more fresh air-fuel mixture. This last stroke is called the **exhaust stroke** and now we're ready to begin the cycle all over again.

Remember, that's a four stroke engine: intake-compression-power-exhaust. It is done over and over again to power our car.

Remember that only during the power stroke is the piston driving the crankshaft. During the other three strokes, the crankshaft drives the piston. So there is one power stroke for every two revolutions of the crankshaft.

That means that in an eight cylinder car there are four power strokes for every one revolution of the crankshaft.

Let's discuss the compression stroke for a minute (Figure 17). You always hear the term **"high compression"** or **"compression ratio."** What does it mean?

It is the measure of how much we can squeeze the air-fuel mixture. If the piston holds 100 cubic inches when the piston is at the bottom of its

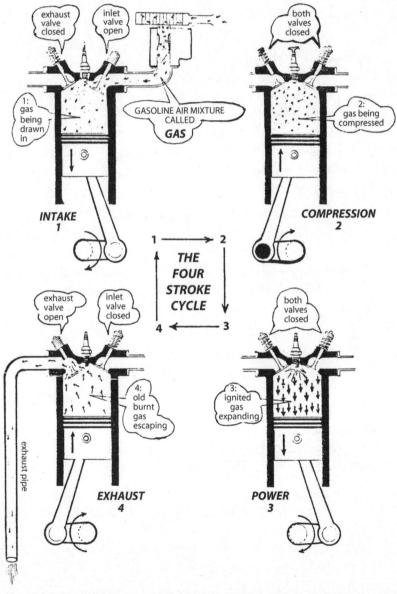

Figure 16

stroke, called "**bottom-dead center**" (**BDC**), and then holds 10 cubic inches at the top of its stroke called "**top-dead center**" (**TDC**), then the compression ratio is 10:1. The mixture is now compressed into a space 10 times smaller than it was at the beginning of the stroke. 5 to 1 compression ratios were common many years ago, now 8 or 9 to 1 is the average, with some engines going as high as 12:1. The more compression, the more power will be generated in the cylinder.

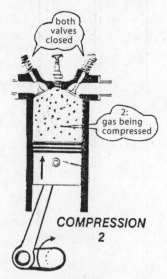

COMPRESSION 2

Figure 17

By now you probably figured out that all this exploding, occurring many times per second, generates a lot of heat. Well, you're right! Our air-fuel mixture burns in the cylinder at 4,000 to 5,000 degrees Fahrenheit. That's hot. So, we have to keep our engine cool or we could actually melt it because iron melts at 2,000 to 2,500 degrees Fahrenheit. So, let's put a blanket of cool water around our hot engine.

Look at Figure 18. As you can see, most engines have canals inside the engine block which carry water from the **radiator** to the hottest parts of the engine, usually the cylinder area, then back to the radiator. These canals are called **water jackets**. The hot water from each cylinder area is circulated by a **water pump**. Once back at the radiator, the outside air cools the water before it's sent back to the hot cylinder area.

In addition to cooling our engine with water, we need an **oil lubrication system** like the one in Figure 19 to keep the metal parts which move against each other from heating up and sticking together. The oil will coat the metal surfaces and keep them lubricated and moving freely. So we have a reservoir of oil in the bottom of the engine in the crankcase. From here, a pump pushes the oil to key points of the engine and circulates it over the moving metal parts. Holes drilled in the connecting rods and crankshaft allow oil to reach bearings and other important areas.

Even though our engine will run on its own, we need to have a way to start it turning. Let's look at Figure 20. This is done using a little **starter motor** attached to the engine block. The ignition key is the "on" switch and the battery supplies the electricity to the motor to turn it on. Once the engine starts, the starter motor stops running.

One more piece of important electrical equipment is the **alternator**.

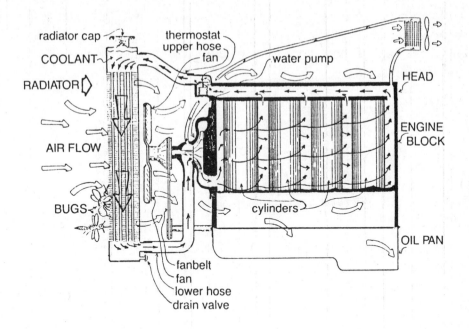

Figure 18

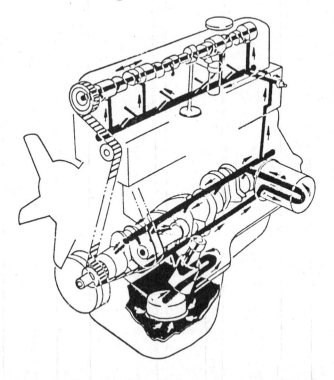

Figure 19 — Understanding the oiling circuit is never more critical than for ohc engines. This particular design employs a hollow cam and individual oil ports—with tiny metering holes—at the lobes.

The alternator is driven by the engine and its job is to supply electricity for running the electrical components of the car, such as the lights and radio. It also re-supplies the battery with the electricity needed to continually re-start the engine.

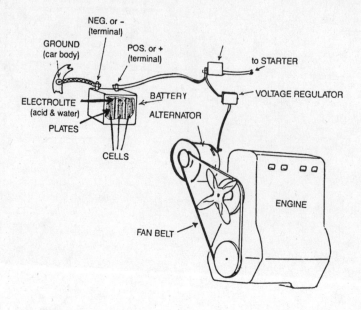

Figure 20

Before we run our engine there is one more area we must be concerned with and that is the **emission control system** used to control the emission of pollutants into the atmosphere. If you've ever been stuck in traffic or inside a parking garage or tunnel, you know what exhaust pollution can smell like.

Automotive engineers are constantly working on systems to reduce exhaust pollutants. The three major pollutants emitted from automobiles are **hydrocarbons (HC), carbon monoxide (CO),** and **oxides of nitrogen (NO_x).** Hydrocarbons are essentially unburned gasoline which comes from the exhaust pipe and the engine's crankcase as a result of the combustion process. Carbon monoxide comes from an over rich fuel-air mixture, which means too much fuel in the mixture, which doesn't allow complete combustion all the way to carbon dioxide and leaves fuel unburned. Oxides of nitrogen are gases formed during combustion as a result of the high combustion temperatures.

There are several methods used to control these emission pollutants. The first was the **PVC system** or **positive crankcase ventilation**. This system redirected the HC pollutants from the crankcase back into the intake system where they would be burned in the combustion chambers. The **air injection system** (Figure 21) controlled CO pollutants by injecting air into the engine exhaust ports to cause further burning of the hot gasoline vapors before they pass out of the exhaust pipe.

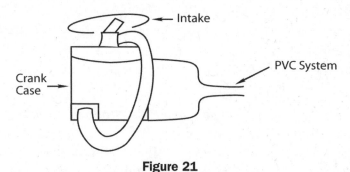

Figure 21

The latest and most effective system is the catalytic converter seen in Figure 22. First introduced in 1975, the system reduces the emission of HC and CO pollutants by oxidizing them into harmless water vapors as the pollutants pass through a cannister of pellets, located in the exhaust system.

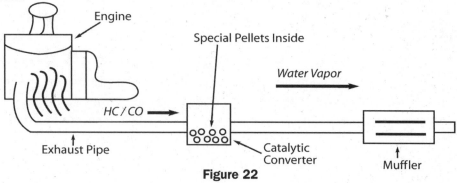

Figure 22

These pellets are coated with a special chemical which causes the HC and CO pollutants to continue oxidizing at a lower temperature and eventually changes them into harmless water vapor before leaving the exhaust pipe.

The third pollutant, NO_x, is controlled by diluting the air-fuel mixture entering the combustion chamber to reduce peak combustion temperature. We can do this by re-circulating exhaust gases back into the intake system in small amounts to dilute the mixture. The emission control system must always be kept in good running order to ensure peak engine performance and maximize emission control.

Engine Summary

In summary, our automobile engine consists of a number of *cylinder/piston* assemblies arranged either *in-line* or in a *V-pattern*. The movable piston acts like our knee pedaling a bicycle. A specific amount of *air-fuel mixture* is admitted into the cylinder through a set of *valves*. The air-fuel mixture is controlled by the *carburetor* or *electronic fuel injection system*. An electrical signal to the *spark plug* in each cylinder causes the air-fuel to explode, sending the piston downward on its *power stroke*. The other three strokes of our *four-stroke engine* are the *intake, compression,* and *exhaust* stroke.

The moving piston turns the *connecting rod* and *crankshaft* arrangement which eventually turns the drive shaft leading to the rear wheels. A *water jacket* and *radiator system* keep the cylinder/piston area cool and friction between moving metal parts is reduced using an *oil lubrication system*.

Burnt gases from the engine which could harm our environment are passed through *emission control devices* like the *catalytic converter, PVC system,* and *air-injection system* to reduce NO_x, *CO,* and *HC pollutants* before they are released into the atmosphere.

DRIVE SYSTEM

Now that the engine is running, we need a way to get the power to the rear wheels to move our automobile. The first drive component is the **transmission**. The power transmission allows us to couple the engine to the rear wheels for driving power and also to vary the speed of the engine depending on how fast we want to travel and in what direction—forward or backward.

Manual Transmission

We'll begin with a manual transmission, sometimes called a stickshift. Imagine a large metal disc, like a dinner plate, attached to the rear of our engine, turning at the same speed as the engine runs. This plate is called the **flywheel**. See Figure 23.

Now imagine another disc attached to a transmission shaft leading to the rear wheels. This disc is called the **transmission disc** or **pressure plate**. We need something between these two plates so we can connect and disconnect the engine to the transmission as we see fit. When we want the engine to spin freely, like at a stop light, we'll disconnect it from the transmission disc. When we want to move our car, we'll connect the

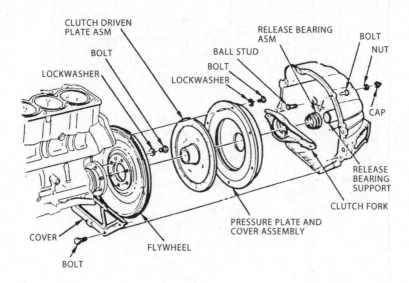

Figure 23 — Clutch, pressure plate, and bellhousing. Note that the clutch disk may have a front and rear face, defined by the distance the splined hub extends out of the unit. Also of interest in this drawing is the open deck construction of the engine block. Water jackets are roofed by the cylinder head. The GM Quad-4 is built on the same pattern.

transmission disc to the spinning engine disc and drive away.

To do this, we use a third disc between these two other plates, called a **clutch plate**. By using a heavy spring triggered by the clutch pedal, we can squeeze the clutch plate and transmission plate against the spinning engine plate and the whole assembly will turn as one unit with the engine. It's like a sandwich with the clutch plate holding the two pieces of bread together! Now the rear wheels will turn with the engine. When we want to disconnect the engine from the wheels to stop the car or change gears, we'll step on the clutch pedal and separate the two plates from each other. The clutch disc in the middle is simply a way of doing this connecting and disconnecting smoothly without jarring or banging the plates together. Friction clutches are only found in manual transmissions.

Now that our car is moving, let's speed it up and slow down by changing gears. Assume our manual transmission has three forward gears (first, second, and third) and one reverse gear like the one in Figure 24. Suppose we had a driving gear with 12 teeth and a driving gear with 24

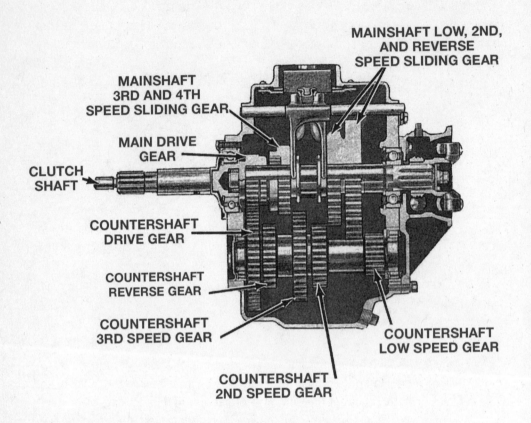

MAINSHAFT LOW, 2ND, AND REVERSE SPEED SLIDING GEAR

MAINSHAFT 3RD AND 4TH SPEED SLIDING GEAR

MAIN DRIVE GEAR

CLUTCH SHAFT

COUNTERSHAFT DRIVE GEAR

COUNTERSHAFT REVERSE GEAR

COUNTERSHAFT 3RD SPEED GEAR

COUNTERSHAFT LOW SPEED GEAR

COUNTERSHAFT 2ND SPEED GEAR

Figure 24

teeth. If the driving gear makes one revolution then the driven gear would only turn one-half revolution because it has twice as many teeth. So the driven gear would turn slowly but with lots of twisting force or torque. If the slowly turning driven gear were connected to the rear wheels, the car would move slowly, like leaving a stoplight, but with lots of power or torque because our engine is turning at a relatively fast rate. We need lots of power to start our car moving because it is so heavy and there's a lot of resistance to getting it moving. Once the car is moving, obviously, we need less power but more engine speed to keep it moving.

Now as we pick up speed, we change gears to second gear, which is another set of gears slightly smaller in number of teeth than the first gear but still bigger than the driving gear. So second gear turns the rear wheels faster but with a little less torque. Now we're probably moving 15–35 miles per hour. If we wanted to go even faster, we'd shift to third gear, which is basically the same size as the driving gear and turns at the same speed as the engine. This gear would be appropriate for cruising down the highway. In our manual transmission, each time we shift gears, we step on the clutch to separate the engine plate from the transmission plate, then we select a new gear to attach to the back of the transmission plate and then release the clutch pedal slowly to re-engage the transmission plate to the engine plate and keep the car moving. Of course, if we wanted to go in reverse, we'd select another set of gears with an idler gear designed to make the transmission shaft spin in the opposite direction from the forward gears.

That is a basic transmission.

Automatic Transmission

In some transmissions, the shifting of forward gears is done automatically, without a clutch pedal or friction disc. These transmissions are called **automatic transmissions** or fluid drive transmissions because they use hydraulic fluid instead of a friction plate to connect and disconnect the power from the engine to the transmission and rear wheels. Imagine that our engine plate and transmission plate are now shaped like two halves of a doughnut. Inside each half are blades, like the blades of a fan. The whole assembly is sealed up and filled with oil. The half attached to the engine is now called the **pump half** and the side attached to the transmission is called the **turbine**. Between the two halves, instead of the clutch plate, we put a third fan-like arrangement called the **stator**.

Now put the gear selector into drive or D and here's what happens. The pump half spins with the engine and throws oil in a clockwise direction against the turbine. This action causes the turbine to also turn in a clockwise direction, like wind blowing a windmill. The job of the stator, as in Figure 26, is to keep oil going back to the pump in the same clockwise direction so the pump can send it back to the turbine in the same direction. This causes a kind of pyramid or multiplying effect and makes the pump turn faster and faster.

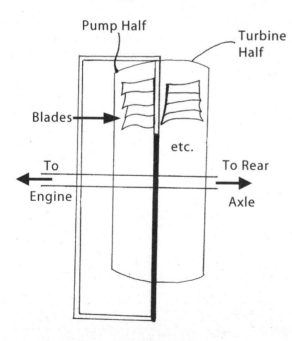

Figure 25

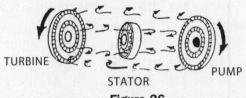

TURBINE

STATOR PUMP

Figure 26

Eventually, the pump half and the turbine half will be turning at the same high rate of speed and the stator will no longer be needed. At this point, our car is up to speed and moving easily down the street. Now let's add transmission gears as before to speed up and slow down. Different from manual transmissions, an automatic transmission has gears arranged in a planetary fashion as shown in Figure 27. These gears are different sizes and represent first, second, third, and reverse. Not all the gears are used at the same time. Different gear ratios are selected using hydraulic controls to grab and hold different gears stationary while allowing others to turn freely. Of course, these various gears can be selected manually if desired, depending on road conditions.

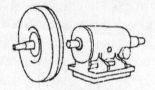

Figure 27

Next, between the transmission and the rear wheels is the **drive shaft** and **rear differential**. (See Figure 28.) The drive shaft is a solid or tubular shaft designed to transmit power from the transmission shaft to the driving wheels. At each end there is a set of

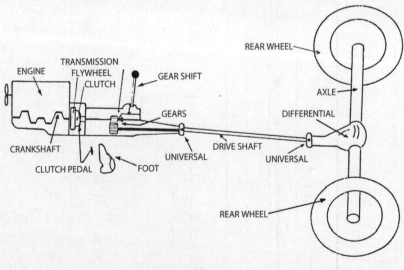

Figure 28

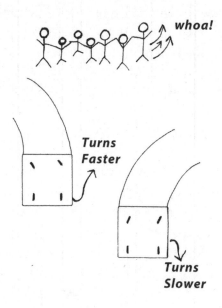

Turns Faster

Turns Slower

whoa!

Figure 29

universal joints which allow the shaft to move up and down while turning without breaking. This feature allows us to drive up driveways or through potholes or over bumps without breaking our drive shaft.

The gear differential has two sets of gears. It is part of the rear axle assembly (or front axle if our car is front wheel drive). The first set of gears is a ring and pinion gear designed to transmit power from the shaft through a 90° turn to drive the rear axle and wheels.

This ring and pinion arrangement would be fine if we only needed to go in a straight line. But when we turn a corner one wheel will turn faster than the other. The outside wheel will always turn faster than the wheel at the inside of the turn. It's like a group of your friends roller skating in a line and going around a corner. The person at the end of the line will be whipped around the turn faster than the person at the head of the line or the inside of the turn. So to help adjust the speed of the wheels when turning, another set of gears is added to the ends of each half of the rear axle (Figure 30). These gears consist of two small bevel gears for each half of the axle and a bevel gear attached to the frame of the differential. As the car

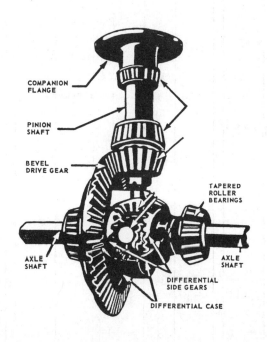

COMPANION FLANGE

PINION SHAFT

BEVEL DRIVE GEAR

TAPERED ROLLER BEARINGS

AXLE SHAFT

AXLE SHAFT

DIFFERENTIAL SIDE GEARS

DIFFERENTIAL CASE

Figure 30 — Differential with part of case cut away.

turns a corner, the bevel gears will rotate relative to each other at different speeds. The bevel gear attached to the frame is basically an idler gear and allows one half of the rear axle to turn slowly while the other half turns faster by the same amount. It doesn't matter whether we turn to the right or the left. If one wheel speeds up by 10% going around a corner, the other wheel will slow down by 10% to match.

Drive System Summary

To review, once our engine is running, the power from the engine is transmitted to the rear wheels through the *drive system* which consists of the *transmission, drive shaft, differential,* and *rear (or front) drive axle.*

Remember that the transmission can be either *manual* or *automatic.* In the manual transmission, a *manual clutch* and *drive plate* arrangement is used to couple and uncouple the moving *engine shaft* from the *transmission shaft.* The driver first steps on the *clutch pedal* to disengage the engine from the transmission then selects a *transmission gear* either forward or reverse and finally releases the pedal to re-engage the engine and transmission to move the car.

In the *automatic transmission,* the engine and transmission are coupled and uncoupled *hydraulically,* using two halves of a large doughnut fan-like arrangement called the *pump half* and *turbine half.* The gears are pre-selected by the driver.

The *drive shaft* transmits power from the transmission to the *differential.* The *differential* then distributes power to the *drive axle* in either equal amounts or in varying percentages depending on whether the car is moving in a straight line or around a corner.

BRAKES

Now that our car is moving at different speeds, forward and reverse, and going around corners, we need to be able to stop it when we want. Let's add brakes.

There are two types of brakes—**drum brakes** and **disc brakes** as in Figure 31. Drum brakes consist of two rounded halves of special friction material called **brake shoes** which fit inside the **brake drum**. The drum is attached to the wheel rim and turns with the wheel. The idea is to scrape something against the drum to slow it down and stop it from turning. This is similar to dragging your foot across the ground while on your bicycle. So why not scrape the special friction material of the shoes against the drum and slow it down? We step on the **brake pedal** which forces hydraulic fluid into a **master pump**. The pump builds up pressure in the hydraulic lines and sends the fluid out to the brake shoes and pushes them out against the rotating drum. The friction material on the surface of the shoe sticks to the drum and causes it to slow and stop, if we kept pressure on the brake pedal. Now release the brake pedal and the shoes retract away from the inside of the drum and now the drum is free to turn easily again. As you can imagine all this scraping and grinding causes tremendous heat build-up, so proper design and frequent replacement of shoes is vital.

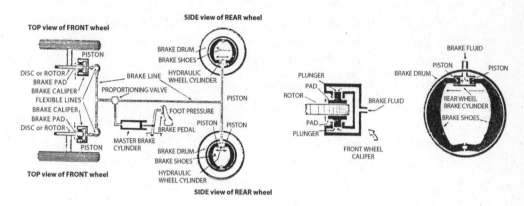

Figure 31

Also, to alert drivers behind us that we are slowing down or stopping our car, **red brake lights** are attached to the rear of our car. Keyed to the movement of the brake pedal, the brake lights come on each time we step on the brake pedal and stay on as long as our foot is on the pedal. An electric microswitch is attached to the brake pedal and sends an electronic signal to the brake lights to turn on when the pedal is stepped on and to go out when the pedal returns to its resting position.

Disc brakes work like the brakes on your ten-speed or road bike. Disc brakes squeeze a turning **rotor** attached to the wheel, between two pads to slow the wheel down. It's just like spinning your bicycle tire between your thumb and forefinger, then squeezing your fingers together to stop the wheel. Instead of shoes, there are little round brake pads or **pucks** located in a metal housing called the brake **caliper**. A rotor attached to the wheel spins between the two pads like spinning between your two fingers. When you step on the brake pedal, the same hydraulic reaction occurs as before only now instead of forcing the brake shoes out against the inside of the drum, the two pads are forced to close against the spinning rotor to slow it down as before.

Because brakes are so vital to the operating of an automobile and our safety, a back-up hydraulic system is included in case of any hydraulic leaks or loss of brake fluid. An **emergency brake** is also part of the system and is run purely mechanically, without any brake fluid.

Brake Summary

The *brake system,* in summary, stops our automobile once it is moving. There are two types of braking systems: *drum brakes* or *disc brakes.* Drum brakes consist of movable *brake shoes* inside of a rotating *brake drum* attached to the wheel. When the brake pedal is depressed, the brake shoes are forced out against the brake drum because of *hydraulic pressure* in the brake lines from the *master cylinder.* The brake shoes rub against the brake drum to slow down the turning of the wheel and, if desired, stop it completely.

The *disc brake system* incorporates a rotating disc called a *rotor* attached to the spinning wheel of the automobile. The rotor turns between a *brake caliper* which holds two *brake pads,* one on each side of the rotor. When the brake pedal is depressed, the same hydraulic pressure now forces the brake pads together and squeezes the rotor between them. This squeezing action causes the rotor to slow down and thereby slows down the turning wheel.

Both systems incorporate *brake lights* at the rear of the automobile which come on each time the pedal is depressed.

That's our automobile, ready to run, turn, stop, and take us places we've never been or places we always visit. The only item missing is a driver—you. As complicated as it may seem, it can be very easy to drive but also very dangerous. Automobiles and driving should never be taken lightly and carelessly. Always drive with respect for the road and others around you. But above all, enjoy.

TROUBLESHOOTING GUIDE

Here are some troubleshooting tips to help you solve some common automotive mechanical problems:

Engine

I. If your engine turns over or cranks but does not start then

    a. check your gas gauge, do you have enough gasoline?

    b. are you using the correct starting procedure?

    c. check for the smell of gasoline around the engine and passenger compartment. If present, then the engine may be flooded, wait one minute then follow correct starting procedure.

    d. maybe the fuel line or fuel filter is clogged and gasoline is not flowing properly.

II. If your engine stalls:

    a. then check if your idle switch or fuel mixture is properly adjusted.

    and the engine is hot then:

    b. check for fuel line leaks or air leaks.

    c. check to see if the fuel pump pressure is too high.

    and the engine is cold then:

    d. check the choke system for improper adjustment.

    e. check for leaking or misaligned carburetor float.

Clutch

III. If you experience clutch chatter then

    a. engine mounts may be loose.

    b. clutch linkage or cable may be binding.

    c. there may be grease on the driven plate (disc) facing.

    d. the facings on the driven plate (disc) may be damaged or loose.

Manual Transmission

IV. If the transmission jumps out of gear check for

    a. worn pilot bearing in crankshaft.

    b. bent transmission shaft.

    c. worn high speed sliding gear.

    d. a bent or loose shifter fork.

    e. worn gear teeth.

    f. gears to see if they are engaging completely.

V. If the transmission is noisy in all gears then

    a. there may be insufficient lubricant or improper lubricant.

    b. the counter gear bearings may be worn.

    c. the main drive gear or mainshaft bearings may be damaged.

Lights

VI. If one or more of the lights don't work but others do then

    a. the light bulbs may be defective.

    b. some of the fuses may be blown, check the fuse box.

    c. the light sockets or fuse clips may be broken or dirty.

    d. check the electrical circuit for poor grounding.

Disc Brakes

VII. If your disc brakes grab or pull the car to one side or the other then

    a. the master cylinder may be low on brake fluid.

    b. there may be air in the hydraulic lines.

    c. the brake pads may be distorted.

    d. the front end may be out of alignment.

    e. check the brake caliper pistons for sticking.

    f. check for soft or broken caliper seals.

Drum Brakes

VIII. If your drum brakes grab or pull to one side then

    a. the brake drums are out of round.

    b. check for unmatched brake shoe lining.

    c. the brake lining may be glazed over.

    d. check for excessive brake lining dust.

    e. check for low or incorrect tire pressure.

    f. the brake return springs may be weak.

    g. the brakes are improperly adjusted.

Tire Wear

IX. Use the following guide to rear tire wear

    a. *Over-inflation*—If the tire tread is worn away in the middle of the tire but not along the edges, then the tire is over-inflated. Check the tire pressure and reduce the pressure to the recommended levels. If required, replace the tires.

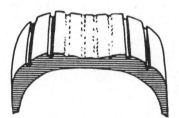

Figure 1 — Over-inflation   **Figure 2** — Under-inflation

    b. *Under-inflation*—If the tire tread is worn along the outside edges but not in the center, then the tire is under-inflated. Add air pressure until the level matches the level specified in the manual or along the side of the tire. If the tire pressure is correct, then check for improper wheel alignment.

    c. *One side wear*—If the inner or outer edge wears faster than the rest of the tread, then a wheel adjustment is needed. The front suspension may have excessive camber or the ball joints could be worn. Also check the control arm bushings for wear or sagging suspension springs.

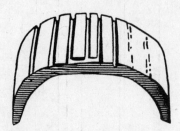

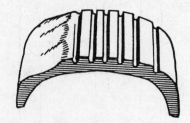

Figure 3 — One side wear   **Figure 4** — Cupping

d. *Cupped or scalloped tread*—If there are scalloped digs or cups around the edge of the tread, then the suspension parts may be bent or worn. Check and replace all worn suspension parts.

BASIC SHOP REVIEW

COMMON HANDTOOLS

Tools are designed to make a job easier and enable the craftsman to work more efficiently. (A craftsman is a master of any one of a number of trades, such as a machinist, carpenter, hull technician, builder, or steelworker.) If the tools are not used properly or cared for, their advantages will be lost.

Striking Tools

Hammers, mallets, and sledges are used to apply a striking force.

Hammers

Carpenter's hammer. The primary use of the carpenter's hammer is to drive or draw (pull) nails. Note the names of the various parts of the hammer shown in Figure 1. The carpenter's hammer has either a curved or straight claw. The face may be either bell-faced or plain-faced, and the handle may be made of wood or steel.

Machinist's hammer. Machinist's hammers are mostly used by people who work with metal or around machinery. These hammers are

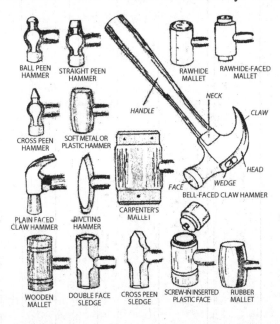

Figure 1 — Hammers, mallets, and sledges

distinguished from carpenter's hammers by a variable-shaped peen, rather than a claw, at the opposite end of the face (Figure 1). The ball-peen hammer is probably most familiar to you.

The ball-peen hammer, as its name implies, has a ball which is smaller in diameter than the face. It is therefore useful for striking areas that are too small for the face to enter.

Ball-peen hammers are made in different weights, usually 4, 6, 8, and 12 ounces and 1, $1^1/_2$, and 2 pounds. For most work, a $1^1/_2$-pound and a 12-ounce hammer will suffice. However, a 4- or 6-ounce hammer will often be used for light work such as tapping a punch to cut gaskets out of sheet gasket material.

Machinist's hammers may be further divided into hard-face and soft-face classifications. The hard-faced hammer is made of forged tool steel while the soft-faced hammers have a head made from brass, lead, or a tightly rolled strip of rawhide. Plastic-tipped hammers, or solid plastic with a lead core for added weight, are becoming increasingly popular.

Soft-faced hammers (Figure 1) should be used when there is danger of damaging the surface of the work, as when pounding on a machined surface. Most soft-faced hammers have heads that can be replaced as the need arises. Lead-faced hammers, for instance, quickly become battered and must be replaced, but have the advantage of striking a solid, heavy, nonrebounding blow that is useful for such jobs as driving shafts into or out of tight holes. If a soft-faced hammer is not available, the surface to be hammered may be protected by covering it with a piece of soft brass, copper, or hard wood.

Mallets and Sledges

The mallet is a short-handled tool used to drive wooden-handled chisels, gouges, wooden pins, or form or shape sheet metal where hard-faced hammers would mar or injure the finished work. Mallet heads are made from a soft material, usually wood, rawhide, or rubber. For example, a rubber-faced mallet is used for knocking out dents in an automobile. It is cylindrically shaped with two flat driving faces that are reinforced with iron bands. (See Figure 1.) Never use a mallet to drive nails, screws, or any object that may cause damage to the face.

The sledge is a steel-headed, heavy duty driving tool that can be used for a number of purposes. Short-handled sledges are used to drive bolts, driftpins, and large nails, and to strike cold chisels and small hand rock drills. Long-handled sledges are used to break rock and concrete, to drive spikes, bolts, or stakes, and to strike rock drills and chisels.

Turning Tools (Wrenches)

A wrench is a basic tool that is used to exert a twisting force on bolt heads, nuts, studs, and pipes. The special wrenches designed to do certain jobs are, in most cases, variations of the basic wrenches that will be described in this section.

The size of any wrench used on bolt heads or nuts is determined by the size of the opening between the jaws of the wrench. The opening of a wrench is manufactured slightly larger than the bolt head or nut that it is designed to fit. Hex-nuts (six-sided) and other types of nut or bolt heads are measured across opposite flats (Figure 2).

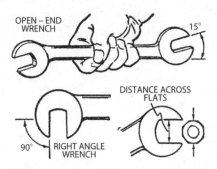

Figure 2 — Open-end wrenches

Open-End Wrenches

Solid, nonadjustable wrenches with openings in one or both ends are called open-end wrenches. (See Figure 2.) Usually they come in sets of six to ten wrenches with sizes ranging from $5/16$ to 1 inch. Wrenches with small openings are usually shorter than wrenches with large openings.

Open-end wrenches may have their jaws parallel to the handle or at angles anywhere up to 90°. The average angle is 15° (Figure 2). This angular displacement variation permits selection of a wrench suited for places where there is room to make only a part of a complete turn of a nut or bolt.

Box Wrenches

Box wrenches (Figure 3) are safer than open-end wrenches since there is less likelihood they will slip off the work. They completely surround or box a nut or bolt head.

The most frequently used box wrench has 12 points or notches arranged in a circle in the head and can be used with a minimum swing angle of 30°. Six- and 8-point wrenches are used for heavy, 12 for medium, and 16 for light duty only.

Figure 3 — 12-point box-end wrench

Combination Wrench

After a tight nut is broken loose, it can be unscrewed much more quickly with an open-end wrench than with a box wrench. This is where a combination box-open end wrench (Figure 4) comes in handy. You can use the box-end for breaking nuts loose or for snugging them down, and the open-end for faster turning.

The box-end portion of the wrench can be designed with an offset in the handle. Notice in Figure 4 how the 15° offset allows clearance over nearby parts.

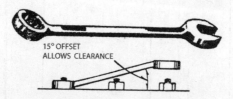

Figure 4 — Combination wrench

Socket Wrench

The socket wrench is one of the most versatile wrenches in the toolbox. Basically, it consists of a handle and a socket-type wrench which can be attached to the handle.

The "Spintite" wrench shown in Figure 5 is a special type of socket wrench. It has a hollow shaft to accommodate a bolt protruding through a nut, has a hexagonal head, and is used like a screwdriver. It is supplied in small sizes only and is useful for assembly and electrical work. When used for the latter purpose, it must have an insulated handle.

A complete socket wrench set consists of several types of handles along with bar extensions, adapters, and a variety of sockets (Figure 5).

Sockets. A socket (Figure 6) has a square opening cut in one end to fit a square drive lug on a detachable handle. In the other end of the socket is

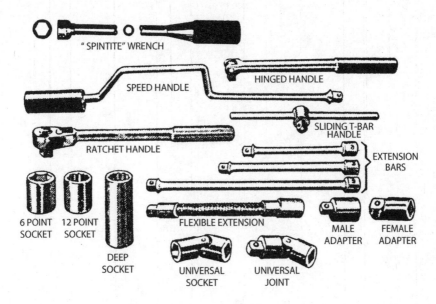

Figure 5 — Socket set components

a 6-point or 12-point opening very much like the opening in the box-end wrench.

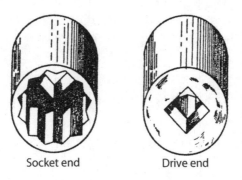

Socket end   Drive end

Figure 6 — 12-point sockets

Torque Wrenches

There are times when, for engineering reasons, a definite force must be applied to a nut or bolt head. In such cases a torque wrench must be used. For example, equal force must be applied to all the head bolts of an engine. Otherwise, one bolt may bear the brunt of the force of internal combustion and ultimately cause engine failure.

The three most commonly used torque wrenches are the Deflecting Beam, Dial Indicating, and Micrometer Setting types (Figure 7).

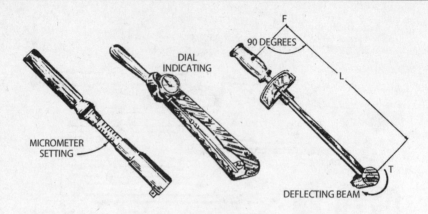

Figure 7 — Torque wrenches

Adjustable Wrenches

A handy all-round wrench that is generally included in every toolbox is the adjustable open-end wrench. This wrench is not intended to take the place of the regular solid open-end wrench. Additionally, it is not built for use on extremely hard-to-turn items. Its usefulness is achieved by being capable of fitting odd-sized nuts. This flexibility is achieved although one jaw of the adjustable open-end wrench is fixed, because the other jaw is moved along a slide by a thumbscrew adjustment (Figure 8). By turning the thumbscrew, the jaw opening may be adjusted to fit various sizes of nuts.

Adjustable wrenches are available in varying sizes ranging from 4 to 24 inches in length. The size of the wrench selected for a particular job is dependent upon the size of the nut or bolt head to which the wrench is to be applied. As the jaw opening increases the length of the wrench increases.

Figure 8 — Adjustable wrenches

Pipe wrench (Stillson). When rotating or holding round work, an adjustable pipe wrench (Stillson) may be used (Figure 9). The movable jaw on a pipe wrench is pivoted to permit a gripping action on the work. This tool must be used with discretion, as the jaws are serrated and always make marks on the work unless adequate precautions are taken. The jaws should be adjusted so the bite on the work will be taken at about the center of the jaws.

Figure 9 — Adjustable pipe wrench

Chain pipe wrench. A different type pipe wrench, used mostly on large sizes of pipe, is the chain pipe wrench (Figure 10). This tool works in one direction only, but can be backed partly around the work and a fresh hold taken without freeing the chain. To reverse the operation the grip is taken on the opposite side of the head. The head is double-ended and can be reversed when the teeth on one end are worn out.

Figure 10 — Chain pipe wrench

Strap wrench. The strap wrench (Figure 11) is similar to the chain pipe wrench but uses a heavy web strap in place of the chain. This wrench is used for turning pipe or cylinders where you do not want to mar the surface of the work. To use this wrench, the webbed strap is placed around the cylinder and passed through the slot in the metal body of the wrench. The strap is then pulled up tight and as the mechanic turns the wrench in the desired direction, the webbed strap tightens further around the cylinder. This gripping action causes the cylinder to turn.

Spanner Wrenches

Many special nuts are made with notches cut into their outer edge. For those nuts a hook spanner (Figure 12) is required. This wrench has a

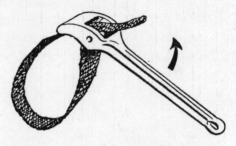

Figure 11 — Strap wrench

curved arm with a lug or hook on the end. This lug fits into one of the notches of the nut and the handle turns to loosen or tighten the nut. This spanner may be made for just one particular size of notched nut, or it may have a hinged arm to adjust it to a range of sizes.

Another type of spanner is the pin spanner. Pin spanners have a pin in place of a hook. This pin fits into a hole in the outer part of the nut.

Face pin spanners are designed so that the pins fit into holes in the face of the nut (Figure 12).

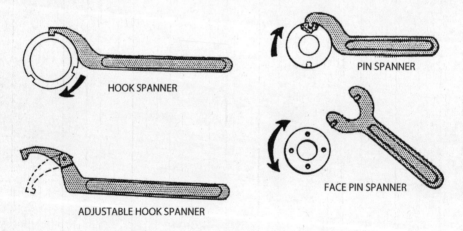

HOOK SPANNER

PIN SPANNER

ADJUSTABLE HOOK SPANNER

FACE PIN SPANNER

Figure 12 — General-purpose spanner wrenches

Setscrew Wrenches (Allen and Bristol)

In some places it is desirable to use recessed heads on setscrews and capscrews. One type (Allen) screw is used extensively on office machines and in machine shops. The other type (Bristol) is used infrequently.

Recessed head screws usually have a hex-shaped (six-sided) recess. To remove or tighten this type of screw requires a special wrench that will fit in the recess. This wrench is called an Allen-type wrench. Allen-type wrenches are made from hexagonal, L-shaped bars of tool steel (Figure 13). They range in size up to $3/4$ inch. When using the Allen-type wrench make sure you use the correct size to prevent rounding or spreading the head of the screw. A snug fit within the recessed head of the screw is an indication that you have the correct size.

The Bristol wrench is made from round stock. It is also L-shaped, but one end is fluted to fit the flutes or little splines in the Bristol setscrew (Figure 13).

Figure 13 — Allen and Bristol-type wrenches

METAL CUTTING TOOLS

Snips and Shears

Snips and shears are used for cutting sheet metal and steel of various thicknesses and shapes. Normally, the heavier or thicker materials are cut by shears.

One of the handiest tools for cutting light (up to $^1/_{16}$ inch thick) sheet metal is the hand snip (tip snips). The straight hand snips shown in Figure 14 have blades that are straight and cutting edges that are sharpened to an 85° angle. Snips like this can be obtained in different sizes ranging from the small 6-inch to the large 14-inch snip. Tin snips will also work on slightly heavier gages of soft metals such as aluminum alloys.

It is hard to cut circles or small arcs with straight snips. There are snips

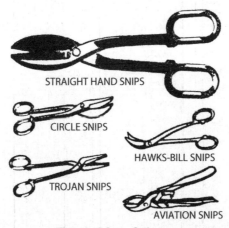

Figure 14 — Snips

especially designed for circular cutting. They are called circle snips, hawks-bill snips, trojan snips, and aviation snips (Figure 14).

Bolt Cutters

Bolt cutters (Figure 15) are giant shears with very short blades and long handles. The handles are hinged at one end. The cutters are at the ends of extensions which are jointed in such a way that the inside joint is forced outwards when the handles are closed, thus forcing the cutting edges together with great force.

Bolt cutters are made in lengths of 18 to 36 inches. The larger ones will cut mild steel bolts and rods up to $1/2$ inch. The material to be cut should be kept as far back in the jaws as possible. Never attempt to cut spring wire or other tempered metal with bolt cutters. This will cause the jaws to be sprung or nicked.

Adjusting screws near the middle hinges provide a means for ensuring that both jaws move the same amount when the handles are pressed together. Keep the adjusting screws just tight enough to ensure that the cutting edges meet along their entire length when the jaws are closed. The hinges should be kept well oiled at all times.

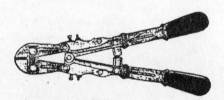

Figure 15 — Bolt cutters

Hacksaws

Hacksaws are used to cut metal that is too heavy for snips or bolt cutters. Thus, metal bar stock can be cut readily with hacksaws.

There are two parts to a hacksaw: the frame and the blade. Common hacksaws have either an adjustable or solid frame (Figure 16). Adjustable frames can be made to hold blades from 8 to 16 inches long, while those with solid frames take only the length blade for which they are made. This length is the distance between the two pins that hold the blade in place.

Hacksaw blades are made of high-grade tool steel, hardened and tempered. There are two types, the all-hard and the flexible. All-hard blades are hardened throughout, whereas only the teeth of the flexible blades are hardened. Hacksaw blades are about $1/2$ inch wide, have from 14 to 32 teeth per inch, and are from 8 to 16 inches long. The blades have a hole at each end which hooks to a pin in the frame. All hacksaw frames which hold the blades either parallel or at right angles to the frame are provided with a wing nut or screw to permit tightening or removing the blade.

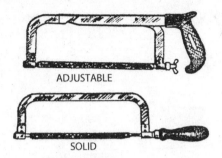

Figure 16 — Hacksaws

Chisels

Chisels are tools that can be used for chipping or cutting metal. They will cut any metal that is softer than the materials of which they are made. Chisels are made from a good grade tool steel and have a hardened cutting edge and beveled head. Cold chisels are classified according to the shape of their points, and the width of the cutting edge denotes their size. The most common shapes of chisels are flat (cold chisel), cape, round-nose, and diamond-point (Figure 17).

The type of chisel most commonly used is the flat cold chisel, which serves to cut rivets, split nuts, chip castings, and cut thin metal sheets. The cape chisel is used for special jobs like cutting keyways, narrow grooves, and square corners. Round-nose chisels make circular grooves and chip inside corners with a fillet. Finally, the diamond-point is used for cutting V-grooves and sharp corners.

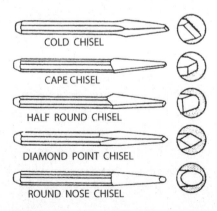

Figure 17 — Types of points on metal cutting chisel

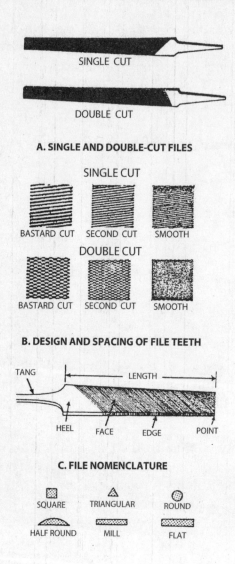

Figure 18 — File information

Files

There are a number of types of files for common use, and each type may range in length from 3 to 18 inches.

Grades. Files are graded according to the degree of fineness, and according to whether they have single- or double-cut teeth. The difference is apparent when you compare the files in Figure 18A.

Single-cut files have rows of teeth cut parallel to each other. These teeth are set at an angle of about 65° with the centerline. You will use single-cut files for sharpening tools, finish filing, and drawfiling. They are also the best tools for smoothing the edges of sheet metal.

Files with crisscrossed rows of teeth are double-cut files. The double cut forms teeth that are diamond-shaped and fast cutting. You will use double-cut files for quick removal of metal and for rough work.

Files are also graded according to the spacing and size of their teeth, or their coarseness and fineness. Some of these grades are pictured in Figure 18B. In addition to the three grades shown, you may use some dead smooth files, which have very fine teeth, and some rough files with very coarse teeth. The fineness or coarseness of file teeth is also influenced by the length of the file. (The length of a file is the distance from the tip to the heel, and does not include the tang (Figure 18C).) When you have a chance, compare the actual size of the teeth of a 6-inch, single-cut smooth file and a 12-inch, single-cut smooth file; you will notice the 6-inch file has more teeth per inch than the 12-inch file.

Shapes. Files come in different shapes. Therefore, in selecting a file for a job, the shape of the finished work must be considered. Some of the cross-sectional shapes are shown in Figure 18.

Triangular files are tapered (longitudinally) on all three sides. They are used to file acute internal angles and to clear out square corners. Special triangular files are used to file saw teeth.

Mill files are tapered in both width and thickness. One edge has no teeth and is known as a safe edge. Mill files are used for smoothing lathe work, drawfiling, and other fine, precision work. Mill files are always single-cut.

Flat files are general-purpose files and may be either single- or double-cut. They are tapered in width and thickness. Hard files, not shown, are somewhat thicker than flat files. They taper slightly in thickness, but their edges are parallel.

The flat or hard files most often used are the double-cut for rough work and the single-cut, smooth file for finish work.

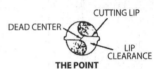

Square files are tapered on all four sides and are used to enlarge rectangular-shaped holes and slots. Round files serve the same purpose for round openings. Small round files are often called "rattail" files.

The half round file is a general-purpose tool. The rounded side is used for curved surfaces and the flat face on flat surfaces. When you file an inside curve, use a round or half-round file whose curve most nearly matches the curve of the work.

Twist Drills

Making a hole in a piece of metal is generally a simple operation, but in most cases it is an important and a precise job. A large number of different tools and machines have been designed so that holes may be made speedily, economically, and accurately in all kinds of material.

The principal parts of a twist drill are the body, the shank, and the point (Figure

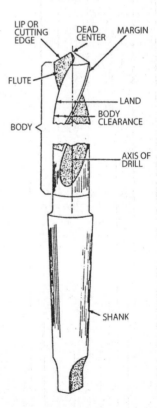

Figure 19 — Twist drill nomenclature

19). The dead center of a drill is the sharp edge at the extreme tip end of the drill. It is formed by the intersection of the cone-shaped surfaces of the point and should always be in the exact center of the axis of the drill. The point of the drill should not be confused with the dead center. The point is the entire cone-shaped surface at the end of the drill.

The lip or cutting edge of a drill is that part of the point that actually cuts away the metal when drilling a hole. It is ordinarily as sharp as the edge of a knife. There is a cutting edge for each flute of the drill.

The lip clearance of a drill is the surface of the point that is ground away or relieved just back of the cutting edge of the drill. The strip along the inner edge of the body is called the margin. It is the greatest diameter of the drill and extends the entire length of the flute. The diameter of the margin at the shank end of the drill is smaller than the diameter at the point. This allows the drill to revolve without binding when drilling deep holes.

The shank is the part of the drill that fits into the socket, spindle, or chuck of the drill press. Several types exist.

Twist drills are provided in various sizes. They are sized by letters, numerals, and fractions.

Countersinks

Countersinking is the operation of beveling the mouth of a hole with a rotary tool called a countersink (Figure 20). The construction of the countersink is similar to the twist drill. There are four cutting edges, which are taper ground to the angle marked on the body.

A countersink is used primarily to set the head of a screw or rivet flush with the material in which it is being placed. Countersinks are made in a number of sizes. One size usually takes care of holes of several different sizes. That is, the same countersink can be used for holes from $1/4$ inch to $1/2$ inch in diameter. Remove only enough metal to set the screw or rivet head flush with the material. If you remove too much material, the hole will enlarge and weaken the work.

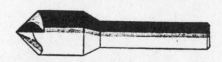

Figure 20 — Countersink

Select the countersink with the correct lip angle to correspond with the screw or rivet head being used. These countersinks can be turned by any machine that will turn a twist drill.

Reamers

Reamers are used to enlarge and true a hole. The reamer consists of three parts—the body, the shank, and the blades. The shank has a square tang to allow the reamer to be held with a wrench for turning. The main purpose of the body is to support the blades.

Reamers of the types shown in Figure 21 are available in any standard size. They are also available in size variations of .001" for special work. A solid straight flute reamer lasts longer and is less expensive than the expansion reamer. However, the solid spiral flute reamer is preferred by craftsmen because it is less likely to chatter.

Figure 21 — Above—solid spiral flute reamer
Below—solid straight flute reamer

For general purposes, an expansion reamer (Figure 22) is the most practical. This reamer can usually be obtained in standard sizes from $1/4$ inch to 1 inch, by 32nds. It is designed to allow the blades to expand $1/32$ of an inch. For example, the $1/4$-inch expansion reamer will ream a $1/4$-inch to a $9/32$-inch hole. A $9/32$-inch reamer will enlarge the hole from $9/32$ inch to $5/16$ inch. This range of adjustment allows a few reamers to cover sizes up to 1 inch.

Figure 22 — Expansion reamer

Punches

A hand punch is a tool that is held in the hand and struck on one end with a hammer. There are many kinds of punches designed to do a variety of jobs. Figure 23 shows several types of punches. Most punches are made of tool steel. The part held in the hand is usually octagonal shaped, or it may be knurled. This prevents the tool from slipping around in the hand. The other end is shaped to do a particular job.

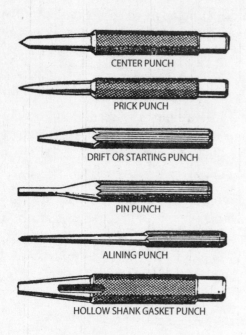

CENTER PUNCH

PRICK PUNCH

DRIFT OR STARTING PUNCH

PIN PUNCH

ALINING PUNCH

HOLLOW SHANK GASKET PUNCH

Figure 23 — Punches

The center punch, as the name implies, is used for marking the center of a hole to be drilled. If you try to drill a hole without first punching the center, the drill will "wander" or "walk away" from the desired center.

The point of a center punch is accurately ground central with the shank, usually at a 60–90° angle, and is difficult to regrind by hand with any degree of accuracy. It is therefore advisable to take care of a center punch and not to use it on extremely hard materials. When extreme accuracy is required, a prick punch is used. Compare the point angle of the center and prick punches.

Drift punches, sometimes called "starting punches," have a long taper from the tip to the body. They are made that way to withstand the shock of heavy blows. They may be used for knocking out rivets after the heads have been chiseled off, or for freeing pins which are "frozen" in their holes.

After a pin has been loosened or partially driven out, the drift punch may be too large to finish the job. The follow-up tool to use is the pin punch. It is designed to follow through the hole without jamming. Always use the largest drift or pin punch that will fit the hole. These punches usually come in sets of three to five assorted sizes. Both of these punches will have flat points, never edged or rounded.

For assembling units of a machine, an alinement (alining) punch is invaluable. It is usually about one foot long and has a long, gradual taper. Its purpose is to line up holes in mating parts.

Hollow metal cutting punches are made from hardened tool steel. They are made in various sizes and are used to cut holes in light gage sheet metal.

Taps and Dies

Taps and dies are used to cut threads in metal, plastics, or hard rubber. The taps are used for cutting internal threads, and the dies are used to cut external threads. There are many different types of taps. However, the most common are the taper, plug, bottoming, and pipe taps (Figure 24).

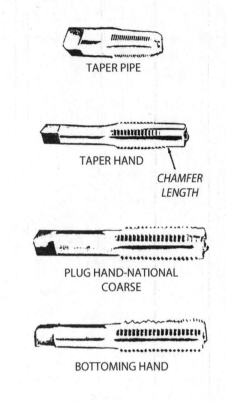

The taper (starting) hand tap has a chamfer length of eight to ten threads. These taps are used when starting a tapping operation and when tapping through holes.

Plug hand taps have a chamfer length of three to five threads and are designed for use after the taper tap.

Figure 24 — Types of common taps

Bottoming hand taps are used for threading the bottom of a blind hole. They have a very short chamfer length of only 1 to 1-$\frac{1}{2}$ threads for this purpose. This tap is always used after the plug tap has already been used. Both the taper and plug taps should precede the use of the bottoming hand tap.

Pipe taps are used for pipe fittings and other places where extremely tight fits are necessary. The tap diameter, from end to end of threaded portion, increases at the rate of $\frac{3}{4}$ inch per foot. All the threads on this tap do the cutting, as compared to the straight taps where only the nonchamfered portion does the cutting.

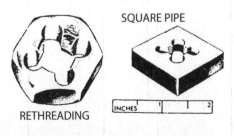

Figure 25 — Types of solid dies

Dies are made in several different shapes and are of the solid or adjustable type. The square pipe die (Figure 25) will cut American Standard Pipe Thread only. It comes in a variety of sizes for cutting threads on pipe with diameters of $1/8$ inch to 2 inches.

A rethreading die (Figure 25) is used principally for dressing over bruised or rusty threads on screws or bolts. It is available in a variety of sizes for rethreading American Standard Coarse and Fine threads. These dies are usually hexagonal in shape and can be turned with a socket, box, open-end, or any wrench that will fit. Rethreading dies are available in sets of six, 10, 14, and 28 assorted sizes in a case.

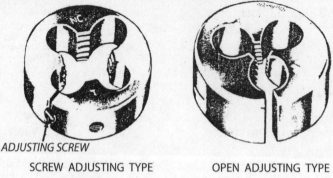

SCREW ADJUSTING TYPE   OPEN ADJUSTING TYPE

Figure 26 — Types of adjustable dies

Round split adjustable dies (Figure 26) are called "button" dies and can be used in either hand diestocks or machine holders. The adjustment in the screw adjusting type is made by a fine-pitch screw which forces the sides of the die apart or allows them to spring together. The adjustment in the open adjusting types is made by means of three screws in the holder, one for expanding and two for compressing the dies. Round split adjustable dies are available in a variety of sizes to cut American Standard Coarse and Fine threads, special form threads, and the standard sizes of threads that are used in Britain and other European countries. For hand threading, these dies are held in diestocks (Figure 27). One type diestock has three pointed screws that will hold round dies of any construction, although it is made specifically for open adjusting-type dies.

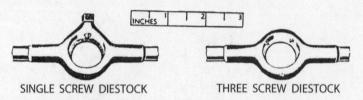

SINGLE SCREW DIESTOCK   THREE SCREW DIESTOCK

Figure 27 — Diestocks

Pipe and Tubing Cutters and Flaring Tools

Pipe cutters (Figure 28) are used to cut pipe made of steel, brass, copper, wrought iron, and lead. Tube cutters (Figure 28) are used to cut tubing made of iron, steel, brass, copper, and aluminum. The essential difference between pipe and tubing is that tubing has considerably thinner walls. Flaring tools (Figure 29) are used to make single or double flares in the ends of tubing.

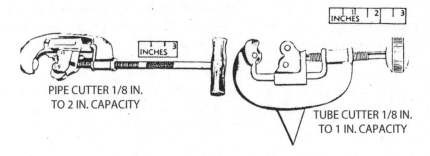

Figure 28 — Pipe and tubing cutters

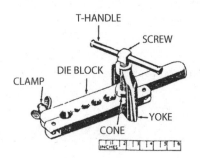

Figure 29 — Single flaring tool

WOODCUTTING HANDTOOLS

Handsaws

The most common carpenter's handsaw consists of a steel blade with a handle at one end. The blade is narrower at the end opposite the handle. This end of the blade is called the "point" or "toe." The end of the blade nearest the handle is called the "heel" (Figure 30). One edge of the blade has teeth, which act as two rows of cutters. When the saw is used, these teeth cut two parallel grooves close together. The chips (sawdust) are pushed out from between the grooves (kerf) by the beveled part of the teeth. The teeth are bent alternately to one side or the other to make the kerf wider than the thickness of the blade. This bending is called the "set" of the teeth (Figure 31).

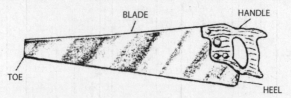

Figure 30 — Nomenclature of a handsaw

The number of teeth per inch, the size and shape of the teeth, and the amount of set depend on the use to be made of the saw and the material to be cut. Carpenter's handsaws are described by the number of points per inch. By custom, there is always one more point than there are teeth per inch. A number stamped near the handle gives the number of points of the saw.

Figure 31 — "Set" of handsaw teeth

Crosscut and ripsaws. Woodworking handsaws designed for general cutting consist of ripsaws and crosscut saws. Ripsaws are used for cutting with the grain and crosscut saws are for cutting across grain.

The major difference between a ripsaw and a crosscut saw is the shape of the teeth. A tooth with a square-faced chisel-type cutting edge, like the ripsaw tooth shown in Figure 32, does a good job of cutting with the grain (called ripping), but a poor job of cutting across the grain (called crosscutting). A tooth with a beveled, knifetype cutting edge, like the crosscut saw tooth shown in the same figure, does a good job of cutting across the grain, but a poor job of cutting with the grain.

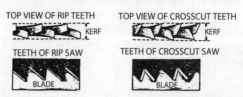

Figure 32 — Comparing rip and crosscut saw teeth

Special-purpose saws. The more common types of saws used for special purposes are shown in Figure 33. The backsaw is a crosscut saw designed for sawing a perfectly straight line across the face of a piece of stock. A heavy steel backing along the top of the blade keeps the blade perfectly straight.

The dovetail saw is a special type of backsaw with a thin, narrow blade and a chisel-type handle.

The compass saw is a long, narrow, tapering ripsaw designed for cutting out circular or other non-rectangular sections from within the margins of a board or panel. A hole is bored near the cutting line to start the saw. A key-hole saw is simply a finer, more narrow compass saw.

The coping saw is used to cut along curved lines as shown in Figure 33.

Planes

The plane is the most extensively used of the hand shaving tools. Most of the lumber handled by anyone working with wood is dressed on all four sides, but when performing jobs, such as fitting doors and sash, and interior trim work, planes must be used.

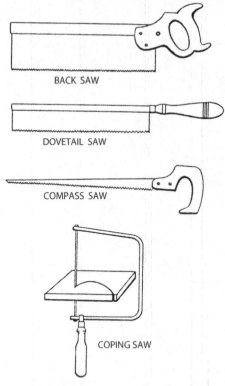

Figure 33 — Special saws

Bench and block planes are designed for general surface smoothing and squaring. Other planes are designed for special types of surface work.

The principal parts of a bench plane and the manner in which they are assembled are shown in Figure 34. The part at the rear that you grasp to push the plane ahead is called the handle; the part at the front that you grasp to guide the plane along its course is called the knob. The main body of the plane, consisting of the bottom, the sides, and the sloping part that carries the plane iron, is called the frame. The bottom of the frame is called the sole, and the opening in the sole, through which the blade emerges, is called the mouth. The front end of the sole is called the toe; the rear end, the heel.

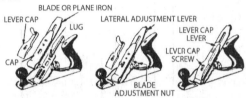

Figure 34 — Parts of a bench plane

There are three types of bench planes (Figure 35): the smooth plane, the jack plane, and the jointer plane (sometimes called the fore plane or the gage plane). All are used primarily for shaving and smoothing with the

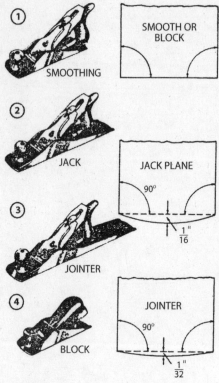

Figure 35 — Types of bench planes and block plane

grain; the chief difference is the length of the sole. The sole of the smooth plane is about 9 inches long, the sole of the jack plane about 14 inches long, and the sole of the jointer plane from 20 to 24 inches long.

The longer the sole of the plane is, the more uniformly flat and true the planed surface will be. Consequently, which bench plane you should use depends upon the requirements with regard to surface trueness. The smooth plane is, in general, smoother only; it will plane a smooth, but not an especially true surface in a short time. It is also used for cross-grain smoothing and squaring of end-stock.

The jack plane is the general "jack-of-all-work" of the bench plane group. It can take a deeper cut and plane a truer surface than the smooth plane. The jointer plane is used when the planed surface must meet the highest requirements with regard to trueness.

A block plane and the names of its parts are shown in Figure 36. Note that the plane iron in a block plane does not have a plane iron cap, and also that, unlike the iron in a bench plane, the iron in a block plane goes in bevel-up.

The block plane, which is usually held at an angle to the work, is used chiefly for cross-grain squaring of end-stock. It is also useful, however, for smoothing all plane surfaces on very small work.

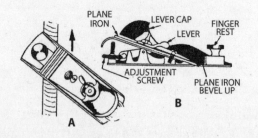

Figure 36 — Block plane nomenclature

Boring Tools

When working with wood, you will frequently be required to bore holes. It is important, therefore, that you know the proper procedures and tools used for this job. Auger bits and a variety of braces and drills are used extensively for boring purposes.

Auger bits. Bits are used for boring holes for screws, dowels, and hardware, as an aid in mortising (cutting a cavity in wood for joining members) and in shaping curves and for many other purposes. Like saws and planes, bits vary in shape and structure with the type of job to be done. Some of the most common bits are described in this section.

Auger bits are screw-shaped tools consisting of six parts: the cutter, screw, spur, twist, shank, and tang (Figure 37). The twist ends with two sharp points called the spurs, which score the circle, and two cutting edges which cut shavings within the scored circle. The screw centers the bit and draws it into the wood. The threads of the screw are made in three different pitches: steep, medium, and fine. The steep pitch makes for quick boring and thick chips, and the fine or slight pitch makes for slow boring and fine chips. For endwood boring, a steep- or medium-pitch screw bit should be used because endwood is likely to be forced in between the fine screw threads, and that will prevent the screw from taking hold. The twist carries the cuttings away from the cutters and deposits them in a mound around the hole.

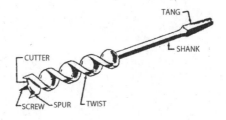

Figure 37 — Nomenclature of an auger bit

The sizes of auger bits are indicated in sixteenths of an inch and are stamped on the tang (Figure 38). A number 10 stamped on the tang means $10/16$ or $5/8$ inch; number 5 means $5/16$ inch and so on. The most common woodworker's auger bit set ranges in size from $1/4$ to one inch.

Ordinarily auger bits up to one inch in diameter are from 7 to 9 inches long. Short auger bits that are about $3^1/2$ inches long are called dowel bits.

Expansive auger bits have adjustable cutters for boring holes of different diameters (Figure 39). Expansive bits are generally made in two different sizes. The largest size has three cutters and bores holes up to 4 inches

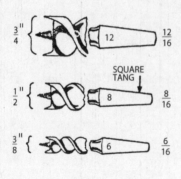

Figure 38 — Size markings on auger bits

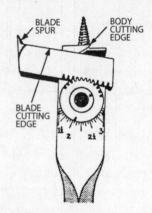

Figure 39 — Expansive bit

in diameter. A scale on the cutter blade indicates the diameter of the hole to be bored.

Braces and drills. The auger bit is the tool that actually does the cutting in the wood; however, it is necessary that another tool be used to hold the auger bit and give you enough leverage to turn the bit. The tools most often used for holding the bit are the carpenter's brace, breast drill, and push drill (Figure 40).

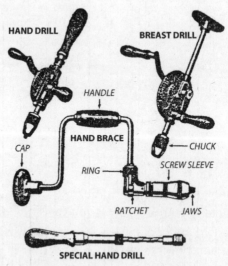

Figure 40 — Brace and drills

Wood Chisels

A wood chisel is a steel tool fitted with a wooden or plastic handle. It has a single beveled cutting edge on the end of the steel part, or blade. According to their construction, chisels may be divided into two general classes: tang chisels, in which part of the chisel enters the handle, and socket chisels, in which the handle enters into a part of the chisel (Figure 41).

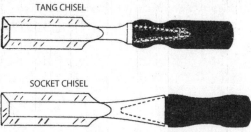

Figure 41 — Tang and socket wood chisels

A socket chisel is designed for striking with a wooden mallet (never a steel hammer), while a tang chisel is designed for hand manipulation only.

Wood chisels are also divided into types, depending upon their weights and thicknesses, the shape or design of the blade, and the work they are intended to do.

The shapes of the more common types of wood chisels are shown in Figure 42. The firmer chisel has a strong, rectangular cross-section blade, designed for both heavy and light work. The blade of the paring chisel is relatively thin and is beveled along the sides for the fine paring work. The butt chisel has a short blade, designed for work in hard-to-get-at places.

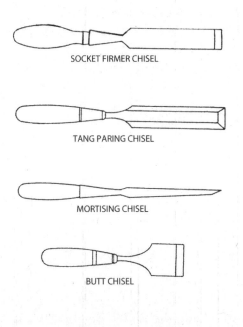

Figure 42 — Shapes of common types of wood chisels

The butt chisel is commonly used for chiseling the gains (rectangular depressions) for the butt hinges on doors, hence the name. The mortising chisel is similar to a socket firmer but has a narrow blade, designed for chiseling out the deep, narrow mortises for mortise-and-tenon joints. This work requires a good deal of levering out of chips; consequently, the mortising chisel is made extra thick in the shaft to prevent breaking.

A framing chisel is shaped like a firmer chisel, but has a very heavy, strong blade designed for work in rough carpentry.

SCREWDRIVERS

A screwdriver is one of the most basic of handtools. It is also the most frequently abused of all handtools. It is designed for one function only—to drive and remove screws. A screwdriver should not be used as a pry bar, a scraper, a chisel, or a punch.

Standard

There are three main parts to a standard screwdriver. The portion you grip is called the handle, the steel portion extending from the handle is the shank, and the end that fits into the screw is called the blade (Figure 43).

The steel shank is designed to withstand considerable twisting force in proportion to its size, and the tip of the blade is hardened to keep it from wearing.

Standard screwdrivers are classified by size, according to the combined length of the shank and blade. The most common sizes range in length from $2^1/2$ to 12 inches. There are many screwdrivers smaller and some larger for special purposes. The diameter of the shank, and the width and thickness of the blade are generally proportionate to the length, but again there are special screwdrivers with long thin shanks, short thick shanks, and extra wide or extra narrow blades.

Screwdriver handles may be wood, plastic, or metal. When metal handles are used, there is usually a wooden hand grip placed on each side of the handle. In some type of wood- or plastic-handled screwdrivers the shank extends through the handle, while in others the shank enters the handle only a short way and is pinned to the handle. For heavy work, special types of screwdrivers are made with a square shank. They are designed this way so that they may be gripped with a wrench, but this is the only kind on which a wrench should be used.

When using a screwdriver it is important to select the proper size so that the blade fits the screw slot properly. This prevents burring the slot and reduces the force required to

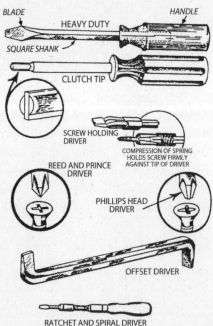

BLADE HANDLE
HEAVY DUTY
SQUARE SHANK
CLUTCH TIP
SCREW HOLDING DRIVER
COMPRESSION OF SPRING HOLDS SCREW FIRMLY AGAINST TIP OF DRIVER
REED AND PRINCE DRIVER
PHILLIPS HEAD DRIVER
OFFSET DRIVER
RATCHET AND SPIRAL DRIVER

Figure 43 — Screwdrivers

hold the driver in the slot. Keep the shank perpendicular to the screw head.

Recessed

Recessed screws are now available in various shapes. They have a cavity in the head and require a specially shaped screwdriver. The clutch tip (Figure 43) is one shape, but the more common include the Phillips, Reed and Prince, and newer Torq-set types (Figure 44). The most common type found is the Phillips head screw. This requires a Phillips-type screwdriver (Figure 43).

Phillips screwdriver. The head of a Phillips-type screw has a four-way slot into which the screwdriver fits. This prevents the screwdriver from slipping. Three standard sized Phillips screwdrivers handle a wide range of screw sizes. Their ability to hold helps to prevent damaging the slots or the work surrounding the screw. It is a poor practice to try to use a standard screwdriver on a Phillips screw because both the tool and screw slot will be damaged.

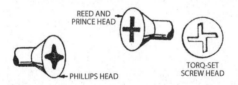

Figure 44 — Comparison of Phillips, Reed and Prince, and Torq-set screw heads

Reed and Prince screwdriver. Reed and Prince screwdrivers are *not* interchangeable with Phillips screwdrivers. Therefore, always use a Reed and Prince screwdriver with Reed and Prince screws and a Phillips screwdriver with Phillips screws, or a ruined tool or screw head will result.

The Phillips screwdriver has about 30° flukes and a blunt end, while the Reed and Prince has 45° flukes and a sharper, pointed end. The Phillips screw has beveled walls between the slots; the Reed and Prince, straight, pointed walls. In addition, the Phillips screw slot is not as deep as the Reed and Prince slot. Refer to Figure 45.

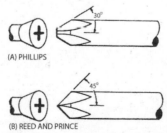

Figure 45 — Matching cross-slot screws and drivers

"Torq-set" screws. "Torq-set" machine screws (offset cross-slot drive) have recently begun to appear in new equipment. The main advantage of the newer type is that more torque can be applied to its head while tightening or loosening than any other screw of comparable size and material without damaging the head of the screw.

Offset screwdrivers. An offset screwdriver (Figure 43) may be used where there is not sufficient vertical space for a standard or recessed screwdriver. Offset screwdrivers are constructed with one blade forged in line and another blade forged at right angles to the shank handle. Both blades are bent 90° to the shank handle. By alternating ends, most screws can be seated or loosened even when the swinging space is very restricted. Offset screwdrivers are made for both standard and recessed head screws.

Ratchet screwdriver. For fast, easy work the ratchet screwdriver (Figure 43) is extremely convenient, as it can be used one-handed and does not require the bit to be lifted out of the slot after each turn. It may be fitted with either a standard type bit or a special bit for recessed heads. The ratchet screwdriver is most commonly used by the woodworker for driving screws in soft wood.

PLIERS

Pliers are made in many styles and sizes and are used to perform many different operations. Pliers are used for cutting purposes as well as holding and gripping small articles in situations where it may be inconvenient or impossible to use hands. Figure 46 shows several different kinds.

The combination pliers are handy for holding or bending flat or round stock. The long-nosed pliers are less rugged and break easily if you use them on heavy jobs. Long-nosed pliers, commonly called needle-nose pliers, are especially useful for holding small objects in tight places and for making delicate adjustments. The round-nosed kind are handy when you

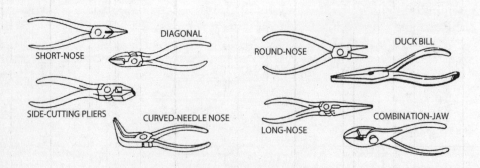

Figure 46 — Pliers

need to crimp sheet metal or form a loop in a wire. The diagonal cutting pliers, commonly called "diagonals" or "dikes," are designed for cutting wire and cotter pins close to a flat surface and are especially useful in the electronic and electrical fields. Duckbill pliers are used extensively in aviation areas.

Slipjoint Pliers

Slipjoint pliers (Figure 47) are pliers with straight, serrated (grooved) jaws, and the screw or pivot with which the jaws are fastened together may be moved to either of two positions, in order to grasp small- or large-sized objects better.

To spread the jaws of slipjoint pliers, first spread the ends of the handles apart as far as possible. The slipjoint, or pivot, will now move to the open position. To close, again spread the handles as far as possible, then push the joint back into the closed position.

Slipjoint combination pliers (Figure 48) are pliers similar to the slipjoint pliers just described, but with the additional feature of a side cutter at the junction of the jaws. This cutter consists of a pair of square-cut notches, one on each jaw, which act like a pair of shears when an object is placed between them and the jaws are closed.

The cutter is designed to cut material such as soft wire and nails. To use the cutter, open the jaws until the cutter on either jaw lines up with the other. Place the material to be cut as far back as possible into the opening formed by the cutter, and squeeze the handles of the pliers together. Do not attempt to cut hard material such as spring wire or hard rivets with the combination pliers. To do so will spring the jaws; and if the jaws are sprung, it will be difficult thereafter to cut small wire with the cutters.

 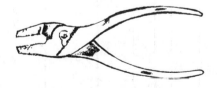

Figure 47 — Slipjoint pliers   **Figure 48** — Slipjoint combination pliers

Wrench (Vise-grip) Pliers

Vise-grip pliers (Figure 49) can be used for holding objects regardless of their shape. A screw adjustment in one of the handles makes them

Figure 49 — Vise-grip pliers

suitable for several different sizes. The jaws of vise-grips may have standard serrations such as the pliers just described or may have a clamp-type jaw. The clamp-type jaws are generally wide and smooth and are used primarily when working with sheet metal.

Vise-grip pliers have an advantage over other types of pliers in that you can clamp them on an object and they will stay. This will leave your hands free for other work.

Vises and Clamps

Vises are used for holding work when it is being planed, sawed, drilled, shaped, sharpened, or riveted, or when wood is being glued. Clamps are used for holding work that cannot be satisfactorily held in a vise because of its shape and size, or when a vise is not available. Clamps are generally used for light work.

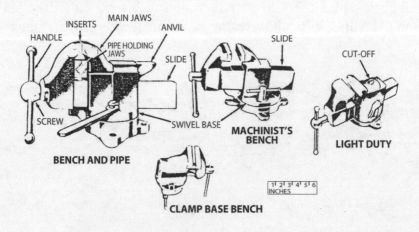

Figure 50 — Common types of bench vises

Figure 50 shows common bench vises.

A machinist's bench vise is a large steel vise with rough jaws that prevent the work from slipping. Most of these vises have a swivel base with jaws that can be rotated, while others cannot be rotated. A similar light duty model is equipped with a cutoff. These vises are usually bolt-mounted onto a bench.

The bench and pipe vise has integral pipe jaws for holding pipe from $3/4$ inch to 3 inches in diameter. The maximum working main jaw opening is usually 5 inches, with a jaw width of 4 to 5 inches. The base can be swiveled to any position and locked. These vises are equipped with an anvil and are also bolted onto a workbench.

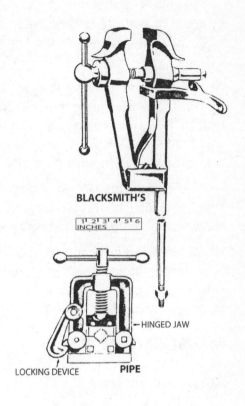

Figure 51 — Blacksmith's and pipe vises

The clamp base vise usually has a smaller holding capacity than the machinist's or the bench and pipe vise and is usually clamped to the edge of a bench with a thumbscrew. These type vises can be obtained with a maximum holding capacity varying between $1^1/_2$ inch and 3 inches. These vises normally do not have pipe holding jaws.

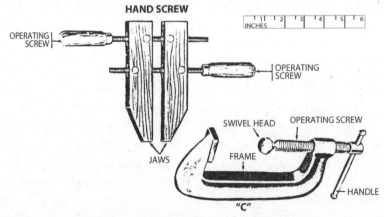

Figure 52 — C-Clamp and handscrew clamp

The blacksmith's vise (Figure 51) is used for holding work that must be pounded with a heavy hammer. It is fastened to a sturdy workbench or wall, and the long leg is secured into a solid base on the floor.

The pipe vise (Figure 51) is specifically designed to hold round stock or pipe. The vise shown has a capacity of 1 to 3 inches. One jaw is hinged so that the work can be positioned and then the jaw brought down and locked. This vise is also used on a bench. Some pipe vises are designed to use a section of chain to hold down the work. Chain pipe vises range in size from $1/8$- to $2^1/2$ inch pipe capacity up to $1/2$- to 8-inch pipe capacity.

A C-clamp (Figure 52) is shaped like the letter c. It consists of a steel frame threaded to receive an operating screw with a swivel head. It is made for light, medium, and heavy service in a variety of sizes.

A hand screw clamp (Figure 52) consists of two hard maple jaws connected with two operating screws. Each jaw has two metal inserts into which the screws are threaded. The hand screw clamp is also issued in a variety of sizes.

MEASURING TOOLS

Rules and Tapes

There are many different types of measuring tools. Where exact measurements are required, a micrometer caliper (mike) is used. Such a caliper, when properly used, gives measurements to within .001 of an inch accuracy. On the other hand, where accuracy is not extremely critical, the common rule or tape will suffice for most measurements.

Figure 53 shows some of the types of rules and tapes commonly used. Of all measuring tools, the simplest and most common is the steel rule. This rule is usually 6 to 12 inches in length, although other lengths are available. Steel rules may be flexible or non-flexible, but the thinner the rule, the easier it is to measure accurately because the division marks are closer to the work.

Generally a rule has four sets of graduations, one on each edge of each side. The longest lines represent the inch marks. On one edge, each inch is divided into 8 equal spaces, so each space represents $1/8$ inch. The other edge of this side is divided into sixteenths. The $1/4$-inch and $1/2$-inch marks are commonly made longer than the smaller division marks to facilitate counting, but the graduations are not, as a rule, numbered individually as they are sufficiently far apart to be counted without difficulty. The opposite side is similarly divided into 32 and 64 spaces per inch, and it is common practice to number every fourth division for easier reading.

There are many variations of the common rule. Sometimes the graduations are on one side only, sometimes a set of graduations is added across one end for measuring in narrow spaces, and sometimes only the first inch is divided into 64ths, with the remaining inches divided into 32nds and 16ths.

A metal or wood folding rule may be used for measuring purposes. These folding rules are usually 2 to 6 feet long. The folding rules cannot be relied on for extremely accurate measurements because a certain amount of play develops at the joints after they have been used for a while.

Steel tapes are made from 6 to about 300 feet in length. The shorter lengths are frequently made with a curved cross section so that they are flexible enough to roll up, but remain rigid when extended. Long, flat tapes require support over their full length when measuring, or the natural sag will cause an error in reading.

The flexible-rigid tapes are usually contained in metal cases into which they wind themselves when a button is pressed, or into which they can be easily pushed. A hook is provided at one end to hook over the object being measured so one person can handle it without assistance. On some models, the outside of the case can be used as one end of the tape when measuring inside dimensions

Figure 53 — Some common types of rules

Simple Calipers

Simple calipers are used in conjunction with a scale to measure diameters (see Figure 54).

Outside calipers for measuring outside diameters are bow-legged; those used for inside diameters have straight legs with the feet turned outward. Calipers are adjusted by pulling or pushing the legs to open or close them. Fine adjustment is made by tapping one leg lightly on a hard surface to close them, or by turning them upside down and tapping on the joint end to open them.

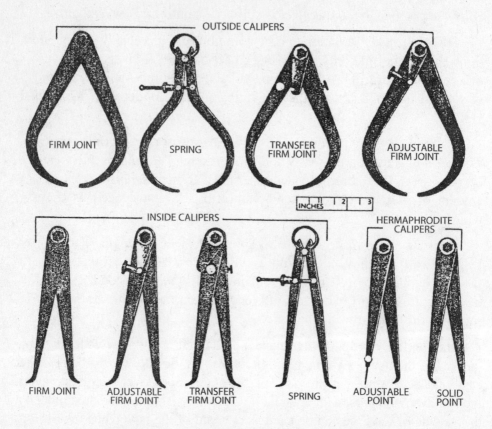

Figure 54 — Simple calipers–noncalibrated

Spring-joint calipers have the legs joined by a strong spring hinge and linked together by a screw and adjusting nut. For measuring chamfered cavities (grooves), or for use over flanges, transfer calipers are available. They are equipped with a small auxiliary leaf attached to one of the legs by a screw. (See Figure 54.) The measurement is made as with ordinary calipers; then the leaf is locked to the leg.

Slide Caliper

The main disadvantage of using ordinary calipers is that they do not give a direct reading of a caliper setting. As explained earlier, you must measure a caliper setting with a rule. To overcome this disadvantage, use slide calipers (Figure 55). This instrument is occasionally called a caliper rule.

Slide calipers can be used for measuring outside, inside, and other dimensions. One side of the caliper is used as a measuring rule, while the scale on the opposite side is used in measuring outside and inside dimensions. Graduations on both scales are in inches and fractions thereof. A locking screw is incorporated to hold the slide caliper jaws in position during use. Stamped on the frame are two words, "in" and "out." These are used in reading the scale while making inside and outside measurements, respectively.

To measure the outside diameter of round stock, or the thickness of flat stock, move the jaws of the caliper into firm contact with the surface of the stock. Read the measurement at the reference line stamped "out."

When measuring the inside diameter of a hole, or the distance between two surfaces, insert only the rounded tips of the caliper jaws into the hole or between the two surfaces. Read the measurement on the reference line stamped "in."

Note that two reference lines are needed if the caliper is to measure both outside and inside dimensions, and that they are separated by an amount equal to the outside dimension of the rounded tips when the caliper is closed.

Pocket models of slide calipers are commonly made in 3-inch and 5-inch sizes and are graduated to read in 32nds and 64ths. Pocket slide calipers are valuable when extreme precision is not required. They are frequently used for duplicating work when the expense of fixed gages is not warranted.

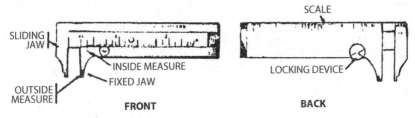

Figure 55 — Caliper square (slide caliper)

Vernier Caliper

A vernier caliper (Figure 56) consists of an L-shaped member with a scale engraved on the long shank. A sliding member is free to move on the bar and carries a jaw that matches the arm of the L. The vernier scale is engraved on a small plate that is attached to the sliding member.

Perhaps the most distinct advantage of the vernier caliper, over other types of caliper, is the ability to provide very accurate measurements over a large range. It can be used for both internal and external surfaces. Pocket models usually measure from zero to 3 inches, but sizes are available to 4 feet. In using the vernier caliper, you must be able to measure with a slide caliper and be able to read a vernier scale.

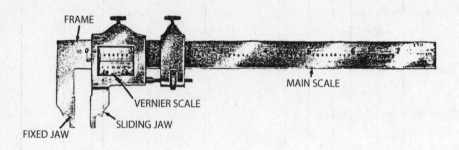

Figure 56 — Vernier caliper

MICROMETER

In much wider use than the vernier caliper is the micrometer, commonly called the "mike." It is important that a person who is working with machinery or in a machine shop thoroughly understand the mechanical principles, construction, use, and care of the micrometer. Figure 57 shows an outside micrometer caliper with the various parts clearly indicated. Micrometers are used to measure distances to the nearest one-thousandth of an inch. The measurement is usually expressed or written as a decimal; so you must know the method of writing and reading decimals.

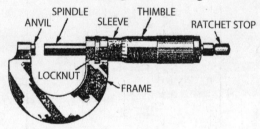

Figure 57 — Nomenclature of an outside micrometer caliper

Types

Three types of micrometers commonly used are the outside micrometer caliper (including the screw thread micrometer), the inside micrometer, and the depth micrometer. The outside micrometer is used for measuring outside dimensions, such as the diameter of a piece of round stock. The screw thread micrometer is used to determine the pitch diameter of screws. The inside micrometer is used for measuring inside dimensions, as for example, the inside diameter of a tube or hole, the bore of a cylinder, or the width of a recess. The depth micrometer is used for measuring the depth of holes or recesses.

SQUARES

Squares are primarily used for testing and checking trueness of an angle or for laying out lines on materials. Most squares have a rule marked on their edge. As a result they may also be used for measuring.

Carpenter's Square

The size of a carpenter's steel square (Figure 58) is usually 12 inches × 8 inches, 24 inches × 16 inches, or 24 inches × 18 inches. The flat sides of the blade and the tongue are graduated in inches and fractions of an inch. (The square also contains information that helps to simplify or eliminate the need for computations in many woodworking tasks.) The most common uses for this square are laying out and squaring up large patterns, and for testing the flatness and squareness of large surfaces. Squaring is accomplished by placing the square at right angles to adjacent surfaces and observing if light shows between the work and the square.

One type of carpenter's square (framing) has additional tables engraved on the square. With the framing square, the craftsman can perform calculations rapidly and lay out rafters, oblique joints, and stairs.

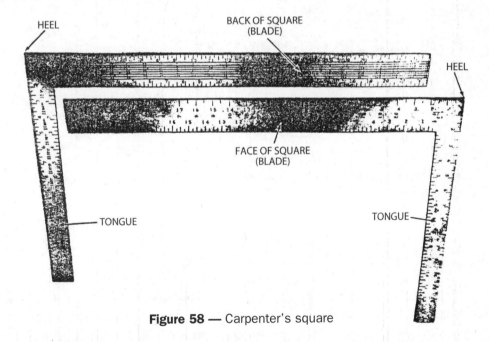

HEEL

BACK OF SQUARE
(BLADE)

HEEL

FACE OF SQUARE
(BLADE)

TONGUE

TONGUE

Figure 58 — Carpenter's square

Try Square

The try square (Figure 59) consists of two parts at right angles to each other; a thick wood or iron stock and a thin, steel blade. Most try squares are made with the blades graduated in inches and fractions of an inch. The blade length varies from 2 inches to 12 inches. This square is used for setting or checking lines or surfaces that must be at right angles to each other.

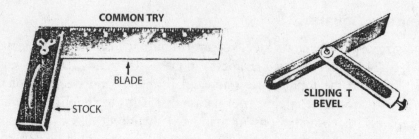

Figure 59 — Common try square   **Figure 60** — Sliding T-bevel

Sliding T-bevel

The sliding T-bevel (Figure 60) is an adjustable try square with a slotted beveled blade. Blades are normally 6 to 8 inches long. The gliding T-bevel is used for laying out angles other than right angles, and for testing constructed angles such as bevels. These squares are made with either wood or metal handles.

MISCELLANEOUS GAGES

There are a number of miscellaneous gages. The depth gage, feeler gage, thread gage, telescoping gage, dividers, and plumb bob are among some of the gages that will be discussed here.

Depth Gage

A depth gage is an instrument for measuring the depth of holes, slots, counterbores, recesses, and the distance from a surface to some recessed part.

Thickness (Feeler) Gage

Thickness (feeler) gages are used for checking and measuring small openings such as contact point clearances, narrow slots, etc. These gages are made in many shapes and sizes and, as shown in Figure 61, thickness gages can be made with multiple blades (usually 2 to 26). Each blade is a specific number of thousandths of an inch thick. This enables the application of one tool to the measurement of a variety of thicknesses. Some thickness gage blades are straight, while others are bent at 45° and 90° angles at the end. Thickness gages can also be grouped so that there are several short and several long blades together. Before using a feeler gage, remove any foreign matter from the blades. You cannot get a correct measurement unless the blades are clean.

Figure 61 — Thickness gages

Thread Gage

Thread gages (screw-pitch gages) are used to determine the pitch and number of threads per inch of threaded fasteners. (See Figure 62.) They consist of thin leaves whose edges are toothed to correspond to standard thread sections. The number of threads per inch is indicated by the numerical value on the blade.

Wire Gage

The wire gage is used for measuring the diameters of wires or the thickness of sheet metal. This gage is circular in shape with cutouts in the outer perimeter. Each cutout gages a different size from No. 0 to No. 36. The larger the gage number, the smaller the diameter or thickness.

Marking Gages

A marking gage is used to mark off guidelines parallel to an edge, end, or surface of a piece of wood or metal. It has a sharp spur or pin that does the marking.

Marking gages (Figure 63) are made of wood or steel. They consist of a graduated beam about 8 inches long on which a head slides. The head can be fastened at any point on the beam by means of a thumbscrew. The thumbscrew presses a brass shoe tightly against the beam and locks it firmly in position. The steel pin or spur that does the marking projects from the beam about $1/_{16}$ inch.

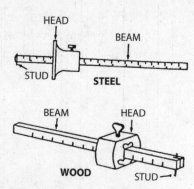

Figure 62 — Screw pitch gage

Figure 63 — Marking gages

Dividers

Dividers are useful instruments for transferring measurements and are frequently used in scribing arcs and circles in layout work.

To lay out a circle with a divider, set the divider at the desired radius, using a rule as shown in Figure 64.

PLUMB BOB

A plumb bob (Figure 65) is a pointed, tapered brass or bronze weight which is suspended from a cord for determining the vertical or plumb line to or from a point on the ground. Common weights for plumb bobs are 6, 8, 10, 12, 14, 16, 18, and 24 ounces.

LEVELS

Levels are tools designed to prove whether a plane or surface is true horizontal or true vertical. Some precision levels are calibrated so that they will indicate in degrees, minutes, and seconds the angle inclination of a surface in relation to a horizontal or vertical surface.

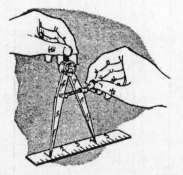

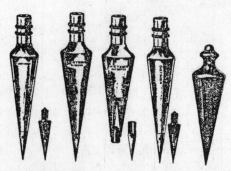

Figure 64 — Setting a divider to a desired radius

Figure 65 — Plumb bobs

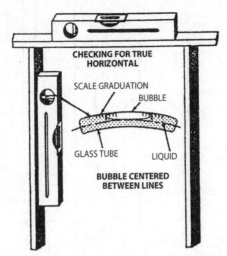

Figure 66 — Horizontal and vertical use of level

The level is a simple instrument consisting of a liquid, such as alcohol or chloroform, partially filling a glass vial or tube so that a bubble remains. The tube is mounted in a frame that may be aluminum, wood, or iron. Levels are equipped with one, two, or more tubes. One tube is built in the frame at right angles to another (Figure 66). The tube indicated in Figure 66 is slightly curved, causing the bubble to seek always the highest point in the tube. On the outside of the tube are two sets of graduation lines separated by a space. Leveling is accomplished when the air bubble is centered between the graduation lines.

FASTENING COMPONENTS

Woodworking Fasteners

Nails

Nails achieve their fastening or holding power when they displace wood fibers from their original position. The pressure exerted against the nail by these fibers, as they try to spring back to their original position, provides the holding power.

The usual type of shank is round, but there are various special-purpose nails with other types of shanks. Nails with square, triangular, longitudinally grooved, and spirally grooved shanks have a much greater holding power than smooth round wire nails of the same size.

The lengths of the most commonly used nails are designated by the penny system. The abbreviation for the word "penny" is the letter "d." Thus the expression "a 2d nail" means a two-penny nail. The penny sizes and corresponding length and thickness (in gage sizes) of the common

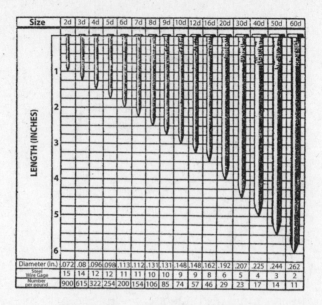

Size	2d	3d	4d	5d	6d	7d	8d	9d	10d	12d	16d	20d	30d	40d	50d	60d
Diameter (in.)	.072	.08	.096	.098	.113	.112	.131	.131	.148	.148	.162	.192	.207	.225	.244	.262
Steel Wire Gage	15	14	12	12	11	11	10	10	9	9	8	6	5	4	3	2
Number per pound	900	615	322	254	200	154	106	85	74	57	46	29	23	17	14	11

Figure 67 — Common nail sizes

nails are shown in Figure 67. The thickness of a nail increases and the number of nails per pound decreases with the penny size.

Nails larger than 20d are called spikes and are generally designated by their length in inches (such as 5 inches or $6^1/_2$ inches); nails smaller than 2d are designated in fractions of an inch instead of in the penny system.

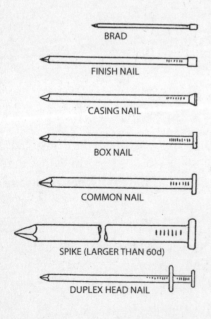

Figure 68 — Nail varieties

Figure 68 shows the more common types of wire nails. The brad and finish nail both have a deep countersink head that is designed to be "set" below the surface of the work. These nails are used for interior and exterior trim-work where the nails are "set" and puttied to conceal their location. The casing nail is used for the same purpose, but because of its flat countersink head, may be driven flush and left that way.

The other nails shown in Figure 68 are all flat-headed, without countersinks. One of these flat-headed nails (called the common nail) is one of the most widely used in general wood construction. Nails with large flat heads are used for nailing roof paper, plaster board, and similar thin or soft materi-

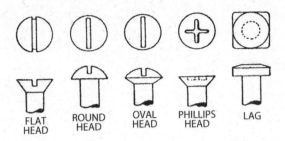

Figure 69 — Wood screw heads

als. Duplex or double-headed nails are used for nailing temporary structures, such as scaffolds, which are eventually to be dismantled. When using the double-headed nail it is driven to the lower head so that it can be easily drawn at a later time.

Wood Screws

Screws have several advantages over nails. They may be easily withdrawn at any time without injury to the material. They also hold the wood more securely, can be easily tightened, and, generally, are neater in appearance.

Wood screws are designated by material, type of head (Figure 69), and size.

Most wood screws are made of steel or brass, but other metals are used as well. Cost or special purpose application will determine the selection of the material to be used.

The size of an ordinary wood screw is indicated by the length and body diameter (unthreaded part) of the screw. Figure 70 shows the nomenclature and the three most common types of wood screws. Notice that the length is always measured from the point to the greatest diameter of the head.

Body diameters are designated by gage numbers, running from 0 (for about a $1/16$ inch diameter) to 24 (for about a $3/8$ inch diameter).

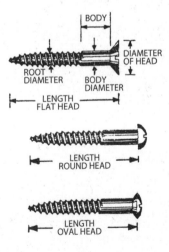

Figure 70 — Nomenclature and types of wood screws

Designation of length and gage number appear as "1$^1/_4$-9." This means a No. 9 screw 1$^1/_4$ inches long.

Metal Fastening Devices

Many mechanisms and devices are held together with metal fasteners.

Metal parts can be fastened together with various fastening devices, such as rivets, bolts, screws, etc. Rivets provide a more permanent type of fastening, whereas bolts and screws are used to fasten together parts that may have to be taken apart later.

Bolts

A bolt is distinguished from a wood screw by the fact that it does not thread into the wood, but goes through and is held by a nut threaded onto the end of the bolt. Figure 71 shows the four common types of bolts used in woodworking. Stove bolts are rather small, ranging in length from $^3/_8$ inch to 4 inch, and in body diameter from $^1/_8$ inch to $^3/_8$ inch. Carriage and machine bolts run from $^3/_4$ inch to 20 inch long, and from $^3/_{16}$ inch to $^3/_4$ inch in diameter. (The carriage bolt has a square section below the head, which is imbedded in the wood to prevent the bolt from turning as the nut is drawn up.) The machine bolt has a hexagon or square head which is held with a wrench to prevent it from turning.

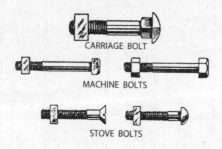

Figure 71 — Bolts

Machine Screws

The term "machine screw" is the general term used to designate the small screws that are used in tapped holes for the assembly of metal parts. Machine screws may also be used with nuts, but usually they are screwed into holes that have been tapped with matching threads.

Machine screws are manufactured in a variety of lengths, diameters, pitches (threads per inch), materials, head shapes, finishes, and thread fits. A complete description of machine screws must include these factors, e.g.,

ROUND — FLAT — OVAL — FILLISTER — WASHER — SQUARE — HEXAGON — SPECIAL — PHILLIPS FLAT HEAD SPEC COUNTERSINK — FLATHEAD SPANNER — FLATHEAD ONE WAY SLOT — FLATHEAD SIDESLOT — SAME FOR ROUND, OVAL, AND FILLISTER HEADS — PHILLIPS BRAZIER HEAD — PHILLIPS WASHER HEAD — PYRAMID HEAD — SPECIAL BINDING HEAD — HEXAGON HEAD — HEXAGON WASHER HEAD — TWIN HEAD WRENCH TYPE — CLOCK HEAD

Figure 72 — Machine screw and capscrew heads

"1/2-inch, 8-32, round head, brass, chromium-plated, machine screw." The first number is the length of the screw. Let's examine some of these other factors.

Diameter and pitch. The diameters of American Standard machine screws are expressed in gage numbers or fractions of an inch. In the preceding paragraph, the "8-32" means that the screw gage is No. 8 and that it has 32 threads per inch. Note, particularly, that the "8" and "32" are two separate numbers, indicating two individual measurements; they are never to be pronounced "eight-thirty-seconds" or written as a fraction such as $8/32$.

Materials and finishes. Most machine screws are made of steel or brass. They may be plated to help prevent corrosion. Other special machine screws made of aluminum or Monel metal are also obtainable.

Head shapes. A variety of common and special machine screw head shapes are shown in Figure 72. Some of the heads require special tools for driving and removing. These special tools are usually included in a kit that comes with the machine or installation on which the screws are used.

Capscrews

Capscrews perform the same functions as machine screws, but come in larger sizes for heavier work. Sizes range up to 1 inch in diameter and 6 inches in length.

Capscrews are usually used without nuts. They are screwed into tapped holes, and are sometimes referred to as tap bolts.

Capscrews may have square, hex, flat, button, or fillister heads (Figure 72). Fillister heads are best for use on moving parts when such heads are sunk into counterbored holes. Hex heads are usually used where the metal parts do not move.

The strongest capscrews are made of alloy steel, and can withstand great stresses, strains, and shearing forces.

Some capscrews have small holes through their heads. A wire, called a safety wire, is run through the holes of several capscrews to keep them from coming loose.

Setscrews

Setscrews are used to secure small pulleys, gears, and cams to shafts, and to provide positive adjustment of machine parts. They are classified by diameter, thread, head shape, and point shape. The point shape is important because it determines the holding qualities of the setscrew.

Setscrews hold best if they have either a cone point or a dog point, shown in Figure 73. These points fit into matching recesses in the shaft against which they bear.

Headless setscrews—slotted, Allen, or Bristol types—are used with moving parts because they do not stick up above the surface. They are threaded all the way from point to head. Common setscrews, used on fixed parts, have square heads. They have threads all the way from the point to the shoulder of the head.

Thumb screws are used for setscrews, adjusting screws, and clamping screws. Because of their design they can be loosened or tightened without the use of tools.

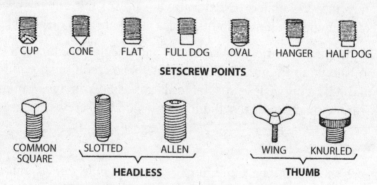

CUP   CONE   FLAT   FULL DOG   OVAL   HANGER   HALF DOG

SETSCREW POINTS

COMMON SQUARE   SLOTTED   ALLEN   WING   KNURLED

HEADLESS   **THUMB**

Figure 73 — Setscrews and thumb screws

Nuts

Square and hexagonal nuts are standard but they are supplemented by special nuts. (See Figure 74.) One of these is the jam nut, used above a

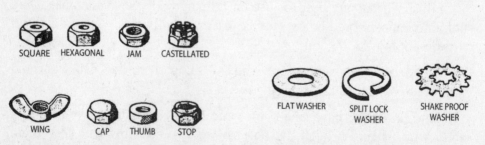

SQUARE   HEXAGONAL   JAM   CASTELLATED

WING   CAP   THUMB   STOP

Figure 74 — Common kinds of nuts

FLAT WASHER   SPLIT LOCK WASHER   SHAKE PROOF WASHER

Figure 75 — Washers

standard hex nut to lock it in position. It is about half as thick as the standard hex nut and has a washer face.

Castellated nuts are slotted so that a safety wire or cotter key may be pushed through the slots and into a matching hole in the bolt. This provides a positive method of preventing the nut from working loose. For example, you will see these nuts used with the bolts that hold the two halves of an engine connecting rod together.

Wing nuts are used where the desired degree of tightness can be obtained by the fingers. Cap nuts are used where appearance is an important consideration. They are usually made of chromium-plated brass. Thumb nuts are knurled, so they can be turned by hand for easy assembly and disassembly.

Elastic stop nuts are used where it is imperative that the nut does not come loose. These nuts have a fiber or composition washer built into them that is compressed automatically against the screw threads to provide holding tension. They are used extensively on radio, sound equipment, fire control equipment, and on aircraft.

Washers

Figure 75 shows various types of washers. Flat washers are used to back up bolt heads and nuts, and to provide larger bearing surfaces. They prevent damage to the surfaces of the metal parts.

Split lock washers are used under nuts to prevent loosening by vibration. The ends of these spring-hardened washers dig into both the nut and the work to prevent slippage.

Shakeproof lock washers have teeth or lugs that grip both the work and the nut. Several patented designs, shapes, and sizes are obtainable.

Keys and Pins

Cotter keys (Figure 76) are used to secure screws, nuts, bolts, and pins. They are also used as stops and holders on shafts and rods. Square keys

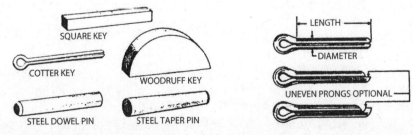

Figure 76 — Keys and pins   **Figure 77** — Types of cotter pins

and woodruff keys are used to prevent hand wheels, gears, cams, and pulleys from turning on a shaft. These keys are strong enough to carry heavy loads if they are fitted and seated properly.

Taper pins are used to locate and position matching parts. They are also used to secure small pulleys and gears to shafts. They usually have a taper of $1/4$-inch per foot. Holes for taper pins must be reamed with tapered reamers. If this is not done, the taper pin will not fit properly.

Dowel pins are used to position and align the units or parts of an assembly. One end of a dowel pin is chamfered, and it is usually .001 to .002 inch greater in diameter than the size of the hole into which the pin will be driven.

Cotter Pins

Some cotter pins are made of low-carbon steel, while others consist of stainless steel and are more resistant to corrosion. Regardless of shape or material, all cotter pins are used for the same general purpose—safetying. Safetying is a process of securing fasteners and other equipment so they do not work loose due to vibration.

Dimension perimeters of a cotter pin are shown in Figure 77. Whenever uneven prong cotter pins are used, the length measurement is to the end of the shortest prong.

Rivets

Rivets are used extensively as a fastening device in aircraft. They are also used to join metal sheet when brazing, welding, or locking techniques will not provide a satisfactory joint.

The major types of rivets used extensively include the standard type and pop rivets. Standard rivets must be driven using a bucking bar whereas the pop rivets have a self heading capability and may be installed where it is impossible to use a bucking bar.

Standard rivets. Wherever possible, rivets should be made of the same material as the material they join. They are classified by lengths, diameters, and their head shape and size. Some of the standard head shapes are shown in Figure 78.

Selection of the proper length of a rivet is important. Should too long a rivet be used, the formed head will be too large, or the rivet may bend or be forced between the sheets being riveted. Should too short a rivet be used, the formed head will be too small or the riveted material will be damaged. The length of the rivet should equal the sum of the thickness of the metal plus $1^1/_2$ times the diameter of the rivet.

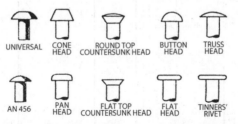

Figure 78 — Some common types of rivets

Pop rivets. Pop rivets have two advantages compared to standard rivets in that they can be set by one person and can also be used for blind fastening. This means that they can be used where there is limited or no access to the reverse side of the work.

LUBRICATION

If you grew up in a large city, perhaps the only connection you had with lubrication was taking the family car to the garage or gasoline station for greasing and an oil change. If you grew up on a farm or had a car that you kept in running condition yourself, you are well aware of the need for regular lubrication of all moving parts. If your car ever burned out a bearing, you've had a lesson you are not likely to forget.

Functions of Lubricants

Lubricants are used as coolants, to reduce friction, to prevent wear, and to protect against corrosion.

Lubricants

Lubricants are of two general classes—oils and greases. Oils are fluids; greases are semisolid at ordinary temperatures. For many applications, liquid lubricants are more suitable than greases, particularly if the lubricant can be retained, as in an oil bath, a gear box, or in a forced-feed system. Where conditions are such that oil is not readily retained, or additional protection against corrosion is needed, greases are used.

It is important that you learn and understand the uses of each tool described in this review. Many of the tools mentioned are directly applicable for use in designing, maintaining, and fixing an automobile.

MATHEMATICS KNOWLEDGE REVIEW

ARITHMETIC

Arithmetic is comprised of four basic operations. These are addition, subtraction, multiplication, and division. Each of these operations will now be reviewed.

Addition

Addition involves adding two or more numbers together. For example,

$$\begin{array}{r} 2 \\ + 7 \\ \hline 9 \end{array}$$

When we add two or more numbers together, the answer is called the sum of the original numbers. Certain properties which hold true for addition are as follows.

The **associative property** states that regrouping numbers being added will not affect the sum. For example,

$$(6 + 4) + 3 = 13 = 6 + (4 + 3)$$

The **commutative property** states that reversing the order of addition will not affect the sum. For example,

$$\begin{array}{r} 3 \\ + 2 \\ \hline 5 \end{array} \quad \text{and} \quad \begin{array}{r} 2 \\ + 3 \\ \hline 5 \end{array}$$

The **additive identity** is 0, and, when added to any number, will result in that number. For example,

$$\begin{array}{r} 7 \\ + 0 \\ \hline 7 \end{array}$$

The **additive inverse** of a number is the negative of that number. When a number is added to its additive inverse, the answer is 0. For example,

$$
\begin{array}{r}
4 \\
+ \ (-4) \\
\hline
0
\end{array}
$$

Subtraction

Subtraction involves subtracting one number from another. For example,

$$
\begin{array}{r}
8 \\
- \ 3 \\
\hline
5
\end{array}
$$

When we subtract one number from another, the answer is called the difference of the two numbers.

In subtraction the identity is 0. For example,

$$
\begin{array}{r}
3 \\
- \ 0 \\
\hline
3
\end{array}
$$

Multiplication

Multiplication involves multiplying two or more numbers together. When we multiply two or more numbers together, the answer is called the product of the numbers. Multiplication is written symbolically in two ways. The symbol × may be used, as in

$$
\begin{array}{r}
2 \\
\times \ 3 \\
\hline
6
\end{array}
$$

Sometimes no symbol is used, as in (2)(3) = 6. As in addition, certain properties hold true for multiplication.

The **associative property** states that regrouping numbers being multiplied will not affect the product. For example,

$$6 \times (4 \times 3) = 6 \times 12 = 72 = 24 \times 3 = (6 \times 4) \times 3$$

The **commutative property** states that reversing the order of multiplication will not affect the product. For example,

$$\begin{array}{r} 3 \\ \times\ 2 \\ \hline 6 \end{array} \text{, and } \begin{array}{r} 2 \\ \times\ 3 \\ \hline 6 \end{array}$$

The **multiplicative identity** is 1, and when multiplied by any number, will result in that number. For example,

$$\begin{array}{r} 7 \\ \times\ 1 \\ \hline 7 \end{array}$$

The **multiplicative inverse** of a number is the reciprocal of that number (one divided by that number). When a number is multiplied by its multiplicative inverse, the answer is 1. For example,

$$4 \times \frac{1}{4} = 1$$

Another property is the **distributive property of multiplication and addition**. This states in general, that

$$a \times (b + c) = ab + ac$$

For example,

$$3 \times (6 + 2) = 24 = (3 \times 6) + (3 \times 2)$$

Division

Division involves dividing one number by another. When we divide one number by another, the answer is called the quotient of the two numbers. For example, $4/2 = 2$. The reciprocal of a number is defined as one divided by that number. For example, 1/2 is the reciprocal of 2. The only number which serves as its own reciprocal is 1.

FRACTIONS

A fraction is a number of the form a/b, where a and b are numbers. Here a is the numerator of the fraction, and b is the denominator. If we multiply both the numerator and the denominator by the same number, then we do not change the numerical value of the fraction. For example,

$$\frac{3a}{3b} = \frac{a}{b}$$

Adding Fractions

Addition of fractions is similar to addition of (whole) numbers or expressions, in that it is carried out on two or more fractions. The difference is that prior to performing this addition, each fraction is required to have the same denominator. For example, one cannot add 1/2 and 3/4 without first finding the least common denominator of these fractions. The two denominators are 2 and 4, and since 2 evenly divides 4, 4 is the least common denominator. We need to find two fractions, each with denominator 4, such that one equals 1/2 and the other equals 3/4. We recall that we may multiply both the numerator and the denominator by the same number without changing the numerical value of the fraction. Thus

$$\frac{1}{2} = \left(\frac{1}{2}\right)\left(\frac{2}{2}\right) = \frac{2}{4} \text{ and } \frac{(3)\,(1)}{(4)\,(1)} = \frac{3}{4}$$

Now we can add 1/2 and 3/4 by adding 2/4 and 3/4. The rule for adding two or more fractions with a common denominator is to add all the numerators and make this the numerator of the sum. The denominator of the sum is the common denominator of each fraction being added. Do not add the denominators! Then

$$\frac{1}{2} + \frac{3}{4} = \frac{2}{4} + \frac{3}{4} = \frac{(2+3)}{4} = \frac{5}{4}$$

Subtracting Fractions

Subtraction of fractions is like subtraction of numbers, but again a common denominator is required. Once we have the fractions over a common denominator, the difference is the first numerator minus the second, divided by the common denominator. For example, 5/8 – 1/5 cannot be solved until we find the least common denominator of the two denominators, 8 and 5. Since 8 and 5 are relatively prime (they have no factors in common), the least common denominator is 8 × 5 = 40. Thus

$$\frac{5}{8} - \frac{1}{5} = \left(\frac{5}{5}\right)\left(\frac{5}{8}\right) - \left(\frac{8}{8}\right)\left(\frac{1}{5}\right)$$

$$= \frac{25}{40} - \frac{8}{40} = \frac{(25-8)}{40} = \frac{17}{40}$$

Multiplying Fractions

Multiplication of fractions is simpler than addition or subtraction of fractions, because it is not necessary to first obtain a common denominator. The product of two fractions is the product of the numerators over the product of the denominators. For example,

$$\left(\frac{3}{4}\right) \times \left(\frac{2}{3}\right) = \frac{(3 \times 2)}{(4 \times 3)} = \frac{6}{12} = \frac{1}{2}$$

after reducing the answer.

Dividing Fractions

Division of fractions, like multiplication of fractions, does not require a common denominator. The quotient of one fraction and another is the product of the first numerator and the second denominator over the product of the first denominator and the second numerator. This may be easier to understand if we consider dividing by (a/b) to actually be multiplying by its reciprocal, (b/a). For example,

$$\left(\frac{4}{5}\right) \div \left(\frac{3}{7}\right) = \left(\frac{4}{5}\right) \times \left(\frac{7}{3}\right) = \frac{(4 \times 7)}{(5 \times 3)} = \frac{28}{15}$$

The quotient of two fractions can be a mixed number, as 28/15 is actually

$$1\frac{13}{15}$$

MIXED NUMBERS

A mixed number is the sum of a whole number and a fraction, such as $5\frac{4}{7}$. For example,

$$\frac{39}{7} = \frac{(35 + 4)}{7}$$

(splitting the numerator of an improper fraction into a part which evenly divides the denominator and the remainder)

$$= \frac{35}{7} + \frac{4}{7}$$

(splitting the sum in the numerator into a sum of fractions)

$$= 5\frac{4}{7}$$

A mixed number will typically result from dividing a larger integer by a smaller one if there is a remainder, or if the smaller integer does not evenly divide the larger one.

Adding Mixed Numbers

Addition of mixed numbers can be carried out by first adding the whole numbers, then adding the fractions, and finally adding the two results together to form the sum. In general,

$$a\frac{b}{c} + d\frac{e}{f} = (a + d) + \left[\frac{b}{c} + \frac{e}{f}\right]$$

For example,

$$2\frac{6}{7} + 3\frac{4}{5} = (2 + 3) + \left[\frac{6}{7} + \frac{4}{5}\right]$$

(adding the integer parts and the fraction parts)

$$= 5 + \left[\left(\frac{6}{7}\right)\left(\frac{5}{5}\right) + \left(\frac{4}{5}\right)\left(\frac{7}{7}\right)\right]$$

(putting the fractions to be added over a common denominator)

$$= 5 + \left[\left(\frac{30}{35}\right) + \left(\frac{28}{35}\right)\right]$$

(simplifying algebraically via multiplication)

$$= 5 + \left[\frac{30 + 28}{35}\right]$$

(adding fractions)

$$= 5 + \left(\frac{58}{35}\right)$$

(simplifying algebraically via addition)

$$= 5 + \left[\frac{35 + 23}{35}\right]$$

(splitting the numerator of an improper fraction into a part which evenly divides the denominator and the remainder)

$$= 5 + \left(\frac{35}{35}\right) + \left(\frac{23}{35}\right)$$

(splitting the sum in the numerator into a sum of fractions)

$$= 5 + 1 + \left(\frac{23}{35}\right)$$

(simplifying algebraically via division)

$$= 6\frac{23}{35}$$

Subtracting Mixed Numbers

Subtraction of mixed numbers can be accomplished by first subtracting the whole number parts, then the fraction parts, and then adding the two results to find the difference. For example,

$$3\frac{6}{7} - 2\frac{4}{9} = (3-2) + \left[\left(\frac{6}{7}\right) - \left(\frac{4}{9}\right)\right]$$

(subtracting integer parts and fraction parts)

$$= 1 + \left[\left(\frac{6}{7}\right)\left(\frac{9}{9}\right) - \left(\frac{4}{9}\right)\left(\frac{7}{7}\right)\right]$$

(putting the fractions over a common denominator)

$$= 1 + \left[\left(\frac{54}{63}\right) - \left(\frac{28}{63}\right)\right]$$

(simplifying algebraically via multiplication)

$$= 1 + \left[\frac{(54-28)}{63}\right]$$

(subtracting fractions)

$$= 1\frac{26}{63}$$

Multiplying Mixed Numbers

Multiplication of mixed numbers is most easily performed by first converting each mixed number to a fraction. The whole number part must be put over the denominator of the fraction part. For example,

$$6\frac{4}{7} = \left(\frac{6}{1}\right)\left(\frac{7}{7}\right) + \left(\frac{4}{7}\right)$$

(putting the integer part of a mixed number over the denominator of the fraction part)

$$= \left(\frac{42}{7}\right) + \left(\frac{4}{7}\right)$$

(simplifying algebraically via multiplication)

$$= \frac{(42 + 4)}{7}$$

(adding fractions by adding their numerators)

$$= \frac{46}{7}$$

After converting each mixed number to a fraction, simply multiply the fractions. For example,

$$6\frac{4}{7} \times 6\frac{5}{7} = \left(\frac{46}{7}\right) \times \left(\frac{47}{7}\right)$$

(converting each mixed number to an improper fraction)

$$= \frac{(46 \times 47)}{(7 \times 7)}$$

(multiplying the two improper fractions)

$$= \frac{2162}{49}$$

(simplifying algebraically via multiplication)

$$= 44\frac{6}{49}$$

Dividing Mixed Numbers

Division of mixed numbers should be done by first converting each mixed number to a fraction, and then multiplying the first fraction by the reciprocal of the second. For example,

$$3\frac{2}{5} \div 2\frac{1}{3} = \left[\left(\frac{3}{1}\right)\left(\frac{5}{5}\right) + \frac{2}{5}\right] \div \left[\left(\frac{2}{1}\right)\left(\frac{3}{3}\right) + \frac{1}{3}\right]$$

(putting each mixed number over a common denominator)

$$= \left[\frac{(3 \times 5) + 2}{5}\right] \div \left[\frac{(2 \times 3) + 1}{3}\right]$$

(combining fractions with the same denominator)

$$= \left[\frac{(15 + 2)}{5}\right] \div \left[\frac{(6 + 1)}{3}\right]$$

(simplifying algebraically via multiplication)

$$= \left(\frac{17}{5}\right) \div \left(\frac{7}{3}\right)$$

(simplifying algebraically via addition)

$$= \left(\frac{17}{5}\right) \times \left(\frac{3}{7}\right)$$

(dividing fractions via multiplication of the first by the reciprocal of the other)

$$= \frac{(17 \times 3)}{(5 \times 7)}$$

(multiplying fractions by multiplying the numerators and denominators)

$$= \frac{51}{35}$$

(simplifying algebraically via multiplication)

$$= \frac{(35 + 16)}{35}$$

(splitting the numerator of an improper fraction into a part which evenly divides the denominator and the remainder)

$$= \left(\frac{35}{35}\right) + \left(\frac{16}{35}\right)$$

(splitting the fraction)

$$= 1\frac{16}{35}$$

PERCENTS

Percents are fractions expressed as part of a whole. For example, 20%, or 20 percent, is 20/100 or 1/5. One-half is 50%, which is 50/100, or 1/2. Further, 100% = 100/100 = 1.

Adding Percents

Since percents are fractions, they could be added as such by converting them to fractions with 100 as the common denominator. This is not necessary, however, as they can be added directly. For example,

$$25\% + 31\% = (25 + 31)\% = 56\%$$

Subtracting Percents

Subtraction of percents can also be done directly. For example,

$$79\% - 42\% = (79 - 42)\% = 37\%$$

Multiplying Percents

To multiply two percents, first multiply the numbers together, then divide this answer by 100 × 100 (or 10,000). For example,

$$25\% \times 50\% = \left(\frac{25}{100}\right) \times \left(\frac{50}{100}\right)$$

(by definition of percent)

$$= \frac{(25 \times 50)}{10,000}$$

(multiplying fractions)

$$= \frac{1,250}{10,000}$$

(simplifying algebraically via multiplication)

$$= \frac{125}{1,000}$$

(reducing the fraction)

$$= \frac{12.5}{100}$$

(putting the fraction over 100 so it can be converted to a percent)

$$= 12.5\%$$

Dividing Percents

To divide one percent by another, it is valid to first multiply each by 100. This changes the percents to actual numbers, and the answer will be an actual number. Thus it suffices to ignore the percentage signs. For example,

$$14\% \div 7\% = \frac{14}{100} \div \frac{7}{100}$$

(definition of percent)

$$= \left(\frac{14}{100}\right) \times \left(\frac{100}{7}\right)$$

(dividing fractions)

$$= \frac{(14 \times 100)}{(100 \times 7)}$$

(multiplying fractions)

$$= \frac{1,400}{700}$$

(simplifying algebraically via multiplication)

$$= 2 \text{ or } 200\%$$

ALGEBRAIC EQUATIONS

An algebraic equation is a statement of equality of two algebraic expressions. An algebraic expression may contain numbers and/or symbols representing numbers. For example, $3x + 2$ is an expression (x represents an unknown number, not the multiplication symbol). If we write $3x + 2 = 8$, then this is an algebraic equation and we can solve it by finding the numerical value of x. There may be more than one unknown, for example $3x + 2y = 9$. The solution of an algebraic equation is an ordered set of values, one for each variable, which makes the equation numerically correct. For example, if

$3x + 2 = 8$, then $x = 2$

is a solution (in fact it is the only solution). If

$3x + 2y = 9$, then $(x = 3, y = 0)$

is a solution, and $(x = 1, y = 3)$ is another solution. In fact, for any value of x there is a value of y which would make this combination a solution, and, likewise, for any value of y, there is a value of x which would make this combination a solution.

To find the solution one must undo to the variable whatever the equation does to it. The idea is to get the variable to one side of the equation. Let us return to our example of $3x + 2 = 8$. We ask ourselves what this equation is doing to the variable. The variable is x, and we see that the equation is first multiplying it by 3, and then adding 2 to it. We first undo the last operation performed on it, so we undo the addition of 2. We do this by subtracting 2. But whatever we do to one side of the equation we must do to the other side as well if we wish to preserve the equality. The answer is $(3x + 2) - 2 = (8) - 2$, or, after simplifying, $3x = 6$. Now we undo the multiplication by 3. We do this by dividing by 3. We obtain $(3x)/3 = (6)/3$, or, after simplifying, $x = 2$. This is our unique solution.

As another example, consider the algebraic equation $(x/2) - 6 = 14$. First we undo the subtraction of 6, and this can be accomplished by adding 6 to both sides. We obtain

$[(x/2) - 6] + 6 = (14) + 6$, or $(x/2) = 20$.

Now we undo the division of 2 by multiplying (both sides of the equation) by 2. We obtain $2(x/2) = 2(20)$, or $x = 40$. This is the unique solution.

EXPONENTS

Exponents symbolize repeated multiplication by the same number. For example, if we write $2^3 = 8$, then this means that two, multiplied by itself three times, will give a result of 8. This simply means that $2 \times 2 \times 2 = 8$.

Bases

In the equation $2^4 = 16$, the base is 2, since 2 is the number being repeatedly multiplied.

Powers

In the equation $2^4 = 16$, the power is 4, since 2 is being multiplied by itself four times, i.e., $2 \times 2 \times 2 \times 2 = 16$.

If 1 is raised to any power, then the answer is still 1. Any number (other than 0) raised to the 0 power is 1. Any number raised to the power of 1 is itself. For example $8^1 = 8$. Multiplying two bases raised to different powers is the same as raising the base to the sum of the powers. For example,

$$2^2 \times 2^3 = 2^{(2+3)} = 2^5 = 32$$

Multiplying different bases raised to the same power is the same as raising the product of the bases to the common power. For example,

$$2^3 \times 4^3 = (2 \times 4)^3 = 8^3 = 512$$

Any number raised to an even power is non-negative. For example,

$$3^2 = 9 \geq 0, \text{ and } (-2)^4 = 16 \geq 0$$

The answer would only equal 0 if the base were 0.

Roots

Roots are bases, except that you try to find them given the other information. For example, the square root of 9 is 3, since

$$3 \times 3 = 9$$

(square means second power). The cube root of 64 is 4, since

$$4 \times 4 \times 4 = 64$$

(cube means third power).

For square roots we usually accept the positive solution as the solution, but there is also a negative one. For example,

$$(-3) \times (-3) = 9$$

also, so -3 is another square root of 9.

Prime Numbers

Prime numbers are numbers which are divisible only by themselves and by 1. A number can be expressed as a product of bases (or roots) raised to appropriate powers (or exponents). For example,

$$54 = 2 \times 27 = 2^1 \times 3^3$$

Obtaining this expression is called factoring a number, since 2 and 3 are the prime factors of 27. A prime number has no factors other than itself and 1, and hence, when factored, is written as itself raised to the power of

1. For example, $13 = 13^1$, and there is no other way to factor 13. No integer other than 1 and 13 can divide 13 without a remainder.

GEOMETRY

Geometry is the study of objects on a line (one-dimensional), in the plane (two-dimensional), or in space (three-dimensional). Typically, you will be asked to find areas, perimeters, lengths, or measures of angles.

Angles

An angle is formed by the intersection of two lines or line segments. The point of intersection is known as the vertex of the angle. Its size is measured in degrees, minutes, and seconds. A degree is 60 minutes, and a minute is 60 seconds.

A right angle is 90 degrees, and a straight angle is 180 degrees. An acute angle is an angle less than 90 degrees, and an obtuse angle is an angle greater than 90 degrees. Two angles which add to 90 degrees are called complimentary, and two angles which add to 180 degrees are called supplementary.

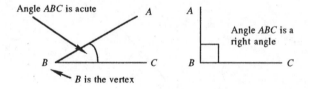

Figure 1

Perimeter

The perimeter of a closed geometric figure in two dimensions is the length of its border. For a triangle or a quadrilateral, this is the sum of the lengths of the sides. For a circle of radius r, the perimeter is $2\pi r$, where π = 3.14159 (approximately). That means that if you made a circle of radius

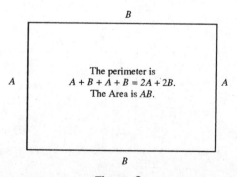

Figure 2

r out of a piece of string, then the length of the string, when the string was straightened out, would be $2\pi r$.

Area

The area of a closed geometric figure in two dimensions is the size of its internal region. Different rectangles with the same area may have different perimeters, and rectangles with the same perimeter may have different areas.

For a rectangle, the area is the product of the lengths of two consecutive sides. For a square, the area is the square of the length of any side. For a circle of radius *r*, the area is πr^2, where $\pi = 3.14159$ (approximately).

Triangles

A triangle is a closed figure with three sides, and hence it also has three angles. These angles sum to 180 degrees.

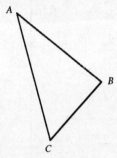

Figure 3 — *ABC* is a triangle. $\angle A + \angle B + \angle C = 180°$.

A right triangle is one in which one of the three angles is a right angle (90 degrees). In a right triangle the Pythagorean Theorem states that the squared length of the hypotenuse (the side opposite the right angle) is equal to the sum of the squared lengths of the two other sides (the legs). By Pythagorean Theorem:

$$\overline{AB}^2 + \overline{BC}^2 = \overline{AC}^2$$

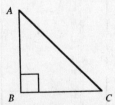

Figure 4 — $\angle B = 90°$, so *ABC* is a right triangle.

The area of a right triangle is one-half of the product of its two legs. Area:

$$\frac{(\overline{AB} \times \overline{BC})}{2}$$

An isosceles triangle is one in which two of the sides are of the same length. The angles opposite from these two sides are also equal. An equilateral triangle is one in which each side is of the same length. In an equilateral triangle each angle is 60 degrees. A scalene triangle has no equal pair of sides or angles.

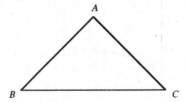

Figure 5 — $\overline{AB} = \overline{AC}$, so *ABC* is an isosceles triangle.

The area of an equilateral triangle with sides of length *s* can be derived as follows: Label the three vertices of an equilateral triangle *A*, *B*, and *C*. Draw a line segment from *C* to the midpoint of side *AB*, and label this midpoint *D*. Now draw a line through *B* which is perpendicular to side *AB* (or is parallel to *CD*), and extend this line past *C*. Draw a line through *C* which is parallel to side *AB* and extend this line until it intersects the previous one you drew. Label this point of intersection *E*. Now *BDCE* is a rectangle whose sides are *BD* (of length *s/2*) and *CD*. By the Pythagorean Theorem, the length of *CD* squared plus the length of *BD* squared equals the length of *BC* squared. But the length of *BC* is *s*, so we obtain

$$\overline{CD}^2 + \overline{BD}^2 = \overline{BC}^2$$

$$\overline{CD}^2 + \left(\frac{s}{2}\right)^2 = s^2$$

$$\overline{CD}^2 = s^2 - \left(\frac{s}{2}\right)^2$$

$$\overline{CD}^2 = s^2 - \frac{s^2}{4}$$

$$= \frac{4s^2 - s^2}{4}$$

$$= \frac{3s^2}{4}$$

Now take $\sqrt{}$ of both sides:

$$CD = \sqrt{\frac{3s^2}{4}}$$

$$= \frac{\sqrt{3}s}{2}$$

$$= \frac{1.7325s}{2}$$

So the area of rectangle *BDCE* is

$$(s/2) \times (1.732s/2) = 1.732s^2/4$$

But the area of triangle *BCD* is half of this, or $1.732s^2/8$. Finally, the area of the original triangle, *ABC*, is twice that of triangle *BCD*, or $1.732s^2/4$.

Note that the area of the *rectangle* is *equal* to the area of the original triangle.

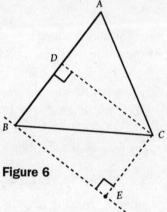

Figure 6

Quadrilaterals

A quadrilateral is a closed figure with four sides. Squares, rectangles, trapezoids, rhombuses, and parallelograms are quadrilaterals.

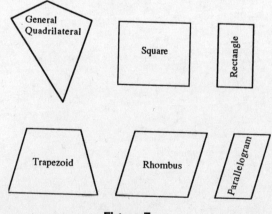

Figure 7

Circles

A circle is the set of points equidistant, or at an equal distance, from a given point. This point is called the center of the circle.

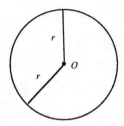

Figure 8 — The distance from any point on the circle to the center is *r*.

MECHANICAL COMPREHENSION REVIEW

A machine is a device that enables man to perform work by changing the magnitude and/or direction of a force or torque (also called the moment of a force, see below) by transforming energy or by transferring motion.

Physicists recognize three basic types of machines: the lever, including simple levers, pulleys, and wheel and axle; the inclined plane, including wedges and screws; and the hydraulic press.

THE LEVER

A lever is made up of a rigid rod pivoted about a certain point called the fulcrum. A common type is shown in Figure 1, with the fulcrum F between the load (or resistance) R and the applied force (or effort) E.

The distances L and l at which the effort and resistance act respectively are known as the lever arms.

This type of lever, with the fulcrum between the resistance and the effort, is called a Class I lever.

In the Class II lever, the resistance is located between the fulcrum and the effort, as in the case of a wheelbarrow, see Figure 2. Generally, the fulcrum is at one end of the lever and the effort is applied at the other end.

In the Class III lever, the effort is applied between the resistance and the fulcrum, as in the case of the human forearm held horizontally with a load in the hand (Figure 3).

The helpful thing about machines is that you can predict the forces required for their operation, as well as the forces they will exert.

Consider, for example, the case of a Class III lever.

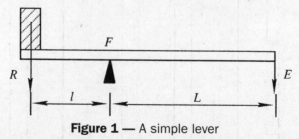

Figure 1 — A simple lever

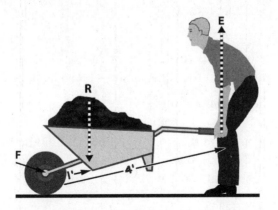

Figure 2 — This makes it easier.

You might know from experience that it takes a big pull at E to overcome a relatively small resistance at R. Just remind yourself of this principle, try closing a door by pushing on it about three or four inches from the hinges (fulcrum).

The relationship between the lever arms L and l, on one hand, and the resistance and effort R and E on the other, can be stated as follows: the length L of the effort arm is the same number of times greater than the length l of the resistance arm, as the resistance R is the same number of times greater than the effort E.

Or, expressed in mathematical terms:

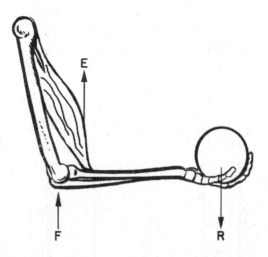

Figure 3 — Your arm is a lever.

$$\frac{L}{l} = \frac{R}{E}.$$

Remember that all distances must be in the same units — such as inches — and all forces must be in the same units — such as pounds.

Consider the following example as a way of applying this principle. Suppose that you want to pry up the lid of a paint can with a 6-inch crowbar, and you know that the average force holding the lid is 50 pounds, see Figure 4. If the distance from the edge of the paint can to the edge of the cover is one inch, what force will you have to apply on the end of the crowbar?

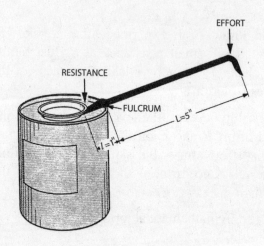

Figure 4 — A first-class job.

According to the formula above,

$$\frac{L}{l} = \frac{R}{E}.$$

Here, $L = 5$ inches, $l = 1$ inch, $R = 50$ pounds, and E is unknown.

Then

$$\frac{5}{1} = \frac{50}{E}$$

and $E = \dfrac{50 \times 1}{5} = 10$ pounds.

You will need to apply a force of only 10 pounds. Note that the resistance *R* is 5 times greater than the effort *E*. We say that this machine has a *mechanical advantage* of 5.

In general, the mechanical advantage (M.A.) for levers is the ratio of the resistance to the applied force, or effort:

$$\text{M.A.} = \frac{R}{E}.$$

Note that by virtue of the formula

$$\frac{R}{E} = \frac{L}{l},$$

the mechanical advantage can also be obtained from the lever arms:

$$\text{M.A.} = \frac{L}{l}$$

BLOCK AND TACKLE

A block (or pulley) and tackle may be considered equivalent to a lever with arms of different lengths. In Figure 5, you will see an illustration of a block. Study it and be familiar with the names of the different parts that go into it. Incidentally, you will often hear the rope or tackle called the fall.

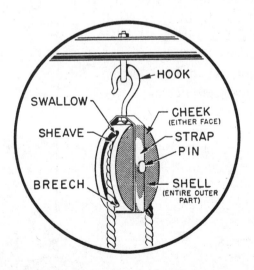

Figure 5 — Look it over.

Mechanical Advantage

A single fixed block is really a first-class lever with equal arms (Figure 6). The arms *EF* and *FR* are equal; hence, the mechanical advantage is one. A single fixed block does not magnify force nor speed.

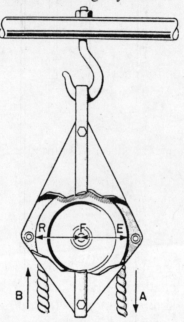

Figure 6 — No advantage.

You can, however, use a single block-and-fall to magnify the force you exert. In Figure 7, the block is not fixed, and the fall is doubled as it supports the 200-pound cask. When rigged this way, a single block-and-fall is called a runner. Each half of the fall carries one-half of the total load, or 100 pounds. Thus, by the use of the runner, the man is lifting a 200-pound cask with a 100-pound pull. The mechanical advantage is two, as can be checked by the formula:

$$\text{M.A.} = \frac{R}{E} = \frac{200}{100}, \text{ or } 2.$$

The single movable block in

Figure 7 — A runner.

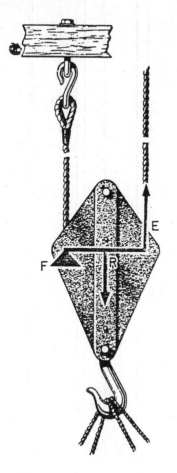

Figure 8 — M.A. is 2 to 1

the previous setup is really a second-class lever. As shown in Figure 8, the effort *E* acts upward upon the arm *EF*, which is the diameter of the sheave, or pulley. The resistance *R* acts downward on the arm *FR*, which is the radius of the sheave. Since the diameter is twice the radius, the mechanical advantage is two.

But, when the effort at *E* moves up two feet, the load at *R* is raised only one foot. That's one thing to remember about blocks and falls — if you are actually getting a mechanical advantage from the system, the length of rope that passes through your hands is greater than the distance that the load is raised.

You can arrange blocks in a number of ways, depending on the job to be done and the mechanical advantage you want to get.

An improvement on the runner shown in Figure 7 can be made by making use of another single block to change the direction of the pull as in Figure 9. This arrangement is known as a gun tackle. Notice that because the second block is fixed, it merely changes the direction of pull, and the mechanical advantage of the whole system remains two.

Another example of a block and tackle machine is the luff tackle, which consists of a double block and a single block, rigged as in Figure 10. Notice that the weight is suspended by the three parts of rope which extend from the movable single block. Each part of the rope carries its share of the load. If the crate weighs 300 pounds, then each of the three parts of the rope supports its share — 100 pounds. You will only have to pull downward with a force of 100 pounds on *A* to lift the crate.

The mechanical advantage is:

$$\text{M.A.} = \frac{R}{E} = \frac{300}{100} = 3$$

A quick rule to estimate the mechanical advantage of most block and tackle machines is:

M.A. = Number of strands of rope supporting movable block of block and tackle.

THE WHEEL AND AXLE

It is obvious that the simple lever, as well as the block and tackle have limitations in that they can only operate through a small angle or a fixed direction. These limitations are overcome by using a continuous rotation of the lever arm in the wheel and axle.

Consider, as an example, the old oaken bucket in Figure 11 raised by a wheel-and-axle arrangement.

Mechanical Advantage

In the example at hand, if the distance from the center of the axle to the handle is 8 inches, and the radius of the drum around which the rope is wound is 2 inches, then you have a theoretical mechanical advantage of 4 as can be found from the formula:

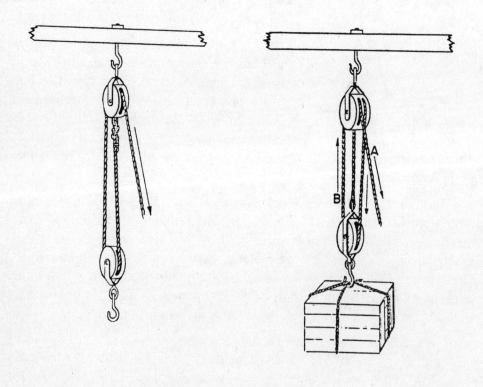

Figure 9 — A gun tackle.   **Figure 10**

$$M.A. = \frac{L}{l} = \frac{R}{E}$$

where: L = radius of the circle through which the handle turns

l = one-half the diameter of the drum, or radius

R = force of the resistance offered by the bucket

E = force of effort applied on the handle

$$M.A. = \frac{8''}{2''} = 4$$

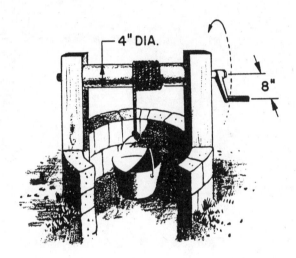

4" DIA.

8"

Figure 11 — The old oaken bucket

MOMENT OF FORCE

Whenever you use a lever, or a wheel and axle, your effort on the lever arm or the rim of the wheel will cause a rotation about the fulcrum or the axle in one direction or another. If the rotation occurs in the same direction as the hands of a clock, that direction is called clockwise, otherwise it's called counterclockwise. You have already seen that the result of a force acting on the lever arm depends not only on the amount of that force but also on the distance from the fulcrum or center of rotation. The product of the force times the distance is known as the **moment of force**, or **torque**. Look at the effect of counterclockwise movement of the capstan in Figure 12. Here the amount of the effort is designated E_1, and the distance from the point where this force is applied to the center of the axle is L_1.

Then $E_1 \times L_1$ is the moment of force. Ordinarily, the distance is measured in feet and the applied force is measured in pounds. Therefore, moments of force are generally measured in foot-pounds (ft-lb).

The usefulness of such a machine is illustrated in the figure below.

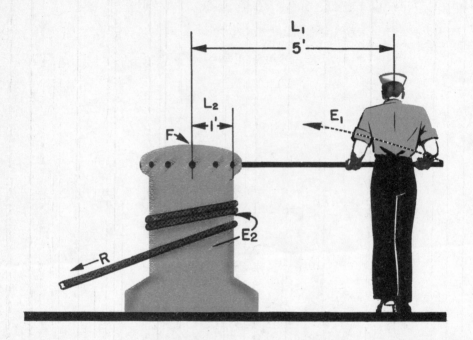

Figure 12 — The capstan

Balancing Moments

The idea of the balance of moments of force can be summed up by the expression

CLOCKWISE MOMENTS = COUNTERCLOCKWISE MOMENTS

This may be written as

$$E_1 \times L_1 = E_2 \times L_2$$

where:

E_1 = force of effort

L_1 = distance from fulcrum or axle to point where force is applied

E_2 = force of resistance

L_2 = distance from fulcrum or center of axle to the point where resistance is applied

EXAMPLE

Put this formula to work on a capstan problem. A single capstan bar is gripped 5 feet from the center of a capstan head with a radius of one foot. A $1/2$-ton anchor is to be lifted. How much effort does the sailor have to exert?

First, write the formula down:

$$E_1 \times L_1 = E_2 \times L_2$$

Here $L_1 = 5$; $E_2 = 1,000$ pounds; and $L_2 = 1$.

Substitute these values in the formula, and it reads.

$$E_1 \times 5 = 1,000 \times 1$$

and

$$E_1 = \frac{1,000}{5} = 200 \text{ pounds}$$

It follows that the mechanical advantage in this case is:

$$\text{M.A.} = \frac{E_2}{E_1} = \frac{L_1}{L_2} = 5$$

and the capstan can be turned against a given resistance by applying a force or effort of only one-fifth its magnitude.

THE COUPLE

Take a look at Figure 13. It's another capstan turning situation. To increase effective effort, a second capstan bar is placed opposite the first and another sailor can now apply a force on the second bar. The two sailors in Figure 13 will apparently be pushing in opposite directions.

But, since they are on opposite sides of the axle, they are actually causing rotation in the same direction. And, if the two sailors are pushing with equal force, the moment of force is twice as great than if only one sailor was pushing. This arrangement is known technically as a **couple** and it is a special example of a wheel and axle.

The moment of force is equal to the product of the total distance L_T between the two points of effort and the force E_1 applied by one sailor. The equation for the couple may be written

$$E_1 \times L_T = E_2 \times L_2$$

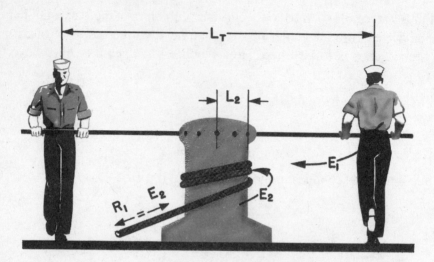

Figure 13 — A couple

THE INCLINED PLANE AND THE WEDGE

Ramps and mountain highways are two simple examples of inclined planes. Large loads can be moved by applying small forces. The wedge is a single or double movable inclined plane.

The Barrel Role

The load is raised to a certain height by applying a relatively small force through a longer distance. Look at Figure 14. Here you see the driver easing the 300-pound barrel up to the bed of the truck, three feet above the sidewalk. He is using a plank nine feet long. If he didn't use the ramp at all, he'd have to apply a 300-pound force straight up through the three-foot distance. With the ramp, however, he can apply his effort over the entire nine feet of the plank as the barrel is slowly rolled up to a height of three feet. It looks, then, as if he could use a force only one-third ($^{3 \text{ feet}}/_{9 \text{ feet}}$) of 300, or 100 pounds, to do the job. The mechanical advantage is therefore 3.

Here's the formula, which is very similar to that of the lever:

$$\text{M.A.} = \frac{L}{l} = \frac{R}{E}$$

Here, however, we have:

L = length of the ramp, measured along the slope

l = height of the ramp

R = weight of object to be raised, or lowered

E = force required to raise or lower object

Applying the formula to this problem:

$$\frac{9}{3} = \frac{300}{E}$$

$$9E = 900$$

$$E = 100 \text{ pounds}$$

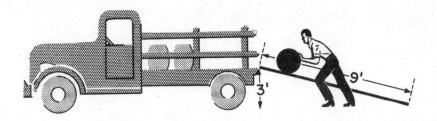

Figure 14

The Wedge

The wedge is a special application of an inclined plane. It consists of two inclined planes, set base to base. By driving the wedge full-length into the material to be cut or split, the material is forced apart a distance equal to the width of the board end of the wedge. See Figure 15.

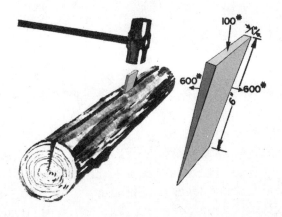

Figure 15 — The wedge

Long, slim wedges give high mechanical advantage. For example, the wedge of Figure 15 has a mechanical advantage of six, found by dividing the length (or depth) of the wedge by its width. It's hard to imagine how one would split a log with other machines such as a system of pulleys instead of a wedge.

THE SCREW

A Modified Inclined Plane

A screw is basically an inclined plane wrapped around a cylindrical shaft that forms a continuous helix. The corrugations of a screw are known as threads, and the distance between any two adjacent threads is called the pitch of the screw, p. See Figure 16.

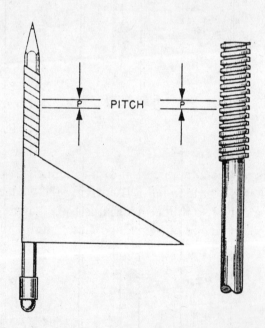

Figure 16 — A screw is an inclined plane in spiral form.

The Jack

A typical example of screw is a jack screw, a machine used to raise a bulky and heavy load. The jack has a lever handle with a length R, see Figure 17. If you pull the lever handle around one turn, its outer end has described a circle. The circumference of this circle is equal to 2π (where π = 3.1416). That is the distance, or the lever arm, through which you effort is applied.

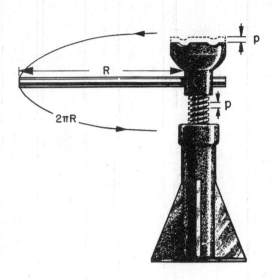

Figure 17 — The jack screw

At the same time, the screw has made one revolution, and in doing so has been raised a height equal to its pitch p. Recalling that the theoretical mechanical advantage is the ratio of the distance through which the effort is applied to the distance the resistance or load is moved, we have:

$$\text{T.M.A.} = \frac{2\pi r}{p}$$

in which

r = length of handle

p = pitch.

Assuming a 2 foot (24") length for the lever arm, and a $\frac{1}{4}$ inch pitch for the thread, you can find the theoretical mechanical advantage by the formula:

$$\text{T.M.A.} = \frac{2 \times 3.1416 \times 24}{\frac{1}{4}} = \frac{150.79}{0.25} = 603.19$$

A 50-pound pull on the handle would result in a theoretical lift of 50 × 603.19 or about 30,000 pounds.

But jacks have considerable friction loss. This is fortunate, however, for if no friction were present, the weight of the load would cause the jack to spin right back down to the bottom as soon as you released the handle.

THE MICROMETER

The micrometer is a useful device for making very accurate small measurements, of the order of a few thousandths of an inch. In Figure 18, you see a cutaway view of a micrometer.

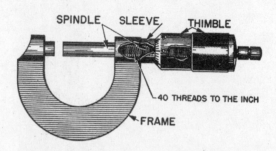

Figure 18 — The micrometer

The thimble turns freely on the sleeve, which is rigidly attached to the micrometer frame. The spindle is attached to the thimble, and is fitted with screw threads which move the spindle and thimble to the right or left in the sleeve when you rotate the thimble. These screw threads are cut 40 threads to the inch. Hence, one turn of the thimble moves the spindle and thimble $1/40$ inch which represents one of the smallest divisions on the micrometer. Also, to allow very fine measurements, the thimble is divided into 25 equal sections laid out by graduation marks around its rim. Since one complete revolution rotating through 25 such sections moves the spindle $1/40$ of an inch, it is easy to see that one of these smaller sections corresponds to a move of the spindle a distance of $1/25$ of $1/40$ inch, or $1/1000$ of an inch.

GEARS

An eggbeater (Figure 19) gives you a simple demonstration of the three things that gears do. They can change the direction of motion; increase or decrease the speed of the applied motion; and magnify or reduce the force which you apply. Gears also give you a positive drive. There can be, and usually is, creep or slip in a belt drive. But gear teeth are always in mesh, and there can be no creep or slip.

Follow the directional changes in Figure 19. Notice that as *B* turns in a clockwise direction, *C* revolves in the opposite direction. Now consider how the gears change the speed of motion. There are 32 teeth on gear *A* and 8 teeth on gear *B*. But the gears mesh, so that one complete revolution of *A* results in four complete revolutions of *B* and *C*. Thus the blades revolve four times as fast as the crank handle.

You have previously learned that third-class levers increase speed at the expense of force. The same thing happens with this eggbeater. The magnitude of the force is changed. The force required to turn the handle is greater than the force applied to the frosting by the blades. Therefore a mechanical advantage of less than one results.

Types of Gears

The most commonly used gears are the straight spur gears. Motion can be transmitted from one parallel shaft to another parallel shaft by means of spur gears. This setup is shown in Figure 20. Spur gears are wheels with mating teeth cut in their surfaces so that one can turn the other without slippage. The mating teeth in this case are cut so that they are parallel to the axis of rotation.

When two gears of unequal size are

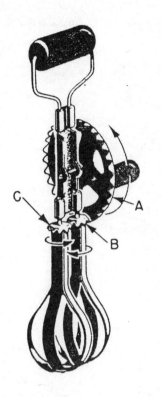

Figure 19 — A simple gear arrangement

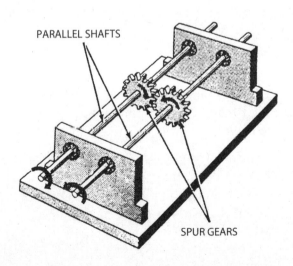

PARALLEL SHAFTS

SPUR GEARS

Figure 20 — Spur gears coupling two parallel shafts

meshed together, the smaller of the two is called a pinion.

Helical gears are another type of spur gear. Study Figure 21 for the types of gears discussed here.

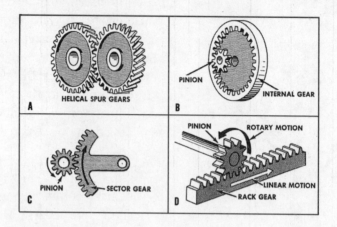

Figure 21 — Gear types

In helical gears, the teeth are cut slant-wise across the working face of the gear. One end of the tooth, therefore, lies ahead of the other.

In the straight spur gears the whole width of the teeth comes in contact at the same time. But with helical (spiral) gears, contact between two teeth starts first at the leading ends and moves progressively across the gear faces until the trailing ends are in contact. Such gears have the disadvantage in that gears tend to thrust or push axially on the shaft, thus requiring a thrust bearing on the shaft to counteract this thrust. But they have the advantage of less lost motion and smoother, quieter action.

Figure 21 also shows three other gear arrangements in common use. The internal gear in Figure 21B has teeth on the inside of a ring, pointing inward toward the axis of rotation. An internal gear is always meshed with an external gear, or pinion, whose center is offset from the center of the internal gear. Either the internal or pinion gear can be the driver gear, and the gear ratio is calculated by counting the number of teeth.

Often only a portion of a gear is needed where the motion of the pinion is limited. In this case the sector gear (Figure 21C) is used to save space and material. The rack and pinion in Figure 21D are both spur gears. This arrangement is useful in changing rotary motion into linear motion.

The Bevel Gear

When shafts are not parallel, the bevel gear is used. It can connect shafts lying at any given angle because they can be beveled to suit the angle.

A special case of the bevel gear is the miter gear, which is used to connect shafts having a 90° angle, which means the gear faces are beveled at a 45° angle.

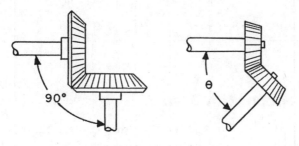

Figure 22 — Bevel gears

You will also run across spiral bevel gears with teeth cut so as to have advanced and trailing ends. Figure 23 shows what they look like. Spiral bevel gears have the same advantage as other spiral (helical) gears — less lost motion and smoother, quieter operation.

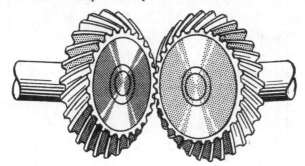

Figure 23 — Spiral bevel gears

The Worm and Worm Wheel

Worm and worm-wheel combinations, like those in Figure 24, have many uses and advantages. Figure 24A shows the action of a single-thread worm. For each revolution of the worm, the worm wheel turns one tooth. Thus if the worm wheel has 25 teeth, the gear ratio is 25:1.

Figure 24B shows a double-thread worm. For each revolution of the worm in this case, the worm wheel turns two teeth. That makes the gear ratio 25:2, if the worm wheel has 25 teeth. Tremendous mechanical advantages can be obtained with such worm gear arrangements.

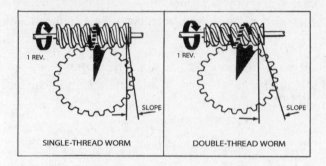

Figure 24 — Worm gears

Changing Direction With Gears

Gears can be used to change the direction of motion. You are familiar with the crankshaft in an automobile engine which turns in only one direction. If you want the car to go backwards, the effect of the engine's rotation must be reversed. This is done by a reversing gear in the transmission, not by reversing the direction in which the crankshaft turns.

Changing Speed

The watch or clock is an example of how gears are used to change the speed of motion. The mainspring slowly unwinds and causes the hour hand to make one revolution in 12 hours. Through a series of gears, the minute hand makes one revolution each hour, while the second hand goes around once per minute.

You can solve any gear speed-reduction problem with this formula:

$$S_2 = S_1 \times \frac{T_1}{T_2}$$

where

S_1 = speed of first shaft in train

S_2 = speed of last shaft in train

T_1 = product of teeth on all drivers

T_2 = product of teeth on all driven gears

Now use the formula on the gear train of Figure 25:

$$S_2 = S_1 \times \frac{T_1}{T_2} = 4 \times \frac{10 \times 20}{40 \times 10} = \frac{800}{400} = 2 \text{ revs. per sec.}$$

Magnifying Force with Gears

Gear trains are used to increase the mechanical advantage. In fact, wherever there is a speed reduction, the effect of the effort you apply is multiplied. Consider the cable winch in Figure 25. The crank arm is 30 inches long, and the drum on which the cable is wound has a 15-inch radius. The small pinion gear has 10 teeth, which mesh with the 60 teeth on the internal spur gear. In order to figure out the mechanical advantage of this machine, we can think of it as a combination of two machines, and then take the product of their mechanical advantages.

Consider the gear and pinion first. The theoretical mechanical advantage of any arrangement of two meshed gears can be found by the following formula:

$$\text{T.M.A.} = \frac{T_o}{T_a}$$

in which,

T_o = number of teeth on driven gear

T_a = number of teeth on driver gear

Figure 25 — This magnifies your effort.

In this case, $T_o = 60$ and $T_a = 10$. Then,

$$\text{T.M.A.} = \frac{T_o}{T_a} = \frac{60}{10} = 6.$$

Now, for the other part of the machine, which is a simple wheel-and-axle arrangement consisting of the crank arm and the drum, the theoretical mechanical advantage can be found by dividing the distance the effort moves, $2\pi R$, by the distance the cable is drawn up, $2\pi r$, in one revolution of the drum:

$$\text{T.M.A.} = \frac{2\pi R}{2\pi r} = \frac{R}{r} = \frac{30}{15} = 2$$

Taking the product of the two mechanical advantages, the overall theoretical mechanical advantage of the winch is 6×2, or 12.

Because of friction, however, the actual mechanical advantage may be only 7 or 8. Even so, by applying a force of 100 pounds on the handle, you could lift a load of 700 or 800 pounds.

WORK AND POWER

Measurement

Work, in the mechanical sense of the term, is done when a resistance is overcome by a force acting through a measurable distance. Notice that two factors are involved: force and movement through a distance. The force is normally measured in pounds, and the distance in feet. Work, therefore, is commonly measured in units called foot-pounds. You do one foot-pound of work when you apply a pound of force on any object through a distance of one foot. Writing this as a formula, it becomes:

WORK = FORCE × DISTANCE

(foot-pounds) = (pounds) × (feet).

Thus, if you lift a 90-pound bag through a vertical distance of 5 feet, you will do

WORK = 90 × 5 = 450 ft-lb.

First, in calculating the work done, you measure the actual resistance being overcome. Second, you have to move the resistance to do any work on it.

You already know about the mechanical advantage of a lever. Now consider it in terms of getting work done easily. Look at Figure 26. The load weighs 300 lbs, and you want to lift it up onto a platform a foot above the deck. How much work must you do on it? The answer is 300 foot-pounds of work. You can't make this work any smaller by the use of any machine. However, if you use the eight-foot plank as shown, you can do that amount of work by applying a smaller force through a longer distance.

Since the mechanical advantage is 3, a 100-pound push down on the end of the plank will raise the 300-pound crate.

Figure 26 — Push 'em up.

Through how long a distance will you have to exert that 100-pound push? Neglecting friction, the work done on the machine is equal to the work done by the machine:

Work put in = Work put out

Thus

$$F_1 \times S_1 = F_2 \times S_2$$

in which

F_1 = effort applied, in pounds

S_1 = distance through which effort moves, in feet

F_2 = resistance overcome, in pounds

S_2 = distance resistance is moved, in feet

Now substitute the known values, and you obtain

$$100 \times S_1 = 300 \times 1$$

or $\qquad S_1 = 3$ feet.

The advantage of using the lever is not that it makes any less work for you, but that it allows you to do the job with the force at your command.

Friction

Friction is the resistance that one surface offers to its movement over another surface.

Wherever you apply force to cause motion, friction makes the actual mechanical advantage fall short of the theoretical mechanical advantage. Because of friction, you have to make a greater effort to overcome the resistance which you want to move.

Rolling friction is always less than sliding friction. You take advantage of this fact whenever you use ball bearings or roller bearings. When it is necessary, you can decrease the friction by the use of lubricants, such as oil, grease, or soap.

Efficiency

Because of friction, it is obvious that you have to put more work into a machine than you get out of it. No machine is 100% efficient.

A simple way to calculate the efficiency of a machine is to divide the output by the input and convert to percentage:

$$\text{Efficiency} = \frac{\text{output}}{\text{input}} \times 100$$

Now go back to the lever problem illustrated in Figure 26. If a friction force of 30 pounds is present, work has to be done to overcome it, so that the input is now 300 lb-ft plus 30 lb × 3 ft = 90 lb-ft, or 390 lb-ft, and the efficiency is then

$$\frac{\text{output}}{\text{input}} \times 100 = \frac{300}{390} \times 100 = 77\%.$$

Power

Power is the rate of doing work. Thus, power always includes the time element. By formula,

$$\text{Power} = \frac{\text{work, in ft-lb}}{\text{time, in minutes}}.$$

The horsepower is the common unit used for measuring power. James Watt, the inventor of the steam engine, found by experiment that an average horse could lift a 330-pound load straight up through a distance of 100 ft in one minute. By agreement among scientists, that figure of 33,000 lb-ft of work done in one minute has been accepted as the unit of power and it is called the horsepower.

Therefore, to obtain the power in units of horsepower, obtain the ratio

$$\frac{\text{Power (in ft-lb per min)}}{33,000}.$$

FORCE AND PRESSURE

Force

A force is a push or a pull exerted on — or by — an object. You apply a force on a machine, and the machine in turn transmits a force to the load.

Weight is a common force due to the pull gravity exerts on an object.

You can readily measure force with a spring scale. An Englishman named Hooke discovered that if you hang a 1-pound weight on a spring, the spring stretches a certain distance. A 2-pound weight stretches the spring twice as much, and 3 pounds three times as much. By attaching a pointer to the spring and putting a face on the scale and marking on the face the positions of the pointer, you have made a spring scale.

Unfortunately, springs get tired when they get old and they don't always snap back to the original position; hence, they will give inaccurate readings. Luckily other types of force-measuring devices are made. You've seen the sign, "Honest Weight – No Springs" on the butchershop scales. Scales of this type are shown in Figure 27.

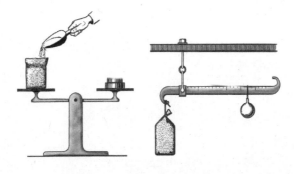

Figure 27 — Balances

Pressure

You know that snowshoes do not reduce the weight, they merely distribute it over a larger area. If you weigh 160 pounds and the area of the soles of your shoes is roughly 60 square inches, each one of those square inches has to carry 160 ÷ 60 = 2.6 pounds of your weight. However, when you put on the snowshoes, you distribute the weight over an area of approximately 900 square inches and now the force on each one of those square inches is equal to only 160 ÷ 900 = 0.18 pound.

Pressure is force per unit area and is measured in pounds per square inch, "psi." With snowshoes on, you exert a pressure of 0.18 psi. To calculate pressure, divide the force by the area over which the force is applied. The formula is

$$\text{Pressure, in psi} = \frac{\text{Force, in lb}}{\text{Area, in sq in}}$$

or $\qquad P = \dfrac{F}{A}$

Measuring Pressure

Fluids — which include both liquids and gases — exert pressure. A fluid at rest exerts equal pressure in all directions. Often it is necessary to

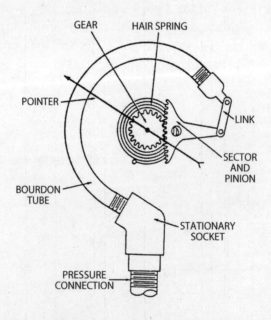

Figure 28 — The Bourdon gage

know the pressure exerted by gas or liquid as in the case of the steam pressure inside a boiler. One device to measure pressure is the Bourdon gage, shown in Figure 28. Its working principle is the same as that of those snakelike paper tubes which you get at a New Year's party. They straighten out when you blow into them.

In the Bourdon gage there is a thin-walled metal tube, somewhat flattened, and bent into the form of a C. Attached to its free end is a lever system which magnifies any motion of the free end of the tube. The fixed end of the gage ends in a fitting which is threaded into the boiler system so that the pressure in the boiler will be transmitted to the tube. Like the paper "snake," the metal tube tends to straighten out when the pressure inside it is increased. As the tube straightens, the pointer is made to move around the dial. Remember, the air is pressing on you all the time. So-called normal atmospheric pressure is 14.7 psi. But as the weather changes, the air pressure may be greater or less than normal. The barometer is a pressure-measuring instrument developed to gather weather data (Figure 29).

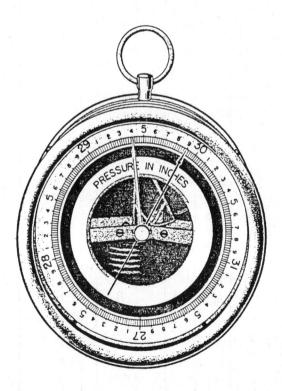

Figure 29 — An aneroid barometer

MACHINE ELEMENTS AND BASIC MECHANISMS

Machine Elements

A machine is made up of one or more basic machine elements or mechanisms. This section will present some of the more familiar elements and mechanisms to be encountered in machinery.

Bearings

You already know that rolling friction is always less than sliding friction. To take advantage of this fact, rollers or bearings are used in machines to reduce friction. Lubricants on bearing surfaces reduce friction even further.

A bearing is a support and guide which carries a moving part of a machine and maintains the proper relationship between the moving part and the stationary part. It usually permits only one form of motion, such as rotation, and prevents any other. There are two basic types of bearings: sliding type (plain bearings), also called friction or guide bearings, and antifrictional type (roller and ball bearings).

Sliding Type (Plain) Bearings

In this type of bearing, a film of lubricant separates the stationary part from the moving part. There are three types of sliding motion bearings in common use: reciprocal motion bearings, thrust bearings, and journal bearings.

Reciprocal motion bearings provide a bearing surface on which an object slides back and forth. They are found on reciprocating steam pumps where connecting rods slide on bearing surfaces near their connections to the pistons. Such bearings are commonly found on the connecting rods of large internal-combustion engines, and in many mechanisms operated by cams.

Thrust bearings are used on rotating shafts, such as those that support bevel gears, worm gears, propellers, and fans. They are installed to reduce axial movement and resist axial thrust and are found mainly on heavy machinery.

A **journal bearing** is composed of two essential parts, the journal, which is the inner cylindrical or conical part and which usually rotates, and the bearing or surrounding shell, which may be stationary, as in the case of lineshaft bearings, or moving, as in a connecting rod bearing.

Antifrictional or Roller and Ball Bearings

You may have encountered these ball bearings in roller skates, skateboard, or bicycle wheels. If any of the little steel balls came out and were lost, your wheels screeched and groaned. The balls or rollers were of hard, highly polished steel. The typical bearing consisted of two hardened steel rings (called races), the hardened steel balls or rollers, and a separator. The motion occurred between the race surfaces and the rolling elements. Ball bearings of this type have since been replaced by more modern antifrictional bearings.

Springs

Springs are elastic objects generally made of metal which can be twisted, pulled, or stretched by some force, and which have the ability to return to their original shape when released. The metal of which they are made is usually steel, though sometimes it's phosphor bronze, brass, or other alloys. A part that is subject to constant spring pressure or thrust is said to be "spring loaded." However, some components which may appear to be spring loaded are actually under hydraulic or pneumatic pressure, or are moved by weights.

Functions of Springs

Some of the more common functional purposes of springs are listed below. Try to consider applications of them as you read them.

1. To store energy for part of a functioning cycle.

2. To force a component to bear against, to maintain contact with, to engage, to disengage, or to remain clear of, some other component.

3. To counterbalance a weight or thrust (gravitational, hydraulic, etc.). Such springs are usually called equilibrator springs.

4. To maintain electrical continuity.

5. To return a component to its original position after displacement.

6. To reduce shock or impact by gradually checking the motion of a moving weight.

7. To permit some freedom of movement between aligned components without disengaging them. These are sometimes called takeup springs.

Types of Springs

There are basically three types of springs: flat, spiral, and helical or coil. See Figure 9–1 for this discussion.

Flat springs include various forms of elliptic or leaf springs (Figure 30, A (1 & 2)), made up of flat or slightly curved bars, plates, or leaves, and special flat springs (Figure 30, A(3)). A special flat spring is made from a flat strip or bar, into a shape calculated for its purpose.

Spiral springs, also known as clock, power, or coil springs (Figure 30, (B)) are wound and gradually release their power as they unwind. Other books use the qualification "spiral" for helical springs discussed below.

Helical springs, often called coil, but not in this text, are probably the most common type of spring. They may be used in compression (Figure 30, D(1)), extension or tension (Figure 30, D(2)), or torsion (Figure 30, D(3)). A spring used in compression tends to shorten in action, while a tension spring lengthens in action. Torsion springs are made to transmit a twist instead of a direct pull, and operate by a coiling or uncoiling action.

Furthermore, cone, double cone, keg, and volute springs are also classed as helical. These are usually used in compression. A **cone** spring

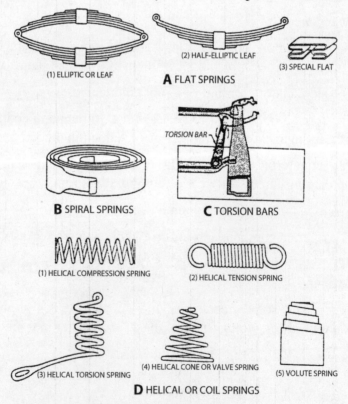

Figure 30 — Types of springs

(Figure 30, D(4)), often called a valve spring because it is frequently used in valves, is shaped by winding the wire on a tapered mandrel instead of a straight one. A **double cone** spring (not illustrated) is composed of two cones joined at the small ends, and a **keg** spring (not illustrated) is two cone springs joined at their large ends.

Volute springs (Figure 30, D(5)) are conical springs made from a flat bar which is wounded so that each coil partially overlaps the adjacent one. The width (and thickness) of the material gives it great strength or resistance. A conical spring can be pressed flat so it requires little space, and it is not likely to buckle sidewise.

Torsion bars (Figure 30, C) are straight bars that are acted on by torsion (twisting force). The bar may be circular or rectangular in cross section, or occasionally, in other shapes such as a tube.

Basic Mechanisms

The Gear Differential

A gear differential is a mechanism that is capable of adding and subtracting the total revolutions of two shafts and delivers the answer by positioning a third shaft. The gear differential will add or subtract any number of revolutions, or very small fractions of revolutions, continuously and accurately. It will produce a continuous series of answers as the inputs change.

Figure 31 is a cutaway drawing of a bevel gear differential showing all its parts and how they are related to each other. Four bevel gears are grouped around the center of the mechanism and are meshed together. The two bevel gears on either side are called end gears. The two bevel gears above and below are called "spider gears." The long shaft running through the end gears and the three spur gears constitute the "spider shaft." The

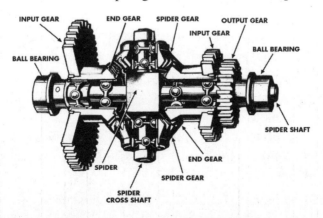

Figure 31 — Bevel gear differential

short shaft running through the spider gears together with the spider gears themselves make up the "spider."

Each of the spider gears and the end gears are bearing-mounted on their shafts and are free to rotate. The spider shaft is rigidly connected with the spider cross shaft at the center block where they intersect. The ends of the spider shaft are secured in flanges or hangers, and they are bearing mounted so the shaft is free to rotate on its axis.

It follows then that to rotate the spider shaft, the spider (consisting of the spider cross shaft and the spider gears) must tumble, or spin, on the axis of the spider shaft, inasmuch as the two shafts are rigidly connected.

The three spur gears shown in Figure 31 are used to connect the two end gears and the spider shaft to other mechanisms. They may be of any convenient size. Each of the two input spur gears is attached to an end gear. An input gear and an end gear together are called a *side* of a differential. The third spur gear is the output gear, as designated in Figure 31. This gear is the only one pinned to the spider shaft. All of the other gears, both level and spur, in the differential are bearing mounted.

Linkages

A linkage may consist of either one or more of the following parts:

1. Rod, shaft, or plunger
2. Lever
3. Rocker arm
4. Bell crank

By combining these parts, it's possible to transmit limited rotary or linear motion. Cams are used with the linkage to change the direction of a motion. For equipment that has to be opened and closed, lever-type linkages are used; for instance, valves in electric-hydraulic systems, gates, clutches, clutch-solenoid interlocks, etc. Another special use of such levers is rocker arms.

Bell cranks are used primarily to transmit motion from a link traveling in one direction to another link which is to be moved in a different direction. The bell crank is mounted on a fixed pivot, and the two links are connected at two points in different directions from the pivot. By locating the connection points properly, the output links can be made to move in any desired direction.

All linkages require occasional adjustments or repair, particularly when they become worn. Typical adjustments consist of lengthening or shortening the rods and shafts by means of a clevis or turnbuckle.

Couplings

A coupling is any device that holds two parts together. Line shafts which are made up of several shafts of different lengths may be held together by any of several types of shaft couplings. The sleeve coupling may be used when shafts are very closely aligned. It is the type with a metal tube slit at each end. These ends enable the clamps to fasten the sleeve securely to the shaft ends. With the clamps tightened, the shafts are held firmly together and turn as one shaft. The sleeve coupling also serves as a convenient device for making adjustments between units. The weight at the opposite end of the clamp from the screw is merely to offset the weight of the screw and clamp arms. By distributing the weight more evenly, shaft vibration is reduced.

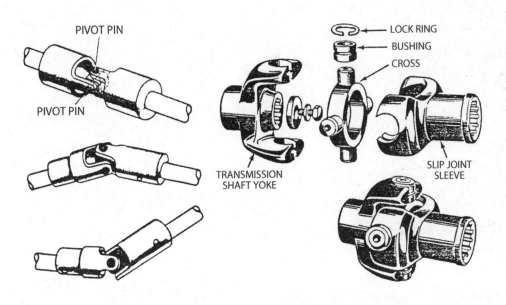

Figure 32 — Universal joint (Hooke type)

Figure 33 — Ring and trunnion universal joint

When two shafts that are not in the same plane, must be coupled, a **universal joint** is needed. Universal joints are used in all types and classes of machinery. An elementary universal joint, sometimes called a Hooke joint (Figure 32), is made up of two U-shaped yokes fastened to the ends of the shafts to be connected. The yokes are held together so that each can bend, or pivot with respect to the other. Figure 33 illustrates a ring and trunnion type of universal joint. This is commonly used in automobile drive shaft systems. Where a smoother torque transmission is desired, and less structural strength required, the Bendix-Weiss universal joint is used (Figure 34). This type of joint transmits motion with constant angular velocity and doesn't have the whipping motion which occurs in the Hooke type; however, it is more expensive and not as strong as the latter.

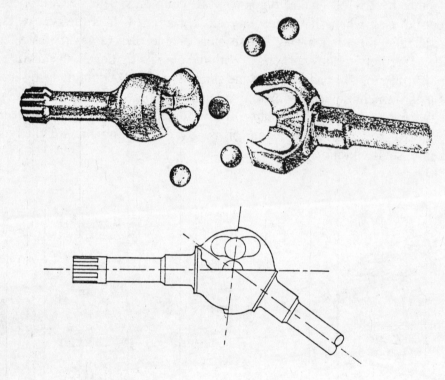

Figure 34 — Bendix-Weiss universal joint

Cam and Cam Followers

A cam is a specially shaped surface, projection, or groove whose movement with respect to a part in contact with it (cam follower) drives the cam follower in another movement in response.

Cams are not ordinarily used to transmit power in the sense that gear trains are. They are generally used to modify mechanical movement, the power for which is furnished through other means. A cam may be a projection on a revolving shaft (or on a wheel) for the purpose of changing the direction of motion from rotary to up-and-down, or vice versa. It may also be a sliding piece or a groove to impart an eccentric motion. Some cams do not make any movement at all, but change the motion of a piece in contact with it.

CLUTCHES

Types

A clutch is a form of coupling which is designed to connect or disconnect a driving and a driven member for starting or stopping the driven part. There are two general classes of clutches — friction clutches and positive clutches, see Figure 35.

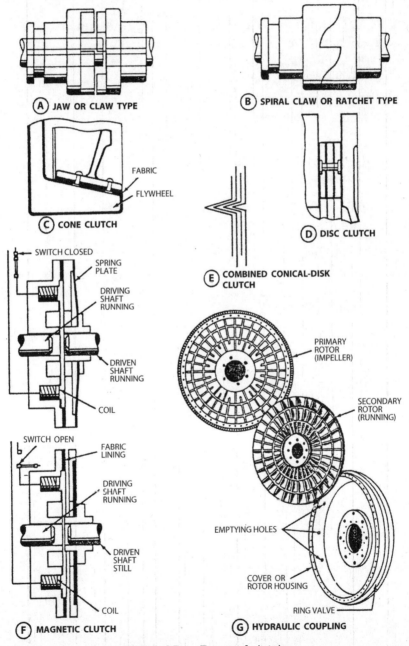

Ⓐ JAW OR CLAW TYPE

Ⓑ SPIRAL CLAW OR RATCHET TYPE

FABRIC

FLYWHEEL

Ⓒ CONE CLUTCH

Ⓓ DISC CLUTCH

Ⓔ COMBINED CONICAL-DISK CLUTCH

SWITCH CLOSED

SPRING PLATE

DRIVING SHAFT RUNNING

DRIVEN SHAFT RUNNING

COIL

PRIMARY ROTOR (IMPELLER)

SECONDARY ROTOR (RUNNING)

SWITCH OPEN

FABRIC LINING

DRIVING SHAFT RUNNING

DRIVEN SHAFT STILL

EMPTYING HOLES

COVER OR ROTOR HOUSING

RING VALVE

COIL

Ⓕ MAGNETIC CLUTCH

Ⓖ HYDRAULIC COUPLING

Figure 35 — Types of clutches

The purpose of a friction clutch is to connect a rotating member to one that is stationary and to bring it up to speed, and to transmit power with a minimum of slippage. Figure 35C shows a cone clutch commonly used in motor trucks. They may be single-cone or double-cone. Figure 35D shows a disc clutch, also used in autos. A disc clutch may also have a number of plates and is then known as a multiple-disc clutch. You may have encountered a multiple-disc clutch on your car which is a series of discs, where each driven disc is located between two driving discs.

Figure 35E illustrates a combined conical disc clutch known as the Hele-Shaw clutch. The groove allows for circulation of oil and for cooling. Single-disc clutches are frequently dry clutches (no lubrication), while multiple-disc clutches may be dry or wet (lubricated or run in oil). Magnetic clutches are a recent development in which the friction surfaces are brought together by magnetic force when the electricity is turned on (Figure 35F).

The induction clutch transmits power without contact between driving and driven members.

In diesel engines and transportation equipment, pneumatic and hydraulic clutches are used (Figure 35G).

Positive clutches have teeth which interlock. The simplest is the jaw or claw type (Figure 35A), which is used only at low speeds. The spiral claw or ratchet type (Figure 35B) cannot be reversed. An example of such a clutch is seen in bicycles — it engages the rear sprocket with the rear wheel when the pedals are pushed forward, and lets the rear wheel revolve freely when the pedals are stopped.

ELECTRICAL AND ELECTRONICS REVIEW

Electricity is a very large part of our lives. It is possible that there is nothing used today by the average person that does not operate without electricity. Yet, we rarely pay attention to electricity.

Electrical systems all follow one basic law of electricity: Ohm's Law. This following review will attempt to outline Ohm's Law as well as other laws that are used to define and explain certain electrical phenomena.

OHM'S LAW

Electrical current flow is the basis for all electrical systems. Current is defined as the flow of electrons for a given unit of time. As an equation it is written as:

$$I = \frac{dq}{dt}$$

where dq is the increment of charge passing by for a time dt.

A good way to think of current is to think of water flowing in a pipe — the water in the pipe is analogous to the electrons in a wire. The pressure that pushes the water through the pipe is known as a voltage potential or simply voltage in electrical terms.

The relationship describing the voltage between two points in a wire and the subsequent current flowing through the wire between those two points is shown below by Ohm's Law:

$$(V) = (R) [I] \tag{1}$$

(volts) = (ohms) [amps]

where: V =   the voltage between two points

            I =   the current passing between two points

            R =   the resistance between the two points
(note: the resistance can be natural — from the wire itself or externally added — known as a resistor.)

The symbols used to represent the three quantities V, I, and R are:

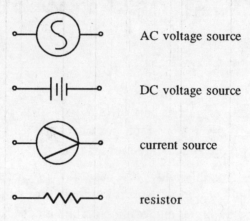

AC voltage source

DC voltage source

current source

resistor

Figure 1

Electrical Power

From Ohm's Law the power relationship can be determined. The power produced or used by an electrical system is quite common to most of us when discussing stereos. A stereo that puts out 200 Watts across a 4-ohm load is producing 100 Watts of power across a resistance of 8 ohms. What does this mean?

First, let us give the power equation.

(Power) = (Voltage) × (Current)

$$P = VI \qquad (2)$$

[Watts] = [volts] [amps]

From Ohm's Law we can arrange the power equation (2) various ways:

$$P = V \cdot I \qquad (2a)$$

$$= RI^2 \qquad (2b)$$

$$= \frac{V^2}{R} \qquad (2c)$$

Now let's go back to our stereo — 200 Watts across a 4-ohm load. The reason the power is given with respect to a load resistance should be obvious from equation (2c). If the resistance, R, changes so will the output P. Therefore, when purchasing a stereo, always make sure the power output given is for the load that you will be using. The difference between speakers that are 4 ohms and 8 ohms is 100 Watts — that is a lot of power.

Electrical Circuits

Ohm's Law can be applied to all electrical systems. It is the basis for solving and understanding electrical circuits.

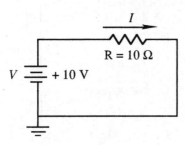

Figure 2

The above figure is a simple circuit containing a battery (the voltage source) and a resistor. If the voltage source (they are also known as generators by some) is 10 V and the resistor is 10 ohms (also shown as 10 Ω), how much current flows through the resistor R?

Using Ohm's Law

$$V = RI$$

$$10 \text{ V} = 10 \ \Omega \ I$$

$$\frac{10 \text{ V}}{10 \ \Omega} = I = 1 \text{ amp}$$

From here all circuit solving methods are just extensions of what we know. Here are some fundamental rules:

Simple Circuit Rules

1. Resistors in series are added.

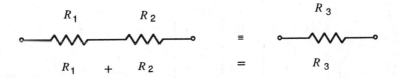

Figure 3

2. Resistors in parallel are the inverse of the added reciprocals.

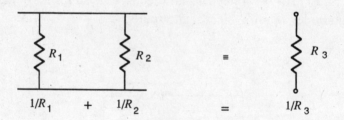

$$1/R_1 \quad + \quad 1/R_2 \qquad = \qquad 1/R_3$$

Figure 4

Note: It doesn't matter if there are 2 resistors or 5,000, the rules are the same.

Electrical Measurements

Electrical measurements are performed by various pieces of equipment.

1. A voltmeter measures voltage.

2. An ammeter measures amps.

3. An ohmmeter measures ohms.

Electrical Effects

As current passes through a wire, a heating phenomenon occurs. If too much current passes through a thin wire, it is possible for the wire to overheat and burn up. It is for this reason that there are national codes. The larger the wire the more current that can be put through it. The reason for this is that all conductors (wires) have some resistance to it.

DC and AC Voltage

DC and AC are acronyms for direct current and alternating current, respectively. A current that remains constant and does not vary over time is known as direct current (or DC) and produces a DC voltage. An alternating current (AC) varies with time periodically and produces a AC voltage.

Electronic Components

Below is a list of electrical components used in circuits.

1. BST — a transistor amplifies current

2. L — an inductor stores voltage

3. C — a capacitor stores charge

4. ⊐Ɛ — a transformer is used to increase or decrease AC voltages and currents in circuits

4. D — a diode rectifies current — in other words, it allows current to pass in one direction and not the other

6. ⊥ — a ground symbol

7. R — a resistor impedes current flow

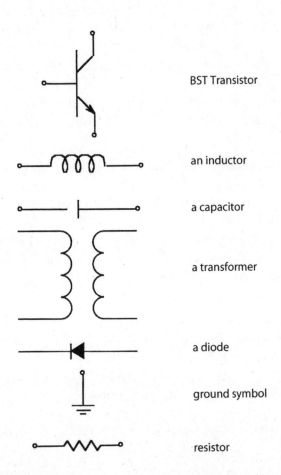

BST Transistor

an inductor

a capacitor

a transformer

a diode

ground symbol

resistor

ASSEMBLING OBJECTS REVIEW

Assembling Objects is a portion of the test that examines a person's spatial abilities. The term *spatial abilities* usually refers to how we see the world visually. This part of the test examines a person's ability to see overall patterns as well as detailed forms. This test is a measure of an aptitude or an ability. The goal of this test is to see what you might be good at doing. The reason these questions are given is to see if you would do well at tasks that involve putting things together, be it in your mind or with your hands.

Most of this portion of the test involves arranging objects into a pattern. For example, small blocks are made into bigger shapes. Some of the test examines the ability to read simple constructional diagrams. Here, the questions will ask the test-taker to arrange objects by using "blueprint" instructions. Some of these questions will involve familiar shapes such as triangles, circles, and rectangles. There may be other shapes that are a little more unusual such as trapezoids and some shapes that are completely unique. The key is to think of this portion of the test as "Legos" or some other similar assembly project. We are all familiar with blocks from playing with them as children. Use what you remember from playing with blocks and you will do well.

The key to answering these questions is first getting comfortable with the directions. You must realize what the test wants you to answer before moving on. Take your time to make sure you understand the question and what is being asked. With Legos, there are two ways to "play". The first is to build whatever the Legos kit was designed for. For example, one would buy a box of Legos that were meant to be turned into a spaceship. To build the spaceship, you read each step of the construction process and you try to emulate what is in the diagram.

The second way to play with Legos is to build a shape out of a set of blocks without instructions. Here you imagine something that you want to have built and you find the correct blocks to build it. However, the task can also be that you have a few Lego blocks and you try to see what they will make. This is the type of question to look at first. We will call these the "Fitting Pieces" questions.

Fitting Pieces:

The goal is to make a whole object out of parts. For example, the question will be **Using the blocks on the left, which shape is possible?**:

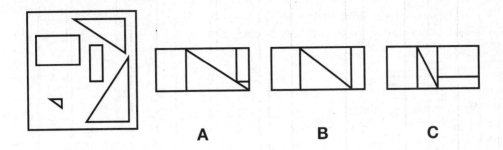

Here we have 5 pieces that can be arranged to make up one of the 3 possible shapes A, B, or C. You must decide which answer works. You may be familiar with these types of questions or this may be something new to you. There are a few tips that will help you answer these questions.

First, you can count the number of objects that make up the shapes. Sometimes this is an easy way to eliminate possible answers.

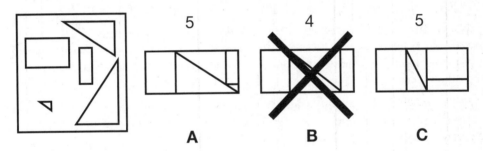

You can see that the shape must have 5 objects. If there are not 5 objects, eliminate the shape. Because B has only 4 objects, it can be eliminated. This is a quick way to eliminate some of the possible answers.

Second, find the biggest, or most unique object. Once you do this, look for that object in each of the shapes. For example:

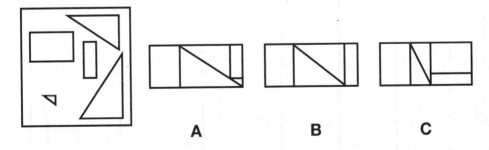

Here the large triangle is highlighted. It is easy to look for this big object and see that it is in A but not in B or C. Notice how this makes it easy to eliminate choices.

Third, a more complicated but thorough strategy is to number each of the objects. Start out by numbering each object in the left and seeing how those numbers correspond:

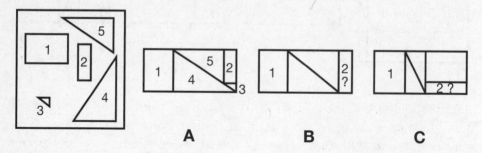

Again, label all of the objects on the left first. Then, try to find those objects in the corresponding pieces. Number 1 is found in all of the objects. Notice that there was a question mark put next to some of the '2s'. This is a notation that is useful. Put a question mark next to the shapes that may or may not correspond. You can always go back and check if needed later. In this example, you do not need to because there is definitely no "3s" in any of the shapes except for A. It is recommended that you fill in all the numbers for the shape you are selecting. In other words, a check for your answer is that all 5 objects should be in shape A. The numbering system is the best and it is recommended if you have the time to do it. Work quickly but efficiently on numbering. When you are unsure if a shape corresponds, put a question mark by it and come back to it later.

Blueprint

The easier of the assembling objects questions are the "Blueprint" questions. Here, you are asked to assemble objects based on looking at a blueprint type diagram. For example, consider the following:

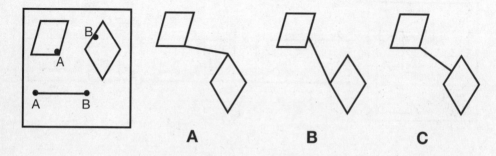

Given the "instructions" from the left panel, which object is the correct construction, A, B, or C?. Here, the correct answer is "C". Using the lines and the markers, you should be connecting the corner of the parallelogram with the middle of the diamond. The line connects point A and B.

There is a very easy way to answer these problems. For each shape, mark a circle on the correct placement. Therefore, for the parallelogram, make circles as follows:

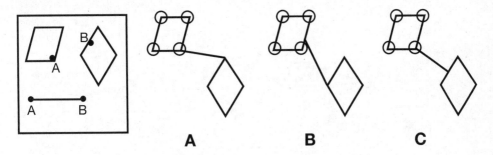

Then make marks for the diamond:

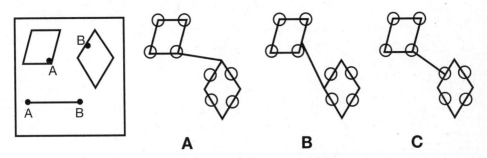

The line will only intercept the circles in one of the cases. Notice that "C" has a line intercepting the circles for both the parallelogram and the diamond. Using this method, you will be more accurate and you will save a lot of time.

ASVAB

Armed Services Vocational Aptitude Battery

Test 2

GENERAL SCIENCE
TEST 2

Time: 11 Minutes
   25 Questions

(Answer sheets appear in the back of this book.)

DIRECTIONS: This is a test of 25 questions to find out how much you know about general science as usually covered in high school courses. Pick the best answer for each question, then blacken the space on your answer form which has the same number and letter as your choice.

---

1. All of the following are true of vascular plants except they

   1–A   lack tubes, true roots, leaves, and stems.

   1–B   can live far from water.

   1–C   can be very large.

   1–D   may produce seeds.

2. Roundworms belong to the phylum

   2–A   Mollusca.   2–C   Chordata.

   2–B   Nematoda.   2–D   Porifera.

3. Ferns do not have

   3–A   spores.   3–C   roots.

   3–B   leaves.   3–D   seeds.

4. The blood component responsible for producing antibodies is

   4–A   red blood cells.   4–C   platelets.

   4–B   white blood cells. 4–D   plasma.

5. A person suffering from night blindness might be able to improve his/her condition by increasing consumption of

5–A vitamin A.   5–C vitamin C.

5–B vitamin B_{12}.   5–D vitamin D.

6. The normal number of chromosomes in a human cell is

6–A 52.   6–C 30.

6–B 108.   6–D 46.

7. In an ecosystem, an example of a producer is a

7–A fungus.   7–C wolf.

7–B maple tree.   7–D rock.

8. Animal cells do not contain

8–A cell membranes.   8–C chloroplasts.

8–B ribosomes.   8–D mitochondria.

9. A weight lifter presses 150 pounds two feet into the air. The work he does is equal to

9–A 75 newton-meters   9–C 148 newton-meters.

9–B 152 foot-pounds.   9–D 300 foot-pounds.

10. When a match burns,

10–A all chemical energy is destroyed.

10–B all kinetic energy is destroyed.

10–C mechanical energy changes to light energy.

10–D chemical energy is changed to heat energy.

11. Among the following substances, the best insulator is

11–A copper.   11–C water.

11–B air.   11–D aluminum.

12. When wire is moved through a magnetic field, _____ is produced.

12–A current   12–C mass

12–B light   12–D charge

13. Which color is not present when sunlight creates a spectrum by passing through a prism?

    13–A Brown   13–C Violet

    13–B Indigo   13–D Orange

14. A high-pitched sound has a greater _____ than a low-pitched sound.

    14–A amplitude   14–C speed

    14–B frequency   14–D hertz

15. The atomic number of a compound indicates the

    15–A mass of an atom.

    15–B number of protons in an atom.

    15–C charge of an atom.

    15–D energy level of an atom.

16. Molecules have the lowest average kinetic energy in a

    16–A plasma.   16–C liquid.

    16–B gas.   16–D solid.

17. The most common solvent is

    17–A air.   17–C salt.

    17–B water.   17–D oxygen.

18. In the equation $C + O_2 \longrightarrow CO_2$, CO_2 can be called a (n)

    18–A reactant.   18–C solute.

    18–B ion.   18–D product.

19. The thickest layer of the earth is called the

    19–A crust.   19–C mantle.

    19–B core.   19–D lava.

20. Life is most abundant in which atmospheric layer?

    20–A Ionosphere

    20–B Thermosphere

    20–C Stratosphere

    20–D Troposphere

21. One rotation of the earth takes

    21–A 24 hours.

    21–B $27^1/3$ days.

    21–C $365^1/4$ days.

    21–D one year.

22. Rock formed by the cooling and hardening of molten material is called

    22–A igneous.

    22–B crystal.

    22–C metamorphic.

    22–D sedimentary.

23. The smallest part of an element that still has the properties of that element is a(n)

    23–A atom.

    23–B molecule.

    23–C proton.

    23–D compound.

24. In photosynthesis, what is formed?

    24–A Glucose

    24–B Carbon dioxide

    24–C Water

    24–D Chlorophyll

25. The bicep muscle is made of

    25–A cardiac muscle.

    25–B involuntary muscle.

    25–C voluntary muscle.

    25–D smooth muscle.

ARITHMETIC REASONING
TEST 2

Time: 36 Minutes
      30 Questions

(Answer sheets appear in the back of this book.)

DIRECTIONS: Each question has four multiple-choice answers, labeled by the number of the question and the letters A, B, C, or D. Select the single best answer.

---

1. Bill buys seven bags of chips for a party. Each bag costs $0.89. What is the total cost?

    1–A $5.23   1–C $6.23

    1–B $6.32   1–D $6.30

2. Scott earns $35,000 per year, and pays 28% tax. How much does he pay in tax per year?

    2–A $10,500   2–C $9,000

    2–B $10,000   2–D $9,800

3. A lion runs 50 miles per hour in pursuit of a zebra running at 40 miles per hour. If the initial distance between them was a quarter of a mile, how long will it take for the lion to catch the zebra?

    3–A   1.5 minutes   3–C   2 minutes

    3–B   1 minute   3–D   1.5 hours

4. Jeff opens a savings account (paying 5% interest) with $1,000 and a CD (paying 6% interest) with $2,000. After one year, how much interest does he earn?

    4–A $17   4–C $120

    4–B $50   4–D $170

5. A family bought a house for $120,000 and sold it two years later for $155,000. How much profit did they make?

5–A $30,000   5–C $40,000

5–B $35,000   5–D $50,000

6. A company had 500 employees. It laid off 68 of them, then hired back 43 of those. How many employees does the company now have?

6–A 475   6–C 543

6–B 432   6–D 568

7. An omelette requires three eggs. Six people meet for breakfast. How many eggs would be required if they all wanted omelettes?

7–A 16   7–C 18

7–B 17   7–D 19

8. A family of four has 12 rolls to serve as part of dinner. How many rolls will each person receive?

8–A 1   8–C 4

8–B 2   8–D 3

9. An athlete runs two miles in 13.5 minutes. How many minutes is this per mile?

9–A 6.5 minutes   9–C 7 minutes

9–B 6.75 minutes   9–D 7.5 minutes

10. Tracy has a 160 mile drive. She leaves at 8:00 and drives at 40 miles per hour. When will she arrive?

10–A 12:00   10–C 11:30

10–B 11:00   10–D 12:30

11. A running back averages 8.5 yards per carry in a football game. If he rushed for 136 yards in the game, then how many times did he carry the ball?

11–A 14   11–C 16

11–B 15   11–D 17

12. Twelve people go to a dance. Half of them are females, and half of the females are wearing black. How many females are wearing black?

12–A 4   12–C 2

12–B 1   12–D 3

13. Sandy earns $12 per hour. If she works overtime she earns time and a half. How much would she earn for two hours of overtime?

13–A $24   13–C $18

13–B $36   13–D $12

14. Marie's car gets 30 miles to the gallon of gas. If gas cost $1.29 per gallon and Marie wants to drive 20 miles, how much will this cost in gas?

14–A $0.86   14–C $25.80

14–B $2.58   14–D $38.70

15. Jimmy has $7 and spends $3.58 for lunch. How much does he have left?

15–A $3.58   15–C $3.42

15–B $3.40   15–D $3.50

16. Sam has to read 21 pages for homework in history, 16 pages in English, and 13 pages in math. How many pages must Sam read?

16–A 29   16–C 37

16–B 34   16–D 50

17. In a soccer league the record for most goals in a season is 21. Brian has already scored 17, and there are two games left. How many goals must he average per game to tie the record?

17–A 1   17–C 3

17–B 2   17–D 4

18. Grace has six skirts and four blouses. If she mixes and matches, how many combinations can she come up with?

18–A 24   18–C 15

18–B 10   18–D 20

19. If there are 24 hours in a day and seven days in a week, then how many hours are there in a week?

19–A 152   19–C 168

19–B 160   19–D 240

20. A boat usually goes 20 miles per hour, but now there is a wind of five miles per hour working against it. How long will it take this boat to travel 30 miles?

20–A 2 hours   20–C 3 hours

20–B 1.5 hours   20–D 2.5 hours

21. Each soccer team in a league has four defenders, but the all-star team will only have three defenders. If there are 16 teams, then how many defenders will not make the all-star team?

21–A 3   21–C 61

21–B 60   21–D 64

22. A grocer buys candy for 10¢ per package, then marks it up by 100% and then charges 10% tax. What is the final cost?

22–A 19¢   22–C 21¢

22–B 20¢   22–D 22¢

23. A towel manufacturer sells sets which consist of two towels and three wash clothes. If he has 24 towels and 31 wash clothes, how many sets can he sell?

23–A 9   23–C 11

23–B 10   23–D 12

24. Jackie comes to work at 8:30 AM, takes 45 minutes for lunch, and leaves at 5:15 PM. How long did she work?

24–A 8 hours   24–C 8.5 hours

24–B 7.5 hours   24–D 9 hours

25. On a winter morning it is –24 degrees in Detroit and 68 degrees in Los Angeles. How much colder is Detroit than Los Angeles?

    25–A 44 degrees   25–C 92 degrees

    25–B 24 degrees   25–D 68 degrees

26. In a school there are twice as many seniors as freshman, and each class is half male and half female. If there are 300 male freshman, then how many female seniors are there?

    26–A 900   26–C 1,200

    26–B 300   26–D 600

27. Mel does 80 push-ups everyday for a week. How many did he do in that week?

    27–A 80   27–C 560

    27–B 160   27–D 800

28. A quarterback throws 30 passes in a game and completes 60%. How many were incomplete?

    28–A 12   28–C 18

    28–B 15   28–D 20

29. A company has 74 pads of paper in stock. The Accounting Department takes 16 pads, the Finance Department takes 12, and Research & Development takes 29. How many pads are left?

    29–A 29   29–C 17

    29–B 33   29–D 46

30. An independent auditor monitors the outgoing phone calls of employees in a small firm during a one week period. One particular employee is on the phone for 24 minutes on Monday, 21 minutes on Tuesday, 13 minutes on Wednesday, 17 minutes on Thursday, and 15 minutes on Friday. What is this employee's average daily time on the phone?

    30–A 16 minutes   30–C 18 minutes

    30–B 17 minutes   30–D 19 minutes

WORD KNOWLEDGE
TEST 2

Time: 11 Minutes
   35 Questions

(Answer sheets appear in the back of this book.)

DIRECTIONS: The ASVAB Word Knowledge Test is a test of your vocabulary. The test consists of 35 questions, each containing an underlined word. Pick one word from the four choices that you believe is the best synonym for the underlined word. A synonym is a word that has the same or nearly the same meaning as, in this case, the underlined word. On your answer sheet, mark the space that matches your choice. Be sure you are marking your answer in the space that represents the proper question number.

Following are two sample questions.

S1. The policeman thought the report of a UFO sighting in broad daylight was <u>curious</u>.

S1–A Odd   S1–C Remote

S1–B Obscure   S1–D Miraculous

S1. **(A)** ODD is the correct answer. Odd has several meanings; in context, odd means unexpected, peculiar, or strange. (B) OBSCURE means vague, remote, not well known, or ambiguous; (C) REMOTE means distant in space or time, out of the way, slight, or aloof; (D) MIRACULOUS means extraordinary—but this word implies a spiritual or religious association not associated with UFOs.

S2. The best synonym for the word <u>anxious</u> is

S2–A bewildered.   S2–C uneasy.

S2–B careless.   S2–D alert.

S2. **(C)** UNEASY is the correct answer. Of the word choices given, only uneasy (meaning difficult, discomforting, awkward, embarrassing, or worried) can sometimes be used as a synonym for anxious. (A) BEWILDERED means confused; (B) CARELESS means untroubled, indifferent, negligent, or spontaneous; (D) ALERT means active, watchful, intelligent.

1. The best synonym for <u>persuade</u> is

   1–A convince.   1–C sweat.

   1–B believe.   1–D permeate.

2. The best synonym for <u>conversion</u> is

   2–A talk.   2–C come together.

   2–B transformation.   2–D revelation.

3. The best synonym for <u>chagrin</u> is

   3–A horror.   3–C grief.

   3–B boredom.   3–D distress.

4. The best synonym for <u>resist</u> is

   4–A save.   4–C live.

   4–B turn off.   4–D oppose.

5. Sandy believed most teenage girls were <u>superficial</u> because of their preoccupation with shopping.

   5–A shallow   5–C flighty

   5–B excessive   5–D important

6. The best synonym for <u>obsolete</u> is

   6–A inconvenient.   6–C unrewarding.

   6–B discontinued.   6–D futile.

7. The best synonym for <u>fitful</u> is

   7–A irregular.   7–C jaunty.

   7–B sound.   7–D undisciplined.

8. The best synonym for <u>humble</u> is

   8–A delicious.   8–C tedious.

   8–B arrogant.   8–D modest.

9. Every five years the rules of the league were reviewed and <u>modified</u> if necessary.

   9–A limited

   9–B obscured

   9–C altered

   9–D updated

10. The best synonym for <u>scold</u> is

    10–A confuse.

    10–B berate.

    10–C weaken.

    10–D flatter.

11. The best synonym for <u>evade</u> is

    11–A intrude.

    11–B elude.

    11–C abandon.

    11–D disappear.

12. The best synonym for <u>deceive</u> is

    12–A get.

    12–B mislead.

    12–C promise.

    12–D create.

13. The secretary had an <u>urgent</u> message to deliver to the company president.

    13–A tempting

    13–B unnecessary

    13–C professional

    13–D important

14. The best synonym for <u>temper</u> is

    14–A pace.

    14–B lure.

    14–C moderate.

    14–D feud.

15. George's <u>fastidious</u> temperament soon drove his roommate crazy.

    15–A rapid-paced

    15–B demanding

    15–C neat

    15–D quirky

16. The best synonym for <u>appeal</u> is

    16–A interest.

    16–B be visible.

    16–C calm.

    16–D repel.

17. The best synonym for <u>virtuoso</u> is

    17–A scholarly.   17–C kindly.

    17–B skillful.   17–D passionate.

18. The best synonym for <u>inadvertent</u> is

    18–A intentional   18–C thoughtless.

    18–B fickle.   18–D whimsical.

19. The best synonym for <u>profess</u> is

    19–A affirm.   19–C work.

    19–B teach.   19–D outline.

20. The best synonym for <u>reconcile</u> is

    20–A settle.   20–C memorize.

    20–B praise.   20–D rest.

21. The crook had been charged several times with being a <u>fraud</u>.

    21–A vandal   21–C imposter

    21–B embezzler   21–D thief

22. Would you care to <u>articulate</u> what you think the problem is?

    22–A solve   22–C communicate

    22–B debate   22–D consider

23. The best synonym for <u>clever</u> is

    23–A knife-like.   23–C dishonest.

    23–B talented.   23–D shrewd.

24. The best synonym for <u>disprove</u> is

    24–A lie.   24–C argue.

    24–B deny.   24–D prohibit.

25. The best synonym for <u>mediocre</u> is

    25–A unsuccessful.   25–C imperfect.

    25–B healthy.   25–D offensive.

26. The best synonym for <u>dismal</u> is

    26–A spirited.   26–C frightening.

    26–B depressing.   26–D weary.

27. The real estate agent said that $85,000 was <u>undoubtedly</u> the best offer the seller could expect.

    27–A improbably   27–C impossibly

    27–B generally   27–D certainly

28. The two girls had been <u>rivals</u> for almost their entire lives.

    28–A colleagues   28–C employers

    28–B servants   28–D competitors

29. The best synonym for <u>discriminate</u> is

    29–A persecute.   29–C separate.

    29–B implicate.   29–D doubt.

30. The best synonym for <u>introspection</u> is

    30–A self-examination.   30–C concentration.

    30–B shyness.   30–D quietness.

31. Characters in soap operas often experience <u>amnesia</u>.

    31–A depression   31–C forgetfulness

    31–B sleeplessness   31–D phobia

32. The best synonym for <u>ignorant</u> is

    32–A inferior.   32–C inexperienced.

    32–B disgraceful.   32–D foolish.

33. The best synonym for <u>covet</u> is

    33–A shelter.   33–C promise.

    33–B steal.   33–D desire.

34. The best synonym for <u>chronic</u> is

    34–A repeat.   34–C acute.

    34–B painful.   34–D brief.

35. The best synonym for <u>deference</u> is

    35–A avoidance.   35–C resistance.

    35–B dissimilarity.   35–D respect.

PARAGRAPH COMPREHENSION TEST 2

Time: 13 Minutes
15 Questions

(Answer sheets appear in the back of this book.)

> **DIRECTIONS:** This test consists of 15 paragraphs that test your ability to understand and retrieve information from passages you have read. Each paragraph is followed by an incomplete question or statement. You must read each of the paragraphs and select the one lettered choice that best completes the statement or question. Your score is based on the number of correct answers. Try to answer every question, but don't spend too much time on any single question.

Here is a sample paragraph.

S1. People use footwear for three basic reasons: to wear to work, to keep up with fashion, and for play. For example, heavy-soled, steel-toed, and high-ankle workboots are the right thing for the construction worker. Well-decorated and fancy high heels may suit the lady about to go out on a date. But thin-soled, washable "tennys" are the only thing for the avid beachcomber in Bermuda.

The reader can infer from this paragraph that

S2–A beachcombers can't wear boots.

S2–B people choose shoes to suit their purpose.

S2–C people would rather go barefoot.

S2–D high heels are out of date.

S1. **(B)** The correct answer is (B), people choose shoes to suit their purpose.

1. In the beginning, honey was mostly an article of local trade. Many farmers and villagers kept a few colonies of bees in box hives to supply their own needs and those of some friends, relatives, and neighbors. Moses Quimby of New York state was the first commercial beekeeper in the United States. As the use of improved hives and new honey-gathering methods became more widespread, commercial beekeeping spread into other states.

   The best title for this passage would be

   1–A   "A History of Beekeeping."

   1–B   "The Development of Commercial Beekeeping."

   1–C   "Moses Quimby—Commercial Beekeeper."

   1–D   "Beekeeping in New York State."

2. Alzheimer's disease includes serious forgetfulness—particularly about recent events—and confusion. At first the individual experiences only minor symptoms that people mistake for emotional upsets and other physical illnesses. Gradually, the victim becomes more forgetful. The affected person may neglect to turn off the oven, may misplace things, or may repeat already answered questions.

   This passage does *not* imply that victims of Alzheimer's disease may

   2–A   not remember childhood events.

   2–B   suffer a gradual worsening of learning abilities.

   2–C   forget recent events.

   2–D   dislike particular foods.

3. Someone with a great desire to learn is said to be highly motivated. Motivation is very important in what one learns and how quickly one learns it. A motivated person will generally learn faster and more efficiently than an unmotivated one. To learn efficiently a person must *intend* to learn.

   According to the passage, in order to learn quickly one must be

   3–A   highly motivated.

   3–B   unmotivated.

   3–C   tired of learning.

   3–D   in need of learning.

4. High tides arise on the sides of the Earth nearest to and farthest from the moon. At times of new moon and full moon, the sun's attraction reinforces that of the moon, producing higher (spring) tides. Halfway between new and full moon, solar attraction does not occur together with lunar attraction and therefore the difference between high and low tides is less; these lesser tides are called neap tides.

"Tides" are

4–A   the lowest level of water.

4–B   the rise and fall of bodies of water.

4–C   sea level measurements.

4–D   the difference between the sun and the moon.

5. Isaac Newton's supreme scientific work was his theory of universal gravitation. He went to a farm in 1665 to avoid the plague, and during this time he worked out the law of gravity and its consequences for the solar system.

According to the passage, the system of universal gravitation is Newton's

5–A   least important scientific work.

5–B   most disputed scientific work.

5–C   most misunderstood scientific work.

5–D   most important scientific work.

6. At present we are forced to look to other bodies in the solar system for hints as to what the early history of the Earth was like. Studies of our moon, Mercury, Mars, and the large satellites of Jupiter and Saturn have provided much evidence that all these large celestial bodies were bombarded by smaller objects shortly after the large bodies had formed.

Which of the following bodies was *not* studied to give evidence that the Earth was bombarded in its early history?

6–A   Mars

6–B   Mercury

6–C   Jupiter

6–D   Earth's moon

7. Solar energy is becoming a logical alternative source of heat as the cost and unavailability of conventional fuels increases. Technology has now made the cost of harnessing the sun more economically possible. Solar heating and solar cooling are good for the environment, providing another reason to switch from conventional fuels.

Solar heat is becoming a logical source of energy because conventional fuels are

7–A   not expensive enough.

7–B   becoming unavailable.

7–C   attractive environmentally.

7–D   are not as close as the sun.

8. Juan Ponce de Leon was the first Spaniard to touch the shores of the present United States. He never dreamed that his "island" of Florida was a peninsular extension of the vast North American continent. After coming to the New World, he led the occupation of Puerto Rico in 1508 and governed it from 1509 to 1512.

From the passage, the reader can assume that a "peninsula" is

8–A   a volcanic island.

8–B   an island completely surrounded by water.

8–C   an extension of land surrounded almost completely by water.

8–D   an island inhabited by Indians.

9. Horse owners who plan to breed one or more mares should know about heredity and know how to care for breeding animals and foals. The number of mares bred that actually conceive varies from about 40 to 85 percent, with the average running less than 50 percent. Some mares that do conceive fail to produce living foals.

To conceive is to

9–A   become sick.

9–B   become pregnant.

9–C   die.

9–D   be born.

10. Animals that produce large amounts of offspring depend upon the sheer size of the litter for the continuance of their species. The young mature very quickly, and are not educated, as the parents are usually involved with obtaining their own food and with reproduction. Should some of the offspring become endangered, the parents will not interfere.

Why would an animal parent *not* be able to care for its litter?

10–A It is busy reproducing and gathering food.

10–B It is busy educating the litter.

10–C It interferes with the litter.

10–D It is busy playing.

11. Phobic reactions are strong fears of specific objects or situations. For example, when a person is extremely fearful of birds, snakes, heights, or closed places when no danger exists, the label phobia is applied to the person's fear and avoidance. A person suffering from a phobia knows what he is afraid of and usually recognizes that his fear is irrational, but cannot control it.

A phobia is a label for

11–A a person's ability to control fear.

11–B a person's fear and avoidance.

11–C a person's love of fear.

11–D a person's dislike of fear.

12. Asbestos millboard in wall and floor protection is a controversial issue because of the health hazard of asbestos fibers in the manufacturing, preparation, and handling of the millboard. The National Fire Protection Association is beginning to remove asbestos as a standard protection from fire. We strongly encourage the use of an alternative protection whenever one is available.

The *overall* implication of the passage is

12–A asbestos is as safe as other building materials.

12–B only touching the asbestos fibers with your hands is harmful.

12–C asbestos can be harmful to one's health.

12–D using asbestos in building materials is fine.

13. From the dawn of civilization, the gaze of humanity has been drawn to the stars. The stars have been relied upon to direct travelers, to make agricultural predictions, to win wars, and to awaken love in the hearts of men and women. Ancient stargazers looking at the nighttime sky saw patterns emerge.

    This passage states that

    13–A man never depends on the stars.

    13–B stars are only for beautifying the skies.

    13–C man has depended on stars at times.

    13–D moons are the same as stars.

14. Try to make the Visitor Center your first stop at any park. There you will find information on attractions, activities, trails, and campsites. Descriptive films, literature, and exhibits will acquaint you with the geology, history, and plant and animal life of the area.

    The background material described includes all the following *except*

    14–A interviews with inhabitants.

    14–B exhibits.

    14–C literature.

    14–D films.

15. The most popular organic gem is the pearl. A pearl occurs when a marine mollusk reacts to an irritating impurity accidentally introduced into its body. A *cultured* pearl is the result of the intentional insertion of a mother-of-pearl bead into a live mollusk. Either way, the pearl-making process is the same: The mollusk covers the irritant with a substance called nacre.

    Nacre is a substance that is

    15–A mechanically manufactured.

    15–B the result of laboratory testing.

    15–C organically secreted by the mollusk.

    15–D present in the chemicals of freshwater ponds.

AUTO & SHOP
TEST 2

Time: 11 Minutes
25 Questions

(Answer sheets appear in the back of this book.)

DIRECTIONS: For each question, read the four possible answers and select the one answer that you believe is correct. Fill in the corresponding letter on your answer sheet.

---

1. Intake and exhaust valves allow air-fuel mixture to flow in and out of the

   1–A intake manifold.   1–C cylinder.

   1–B intake port.   1–D transmission.

2. The flywheel

   2–A maintains the flow of oil through the engine.

   2–B keeps the crankshaft rotating.

   2–C Both (A) and (B)

   2–D None of the above

3. In regard to engines, BDC stands for

   3–A brake design center.   3–C bottom dead center.

   3–B brake dead center.   3–D brake disc caliper.

4. If at TDC the cylinder holds 1 gallon and at BDC holds 10 gallons, then the compression ratio is

   4–A 1:10.   4–C 15:1.

   4–B 20:1.   4–D 10:1.

5. If a four-stroke cycle starts with the compression stroke, then the third stroke would be the

   5–A compression stroke again.

5–B   power stroke.

5–C   intake stroke.

5–D   exhaust stroke.

6. In regard to engines, **ohc** stands for

6–A   overhead crankshaft.   6–C   overhead camshaft.

6–B   overhead caliper.   6–D   none of the above.

7. Which of the following is part of the carburetor?

7–A   Venturi   7–C   Exhaust port

7–B   Camshaft   7–D   None of the above

8. The fuel flow into the float bowl is stopped by the

8–A   throttle valve.   8–C   intake valve.

8–B   choke valve.   8–D   float and needle valve.

9. The air-fuel mixture in a diesel engine is ignited by the

9–A   spark plug.   9–C   compression.

9–B   camshaft.   9–D   None of the above

10. One way to reduce HC is

10–A PCV.   10–C ECS.

10–B air injection.   10–D all of the above.

11. The ratio for direct drive in a five-speed manual transmission is

11–A 15:1.   11–C 3:1.

11–B 10:1.   11–D 1:1.

12. A torque converter is essentially made up of

12–A an axle housing and differential.

12–B a cylinder and piston.

12–C a turbine, pump, and stator.

12–D a clutch and drive shaft.

13. A drive shaft is commonly used with a

    13–A rear-wheel drive system.

    13–B four-wheel drive system.

    13–C front-wheel drive system.

    13–D Both (A) and (B)

14. What is the function of a simple caliper?

    14–A To tighten bolts   14–C Both (A) and (B)

    14–B To bend steel   14–D To measure diameters

15. What is the above tool?

    15–A Allen-type wrench   15–C Bolt cutter

    15–B Screwdriver   15–D Hacksaw

16. What is the above tool?

    16–A Bolt cutter   16–C Straight hand snip

    16–B Bristol wrench   16–D None of the above

17. "Single-cut" is a term which applies to

    17–A hammers.   17–C files.

    17–B chisels.   17–D none of the above.

18. Hollow shank gasket punches are used to

    18–A drill holes.

    18–B cut through heavy gage steel.

18–C Both (A) and (B)

18–D cut holes in light gage sheet metal.

19. Another name for long-nosed pliers is

19–A thin-nosed pliers.

19–C duckbill pliers.

19–B needle-nose pliers.

19–D none of the above.

20. What is the above tool?

20–A Long-nosed pliers

20–C Slipjoint pliers

20–B Duckbill pliers

20–D None of the above

21. Which of the following is part of a carpenter's square?

21–A Tongue

21–C Sleeve

21–B Spindle

21–D All of the above

22. Which of the following is used to determine if a plane or surface is true vertical or true horizontal?

22–A Screw pitch gage

22–C Hammer

22–B Screwdriver

22–D Level

23. In regard to nails, the abbreviation for the word "penny" is

23–A "p"

23–C "r"

23–B "q"

23–D "d"

24. Which of the following is a type of capscrew head?

24–A Fillister

24–C Both (A) and (B)

24–B Hex

24–D None of the above

25. Mallet heads are made from materials such as

25–A steel.

25–C rubber.

25–B wood.

25–D Both (B) and (C)

MATHEMATICS KNOWLEDGE TEST 2

Time: 24 Minutes
25 Questions

(Answer sheets appear in the back of this book.)

DIRECTIONS: Each question has four multiple-choice answers, labeled by the number of the question and the letters A, B, C, or D. Select the single answer which is correct.

---

1. If one angle of a right triangle is 70°, then how many degrees are there in the smallest angle?

    1–A   20°   1–C   30°

    1–B   25°   1–D   35°

2. What is the square root of 196?

    2–A   11   2–C   13

    2–B   12   2–D   14

3. If $-6x > -12$, then which of the following must be true?

    3–A $x > 2$ 3–C $x < 2$

    3–B $x \geq 2$ 3–D $x \leq 2$

4. If the perimeter of a square equals one foot, then what is the area of this square (in square inches)?

    4–A   7   4–C   9

    4–B   8   4–D   10

5. What does $(x - 2)(x - 3)$ equal?

    5–A $x^2 + 5x - 6$ 5–C $x^2 + 5x + 6$

    5–B $x^2 - 5x - 6$ 5–D $x^2 - 5x + 6$

6. If the length of a rectangle is twice the width and the perimeter equals 24, what would the equation look like assuming width equals w?

   6–A $2w = 24$ 6–C $4w = 24$

   6–B $3w = 24$ 6–D $6w = 24$

7. There are 200 girls in the freshman class. This is 40% of the freshman class. How many freshmen are there?

   7–A 300   7–C 700

   7–B 500   7–D 900

8. If $-10x \geq 65$, then which of the following must be true?

   8–A $x < -6.5$ 8–C $x > -6.5$

   8–B $x \leq -6.5$ 8–D $x \geq -6.5$

9. If one side of a right triangle equals one-half a foot and the hypotenuse equals ten inches, then what is the length of the other leg (in inches)?

   9–A 8   9–C 10

   9–B 9   9–D 11

10. If $9y - 26 = -8$, what is y?

   10–A 5   10–C 3

   10–B 4   10–D 2

11. What does $(z + 4)(z - 5)$ equal?

   11–A $z^2 - 9z - 20$ 11–C $z^2 - z - 20$

   11–B $z^2 + 9z - 20$ 11–D $z^2 - z + 20$

12. How many sides does a pentagon have?

   12–A 4   12–C 6

   12–B 5   12–D 7

13. If 60 people like to play basketball and 25% of them also play volleyball, how many play only basketball?

13–A 15

13–C 35

13–B 25

13–D 45

14. If a circle's area is equal to twice its circumference, what is the radius?

14–A 4

14–C 6

14–B 5

14–D 7

15. If $-x/3 > 4$, then which of the following must be true?

15–A $x < 12$

15–C $x > 12$

15–B $x < -12$

15–D $x > -12$

16. Factor $v^2 - 2v - 15$.

16–A $(v - 3)(v + 5)$

16–C $(v + 3)(v + 5)$

16–B $(v - 3)(v - 5)$

16–D $(v + 3)(v - 5)$

17. If a square having side s has the same perimeter as a rectangle with one side equal to four, what is the equation to find the other side, l, of the rectangle?

17–A $4s = 8 + 2l$

17–C $4s = 4 + 3l$

17–B $s = 4 + l$

17–D $4s = 8 + l$

18. If Jane reads ten pages each night for five nights, she will have 40% of her assignment done. How many pages does she have to read for her class?

18–A 100

18–C 150

18–B 125

18–D 175

19. If a right triangle has one angle equal to 25°, what is the difference in the angles formed by the hypotenuse?

19–A 25°

19–C 65°

19–B 40°

19–D 90°

20. What is the product of $(w + 6)(w + 2)$?

20–A $w^2 + 4w + 12$ 20–C $w^2 + 8w + 12$

20–B $w^2 + 6w + 12$ 20–D $w^2 - 8w + 12$

21. If a retailer wants to sell an item at 45% profit, how much must a $1.20 item sell for?

21–A $0.54   21–C $1.65

21–B $0.66   21–D $1.74

22. How many equal angles are there in an isosceles right triangle?

22–A 0   22–C 3

22–B 2   22–D 4

23. What is the square root of 169?

23–A 11   23–C 13

23–B 12   23–D 14

24. If $4x + 12 = 24$, then what is x?

24–A 3   24–C 5

24–B 4   24–D 6

25. If the area of a square is equal to twice its perimeter, what is the length of a side, s?

25–A 2   25–C 6

25–B 4   25–D 8

MECHANICAL COMPREHENSION TEST 2

Time: 19 Minutes
      25 Questions

(Answer sheets appear in the back of this book.)

DIRECTIONS: Choose the best answer to each question and then darken the oval on your answer sheet.

1. In a Class III lever, which of the following is true?

    1–A   The fulcrum is between the resistance and the effort.

    1–B   The effort is between the resistance and the fulcrum.

    1–C   The resistance is between the effort and the fulcrum.

    1–D   The effort is smaller than the resistance.

2. The mechanical advantage in the flag hoist shown is

    2–A   1.

    2–B   2.

    2–C   3.

    2–D   4.

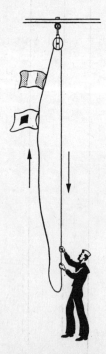

3. In the eggbeater shown, the wheel on the crank handle A has 32 teeth which mesh with the 8 teeth on the horizontal wheel B. What is the relationship between the speeds of the wheels A, B, and C?

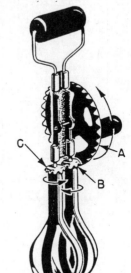

3–A Wheel A revolves four times as fast as wheels B and C.

3–B Wheel A revolves two times as fast as wheels B and C.

3–C Wheel A revolves two times slower than wheels B and C.

3–D Wheels B and C revolve four times as fast as wheel A.

4. The piece of machinery shown here is known as

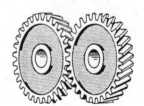

4–A a bevel gear.

4–B a pinion and sector gear.

4–C a worm gear.

4–D a helical spur gear.

5. Cams are devices used to perform which of the following?

5–A To hold two parts together

5–B To modify a mechanical movement, the power for which is furnished through other means

5–C To transmit power from one shaft to another

5–D To connect or disconnect a driving and a driven member for stopping or starting the driven part

6. What is the mechanical advantage of the block-and-tackle system shown here?

6–A   5

6–B   2

6–C   4

6–D   3

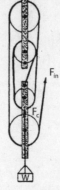

7. What will be the resulting movement of the piston as the crankshaft makes a full turn clockwise?

7–A   The piston moves down one stroke and stops.

7–B   The piston remains stopped, unless the crankshaft is turned counter-clockwise.

7–C   The piston moves down one stroke, then up one stroke, then down a second stroke.

7–D   The piston moves down one stroke, then up one stroke.

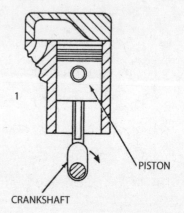

8. Consider the case of Slim (man on the left) and Sam carrying the 300-pound crate slung on a handy 10-foot pole. Slim was smart enough to slide the load up 3 feet from Sam's shoulder. How much load is Sam carrying?

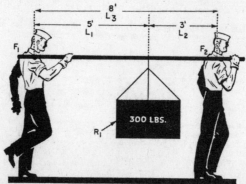

8–A   187.5 pounds   8–C   112.5 pounds

8–B   150 pounds   8–D   500 pounds

9. The function of a gear train is to

    9–A   hold two pieces of machinery together.

    9–B   transmit power from one shaft to another.

    9–C   modify a mechanical movement, the power for which is fur-nished through other means.

    9–D   connect or disconnect a driving and a driven member for stop-ping or starting the driven part.

10. The figure shows one of the dogs used to secure doors aboard a ship. What is the effort E needed to overcome the 200-pound force acting against the slanting face of the wedge?

    10–A 20 pounds

    10–B 800 pounds

    10–C 25 pounds

    10–D 50 pounds

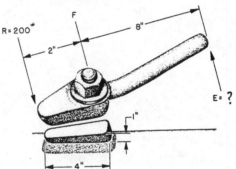

11. In the previous question, what is the force acting on the face of the wedge?

    11–A 800 lb   11–C 50 lb

    11–B 200 lb   11–D 400 lb

12. A ring is to be mounted on a flanged pipe as shown. The maximum angle through which it would be necessary to rotate the ring in order to line up the holes is

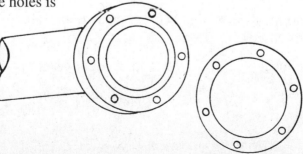

12–A 22.5 degrees.   12–C 60 degrees.

12–B 45 degrees.   12–D 30 degrees.

13. In the diagram below, pulley A drives pulley C which is keyed to the same shaft as pulley B. Pulley B turns pulley D. The diameters of the pulleys are: A = 3 in, B = 4 in, C = 1 in, D = 2 in. When pulley A runs at an rpm of 500, pulley D will make

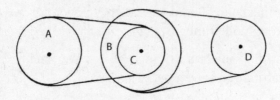

13–A 500 rpm.   13–C 6,000 rpm.

13–B 1,500 rpm.   13–D 3,000 rpm.

14. What will be the resulting movement of the valve if the camshaft makes a full turn?

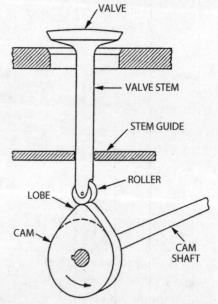

14–A The valve moves up one stroke and down one stroke.

14–B The valve moves down one stroke and then up one stroke.

14–C The valve moves down one stroke and stays down.

14–D The valve moves up one stroke and stays up.

15. In order to transmit motion between non-parallel shafts, which of the following is used?

15–A A clutch   15–C Spur gears

15–B A cam   15–D Bevel gears

16. If gear A is rotating with a speed of 220 rpm, then gear B must be rotating with a speed of

   16–A 220 rpm.

   16–B 360 rpm.

   16–C 134.4 rpm.

   16–D 412.5 rpm.

17. In what direction must the handles (1) and (2) be turned in order to generate the motion shown?

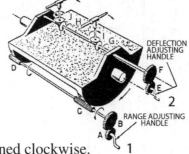

   17–A Both handles must be turned clockwise.

   17–B Both handles must be turned counterclockwise.

   17–C Handle (1) must be turned clockwise and handle (2) counter-clockwise.

   17–D None of the above.

18. A cam is a device used to perform which of the following functions?

   18–A To hold two parts together

   18–B To modify a mechanical movement, the power for which is furnished through other means

   18–C To transmit power from one shaft to another

   18–D To connect or disconnect a driving and a driven member for stopping or starting the driven part

19. The average weight of an adult man is 160 pounds, and the area of his shoe soles is roughly 60 square inches. What must be the size of the area of a pair of snowshoes in order to reduce the pressure under his feet to 0.18 psi?

   19–A 60 sq. in   19–C 450 sq. in

   19–B 120 sq. in   19–D 889 sq. in

20. The gear system shown here is an example of

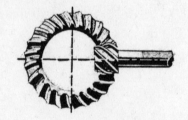

   20–A a worm gear.

   20–B a spiral bevel gear.

   20–C a spur bevel gear.

   20–D a sliding spur gear.

21. The manual drill shown is based on which of the following machine principles?

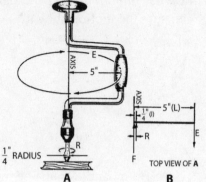

   21–A A third-class lever

   21–B A block and tackle

   21–C The wheel and axle

   21–D The wedge and the inclined plane

22. Refer to the figure in the previous problem to do your work here. The mechanical advantage of the manual drill is

   22–A 10.   22–C 30.

   22–B 20.   22–D 40.

23. Wheel A has 10 teeth which mesh with the 40 teeth on wheel B. Wheel C is rigidly fixed on the same shaft with wheel B. Wheel C, which has 20 teeth, meshes with wheel D which has only 10 teeth. If wheel A turns at a rate of four revolutions per second, which of the following is true?

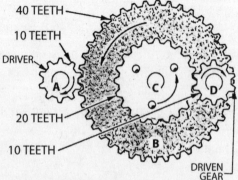

   23–A Wheel B turns at a rate of one revolution per second, and wheel C turns at a rate of 2 revolutions per second.

23–B Wheels B, C, and D turn at a rate of one revolution per second.

23–C Wheels B, C, and D turn at a rate of two revolutions per second.

23–D Wheels B and C turn at a rate of one revolution per second, and wheel D turns at a rate of two revolutions per second.

24. The efficiency of a machine is given by

24–A the ratio $\dfrac{\text{work output} - \text{work input}}{\text{work input}}$.

24–B the ratio $\dfrac{\text{work output}}{\text{work input}}$.

24–C the ratio $\dfrac{\text{work input}}{\text{work output}}$.

24–D the difference of work output – work input.

25. As the air pressure increases, what is the change expected in the barometer shown?

25–A The mercury in the column rises.

25–B The mercury in the column lowers.

25–C The mercury in the column remains unchanged, but the mercury in the lower receptacle rises.

25–D The mercury in the column remains unchanged, but the mercury in the lower receptacle drops.

ELECTRONICS INFORMATION
TEST 2

Time: 9 Minutes
   20 Questions

(Answer sheets appear in the back of this book.)

DIRECTIONS: Choose the best answer to each question by darkening the oval on your answer sheet.

Following are two sample questions.

S1. If the motor at the output needs 5.0 V to run, which of these resistors can be placed in series with it and still allow it to run?

S1–A 1 ohm

S1–B 2 ohms

S1–C 3 ohms

S1–D 10 ohms

S1. **(A)** From Ohm's Law we know two things — the first is that voltages add in series. This means that the voltage across R will take voltage away from the motor. The current through resistor R is 3 amps; thus, a voltage drop of 3 V is dropped across R. This leaves 5 V to be dropped across the motor, therefore, allowing it to work.

S2. Why can birds sit on high voltage wires without fear yet a repairman cannot lean his ladder against the wires and work on them?

S2–A The repairman is not grounded.

S2–B The repairman is grounded.

S2–C The birds are grounded.

S2–D Birds are insulated.

S2. **(B)** The birds are not grounded as they sit on the wires, but the repairman's ladder is usually metal and is grounded. If the repairman has a rubber ladder then he would be fine as well.

1. How much energy does a 75 Watt bulb use in two hours?

    1–A   75 J   1–C   750 J

    1–B   540,000 J   1–D   150 J

2. The fuse box has a breaker of 20 amps on it. Which toaster can be hooked up?

    2–A   Toaster *A* needs 2,000 W to work.

    2–B   Toaster *B* needs 3,000 W to work.

    2–C   Toaster *C* needs 4,000 W to work.

    2–D   Toaster *D* needs 5,000 W to work.

3. How is your house protected against fatal shocks?

    3–A   The house has AC voltage.

    3–B   The house has DC voltage.

    3–C   The electrical system in the house is grounded.

    3–D   The voltage is only 110 volts.

4. What is a diode?

    4–A   A device which passes current in 3 directions.

    4–B   A device which passes current in 2 directions.

    4–C   A device which passes current in 1 direction.

    4–D   A device which will not pass current in any direction.

5. What device produces the voltage-current plot shown?

    5–A   A resistor

    5–B   A transistor

    5–C   A diode

    5–D   A capacitor

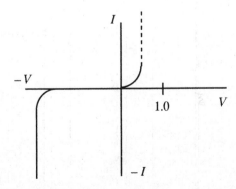

6. What does an ohm stand for?

   6–A Current   6–C Resistance

   6–B Voltage   6–D Weight

7. During an open circuit what occurs?

   7–A The voltage goes to zero.

   7–B The resistance goes to zero.

   7–C The resistance goes to infinity.

   7–D The current goes to infinity.

8. What does a capacitor do?

   8–A Stores charge   8–C Amplifies voltage

   8–B Amplifies current   8–D Follows Ohm's Law

9. What is the voltage between points $A - A'$?

   9–A 2.50 V

   9–B 0.10 V

   9–C 10.0 V

   9–D 3.33 V

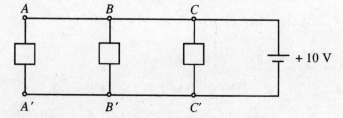

10. What gauge of wire is needed for 20 amps?

   10–A #14   10–C #10

   10–B #12   10–D #6

11. What does the symbol Ω stand for?

   11–A Ohms   11–C Farads

   11–B Mohs   11–D Henrys

12. Metal boxes are used instead of plastic boxes for lighting cabinets because

    12–A metal lasts longer.

    12–B plastic lasts too long and the company wants you to replace them periodically to make money.

    12–C metal cabinets cannot be tampered with.

    12–D metal isolates circuits.

13. Always use a fuse that is

    13–A less than the power needed.

    13–B equal to the power needed.

    13–C greater than the power needed.

    13–D half the current needed.

14. As the wire heats up, its resistance

    14–A becomes larger.

    14–B becomes less.

    14–C does not change.

    14–D passes the heat down the wire and damages other delicate circuits.

15. Which is the symbol for a battery?

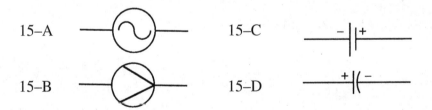

    15–A   15–C

    15–B   15–D

16. What is the best insulator?

    16–A Copper   16–C Dry air

    16–B Iron   16–D Wet air

17. The voltage step ratio for a transformer is

    17–A $\dfrac{V_{primary}}{V_{secondary}} = \dfrac{N_{primary}}{N_{secondary}}$.

    17–B $\dfrac{V_{primary}}{N_{secondary}} = \dfrac{V_{secondary}}{N_{primary}}$.

    17–C $(V_{primary}) \times (V_{secondary}) = (N_{primary}) \times (N_{secondary})$.

    17–D $(V_{primary}) \times (V_{secondary}) \times (N_{primary}) = (N_{secondary})$.

18. In what way does an arc differ from a spark?

    18–A A spark discharges charge to another conductor, while an arc discharges charge to air.

    18–B A spark discharges charge to air while an arc discharges charge to another conductor.

    18–C In no way — they are the same thing.

    18–D A spark is induced while an arc is by accident.

19. What makes a good conductor?

    19–A Current does not flow easily due to high impedance.

    19–B Large voltage drops.

    19–C Current flows easily due to low impedance.

    19–D High resistance.

20. Which of these is a toggle switch?

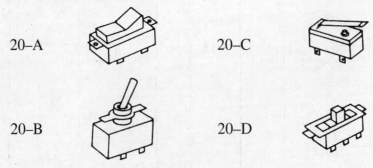

    20–A   20–C

    20–B   20–D

GENERAL SCIENCE
TEST 2

ANSWER KEY

1. (A)	8. (C)	15. (B)	22. (A)
2. (B)	9. (D)	16. (D)	23. (A)
3. (D)	10. (D)	17. (B)	24. (A)
4. (B)	11. (B)	18. (D)	25. (C)
5. (A)	12. (A)	19. (C)	
6. (D)	13. (A)	20. (D)	
7. (B)	14. (B)	21. (A)	

Add up your correct answers and put the number here. _____

Now record your score on pages 451-452.

DETAILED EXPLANATIONS OF ANSWERS

1. **(A)** Vascular means "having tubes." All vascular plants have tubes, true roots, leaves, and stems.

2. **(B)** All worms can be classified as flatworms, roundworms, or segmented worms, each group having its own phylum. Roundworms belong to the phylum Nematoda.

3. **(D)** Ferns are vascular plants, and therefore have leaves (B) and roots (C). They reproduce by spores (A) instead of seeds (D).

4. **(B)** White blood cells (B) produce antibodies. Red blood cells (A) transport oxygen and carbon dioxide. Platelets (C) form clots. Plasma (D) transports dissolved materials.

5. **(A)** Vitamin A deficiency results in night blindness and skin infections.

6. **(D)** A human cell has 46 chromosomes, 23 from each parent.

7. **(B)** Producers make their own food from sunlight energy. Only green plants (like trees) can do this.

8. **(C)** Chloroplasts contain chlorophyll, which converts carbon dioxide, water, and sunlight into glucose and oxygen. Only cells from green plants contain chloroplasts.

9. **(D)** Work = force × distance. Force = weight = 150 pounds. Distance = 2 feet. 150 pounds × 2 feet = 300 foot-pounds.

10. **(D)** Energy is never created or lost; it only changes form. The chemicals in a match head store energy which is released in the form of heat and light.

11. **(B)** Insulators prevent the flow of heat or electricity. Air is a good insulator. Answers (A), (C), and (D) are conductors.

12. **(A)** Electromagnetic induction occurs when a wire is moved through a magnetic field, producing a current in the wire. This is the basis for electrical generators.

13. **(A)** A sunlight spectrum (rainbow) contains red, orange, yellow, green, blue, indigo, and violet.

14. **(B)** Differences in sound volume are related to amplitude differences. Sound intensity is related to amplitude and frequency of sound waves. Speed = Wavelength × Frequency.

15. **(B)** The atomic number of an atom shows how many protons are in the atom's nucleus. Mass (A), charge (C), and energy level (D) of an atom are variable and are not used to define an element (or atom).

16. **(D)** Average kinetic energy is temperature. Materials at very low temperatures are usually solids.

17. **(B)** Solvents are materials in which other chemicals can dissolve. Since water is able to dissolve so many materials, it is sometimes called the "universal solvent."

18. **(D)** In a chemical equation, chemicals to the left of the arrow are called reactants, and those to the right are called products. (The reactants react to produce products.)

19. **(C)** Lava is molten rock at the earth's surface. Core (B), mantle (C), and crust (A) are the three main layers of the earth. The mantle is the thickest layer.

20. **(D)** All the answers are layers of the atmosphere. The troposphere is the layer that touches the surface of the earth, and therefore is the layer where life is most abundant.

21. **(A)** One rotation of the earth takes 24 hours, or one day. One orbit of the moon takes $27^1/_3$ days (B), or one month. One revolution of the earth takes $365^1/_4$ days (C), or one year (D).

22. **(A)** Igneous (A), metamorphic (C), and sedimentary (D) are types of rock, but crystal (B) is not. Igneous rock is formed by the cooling and hardening of molten material.

23. **(A)** Atoms are the smallest particles of an element that retain the properties of that element. Protons (C) are subatomic particles. Molecules (B), which are particles of compounds (D), are made of two or more atoms.

24. **(A)** In photosynthesis, water (C) and carbon dioxide (B) are combined, using sunlight energy and aided by chlorophyll (D), to produce glucose and oxygen.

25. **(C)** The bicep is made of striated muscle which is controlled voluntarily. Smooth muscle (D) is controlled involuntarily (B), as is cardiac muscle (A).

ARITHMETIC REASONING
TEST 2

ANSWER KEY

1. (C)	9. (B)	17. (B)	25. (C)
2. (D)	10. (A)	18. (A)	26. (D)
3. (A)	11. (C)	19. (C)	27. (C)
4. (D)	12. (D)	20. (A)	28. (A)
5. (B)	13. (B)	21. (C)	29. (C)
6. (A)	14. (A)	22. (D)	30. (C)
7. (C)	15. (C)	23. (B)	
8. (D)	16. (D)	24. (A)	

Add up your correct answers and put the number here. _____

Now record your score on pages 451-452.

DETAILED EXPLANATIONS OF ANSWERS

1. **(C)** The answer is (C) because 7 × 89 = 623¢, or $6.23.

2. **(D)** The answer is (D) because 28% of $35,000 is $9,800.

3. **(A)** The answer is (A) because the lion is gaining on the zebra at a rate of 10 miles per hour. He has a quarter mile to go, and each mile takes one-tenth of an hour, or six minutes. Thus, the quarter of a mile will take a quarter of six minutes, or 1.5 minutes.

4. **(D)** The answer is (D) because the savings account pays 5% of $1,000, or $50, and the CD pays 6% of $2,000, or $120. Thus, the total interest is $170.

5. **(B)** The answer is (B) because $155,000 – $120,000 = $35,000.

6. **(A)** The answer is (A) because 500 – 68 + 43 = 475.

7. **(C)** The answer is (C) because 6 × 3 = 18.

8. **(D)** The answer is (D) because 12/4 = 3.

9. **(B)** The answer is (B) because 13.5/2 = 6.75.

10. **(A)** The answer is (A) because at 40 miles per hour the trip will take her four hours. She left at 8:00, so she will arrive at 12:00.

11. **(C)** The answer is (C) because 136/8.5 = 16.

12. **(D)** The answer is (D) because half of the 12 dancers are females, making six females. Half of those, or three of them, were wearing black.

13. **(B)** The answer is (B) because time and a half would be 1.5 × $12/hour = $18/hour. Working two hours, she would earn 2 × $18 = $36.

14. **(A)** The answer is (A) because the car gets 30 miles to the gallon,

and each gallon costs $1.29. So it costs $1.29 to drive 30 miles. Driving 20 miles would cost $1.29 × (20/30), or $0.86.

15. **(C)** The answer is (C) because $7 − $3.58 = $3.42.

16. **(D)** The answer is (D) because 21 + 16 + 13 = 50.

17. **(B)** The answer is (B) because Brian needs 21 − 17 = 4 more goals. He has two games in which to score four goals, so he would need to average 4/2 = 2 goals per game.

18. **(A)** The answer is (A) because 6 × 4 = 24.

19. **(C)** The answer is (C) because 7 × 24 = 168.

20. **(A)** The answer is (A) because the boat will travel 20 − 5 = 15 miles per hour against the wind. At this rate it will take 30/15 = 2 hours to travel 30 miles.

21. **(C)** The answer is (C) because there are 4 × 16 = 64 defenders in the league. If three of them make the all-star team, then 64 − 3 = 61 will not.

22. **(D)** The answer is (D) because the 100% markup will bring the price to 20¢. Then 10% tax is 2¢, so the total is 22¢.

23. **(B)** The answer is (B) because 24 towels is enough for 24/2 = 12 sets, and 31 wash cloths is enough for 31/3 = 10.3, or 10, sets. There will be 10 complete sets, consisting of 20 towels and 30 wash cloths, and four extra towels and one extra wash cloth.

24. **(A)** The answer is (A) because from 8:30 to 12:00 is 3.5 hours. From 12:00 to 5:15 is 5.25 hours. The total is 8.75 hours. But then subtract 45 minutes, or 0.75 hour, for lunch. She worked eight hours.

25. **(C)** The answer is (C) because 68 − (−24) = 68 + 24 = 92 degrees.

26. **(D)** The answer is (D) because there are 300 male freshman, hence 600 freshman. Then there are 1,200 seniors, and half of them, or 600, are females.

27. **(C)** The answer is (C) because 80 × 7 = 560.

28. **(A)** The answer is (A) because 100% – 60% = 40% of the 30 were incomplete. But 40% of 30 is 12.

29. **(C)** The answer is (C) because 74 – 16 – 12 – 29 = 17.

30. **(C)** The answer is (C) because (24 + 21 + 13 + 17 + 15)/5 = 90/5 = 18.

WORD KNOWLEDGE
TEST 2

ANSWER KEY

1. (A)	10. (B)	19. (A)	28. (D)
2. (B)	11. (B)	20. (A)	29. (C)
3. (D)	12. (B)	21. (C)	30. (A)
4. (D)	13. (D)	22. (C)	31. (C)
5. (A)	14. (C)	23. (D)	32. (C)
6. (B)	15. (B)	24. (B)	33. (D)
7. (A)	16. (A)	25. (C)	34. (A)
8. (D)	17. (B)	26. (B)	35. (D)
9. (C)	18. (C)	27. (D)	

Add up your correct answers and put the number here. _____

Now record your score on pages 451-452.

DETAILED EXPLANATIONS OF ANSWERS

1.   **(A)** Persuade means CONVINCE. (B) BELIEVE, meaning to think, to trust, or to have faith in, is not related. (C) SWEAT is synonymous with perspire; (D) PERMEATE is synonymous with pervade.

2.   **(B)** Conversion most closely means a TRANSFORMATION. (A) TALK is synonymous with conversation; (C) COME TOGETHER is synonymous with convergence; (D) REVELATION is synonymous with enlightenment.

3.   **(D)** Chagrin is DISTRESS caused by disappointment. (A) HORROR is extreme fear, dismay, or dread; (B) BOREDOM is restlessness or uninterestedness; (C) GRIEF is a deep distress, a disaster, or an annoyance.

4.   **(D)** Resist means to OPPOSE. (A) SAVE can be synonymous with reserve; (B) TURN OFF can mean to dismiss, evade, sell, accomplish, bore, deviate, or withdraw—but none of these has the same meaning as resist or oppose. (C) LIVE is synonymous for exist.

5.   **(A)** Superficial means SHALLOW or external, having to do only with the surface. (B) EXCESSIVE is synonymous with superfluous. (C) FLIGHTY means frivolous or silly. (D) IMPORTANT is an antonym of superficial.

6.   **(B)** Obsolete means DISCONTINUED or outmoded. (A) INCONVENIENT is not related; (C) UNREWARDING means not valuable or satisfying; (D) FUTILE means serving no useful purpose or frivolous.

7.   **(A)** Fitful means IRREGULAR. When someone has had a fitful night's sleep, he has not slept well. (B) SOUND is the opposite of fitful in the context of sleeping; and (C) JAUNTY and (D) UNDISCIPLINED do not have similar meanings.

8.   **(D)** Humble and MODEST both mean unpretentious or not proud. (A) To "eat humble pie" means to apologize or retract something previously said—but humble does not mean DELICIOUS! (B) ARROGANT,

to put oneself above others or be full of self-importance, is the opposite of humble; (C) TEDIOUS is synonymous with humdrum.

9. **(C)** Modifed means changed or ALTERED. (A) LIMITED means restricted; (B) OBSCURED means hidden or unclear; (D) UPDATED is synonymous with modernized. Modified *may* mean updated, but it *always* means changed, so altered is the best synonym.

10. **(B)** Scold and BERATE both mean to find fault or rebuke. (A) CONFUSE, (C) WEAKEN, and (D) FLATTER (praise excessively) have altogether different meanings.

11. **(B)** Evade and ELUDE both mean to avoid. (A) INTRUDE means to invade; (C) ABANDON can be synonymous with evacuate; (D) DISAPPEAR can be synonymous with evaporate.

12. **(B)** Deceive and MISLEAD mean the same thing. (A) GET is synonymous with receive; (C) PROMISE, meaning to pledge or assure, is an antonym; (D) CREATE is synonymous with conceive.

13. **(D)** Urgent means needing immediate attention; of the choices given, IMPORTANT is closest in meaning. (A) TEMPTING means appealing or enticing; (B) UNNECESSARY is an antonym; (C) PROFESSIONAL means accomplished or skillful.

14. **(C)** The verb "to temper" means to MODERATE, toughen, or condition. (A) PACE means to walk back and forth or set a tempo; (B) LURE is to tempt; (D) FEUD is to wage a long-term quarrel.

15. **(B)** The best synonym for fastidious is DEMANDING. The word also means difficult to please or meticulous (concerned with attention to detail). (A) RAPID-PACED is synonymous with fast, which is not related to fastidious. (C) NEAT means clean and orderly; (D) QUIRKY means peculiar.

16. **(A)** Appeal means to accuse, request, INTEREST, or attract. (B) BE VISIBLE is synonymous with appear; (C) CALM is synonymous with appease; (D) REPEL is the opposite of appeal/attract.

17. **(B)** Virtuoso means SKILLFUL. (A) SCHOLARLY means learned; (C) KINDLY is synonymous with virtuous; (D) PASSIONATE means enthusiastic or easily angered or lustful.

18. **(C)** Inadvertent means unintentional or THOUGHTLESS. (A) IN-TENTIONAL is the opposite of inadvertent; (B) FICKLE means erratic, wishy-washy; (D) WHIMSICAL means unpredictable.

19. **(A)** To profess is to admit, believe, AFFIRM. If you selected (B) TEACH, you were confusing the nouns teacher and profess*or*—a different word. (C) WORK and profess*ion* are sometimes synonymous, but again, the word is different from profess. All three words—profess, professor, and profession—come from the same Latin root, which means to declare publicly. (D) OUTLINE is synonymous with profile, which is not related.

20. **(A)** Reconcile means to SETTLE or resolve differences. (B) PRAISE, (C) MEMORIZE, and (D) REST are not related in meaning.

21. **(C)** A fraud is an IMPOSTER, one who pretends to be something he isn't, a deceiver. (A) a VANDAL destroys or defaces another person's property; (B) an EMBEZZLER, in effect, steals money or property that was entrusted to him; (D) a THIEF is also one who steals.

22. **(C)** To articulate and COMMUNICATE both involve speaking. Neither articulation nor communication *require* a response, although communication implies a two-way exchange. (A) SOLVE means to find a solution for. (B) DEBATE is also a means of communication, but implies an active or animated discussion or argument, which sense isn't contained in either the words articulate or communicate. (D) CONSIDER means to think about, or weigh options.

23. **(D)** Clever and SHREWD both mean cunning and intelligent. (A) KNIFE-LIKE could be synonymous with cleaver, a type of knife; (B) TALENTED means having an ability or skill. *Shrewdness* sometimes borders on being (C) DISHONEST, but cleverness implies getting what you want with intelligence rather than deceit.

24. **(B)** Disprove means to prove to be wrong, to DENY the truth of; deny, therefore, is the best synonym. (A) LIE means to tell an untruth; (C) ARGUE is a synonym for dispute; (D) PROHIBIT means to forbid.

25. **(C)** Mediocre means ordinary, IMPERFECT, or inferior. (A) UN-SUCCESSFUL is not attaining a goal; (B) HEALTHY is not at all related; (D) OFFENSIVE means unpleasant or insulting.

26. **(B)** Dismal means uninteresting or DEPRESSING. (A) SPIRITED

has the opposite meaning; (C) FRIGHTENING is synonymous with dismaying; (D) WEARY means tired.

27. **(D)** Undoubtedly and CERTAINLY mean the same thing. (A) IMPROBABLY means not likely; (B) GENERALLY, meaning usually, is an antonym; (C) IMPOSSIBLY means very incapable of happening.

28. **(D)** A rival is a COMPETITOR. (A) a COLLEAGUE is a professional associate; (B) a SERVANT performs duties for his employer; (C) an EMPLOYER engages the services of workers.

29. **(C)** Discriminate means to distinguish, to perceive the differences of. SEPARATE is the only word choice that has a similar meaning. (A) PERSECUTE means to harass or annoy, especially because of beliefs; (B) IMPLICATE is a synonym for incriminate; (D) DOUBT is to question the truth of.

30. **(A)** Introspection comes from the Latin *introspectus*: *intro* meaning inside, *spectus* to look—or SELF-EXAMINATION, to examine one's own thoughts and beliefs. (B) SHYNESS is synonymous with introversion; (C) CONCENTRATION is the act of focusing one's attention; (D) QUIETNESS is the (small) degree of noise or activity.

31. **(C)** Amnesia is a loss of memory; FORGETFULNESS, meaning failure to remember, is the closest in meaning of the word choices given. (A) DEPRESSION is the state of being sad or inactive; (B) SLEEPLESSNESS is a synonym for insomnia; (D) a PHOBIA is a fear of something.

32. **(C)** Ignorant means unaware or unknowing, lacking knowledge of something; INEXPERIENCED has the closest meaning of the word choices. (A) INFERIOR means lower in status, poor in quality, or below average; (B) DISGRACEFUL means causing a loss of honor, shameful; (D) FOOLISH means absurd or ridiculous.

33. **(D)** To covet is to enviously DESIRE something. (A) To SHELTER, meaning to protect or cover, can be synonymous with keeping something covert (secret); (B) STEAL is not related; (C) to PROMISE may be synonymous with keeping a covenant, or pact.

34. **(A)** Chronic and REPEAT are synonymous. Chronic may also mean long-term. (B) PAINFUL is not related, although a chronic condition may also be painful; (C) ACUTE means sharp or severe; (D) BRIEF, meaning short-term, is an antonym of chronic.

35. **(D)** Deference means a courteous RESPECT or a yielding of opinion or desire. (A) AVOIDANCE is keeping away from; (B) DISSIMILARITY is synonymous with difference; (C) RESISTANCE is a synonym for defiance.

PARAGRAPH COMPREHENSION TEST 2

ANSWER KEY

1. (B)	6. (C)	11. (B)
2. (D)	7. (B)	12. (C)
3. (A)	8. (C)	13. (C)
4. (B)	9. (B)	14. (A)
5. (D)	10. (A)	15. (C)

Add up your correct answers and put the number here. _____

Now record your score on pages 451-452.

DETAILED EXPLANATIONS OF ANSWERS

1. **(B)** The writer concludes the paragraphs by stating that honey-gathering methods became widespread, and that commercial beekeeping spread into other states. Spreading is a kind of development. The paragraph shows a development in time from "In the beginning." Even though the writer talks about some of the history of beekeeping, the point is how it developed and spread to other states.

2. **(D)** Although the victim of Alzheimer's may forget to turn off the oven, the writer says nothing about the victim's disliking any particular food.

3. **(A)** Since a motivated person generally learns faster, the reader can assume that only (A) can be correct. The writer says nothing about "need" (D) or being "tired" (C), or how they affect the learner. To be unmotivated (B) is just the opposite of what the writer says.

4. **(B)** The writer discusses "highs" and "lows" of something nearest to or farthest from the moon. The continents do not get higher and lower because the sun and moon are in different positions. Only the water, or oceans, could react in such a way. Also, the sun and moon are bodies that have relative "attractions" for one another—they do not get higher or lower. Since it is bodies of water—or oceans—that have tides, (B) is the correct answer.

5. **(D)** The writer states that Newton's theory of universal gravitation was his supreme work. "Most important" is close in meaning to supreme. That it was disputed or misunderstood is never discussed by the writer.

6. **(C)** Watch out, this is a little tricky. Notice that the studies were of "the satellites" of Jupiter (i.e., the moons of that planet), not of the planet itself; (C) is correct.

7. **(B)** Solar energy is becoming a logical alternative because of the unavailability of conventional fuels, so (B) must be the answer. The cost of conventional fuels is increasing, so the correct answer can't be (A). Although the writer says solar heating is good for the environment, noth-

ing is mentioned about conventional fuels being good. Conventional fuels (coal, oil, and gas) are much closer than the sun—they are right here on Earth.

8.   **(C)**   The writer implies that de Leon only thought his "island" of Florida was an island. The quotation marks around "island" indicate that the word is used not in its true sense. In fact, Florida is an extension—an outward reaching, but connected part—of the mainland of the American continent. Nothing is said about Indians (D) or volcanoes (A). Answer (B) is incorrect, an island is a body of land completely surrounded by water, and since Florida is not completely surrounded by water, it can't be an island.

9.   **(B)**   Since the "product" of "conceiving" is (to "produce") foals, and since conceiving happens during breeding, conceiving must mean becoming pregnant. "Producing living foals" is not a sickness (A). Here, producing means giving birth to. Although some animals die giving birth (producing), they do not die while conceiving (C).

10. **(A)**   The writer makes it clear that the young are not educated (a form of caring), because the parents are usually involved with gathering their own food and reproducing.

11. **(B)**   The writer clearly states that "the label phobia is applied to the person's fear and avoidance." Phobic persons, according to the writer, cannot control their fears. The writer doesn't say anything about how phobics feel about their fears, only that they experience strong reactions.

12. **(C)**   The topic (T) sentence states that "the health hazard of asbestos fibers" is what makes it a controversial building material.

13. **(C)**   The passage states that the "stars have been relied upon" by travellers and others. Since "relied upon" and "depended upon" mean virtually the same thing, man has depended on stars at times—and (C) is the correct answer.

14. **(A)**   Nothing was said about interviews with inhabitants in the paragraph.

15. **(C)**   "The mollusk covers the irritant with a substance called nacre." Man doesn't do it—the mollusk does. Consequently, the reader can assume that the mollusk must produce this substance naturally, or "organically," to cover any irritant in its system—artificially implanted by man or not.

AUTO & SHOP
TEST 2

ANSWER KEY

1. (C)	8. (D)	15. (A)	22. (D)
2. (B)	9. (C)	16. (C)	23. (D)
3. (C)	10. (D)	17. (C)	24. (C)
4. (D)	11. (D)	18. (D)	25. (D)
5. (D)	12. (C)	19. (B)	
6. (C)	13. (D)	20. (C)	
7. (A)	14. (D)	21. (A)	

Add up your correct answers and put the number here. _____

Now record your score on pages 451-452.

DETAILED EXPLANATIONS OF ANSWERS

1.   **(C)**   Intake and exhaust valves allow the flow of air-fuel mixture in and out of the cylinder, in addition to sealing the air-fuel mixture within the cylinder during combustion. The air-fuel mixture enters and exits the cylinder through the intake and exhaust ports. The intake manifold carries fresh air-fuel mixture from the carburetor to the intake port.

2.   **(B)**   The flywheel is a fairly large, heavy wheel that helps keep the crankshaft rotating, pistons moving, and keeps the engine running smoothly. Once a flywheel starts to rotate, it usually keeps rotating easily because of its weight. The oil pump is what maintains the flow of oil through the engine.

3.   **(C)**   BDC stands for "bottom dead center." BDC is the lowest point a piston can travel during its stroke within the cylinder.

4.   **(D)**   The CR is a measure of how much the air-fuel mixture is squeezed or compressed. The compression ratio (CR) is the ratio between volume in the cylinder when the piston is at BDC and TDC. If at TDC, the volume of air-fuel mixture which the combustion chamber can hold is 1 gallon and at BDC it is 10 gallons, then the CR is equal to 10 to 1 (10:1). This means that the 10 gallons which fill the cylinder at BDC end up being squeezed into a space 1/10th the size of the space which the mixture originally occupied (from 10 *to* 1 gallon).

5.   **(D)**   The third stroke in this case would be the exhaust stroke, where the piston pushes the hot exhaust gases out of the cylinder, clearing it so fresh mixture can enter. When the compression stroke is counted as the first stroke, the order for a four-stroke cycle is compression, power, exhaust, and intake strokes.

6.   **(C)**   The abbreviation **ohc** stands for overhead camshaft. Modern camshaft arrangements often use overhead camshafts. These arrangements are called "overhead" because the camshaft resides in the cylinder head.

7.   **(A)**   The venturi is part of the carburetor. The venturi is hourglass-like in shape, and because of its shape, the air passing through speeds up,

as it squeezes through the thin part of the venturi. When the air speeds up, a slight vacuum is created near the discharge tube which sucks some fuel out of it. The air and fuel mix and are pulled into the cylinder on its intake stroke. The exhaust port (C) is part of the cylinder head and the camshaft (B) is used to open and close valves; neither are part of the carburetor.

8.   **(D)**   The fuel flow into the float bowl is stopped by the needle valve as the attached hollow float rises with rising fuel level. The throttle (A) and choke (B) valves are part of the carburetor but have nothing to do with the float bowl; intake valves (C) are used in cylinder heads not carburetors.

9.   **(C)**   Some internal combustion engines, called *compression-ignition (CI) engines,* or diesel engines, use very high compression ratios to heat air in the combustion chamber so that when fuel is injected, ignition occurs immediately and without a spark from a spark plug.

10.   **(D)**   PCV, air injection, and ECS all help in reducing hydrocarbon (HC) emission which results from either unburned gasoline during combustion or evaporation of gasoline from the carburetor or fuel tank into the atmosphere. Positive crankcase ventilation (PCV) takes gasoline vapors and combustion gases, which escape from the combustion chambers into the crankcase, and discharges them back into the intake manifold to be properly burned along with the fresh incoming air and fuel. Air injection injects compressed air through a nozzle into the engine's exhaust ports to create further burning of partially burned exhaust gases before they exit the exhaust system. An evaporation control system (ECS) uses a pressure-vacuum fuel filler cap, a nonvented fuel tank, a canister filled with charcoal granules, and vent lines (or tubes) to collect and later burn gasoline vapors from the carburetor and fuel tank.

11.   **(D)**   Direct drive is commonly fourth (high) gear in a five-speed manual transmission. In direct drive the transmission output shaft and transmission input shaft (and crankshaft) rotate together because the transmission output shaft slides toward and connects directly to the transmission input shaft. This results is no torque multiplication and a 1:1 gear ratio.

12.   **(C)**   The torque converter is made up of three major parts: the turbine, the pump, and the stator. The turbine and pump resemble two halves of a hollow steel doughnut with blades in each half. The stator resembles a small wheel with blades which is placed between the pump and turbine.

The pump and turbine transfer torque between the crankshaft and transmission input shaft and the stator allows for torque multiplication.

13. **(D)** Rear-wheel drive systems use a drive shaft to transfer torque back to the rear differential. In four-wheel drive systems, a transfer case is often used to transfer torque from the transmission to both a front and rear axle assembly through a pair of drive shafts. Front-wheel drive systems (C) use no drive shaft.

14. **(D)** Simple calipers are used in conjunction with a scale to measure diameters. Outside calipers for measuring outside diameters are bow-legged; those used for inside diameters have straight legs with the feet turned outward. Calipers are adjusted by pulling or pushing the legs to open or close them.

15. **(A)** Recessed head screws usually have a hex-shaped (six-sided) recess. To remove or tighten this type screw requires a special wrench that will fit in the recess. This wrench is called an Allen-type wrench. Allen-type wrenches are made from hexagonal L-shaped bars of tool steel.

16. **(C)** Snips are used for cutting sheet metal and steel. The straight hand snips shown have blades that are straight and cutting edges that are sharpened to an 85° angle.

17. **(C)** Files are graded according to the degree of fineness, and according to whether they have single- or double-cut teeth. Single-cut files have rows of teeth cut parallel to each other. You will use single-cut files for sharpening tools, finish filing, and drawfiling. They are also the best tools for smoothing the edges of sheet metal.

18. **(D)** Hollow metal cutting punches are made from hardened tool steel. They are made in various sizes and are used to cut holes in light gage sheet metal.

19. **(B)** Pliers are used for cutting purposes as well as holding and gripping small articles in situations where it may be inconvenient or impossible to use hands. Long-nosed pliers commonly called needle-nose pliers are especially useful for holding small objects in tight places and for making delicate adjustments.

20. **(C)** Slipjoint pliers are pliers with straight, serrated (grooved) jaws, and the screw or pivot with which the jaws are fastened together may be

moved to either of two positions, in order to grasp small- or large-sized objects better.

21. **(A)** The size of a carpenter's steel square is usually 12 inches × 8 inches, 24 inches × 16 inches, or 24 inches × 18 inches. The flat sides of the blade and the tongue are graduated in inches and fractions of an inch. The most common uses for this square are laying out and squaring up large patterns, and for testing the flatness and squareness of large surfaces.

22. **(D)** Levels are tools designed to prove whether a plane or surface is true horizontal or true vertical. Some precision levels are calibrated so that they will indicate in degrees, minutes, and seconds the angle inclination of a surface in relation to a horizontal or vertical surface. Leveling is accomplished when the air bubble is centered between the graduation lines.

23. **(D)** The lengths of the most commonly used nails are designated by the penny system. The abbreviation for the word "penny" is the letter "d." Thus, the expression "a 2d nail" means a two-penny nail.

24. **(C)** Capscrews may have square, hex, flat, button, or fillister heads. Fillister heads are best for use on moving parts when such heads are sunk into counterbored holes. Hex heads are usually used where the metal parts do not move.

25. **(D)** Mallet heads are made from a soft material, usually wood, rawhide, or rubber. For example, a rubber-faced mallet is used for knocking out dents in an automobile.

MATHEMATICS KNOWLEDGE TEST 2

ANSWER KEY

1. (A)	8. (B)	15. (B)	22. (B)
2. (D)	9. (A)	16. (D)	23. (C)
3. (C)	10. (D)	17. (A)	24. (A)
4. (C)	11. (C)	18. (B)	25. (D)
5. (D)	12. (B)	19. (B)	
6. (D)	13. (D)	20. (C)	
7. (B)	14. (A)	21. (D)	

Add up your correct answers and put the number here. _____

Now record your score on pages 451-452.

DETAILED EXPLANATIONS OF ANSWERS

1. **(A)** The answer is (A) because the third angle equals $180° - 90° - 70° = 20°$ since it is a right triangle.

2. **(D)** The answer is (D) because $14 \times 14 = 196$.

3. **(C)** The answer is (C) because dividing by -6 (and reversing the direction of the inequality) gives $x < 2$.

4. **(C)** The answer is (C) because the perimeter equals 12 inches or each side equals 3 inches and the area is equal to $s^2 = 3 \times 3 = 9$.

5. **(D)** The answer is (D) because $(x - 2)(x - 3) = x^2 - 3x - 2x + 6 = x^2 - 5x + 6$.

6. **(D)** The answer is (D) because the perimeter equals 2 times the length plus 2 times the width. The length is equal to 2 times the width or $2w$. Therefore, the equation is $6w = 24$.

7. **(B)** The answer is (B) because the total freshman class times .40 equals 200 or $200/.40 = 500$ students in the freshman class.

8. **(B)** The answer is (B) because dividing by -10 (and reversing the direction of the inequality) gives $x \le -6.5$.

9. **(A)** The answer is (A) because using the Pythagorean Theorem and letting l be the other leg, $6^2 + l^2 = 10^2$ (because one-half foot equals 6 inches). Then $36 + l^2 = 100$, or $l^2 = 64$. The other leg equals 8 inches.

10. **(D)** The answer is (D) because $(9 \times 2) - 26 = -8$.

11. **(C)** The answer is (C) because $(z + 4)(z - 5) = z^2 - 5z + 4z - 20 = z^2 - z - 20$.

12. **(B)** The answer is (B) because a pentagon has five sides.

13. **(D)** The answer is (D) because 75% or .75 times 60 play only basketball, or .75 × 60 = 45.

14. **(A)** The answer is (A) because the area of the circle is equal to twice the circumference or $2(2\pi r) = \pi r^2$, or $4r = r^2$. Since r cannot equal 0, $r = 4$.

15. **(B)** The answer is (B) because multiplying by –3 (and reversing the direction of the inequality) gives $x < -12$.

16. **(D)** The answer is (D) because factoring $v^2 - 2v - 15$ gives $(v + 3)(v - 5)$.

17. **(A)** The answer is (A) because the perimeter of a square equals $4s$ and the perimeter of a rectangle equals 2 times the length and 2 times the width or $4s = 8 + 2l$.

18. **(B)** The answer is (B) because Jane reads a total of 50 pages in the five nights and this is 40% or .40 of the total assignment. Total assignment = 50/.40 = 125.

19. **(B)** The answer is (B) because the angles formed by the hypotenuse equal 90°, or 90° – 25° = 65°, the other angle is not given. The difference of the two angles is 65° – 25° = 40°.

20. **(C)** The answer is (C) because $(w + 6)(w + 2) = w^2 + 2w + 6w + 12 = w^2 + 8w + 12$.

21. **(D)** The answer is (D) because the final selling cost = 1.20 + .45(1.20) = $1.74.

22. **(B)** The answer is (B) because there are two equal angles in an isosceles triangle.

23. **(C)** The answer is (C) because 13 × 13 = 169.

24. **(A)** The answer is (A) because (4 × 3) + 12 = 24.

25. **(D)** The answer is (D) because $s^2 = 2(4s)$ or $s^2 = 8s$. Since s cannot equal 0, then $s = 8$.

MECHANICAL COMPREHENSION TEST 2

ANSWER KEY

1. (B)	8. (A)	15. (D)	22. (B)
2. (A)	9. (B)	16. (B)	23. (D)
3. (D)	10. (D)	17. (A)	24. (B)
4. (D)	11. (A)	18. (B)	25. (A)
5. (B)	12. (C)	19. (D)	
6. (A)	13. (D)	20. (B)	
7. (D)	14. (B)	21. (C)	

Add up your correct answers and put the number here. _____

Now record your score on pages 451-452.

DETAILED EXPLANATIONS OF ANSWERS

1.   **(B)**   (A) This statement is true for a Class I, not a Class III lever. (B) This is the characteristic, or definition, of a Class III lever. (C) This statement is true for a Class II, not a Class III lever. (D) This is not true because the resistance is further out from the fulcrum than the effort; therefore, the effort has to be greater than the resistance.

2.   **(A)**   Since the effort to lift the flags is equal to the weight of the flags (the resistance) it follows that

$$\text{M.A.} = \frac{E}{R} = \frac{E}{E} = 1.$$

3.   **(D)**   Since the gears mesh, and there are 32 teeth on gear A and 8 teeth on gear B, one complete revolution of A results in four complete revolutions of B. And since gears B and C have the same number of teeth, one revolution of B results in one revolution of C. Thus wheels B and C revolve four times as fast as wheel A.

4.   **(D)**   The figure shows what is known as a helical spur gear. The bevel gear (A) is used for two gears at an angle. The pinion (B) is usually smaller than the other gear; and the worm gear (C) figures a screw-like straight gear driving a regular disk gear.

5.   **(B)**   A cam is a specially shaped surface, projection, or groove whose movement with respect to a part in contact with it (cam follower) drives the cam follower in another movement in response. Cams are not ordinarily used to transmit power in the sense that gear trains are (C). Function (D) is for clutches, while (A) is for couplings.

6.   **(A)**   The mechanical advantage of a block-and-tackle system is given by the number of strands of rope supporting the movable block. In this case, the movable block is supported by five strands of rope.

7.   **(D)**   One half turn of the crankshaft corresponds to one stroke. In the figure, the crankshaft is in a position to force the piston down one stroke

as it makes one half turn clockwise. In the second half turn, the piston is forced up one stroke.

8.   **(A)**   Use Slim's shoulder as a fulcrum F_1. Look at the clockwise moment caused by the 300-pound load. That load is 5 ft away from Slim's shoulder. If R_1 is the load, and L_1 the distance from Slim's shoulder to the load, the clockwise moment M_A is

$$M_A = R_1 \times L_1 = 300 \times 5 = 1,500 \text{ ft-lb.}$$

Sam's effort causes a counterclockwise moment equal to E_2 times L_3 from his shoulder to the fulcrum F_1 at Slim's shoulder:

$$M_B = E_2 \times L_3 = E_2 \times 8 = 8E_2.$$

Hence, equating the moments, we get

$1,500 = 8E_2$ and

$$E_2 = \frac{1,500}{8} = 187.5 \text{ pounds.}$$

9.   **(B)**   Gear trains are ordinarily used to transmit power and change the direction, speed, or size of the force applied. (A) is the function of a coupling, (C) is the function of a cam, and (D) is the function of a clutch.

10.   **(D)**   This is a Class I lever, using the lever formula:

$$\frac{R}{E} = \frac{L}{l}$$

here

$$\frac{200}{E} = \frac{8}{2} = 4 \text{ or}$$

$$E = \frac{200}{4} = 50 \text{ pounds.}$$

(A) is obtained by dividing the resistance by 10 (the length of the whole piece in inches). (B) is obtained by inverting the formula:

$$\frac{E}{R} = 4,$$

and (C) is obtained by dividing $R = 200$ pound by $L = 8"$.

11. **(A)** The wedge is an inclined plane and it multiplies the 200 lb force by about 4. The result is that the net mechanical advantage is about 16: a 50-pound heave actually ends up as an 800 lb force on each wedge to keep the hatch closed.

12. **(C)** The ring and flange both have 6 equally spaced holes; therefore, they must be rotated by an angle of at least

$$\frac{360}{6} = 60 \text{ degrees.}$$

13. **(D)** Since pulley A's diameter is 3 times larger than pulley C's, it follows that one turn of A generates 3 turns of C. But B and C are keyed to the same shaft; therefore, they both turn at the rate of $3 \times 500 = 1,500$ rpm. Now pulley B's diameter is twice that of pulley D. Therefore, D will turn at the rate of $1,500 \times 2 = 3,000$ rpm.

14. **(B)** As the camshaft makes one turn, the cam turns from its lobe to the main disk and then back to the lobe. This process will allow the valve to first move down and then move up again at the end of the turn.

15. **(D)** The clutch (A) is used to connect or disconnect a driving and a driven member for stopping or starting the driven part. A cam (B) is used to modify a mechanical movement, the power for which is furnished through other means. Spur gears (C) are used to couple two parallel shafts, and bevel gears (D) are used to couple two non-parallel shafts.

16. **(B)** The rotation speeds of two meshed gears are related to their number of teeth:

$$\frac{W_A}{W_B} = \frac{N_B}{N_A}$$

where W is the rotation speed (rpm) and N is the number of teeth. Therefore,

$$\frac{220}{W_B} = \frac{11}{18} \text{ and}$$

$$W_B = 220 \times \frac{18}{11} = 360 \text{ rpm.}$$

Thus gear B must be rotating at a faster rate than A, which means (A) and

(C) are wrong. Also, it is wrong to just measure the diameters of the two gear wheels and take the ratio $\dfrac{D_B}{D_A}$ and set it equal to $\dfrac{W_A}{W_B}$ as would be done for pulleys, thus (D) is wrong.

17. **(A)** Since two meshed gears turn in opposite directions and since gears B and F (G is on the same shaft as F, and C is on the same shaft as B) both turn counterclockwise, it follows that gears A and E must be turned clockwise and handles (1) and (2) as well.

18. **(B)** A cam is a device that is designed to modify a mechanical movement, the power for which is supplied through other means. (A) is the function of couplings, (C) is the function of gears, and (D) is the function of the clutch.

19. **(D)** With the regular shoes, each square inch of the soles carries

$160 \div 60 = 2.6$ pounds of weight.

Now the force on the snowshoes remains the same but the area is unknown; the pressure however is known:

$$0.18 \text{ psi} = \frac{160 \text{ lb}}{\text{Area in sq. in}}$$

therefore Area = 889 sq. in.

20. **(B)** The correct name for this gear system is a spiral bevel gear. In spur gears (C), the gears have no curvature. The worm gear (A) is similar but with straight gears at right angles to the plane of the wheel.

21. **(C)** The basis of this machine is the wheel and axle which is an application of the second-class lever since the resistance is between the fulcrum and the effort. The drill bit is based on the wedge and the inclined plane, but not the whole machine.

22. **(B)** From the lever formula:

$$\text{M.A.} = \frac{L}{l} = \frac{R}{E}$$

here $L = 5"$, $l = \frac{1}{4}"$, therefore

$$M.A. = \frac{5}{\frac{1}{4}} = 20.$$

23. **(D)** From the ratio of the number of teeth, $^{40}/_{10} = 4$, wheel B must be turning at $^1/_4$ the rate of wheel A, that is at the rate of one revolution per second. Now since wheel C is rigidly fixed on the same shaft with wheel B, it must be turning at the same rate as wheel B, and from the ratio $^{20}/_{10}$ of its number of teeth to the number of teeth of wheel D, it follows that wheel D must be turning at the rate of two revolutions per second.

24. **(B)** The correct definition of the efficiency of a machine is the ratio of the work output to the work input. (A) always leads to a negative result, (C) is the inverse of the definition, and (D) leads to a negative result which is the deficiency of the machine.

25. **(A)** A rise in pressure is accompanied by a rise in the height of the mercury column because the pressure exerts a force pushing downwards on the mercury that is in the receptacle; thus, the mercury is pushed upwards in the column and its weight acts to balance the force due to the external pressure. This rise is much more noticeable than any change in the lower receptacle.

ELECTRONICS INFORMATION
TEST 2

ANSWER KEY

1. (B)	6. (C)	11. (A)	16. (C)
2. (A)	7. (C)	12. (D)	17. (A)
3. (C)	8. (A)	13. (B)	18. (B)
4. (C)	9. (C)	14. (B)	19. (C)
5. (C)	10. (B)	15. (C)	20. (B)

Add up your correct answers and put the number here. _____

Now record your score on pages 451-452.

DETAILED EXPLANATIONS
OF ANSWERS

1.   **(B)**   Energy is equal to the power × time in seconds:

75 W × 2 hours × 3,600 sec/hr = 540,000 J.

2.   **(A)**   If the voltage in your house is 110 V, then 20 amps is equal to 2,200 Watts. Since only toaster *A* can run on less than 2,200 Watts, this is the toaster.

3.   **(C)**   Your house is grounded to make sure no one gets any stray shocks. The common is grounded.

4.   **(C)**   A diode is known as a rectifier. This means it passes current in only one direction.

5.   **(C)**   The plot shown exemplifies that of a device which rectifies the current passing through it. For a small positive voltage the diode passes current without any drop — for a large reverse voltage the current is not passed through.

6.   **(C)**   The unit of measurement for resistance is an ohm.

7.   **(C)**   An open circuit usually means a current path is broken or open — this would imply infinite resistance.

8.   **(A)**   A capacitor stores charge.

9.   **(C)**   Devices in parallel have an equal voltage across them. The voltage across points $C - C'$, $B - B'$, and $A - A'$ is 10 V.

10.   **(B)**   According to code, the minimum wire gauge needed is #12 for 20 amps.

11.   **(A)** Ω = ohms.

12.   **(D)**   The metal provides a shield from electrical noise that might disrupt the circuits.

13. **(B)**   Always try to use a fuse that can handle the power needed.

14. **(B)**   As wires heat up their resistance drops.

15. **(C)**   The symbol for a battery is sometimes confused with that of a capacitor, but if you keep in mind a battery symbol always has non equal lines and if a capacitor is shown it has a curved line or two equal lines.

16. **(C)**   Air is the best insulator of these items and dry air is much more insulating than wet air because water increases conductivity.

17. **(A)**   By definition the voltage step ratio for a transformer is given by

$$\frac{V_{primary}}{V_{secondary}} = \frac{N_{primary}}{N_{secondary}} = \frac{(\# \text{ of turns})_{primary}}{(\# \text{ of turns})_{secondary}}.$$

18. **(B)**   An arc must discharge to another conductor, but a spark usually will discharge to air.

19. **(C)**   A good conductor has very little voltage drops in it, this implies low resistance, which implies current flows easily.

20. **(B)**   Switch B is a toggle switch because the switch toggles back and forth.

ASVAB

Armed Services Vocational Aptitude Battery

Test 3

GENERAL SCIENCE
TEST 3

Time: 11 Minutes
  25 Questions

(Answer sheets appear in the back of this book.)

DIRECTIONS: This is a test of 25 questions to find out how much you know about general science as usually covered in high school courses. Pick the best answer for each question, then blacken the space on your answer form which has the same number and letter as your choice.

1. Which of the following is not a vertebrate?

   1–A   Fish   1–C   Snails

   1–B   Eagles   1–D   Frogs

2. Insects have

   2–A   2 body regions and 8 legs.

   2–B   3 body regions and 8 legs.

   2–C   2 body regions and 6 legs.

   2–D   3 body regions and 6 legs.

3. Gymnosperms produce

   3–A   fruit.   3–C   seed cones.

   3–B   spores.   3–D   protective seed coverings.

4. The gland that produces insulin is the

   4–A   parathyroid.   4–C   pituitary.

   4–B   thyroid.   4–D   pancreas.

5. Breads and cereals are important sources of

   5–A   protein.   5–C   vitamins.

   5–B   energy.   5–D   minerals.

6. Two brown-eyed parents have a child with blue eyes. Blue eye color is a recessive trait. In terms of eye color, the parents must be genetically

  6–A   both homozygous.

  6–B   both heterozygous.

  6–C   mother homozygous, father heterozygous.

  6–D   mother heterozygous, father homozygous.

7. Omnivores consume

  7–A   everything.   7–C   animals only.

  7–B   plants only.   7–D   both plants and animals.

8. Some cells take materials into their structure by engulfing them. This process is called

  8–A   diffusion.   8–C   respiration.

  8–B   phagocytosis.   8–D   osmosis.

9. One meter equals 100

  9–A   millimeters.   9–C   centimeters.

  9–B   decimeters.   9–D   kilometers.

10. The heat transfer caused when heated liquids or gases rise is called

  10–A conduction.   10–C insulation.

  10–B convection.   10–D radiation.

11. Consumption of electricity is measured in

  11–A volts.   11–C watts.

  11–B amperes.   11–D ohms.

12. Magnetic force between two objects decreases as the amount of _____ the objects increases.

  12–A distance between   12–C electric charge on

  12–B pressure on   12–D insulation between

13. Light waves have a longer wavelength than

    13–A microwaves.   13–C radar.

    13–B radio waves.   13–D x-rays.

14. Sound waves of a loud sound have a greater _____ than those of quiet sounds.

    14–A speed   14–C amplitude

    14–B frequency   14–D intensity

15. Organic compounds are compounds containing

    15–A oxygen.   15–C carbon.

    15–B hydrogen.   15–D water.

16. A material with definite volume but no definite shape is called a

    16–A plasma.   16–C liquid.

    16–B gas.   16–D solid.

17. An acidic solution will have a pH of

    17–A 20.   17–C 7.

    17–B 10.   17–D 5.

18. The equation $C + O_2 \longrightarrow CO_2$ is what type of reaction?

    18–A Synthesis   18–C Displacement

    18–B Decomposition   18–D Double replacement

19. The intensity of an earthquake is measured by a(n)

    19–A thermograph.   19–C telegraph.

    19–B scismograph   19–D oscilloscope.

20. Air pressure is measured with a

    20–A thermometer.   20–C hygrometer.

    20–B barometer.   20–D anemometer.

21. The planet closest to the sun is

    21–A Earth.   21–C Mars.

    21–B Jupiter.   21–D Mercury.

22. In a balanced equation for forming water, $2H_2 + O_2 \longrightarrow$ _____

    22–A H_2O_2.   22–C $2H_2O_2$.

    22–B $2H_2O$.   22–D H_2O.

23. The phylum Chordata includes

    23–A mammals.   23–C mushrooms.

    23–B earthworms.   23–D trees.

24. Otters eat fish. Otters are

    24–A predators.   24–C herbivores.

    24–B prey.   24–D decomposers.

25. Decibels are used to measure

    25–A sound.   25–C distance.

    25–B frequency.   25–D speed.

ARITHMETIC REASONING
TEST 3

Time: 36 Minutes
30 Questions

(Answer sheets appear in the back of this book.)

> **DIRECTIONS:** Each question has four multiple-choice answers, labeled by the number of the question and the letters A, B, C, or D. Select the single best answer.

1. Jimmy is trying to call Carol. Carol is on the phone from 4:00 until 5:18. If Jimmy begins calling at 4:15 and then calls every five minutes, how many calls must be make until Carol's phone is not busy?

   1–A   12   1–C   14

   1–B   13   1–D   15

2. A certain stock changes by four points on one day, then drops six points the next day, and increases by three points the following day. Over the three day period, how much did this stock increase by?

   2–A   –1 point   2–C   7 points

   2–B   –2 points   2–D   1 point

3. Two cars leave the same place at the same time, and both go to the same destination, 40 miles away. One averages 40 miles per hour, and the other averages 60 miles per hour. How much longer will it take the slower car than the faster one?

   3–A   20 minutes   3–C   15 minutes

   3–B   30 minutes   3–D   60 minutes

4. A supermarket makes $1,000 per day in profit. If half of this comes from groceries, 30% from food-related products, and 20% from cigarettes, videos, and newspapers, then how much profit do they make per day from groceries?

   4–A $200   4–C $1,000

   4–B $300   4–D $500

5. Bob earns $5 per hour and double for overtime, which would be any time over 40 hours in a week. How many hours would he need to work to earn $250 in a week?

5–A   40   5–C   50

5–B   45   5–D   55

6. Susan and Phil watch TV one night. Susan watches for three hours and Phil watches for two hours, one of which is with Susan and one is alone. For how many hours was the TV on?

6–A   4   6–C   3

6–B   5   6–D   2

7. A plane flies 3,000 miles in five hours. How far can it go in two hours?

7–A   500 miles   7–C   1,200 miles

7–B   600 miles   7–D   1,800 miles

8. Larry wins $50,000 in a lottery, but has to pay 50% tax. How much does he have left?

8–A $10,000   8–C $20,000

8–B $15,000   8–D $25,000

9. A baseball team wins 20 games, which gives them an 80% winning percentage. How many games did they lose?

9–A   4   9–C   6

9–B   5   9–D   7

10. A rock band with four members gives a concert, and 50,000 fans show up. Tickets cost $10 each and it costs $300,000 to rent the stadium. How much does each band member earn?

10–A $50,000   10–C $60,000

10–B $55,000   10–D $65,000

11. A company has 28 desks in the storeroom. If they hire 16 new employees, and each one needs one desk, then how many desks will they have left in the storeroom?

    11–A 10   11–C 12

    11–B 11   11–D 13

12. On a cold day a family of six is to share three cups of soup. How many cups does each one get?

    12–A 2   12–C 1

    12–B 1.5   12–D 0.5

13. Alice earns $60,000 per year. If she gets a 10% raise, then what is her new salary?

    13–A $65,000   13–C $67,000

    13–B $66,000   13–D $68,000

14. A certain charity sponsors research by funding several workers for $10,000 each per year. If this charity receives donations from four families, and these families give $50,000, $10,000, $5,000, and $25,000, then how many researchers can the foundation support?

    14–A 9   14–C 11

    14–B 10   14–D 12

15. A salesman needs to sell 300 items per week. If he sells 49 on Monday, 61 on Tuesday, 55 on Wednesday, and 45 on Thursday, then how many does he need to sell on Friday?

    15–A 70   15–C 90

    15–B 80   15–D 100

16. A student takes math for four credits, English for three, history for three, and French for three. How many total credits does the student take?

    16–A 10   16–C 12

    16–B 11   16–D 13

17. Jim wants to drive 3,000 miles across the country. He averages 50 miles per hour, and drives 10 hours per day. How many days will it take him to complete his trip?

17–A 5   17–C 7

17–B 6   17–D 8

18. If a football team scores 64 points in their first four games, then how many points do they average per game?

18–A 16   18–C 18

18–B 17   18–D 19

19. A merchant buys fish for $3.00 per pound, then marks it up to earn a 20% profit. What is the retail price per pound?

19–A $3.20   19–C $3.60

19–B $3.40   19–D $3.80

20. In a certain election there are 400,000 voters. If 60% vote for one candidate, then how many votes will he receive?

20–A 240,000   20–C 260,000

20–B 250,000   20–D 270,000

21. Bob lifts weights for six weeks. On the first week he bench presses 100 pounds. The second week, he presses 120 pounds; the third week, 150 pounds; the fourth week, 170 pounds; the fifth week, 210 pounds; and the sixth week, 220 pounds. During which week did he improve the most over his previous week?

21–A Week 3   21–C Week 5

21–B Week 4   21–D Week 6

22. The vice president of the Finance Department of a large company has three directors reporting to him. The first director has four managers under him, the second has three, and the third has three. How many managers are under the vice president?

22–A 7   22–C 9

22–B 8   22–D 10

23. Shirley goes to bed at 11:00 PM and wants to sleep for eight hours. For what time should she set her alarm clock?

    23–A 6:00 AM   23–C 8:00 AM

    23–B 7:00 AM   23–D 9:00 AM

24. In an election there are three candidates, A, B, and C. If A receives half of the votes, B receives one-third of the votes, and C receives 6.67% percent of the votes, then what percent of the population did not vote?

    24–A 10%   24–C 20%

    24–B 15%   24–D 25%

25. In black jack one has a "five card Charlie" if he has five cards whose values sum to 21. If Joe is dealt a 7 and a 4, then hits twice (gets two more cards) and these are a 2 and a 5, then what would the highest fifth card have to be to have a five card Charlie?

    25–A Ace (1)   25–C 3

    25–B 2   25–D 4

26. Andrea has $100 when she goes shopping. She buys some clothes for $39, some tapes for $18, and some food for $12. How much does she have left?

    26–A $22   26–C $28

    26–B $25   26–D $31

27. Victoria walks two miles to her friend's dormitory, then they both walk a mile to the pizza parlor, and then Victoria walks three miles home. How far did she walk?

    27–A 4 miles   27–C 6 miles

    27–B 5 miles   27–D 7 miles

28. If a dozen donuts costs $1.44, then how much does each donut cost?

    28–A $0.12   28–C $0.14

    28–B $0.13   28–D $0.15

29. Bill and Bob each bike for 30 minutes. Bill goes 15 miles and Bob goes 10 miles. How much faster was Bill going than Bob?

    29–A 5 miles per hour   29–C 10 miles per hour

    29–B 15 miles per hour   29–D 20 miles per hour

30. A marathon runner runs 26 miles. How much time would it take to complete this task in order to average six minutes per mile?

    30–A 1 hour and 36 minutes   30–C 2 hours and 36 minutes

    30–B 2 hours and 6 minutes   30–D 3 hours and 6 minutes

WORD KNOWLEDGE
TEST 3

Time: 11 Minutes
   35 Questions

(Answer sheets appear in the back of this book.)

> **DIRECTIONS:** The ASVAB Word Knowledge Test is a test of your vocabulary. The test consists of 35 questions, each containing an underlined word. Pick one word from the four choices that you believe is the best synonym for the underlined word. A synonym is a word that has the same or nearly the same meaning as, in this case, the underlined word. On your answer sheet, mark the space that matches your choice. Be sure you are marking your answer in the space that represents the proper question number.

Following are two sample questions.

S1. Cindy wanted to <u>console</u> Steve on the loss of his job.

   S1–A Comfort   S1–C Acknowledge

   S1–B Annoy   S1–D Revere

S1. **(A)** COMFORT is the best answer; console means to relieve the sadness of. (B) ANNOY is the opposite of console; (C) ACKNOWL-EDGE means to recognize or thank; (D) REVERE means to worship or adore.

S2. The best synonym for the word <u>perceptive</u> is

   S2–A oblivious.   S2–C aware.

   S2–B steadfast.   S2–D stubborn.

S2. **(C)** AWARE is the best choice; perceptive means observant, and one sense of the word aware is to have or show perception, realization, or knowledge. (A) OBLIVIOUS means lacking attention or awareness, and is an antonym; (B) STEADFAST means reliable, loyal, or immovable; (D) STUBBORN means unwilling to give in, resolute.

1. Billy the Kid was an <u>infamous</u> bank robber.

   1–A   well-known   1–C   perfect

   1–B   immature   1–D   evil

2. The best synonym for <u>benign</u> is

   2–A   kind.   2–C   sinister.

   2–B   optimistic.   2–D   suggestive.

3. The best synonym for <u>abet</u> is

   3–A   touch.   3–C   await.

   3–B   vandalize.   3–D   encourage.

4. The instructions for the civil service exam were <u>comprehensive</u>.

   4–A   complete   4–C   difficult

   4–b   understandable   4–D   involved

5. The best synonym for <u>luminous</u> is

   5–A   jazzy.   5–C   energetic.

   5–B   glowing.   5–D   important.

6. Jack the Ripper was truly a <u>malicious</u> character.

   6–A   criminal   6–C   spiteful

   6–B   suspicious   6–D   selfish

7. The best synonym for <u>vicarious</u> is

   7–A   substitute.   7–C   dangerous.

   7–B   lively.   7–D   imaginary.

8. People who don't get enough exercise often feel <u>lethargic</u>.

   8–A   ill   8–C   energetic

   8–B   indifferent   8–D   frustrated

9. The best synonym for <u>facet</u> is

    9–A   visibility.   9–C   brilliance.

    9–B   wit.   9–D   aspect.

10. The best synonym for <u>unwieldy</u> is

    10–A heavy.   10–C large.

    10–B bulky.   10–D immovable.

11. The best synonym for <u>altruism</u> is

    11–A self-indulgence.   11–C charm.

    11–B weakness.   11–D unselfishness.

12. The best synonym for <u>wane</u> is

    12–A fluctuate.   12–C alarm.

    12–B subside.   12–D grow.

13. Margaret tried to make a practice of enjoying life's <u>fleeting</u> moments of happiness to the fullest.

    13–A temporary   13–C eternal

    13–B continuing   13–D simultaneous

14. The best synonym for <u>alleviate</u> is

    14–A relieve.   14–C annoy.

    14–B detour.   14–D dictate.

15. The best synonym for <u>defraud</u> is

    15–A confront.   15–C disgrace.

    15–B thwart.   15–D cheat.

16. The best synonym for <u>facetious</u> is

    16–A exact.   16–C fake.

    16–B sarcastic.   16–D witty.

17. The best synonym for <u>effete</u> is

   17–A bubbly.   17–C doubtful.

   17–B weak.   17–D innocent.

18. The best synonym for <u>benevolent</u> is

   18–A harmless.   18–C charitable.

   18–B blessed.   18–D courteous.

19. Terry especially enjoyed the <u>exotic</u> blooms at the flower show.

   19–A foreign   19–C stylish

   19–B suggestive   19–D weird

20. The best synonym for <u>hazardous</u> is

   20–A secure.   20–C undecided.

   20–B dangerous.   20–D fickle.

21. The best synonym for <u>contrite</u> is

   21–A demanding.   21–C apologetic.

   21–B against.   21–D disagreeable.

22. Her <u>impetuous</u> decisions sometimes produced surprise results.

   22–A distant   22–C impulsive

   22–B crazy   22–D planned

23. The best synonym for <u>apathy</u> is

   23–A indifference.   23–C hope.

   23–B stability.   23–D involvement.

24. The best synonym for <u>volatile</u> is

   24–A pleasant.   24–C angry.

   24–B unstable.   24–D quarrelsome.

25. The best synonym for <u>integrity</u> is

    25–A disdain.   25–C honesty.

    25–B smartness.   25–D fraudulence.

26. The best synonym for <u>consent</u> is

    26–A refuse.   26–C subdue.

    26–B provoke.   26–D agree.

27. The best synonym for <u>avid</u> is

    27–A half-hearted.   27–C eager.

    27–B preventable.   27–D sudden.

28. Because of Mark's <u>gregarious</u> personality, many people invited him to parties.

    28–A insane   28–C puzzling

    28–B bashful   28–D sociable

29. The best synonym for <u>nostalgic</u> is

    29–A homesick.   29–C sympathetic.

    29–B slow.   29–D sad.

30. The furnishings at the palace were designed to impress visitors with the king's <u>opulence</u>.

    30–A tackiness   30–C affluence

    30–B optimism   30–D heaviness

31. The best synonym for <u>awkward</u> is

    31–A unpleasant.   31–C useless.

    31–B ungainly.   31–D graceful.

32. The best synonym for <u>vivid</u> is

    32–A empty.   32–C loud.

    32–B lively.   32–D bright.

33. The best synonym for <u>preservation</u> is

    33–A protection.   33–C gift.

    33–B information.   33–D enforcement.

34. Since Pat was dieting, she <u>opted</u> for a chef's salad.

    34–A wanted   34–C needed

    34–B selected   34–D required

35. The best synonym for <u>appeal</u> is

    35–A be visible.   35–C calm.

    35–B interest.   35–D repel.

PARAGRAPH COMPREHENSION TEST 3

Time: 13 Minutes
15 Questions

(Answer sheets appear in the back of this book.)

DIRECTIONS: This test consists of 15 paragraphs that test your ability to understand and retrieve information from passages you have read. Each paragraph is followed by an incomplete question or statement. You must read each of the paragraphs and select the one lettered choice that best completes the statement or question. Your score is based on the number of correct answers. Try to answer every question, but don't spend too much time on any single question.

Here is a sample paragraph.

S1. Among camp intruders, skunks are the worst. Bears may come and eat scraps from the fire, but most can be shooed away. Raccoons may chew through garbage bags to get at the chicken bones, but a good dog will keep them away. But skunks? Who's going to tell a skunk to go away?

According to this paragraph, "intruders" are

S3–A robbers.

S3–B garbage disposal units.

S3–C animals who barge into campsites.

S3–D stories about animals.

S2. **(C)** The correct answer is (C), animals who barge into campsites.

1. The staff members of the Smithsonian Institution's Family Folklore Project interviewed hundreds of persons about their family folklore. To prepare for these interviews, they used their academic backgrounds in folklore and American studies, and their personal backgrounds as members of families. In addition, they reviewed the major instruction guides in genealogy, oral history, family history, and folklore field-work.

   "Academic background" in this passage refers to

   1–A   life experience.

   1–B   college/university study.

   1–C   fieldwork.

   1–D   travel.

2. Beta blockers are drugs that interfere with the effects of adrenalin. They have been used for heart conditions and for minor stress such as stage fright. Now they are used for test anxiety. These drugs seem to help test-takers who have low scores because of test fright, but not those who do not know the material.

   According to the passage

   2–A   beta blockers are adrenalin.

   2–B   beta blockers cause heart attacks.

   2–C   beta blockers work only on test anxiety.

   2–D   beta blockers work to improve test scores only if the test-taker truly knows the material.

3. We can no longer say the increasing decline in our wild animals and plant species is due only to "natural" processes. Many species are dying out because of exploitation, habitat alteration or destruction, pollution, or the introduction of new species of plants and animals to an area.

   According to this passage,

   3–A   man is the cause of some animal extinction.

   3–B   animals often bring about their own extinction.

   3–C   Congress can absolutely end extinction of animals.

   3–D   a law is more important than human responsibility.

4. The Earth's rapid spin and molten nickel-iron core give rise to a magnetic field which, coupled with the atmosphere, shields us from nearly all of the harmful radiation coming from the sun and other stars. Most meteors burn up in the Earth's atmosphere before they can strike the surface.

    According to this passage, two elements shield us from harmful radiation on Earth:

    4–A spinning nickel and spinning iron.

    4–B a magnetic field and meteors.

    4–C a magnetic field and molten nickel core.

    4–D a magnetic field and the atmosphere.

5. Stress is with us all the time. It comes from mental or emotional activity as well as physical activity. Too much emotional stress can cause physical illnesses such as high blood pressure, ulcers, or even heart disease.

    A source of stress *not* mentioned in this passage is

    5–A physical activity.

    5–B educational activity.

    5–C mental activity.

    5–D emotional activity.

6. Prolific evidence of early man's interest in caves has been discovered in caves scattered throughout the world. Fragments of skeletons of some of the earliest manlike creatures have been discovered in cave deposits. Neanderthal man was found in a cave in the Neander Valley of Germany. Cro-Magnon man created remarkable murals on the walls of caves in southern France more than 10,000 years ago.

    In this passage, "prolific" means

    6–A confusing.

    6–B abundant.

    6–C evil.

    6–D unpleasant smelling.

7. Each child has an individual pattern of social, as well as physical, development. Some of it depends on his home life and his relationships with the people who love him. An only child, on the other hand, may have to learn his lessons in social living through hard experiences on the playground or in the classroom.

Where does this passage say the only child learns his social lessons?

7–A   Home and school

7–B   Playground and classroom

7–C   Playground and home

7–D   All of the above

8. Studies have shown that the environmental impact of wind energy systems is small compared to that of conventional electric power systems. Wind-powered systems do not need to flood large land areas or alter the natural ecology, as do hydroelectric systems. Furthermore, they produce no waste products or thermal or chemical waste, as do fossil-fueled and nuclear-fueled systems.

According to this passage,

8–A   wind energy is more efficient than electric power.

8–B   wind energy is less expensive than electric power.

8–C   wind energy does not have as great an environmental impact as electric power.

8–D   wind energy is more expensive than electric power.

9. The "karat" marking on jewelry tells you what proportion of gold is mixed with other metals. If 14 parts of gold are mixed with 10 parts of base metal, the combination is called 14 karat (14K) gold. The higher the karat rating, the higher the proportion of gold in the object. The lowest karat rating of gold that can be marketed in the United States is 10 karat.

"Karat," as it is used in the jewelry industry, refers to

9–A   jeweler's appraisal.

9–B   U.S. registered trademark.

9–C   amount of gold mixed with other metals.

9–D   money value.

10. Our reliance on wood as fuel declined to less than one percent by 1970. But after the 1973 oil embargo, more and more people began returning to wood as a fuel. In 1976, for example, over six percent of New England's home heating was totally supplied by wood.

According to this passage, the use of wood as a basic fuel has

10–A decreased since the 1973 embargo.

10–B supplied the total population of New England.

10–C become cheaper.

10–D increased to more than six percent in New England.

11. Once a child has been identified as having a speech or language disorder, successful treatment involves a team of experts. An audiologist, an expert in hearing, evaluates those with hearing disorders. This scientist may work with a doctor who specializes in ear, nose, and throat disorders. These two professionals determine which hearing conditions can be treated.

An "audiologist" is

11–A a team of experts.

11–B someone who specializes in hearing processes.

11–C a child with a hearing problem.

11–D a diagnostic tool.

12. Parental love should be special in two respects: First, it should be constant and unconditional—which means it is always present, even when the child is acting in an unlovable manner. Second, parents should be open in expressing and showing love, so children are never uncertain about its presence.

According to this passage, a parent should

12–A love a child only when s/he is good.

12–B love children by being inconsistent.

12–C love a child all the time.

12–D love a child by hiding your love sometimes.

13. AIDS (acquired immune deficiency syndrome) is a disease caused by a virus that destroys a person's defenses against infections. These defenses are known as the immune system. The AIDS virus, known as human immunodeficiency virus, or HIV, can so weaken a person's immune system that he or she cannot fight off even mild infections and eventually becomes vulnerable to life-threatening infections and cancers.

According to this passage, which of the following probably does not result from contracting AIDS?

13–A Life-threatening infections

13–B Skin cancer

13–C Lymphatic cancer

13–D Pregnancy

14. Drugs can affect the way the body uses food. Drugs may act to impair proper nutrition, either by hastening elimination of certain nutrients, by hindering absorption of nutrients, or by interfering with converting nutrients to usable form. For those taking drugs over long periods of time, these interactions can lead to deficiencies of certain vitamins and minerals.

In this passage, "impair" means

14–A to separate.

14–B to put together.

14–C interfere with.

14–D speed up.

15. Several of the major Co-op institutions offer five-year programs with cooperative education required as part of the curriculum. In this arrangement, the student alternates being either on campus or on Co-op. Students in this program graduate with a traditional four-year education augmented by up to two years of Co-op experiences.

According to this passage, a person who enters a Co-op program will spend

15–A more time on campus.

15–B more years studying both on campus and off.

15–C fewer years on campus.

15–D fewer years on Co-op.

AUTO & SHOP
TEST 3

Time: 11 Minutes
   25 Questions

(Answer sheets appear in the back of this book.)

DIRECTIONS: For each question, read the four possible answers and select the one answer that you believe is correct. Fill in the corresponding letter on your answer sheet.

---

1. The clutch

    1–A   maintains the flow of oil throughout the engine.

    1–B   keeps the crankshaft rotating.

    1–C   is the device which connects/disconnects the flow of power between engine and transmission.

    1–D   None of the above

2. In regard to engines, what does SI stand for?

    2–A   Spark-ignition   2–C   Spark idle

    2–B   System ignition   2–D   None of the above

3. Universal joints allow the drive shaft to

    3–A   break apart as necessary.

    3–B   bend.

    3–C   move up and down.

    3–D   Both (A) and (B).

4. An air-fuel ratio, by weight, of 20:1 is called a

    4–A   lean ratio.   4–C   clean ratio.

    4–B   rich ratio.   4–D   None of the above

5. Which of the following is part of the carburetor?

    5–A   Discharge tube   5–B   Camshaft

5–C   Exhaust port   5–D   None of the above

6. Venting helps brakes

   6–A   stay warm.   6–C   stay cool.

   6–B   stay wet.   6–D   None of the above

7. With respect to engines, rpm stands for

   7–A   revolutions per microsecond.

   7–B   reverse pinion mixture.

   7–C   revolutions per minute.

   7–D   none of the above.

8. Fuel flows from the fuel tank to the float bowl due to the

   8–A   throttle valve.   8–C   intake valve.

   8–B   choke valve.   8–D   fuel pump.

9. The radiator

   9–A   heats the coolant from the engine.

   9–B   cools the coolant from the engine.

   9–C   pumps the coolant.

   9–D   Both (B) and (C)

10. Oil

   10–A reduces friction (lubricates).

   10–B cools the engine.

   10–C Both (A) and (B)

   10–D None of the above

11. Select the method or device used to reduce CO emission.

   11–A Catalytic converter   11–C ECS

   11–B Air injection   11–D Both (A) and (B)

12. The larger the first number in the gear ratio

   12–A the higher the gear ratio.   12–C the lower the gear ratio.

   12–B the higher the top speed.   12–D None of the above

13. An exhaust manifold made up of six pipes going into one pipe is called a

    13–A twelve-into-one exhaust system.

    13–B six-into-one exhaust system.

    13–C three-into-one exhaust system.

    13–D All of the above

14. The temperature within the cylinder can reach more than

    14–A 2,000° F.   14–C 4,000° F.

    14–B 10,000° F.   14–D 300° F.

15. Two gears are meshed together. The larger gear

    15–A has less torque.   15–C has more torque.

    15–B moves slower.   15–D Both (B) and (C)

16. The tool shown above is a(n)

    16–A spring caliper.   16–C screwdriver.

    16–B open-end wrench.   16–D None of the above

17. The above tool is a(n)

    17–A solid hacksaw.   17–C screwdriver.

    17–B open-end wrench.   17–D None of the above

18. Which of the following is a type of torque wrench?

    18–A Twist wrench   18–C Deflecting beam wrench

    18–B Combination wrench   18–D None of the above

19. An advantage of a box wrench is that it is

    19–A faster.   19–C both (A) and (B).

    19–B safer.   19–D none of the above.

20. The above tool is a(n)

    20–A six-point socket.   20–C extension bar.

    20–B speed handle.   20–D None of the above

21. What is the above tool?

    21–A Allen-type wrench   21–C Box wrench

    21–B Bristol wrench   21–D None of the above

22. Taps are used for

    22–A cutting internal threads.   22–C both (A) and (B).

    22–B cutting external threads.   22–D none of the above.

23. What is the above tool?

    23–A Center punch   23–C Pin punch

    23–B Alining punch   23–D None of the above

24. Vises are used to hold work during

    24–A sawing.   24–C shaping.

    24–B drilling.   24–D all of the above.

25. Auger bits are used for

    25–A cutting.   25–C both (A) and (B).

    25–B boring.   25–D none of the above.

MATHEMATICS KNOWLEDGE
TEST 3

Time: 24 Minutes
25 Questions

(Answer sheets appear in the back of this book.)

DIRECTIONS: Each question has four multiple-choice answers, labeled by the number of the question and the letters A, B, C, or D. Select the single answer which is correct.

1. What does $(x + 3)\,(x - 3)$ equal?

   1–A $x^2 - 6x - 9$ 1–C $x^2 - 9$

   1–B $x^2 + 6x - 9$ 1–D $x^2 + 9$

2. What is the square root of 625?

   2–A   25   2–C   35

   2–B   15   2–D   45

3. How many sides does an octagon have?

   3–A   7   3–C   9

   3–B   8   3–D   10

4. If $12y > 84$, then which of the following must be true?

   4–A $y < 7$ 4–C $y > 7$

   4–B $y > -7$ 4–D $y = 7$

5. If $11x + 34 = 1$, then what is x?

   5–A -3 5–C   2

   5–B -2 5–D   3

6. What does $(y + 6)\,(y - 3)$ equal?

   6–A $y^2 - 3y - 18$ 6–C $y^2 - 3y + 18$

   6–B $y^2 + 3y + 18$ 6–D $y^2 + 3y - 18$

7. If 75 teenagers go to a concert and $33^1/_3\%$ of them are girls, how many boys went to the concert?

   7–A   55   7–C   40

   7–B   50   7–D   25

8. Factor $w^2 + 3w - 10$.

   8–A $(w - 5)(w + 2)$ 8–C $(w + 5)(w - 2)$

   8–B $(w + 5)(w + 2)$ 8–D $(w - 5)(w - 2)$

9. If a square having side s equals one-half the area of a rectangle with one side equal to six, what is the equation to find the other side, l, of the rectangle?

   9–A $s^2 = 3l$ 9–C $s^2 = 12l$

   9–B $s^2 = 6l$ 9–D $s^2 = 4l$

10. If $-{}^x/_4 < 2$, then which of the following must be true?

    10–A $x < 8$ 10–C $x > -8$

    10–B $x = -8$ 10–D $x < -8$

11. If one side of a right triangle equals one foot and the hypotenuse equals 15 inches, then what is the length of the other leg (in inches)?

    11–A 9   11–C 13

    11–B 11   11–D 14

12. The original cost of a coat is $64. There is a 30% off end-of-the-season sale. How much does the coat cost on sale?

    12–A $40.80   12–C $50.80

    12–B $44.80   12–D $54.80

13. What does the sum of the angles of a triangle and the angles of a square equal?

    13–A 180   13–C 540

    13–B 360   13–D 720

14. What does $(x + 7)(x - 5)$ equal?

    14–A $x^2 - 2x + 35$ 14–C $x^2 + 2x - 35$

    14–B $x^2 + 2x + 35$ 14–D $x^2 - 2x - 35$

15. If $3x + 16 = 40$, then what is x?

    15–A 6   15–C 8

    15–B 7   15–D 9

16. What is the square root of 256?

    16–A 14   16–C 18

    16–B 16   16–D 20

17. How many equal sides does an isosceles triangle have?

    17–A 0   17–C 3

    17–B 2   17–D 5

18. Factor $y^2 + 5y + 6$.

    18–A $(y - 2)(y + 3)$ 18–C $(y + 2)(y + 3)$

    18–B $(y + 2)(y - 3)$ 18–D $(y - 2)(y - 3)$

19. If a circle's area is equal to its circumference, what is the radius?

    19–A $1/2$ 19–C 2

    19–B 1   19–D 3

20. If 90 boys make up 45% of the senior class, how many girls are there in the senior class?

    20–A 110   20–C 150

    20–B 130   20–D 160

21. How many pairs of equal sides does a rectangle have?

    21–A 0   21–C 2

    21–B 1   21–D 3

22. If the perimeter of a rectangle equals twice the area of the rectangle and one side equals four, what would the equation look like to find the length, l?

22–A $2l + 8 = 8l$ 22–C $l + 4 = 8l$

22–B $2l + 8 = 4l$ 22–D $4l + 32 = 4l$

23. If $5x - 39 = -14$, then what is x?

23–A 8   23–C 6

23–B 7   23–D 5

24. If $x/5 \leq -2$, then which of the following must be true?

24–A $x \leq 10$ 24–C $x \leq -10$

24–B $x < -10$ 24–D $x \geq -10$

25. If Joe does five pages of work each day and after six days he has 60% of his assignment done, how many more pages does he have to do to finish his assignment?

25–A 20   25–C 30

25–B 25   25–D 35

MECHANICAL COMPREHENSION TEST 3

Time: 19 Minutes
     25 Questions

(Answer sheets appear in the back of this book.)

DIRECTIONS: Choose the best answer to each question and then darken the oval on your answer sheet.

1. The improvised drill press shown is an example of which type of machine?

   1–A   A first-class lever

   1–B   A second-class lever

   1–C   A third-class lever

   1–D   A runner

2. In the previous example, if the resistance is 100 pounds, the distance to the fulcrum from the drill is 2 feet. What must be the effort applied at the other end in order to have a mechanical advantage of 4?

   2–A   25 pounds   2–C   50 pounds

   2–B   400 pounds   2–D   200 pounds

3. In the previous two problems, how far from the drill must the effort be applied?

   3–A   2 ft   3–C   10 ft

   3–B   0.5 ft   3–D   8 ft

4. The mechanical advantage in the block-and-tackle system shown is

    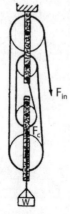

    4–A 5.

    4–B 4.

    4–C 3.

    4–D 2.

5. In the previous problem, what must be the effort applied if the load is 400 pounds?

    5–A 80 pounds   5–C 100 pounds

    5–B 200 pounds   5–D 1,600 pounds

6. In the last two problems, what length does the rope have to be pulled in order to lift the load a height of 5 feet?

    6–A 20 ft   6–C 25 ft

    6–B 1.25 ft   6–D 10 ft

7. The machine element shown is a type of

    7–A pinion and internal gear.

    7–B pinion and sector gear.

    7–C pinion and rack gear.

    7–D spiral bevel gear.

8. As shown here, a jackscrew has a lever arm of 40 cm and a pitch of 5 mm. If the force required to lift a load w of 400 kg is equal to 2 kg, what is the efficiency of the jackscrew?

    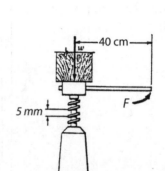

8–A 250%   8–C 25%

8–B 40%   8–D 4%

9. Which of the following statements is true about the pressure exerted by the sea water on the submarine:

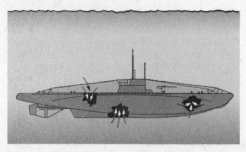

9–A The pressure is exerted on the top and bottom only.

9–B The pressure is exerted on the bottom and sides only.

9–C The pressure is exerted on the top and sides only.

9–D The pressure is exerted on all sides of the submarine.

10. What must be the area of the right tube, if equilibrium is to be maintained?

10–A 1 sq in

10–B 100 sq in

10–C 2 sq in

10–D 5 sq in

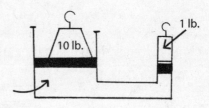

11. Consider the cable winch in the figure shown. The crank arm is 30 inches long, and the drum on which the cable is wound has a 15-inch radius. The small pinion gear has 10 teeth that mesh with the 60 teeth on the internal spur gear. What is the mechanical advantage of the two meshed gears?

11–A $1/6$ 11–C 2

11–B 6   11–D $1/2$

12. In the previous problem, what is the mechanical advantage of the wheel-and-axle arrangement alone?

    12–A 6   12–C $1/6$

    12–B $1/2$ 12–D 2

13. What is the overall mechanical advantage of the cable winch?

    13–A 8   13–C 3

    13–B 4   13–D 12

14. What will be the resulting movement of the piston as the crankshaft starts to turn clockwise and makes a half turn?

    14–A The piston moves up and down two strokes.

    14–B The piston moves down one stroke and then up one stroke.

    14–C The piston moves up one stroke.

    14–D The piston moves down one stroke.

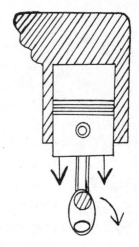

15. The gear system shown here is known as

    15–A a spur bevel gear.

    15–B a spiral bevel gear.

    15–C a worm gear.

    15–D a rack gear.

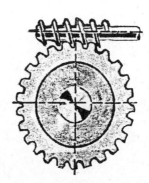

16. How many turns of the windlass drum are necessary in order to move the weight up 9 feet and 5 inches?

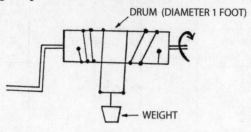

DRUM (DIAMETER 1 FOOT)

WEIGHT

16–A 3   16–C 4

16–B 2   16–D 1.5

17. In the cam-driven valve shown, what is the maximum height the valve will be lifted off the valve seat?

17–A R

17–B r

17–C $R + r$

17–D $R - r$

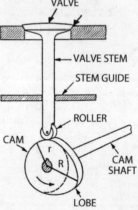

VALVE

VALVE STEM

STEM GUIDE

ROLLER

CAM

r

R

CAM SHAFT

LOBE

18. The chain hoist, or differential pulley, is based on the combination of the block and tackle, and the wheel and axle as shown. When a load is hoisted, the part that remains stationary is

18–A the load.

18–B the lower block.

18–C the chain.

18–D the upper block and wheel.

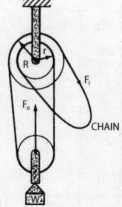

r

R

F_i

F_o

CHAIN

W

19. Determine the force required to lift a 100-lb load with the pulley system shown.

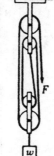

    19–A 50 lb

    19–B 20 lb

    19–C 25 lb

    19–D 400 lb

20. Which hydraulic press requires the least force to keep the weight in equilibrium?

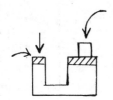 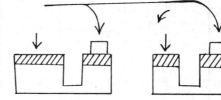

    20–A 1

    20–B 2

    20–C 3

    20–D All three require the same force.

21. The machine element shown here is a type of

    21–A universal joint.

    21–B spiral spring.

    21–C disk clutch.

    21–D ball bearing.

22. A universal joint is a type of

    22–A sliding type bearing.

    22–B helical spring.

    22–C gear differential.

    22–D coupling.

23. The jackscrew shown in the figure has a pitch of $1/_8$ inch and a handle 25 inches long. Thus, the theoretical mechanical advantage is TMA = 1257. In reality, however, it is found that a force of 6 lb must be applied on the handle in order to lift a 2500-lb load. Calculate the actual mechanical advantage (AMA) and the efficiency of the jack-screw.

23–A AMA = 417 and effi-ciency = 33%

23–B AMA = 0.0024 and effi-ciency = 0.08%

23–C AMA = 33 and efficiency = 417%

23–D AMA = 1257 and effi-ciency = 100%

24. The sailor shown in this figure has lugged 3 tons of bricks up to the second deck, which is 15 feet higher than ground. The work performed is

24–A 45,000 ft-lb.

24–B 90,000 ft-lb.

24–C 2.7 hp.

24–D 1.36 hp.

25. In the previous question, if it took the sailor three 10-hour days to do the job, what is the power?

25–A 50 ft-lb per minute

25–C 21 ft-lb per minute

25–B 50 hp

25–D 25 hp

ELECTRONICS INFORMATION
TEST 3

Time: 9 Minutes
20 Questions

(Answer sheets appear in the back of this book.)

DIRECTIONS: Choose the best answer to each question by darkening the oval on your answer sheet.

S1. Which uses the least electricity? (Assume all are efficient.)

S1–A 5 Watt lamp   S1–C 10 Watt lamp

S1–B 50 Watt lamp   S1–D 0.5 Watt lamp

S1. **(D)** The greater the power produced, the greater the current needed. Thus, a 1/2 Watt lamp would use the least power.

S2. Your stereo puts out 100 Watts for your old speakers. You buy new speakers. Your old speakers were 4Ω and the new ones are 8Ω. What is your power out now?

S2–A 100 Watts   S2–C 200 Watts

S2–B 50 Watts   S2–D 10 Watts

S2. **(B)** From the power equation:

$$P = VI = \frac{V^2}{R}$$

If the resistance is doubled from 4Ω to 8Ω, the power will be found to decrease by half to 50 Watts.

1. What is a kilowatt hour?

   1–A   100 Watts of electricity consumed in one hour.

   1–B   10 Watts of electricity consumed in one hour.

   1–C   1 Watt of electricity consumed in one hour.

   1–D   1,000 Watts of electricity consumed in one hour.

2. If the current is tripled in the cable, the heat generated will increase

   2–A   three times.   2–C   nine times.

   2–B   six times.   2–D   12 times.

3. A short circuit has

   3–A   infinite current.   3–C   zero current.

   3–B   infinite voltage.   3–D   infinite resistance.

4. A light switch on your wall has OFF and ON positions; what kind of switch is it?

   4–A   Single-pole switch   4–C   Triple-pole switch

   4–B   Double-pole switch   4–D   Quadruple-pole switch

5. Why is electrical tape used to cover electrical connections instead of masking tape?

   5–A   Better conductivity   5–C   It is waterproof

   5–B   Better adhesion   5–D   Better insulator

6. Which device has the *V/I* output shown below?

   6–A   A diode

   6–B   A resistor

   6–C   A capacitor

   6–D   An inductor

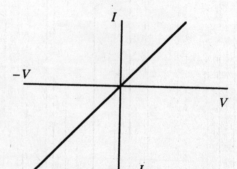

7. What does an impedance load measure?

   7–A   Output voltage   7–C   Output power

   7–B   Output current   7–D   Output resistance

8. When connecting two wires with shielding cable, how should you connect them?

   8–A   Conductor to shield

   8–B   Conductor to conductor to floating shield

   8–C   Conductor to conductor and ground shield

   8–D   Conductor to conductor and remove shield completely

9. What is the current through the *A* leg if all resistances are equal?

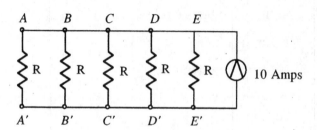

   9–A   9 amps

   9–B   2 amps

   9–C   5 amps

   9–D   Can't determine — not enough information

10. What kind of fuse is shown in the figure?

    Fusible link

    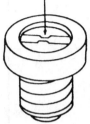

    10–A Resettable

    10–B Plug

    10–C Cartridge

    10–D Ferrite

11. What is the relationship between power and voltage?

    11–A $P = VR$ 11–C $P = V^2I$

    11–B $P = V^2$ 11–D $P = VI$

12. Metal is not put into microwave ovens because

    12–A it will cause an electrical storm.

    12–B it needs to be tempered first.

    12–C metal is not gold or silver.

    12–D current will flow on the surface of the metal causing it to react with your food.

13. What gauge of wire is needed for 55 amps?

    13–A #14   13–C #12

    13–B #10   13–D #6

14. Why are type S-fuses also known as safety fuses?

    14–A The fuse is in the shape of an S, distributing the power equally.

    14–B The fuse is a time delay fuse.

    14–C The fuse is resettable.

    14–D The S-fuse adapters will only allow a fuse equal to or less than to replace it.

15. Which of these is the symbol for a current source?

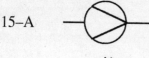

    15–A   15–C

    15–B   15–D

16. Which is the best conductor?

    16–A Copper   16–C Glass

    16–B Dry air   17–D Oil

17. The primary to secondary current ratio is equal to

    17–A $\quad \dfrac{I_{prim}}{I_{sec}} = \dfrac{N_{sec}}{N_{prim}}.$

    17–B $\quad (I_{prim}) \times (I_{sec}) = (N_{sec}) \times (N_{prim}).$

17–C $(I_{prim}) \times (I_{sec}) \times (N_{sec}) = N_{prim}.$

17–D $\dfrac{I_{prim}}{I_{sec}} = \dfrac{N_{prim}}{N_{sec}}.$

18. What is a line drop?

18–A When the electrician drops the line

18–B When the resistance decreases along the line

18–C When the current decreases along the line

18–D When the voltage decreases along the line

19. A universal motor is

19–A a motor that can run on AC or DC.

19–B a motor that can run on AC only.

19–C a motor that can run on DC only.

19–D a motor that can run backwards and forwards.

20. From the figure, determine what the net voltage would be if voltage outputs *A* and *B* were in series with each other.

20–A 3 V

20–B 2 V

20–C 1 V

20–D 0 V

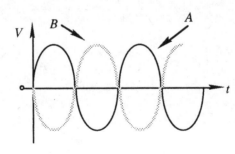

GENERAL SCIENCE
TEST 3

ANSWER KEY

1. (C)	8. (B)	15. (C)	22. (B)
2. (D)	9. (C)	16. (C)	23. (A)
3. (C)	10. (B)	17. (D)	24. (A)
4. (D)	11. (C)	18. (A)	25. (A)
5. (B)	12. (A)	19. (B)	
6. (B)	13. (D)	20. (B)	
7. (D)	14. (C)	21. (D)	

Add up your correct answers and put the number here. _____

Now record your score on pages 451-452.

DETAILED EXPLANATIONS OF ANSWERS

1.   **(C)**   Snails are invertebrates because they have no backbone.

2.   **(D)**   Insects have 3 body regions and 6 legs. Arachnids have 2 body regions and 8 legs (A). Answers (B) and (C) do not characterize any living creature.

3.   **(C)**   Gymnosperms produce seeds without protective seed coverings. The seeds are found in seed cones, not fruits.

4.   **(D)**   The pancreas produces insulin and glucagon. The other choices are also endocrine glands that produce other hormones.

5.   **(B)**   Breads and cereals are principal sources of starches, which provide energy.

6.   **(B)**   The trait for brown eyes is dominant. Therefore, a brown-eyed parent may be genetically BB (homozygous) or Bb (heterozygous). A blue-eyed child must be bb, because blue eyes are recessive. Two brown-eyed parents could produce a blue-eyed child only if both parents were Bb (heterozygous).

7.   **(D)**   Herbivores eat plants (B). Carnivores eat animals (C). Omnivores eat plants and animals.

8.   **(B)**   Phagocytosis is the process of engulfing particles to incorporate them in a cell. Engulfing occurs when the cell membrane flows around an object, causing a bubble, or vacuole, to occur in the cytoplasm. The bubble contains the object engulfed.

9.   **(C)**   1 meter = 100 cm = 1000 mm = 10 dm = $\dfrac{1}{1000}$ km

10.   **(B)**   Convection is the correct answer because it is the definition of heat transfer when dealing with heated liquids or gases.

11. **(C)** All the answers represent electrical units that are used to measure various aspects of electrical current. Watts measure electrical consumption.

12. **(A)** Increasing distance between two objects decreases magnetic force between them. Increasing electrical charge (C) between two objects increases electrostatic force. Answers (B) and (D) do not affect magnetic force.

13. **(D)** All the choices represent electromagnetic waves. X-rays have a shorter wavelength than that of light, while the rest have longer wavelengths.

14. **(C)** Differences in sound volume are related to amplitude differences. Sound intensity is related to amplitude and frequency of sound waves. Speed = Wavelength × Frequency.

15. **(C)** Organic compounds must contain carbon. They may include any other element, including those listed as the other answers.

16. **(C)** All choices represent states of matter. Liquids have a definite volume but no definite shape. Gases (B) and plasmas (A) have no definite volume. Solids (D) have a definite shape.

17. **(D)** The relative acidity or basicity of a solution is measured by pH. Neutral is indicated by a pH of 7. Acid is shown by a pH less than 7. Base is shown by a pH greater than 7.

18. **(A)** All the answers represent types of reactions. In a synthesis reaction, new chemicals (e.g., CO_2) are synthesized, or made from other smaller chemicals.

19. **(B)** All the answer choices represent machines. The seismograph measures the intensity of an earthquake by measuring and graphing the size of vibrations in the ground.

20. **(B)** All the answer choices are machines used to measure weather: thermometer/temperature (A), barometer/air pressure (B), hygrometer/humidity (C), anemometer/wind speed (D).

21. **(D)** The planets that are nearest from the sun to farthest are: Mercury, Venus, Earth, Mars, Jupiter, Saturn, Uranus, Neptune, Pluto.

22. **(B)** The formula for water is H_2O. Since the left side of the equation has 4 hydrogens, 2 water molecules must be placed on the right of the equation to provide 4 hydrogens there.

23. **(A)** The phylum Chordata includes all animals with backbones. Mammals are one of five classes of Chordates.

24. **(A)** Predators are animals that eat other living things. Prey (B) are living things that are eaten. Decomposers (D) are organisms that eat dead plants and animals. Herbivores (C) eat plants.

25. **(A)** Decibels measure the intensity of sound. Sound intensity is related to amplitude and frequency of sound waves.

ARITHMETIC REASONING
TEST 3

ANSWER KEY

1.	(C)	9.	(B)	17.	(B)	25.	(C)
2.	(D)	10.	(A)	18.	(A)	26.	(D)
3.	(A)	11.	(C)	19.	(C)	27.	(C)
4.	(D)	12.	(D)	20.	(A)	28.	(A)
5.	(B)	13.	(B)	21.	(C)	29.	(C)
6.	(A)	14.	(A)	22.	(D)	30.	(C)
7.	(C)	15.	(C)	23.	(B)		
8.	(D)	16.	(D)	24.	(A)		

Add up your correct answers and put the number here. _____

Now record your score on pages 451-452.

DETAILED EXPLANATIONS
OF ANSWERS

1. **(C)** The answer is (C) because Jimmy calls at 4:15, 4:20, …, and his tenth call is at 5:00. He will then make four more calls (at 5:05, 5:10, 5:15, and 5:20) for a total of 14.

2. **(D)** The answer is (D) because $4 - 6 + 3 = 1$.

3. **(A)** The answer is (A) because the slower car goes 40 miles in an hour, and the faster car goes 40 miles at 60 miles an hour, which takes 40 minutes. Thus, the difference is 20 minutes.

4. **(D)** The answer is (D) because half of $1,000 is $500.

5. **(B)** The answer is (B) because in the first 40 hours Bob earns $40 \times \$5 = \$200$. After that he needs to earn $\$250 - \$200 = \$50$, at $10 per hour. This will take $50/10 = 5$ hours more, for a total of $40 + 5 = 45$ hours.

6. **(A)** The answer is (A) because Phil watches alone for one hour, Susan watches alone for two hours, and they watch together for one hour. In total, $1 + 2 + 1 = 4$ hours.

7. **(C)** The answer is (C) because $3,000 \times 2/5 = 6,000/5 = 1,200$ miles.

8. **(D)** The answer is (D) because 50% of $50,000 = $25,000.

9. **(B)** The answer is (B) because $80\% = 4/5$, so they won four of five games. They played $20 \times 5/4 = 25$ games, so they lost $25 - 20 = 5$ games.

10. **(A)** The answer is (A) because they bring in $\$10 \times 50,000 = \$500,000$, and they pay out $300,000. This leaves $200,000 profit, to be split four ways. Each member earns $\$200,000/4 = \$50,000$.

11. **(C)** The answer is (C) because $28 - 16 = 12$.

12. **(D)** The answer is (D) because $3/6 = 0.5$.

13. **(B)** The answer is (B) because 10% of $60,000 is $6,000, so the new salary is $60,000 + $6,000 = $66,000.

14. **(A)** The answer is (A) because $50,000 + $10,000 + $5,000 + $25,000 = $90,000. This will support $90,000/$10,000 = 9 researchers.

15. **(C)** The answer is (C) because 300 − 49 − 61 − 55 − 45 = 90.

16. **(D)** The answer is (D) because 4 + 3 + 3 + 3 = 13.

17. **(B)** The answer is (B) because he drives 50 × 10 = 500 miles per day. It will take him 3,000/500 = 6 days.

18. **(A)** The answer is (A) because 64/4 = 16.

19. **(C)** The answer is (C) because $3.00 × 120% = $3.60.

20. **(A)** The answer is (A) because 60% of 400,000 is 240,000.

21. **(C)** The answer is (C) because his improvements are 20 pounds for Week 2, 30 for Week 3, 20 for Week 4, 40 for Week 5, and 10 for Week 6.

22. **(D)** The answer is (D) because 4 + 3 + 3 = 10.

23. **(B)** The answer is (B) because it is one hour from 11:00 to 12:00, then seven from 12:00 to 7:00.

24. **(A)** The answer is (A) because 100% − 50% − 33.33% − 6.67% = 10%.

25. **(C)** The answer is (C) because 21 − 7 − 4 − 2 − 5 = 3.

26. **(D)** The answer is (D) because $100 − $39 − $18 − $12 = $31.

27. **(C)** The answer is (C) because 2 + 1 + 3 = 6.

28. **(A)** The answer is (A) because $1.44/12 = $0.12.

29. **(C)** The answer is (C) because Bill was going (15 miles)/(0.5 hour) = 30 miles per hour, and Bob was going (10 miles)/(0.5 hour) = 20 miles per hour. The difference is 10 miles per hour.

30. **(C)** The answer is (C) because 26 × 6 = 156 minutes, or two hours and 36 minutes.

WORD KNOWLEDGE
TEST 3

ANSWER KEY

1. (D)	10. (B)	19. (A)	28. (D)
2. (A)	11. (D)	20. (B)	29. (A)
3. (D)	12. (B)	21. (C)	30. (C)
4. (A)	13. (A)	22. (C)	31. (B)
5. (B)	14. (A)	23. (A)	32. (B)
6. (C)	15. (D)	24. (B)	33. (A)
7. (A)	16. (D)	25. (C)	34. (B)
8. (B)	17. (B)	26. (D)	35. (B)
9. (D)	18. (C)	27. (C)	

Add up your correct answers and put the number here. _____

Now record your score on pages 451-452.

DETAILED EXPLANATIONS OF ANSWERS

1. **(D)** Infamous means having the reputation of being an EVIL-doer or criminal of the worst kind. Infamous people are known *specifically* for their heinous deeds; therefore, evil is a closer synonym than (A) WELL-KNOWN. (B) IMMATURE means not completely grown or developed, unfinished; (C) PERFECT can be synonymous with infallible.

2. **(A)** Benign means KIND, gentle, gracious, favorable, or not life threatening. (B) OPTIMISTIC means positive; (C) SINISTER is the opposite of benign; (D) SUGGESTIVE means risque or thought-provoking.

3. **(D)** Abet means to ENCOURAGE or assist. (A) TOUCH is synonymous with abut; (B) VANDALIZE means to deface or destroy; (C) AWAIT is synonymous with abide.

4. **(A)** Comprehensive and COMPLETE mean the same thing. (B) UNDERSTANDABLE is synonymous with comprehensible; (C) DIFFICULT is synonymous with complex; (D) INVOLVED is synonymous with complicated.

5. **(B)** Luminous most closely means GLOWING. It comes from the Latin root *luminosus*, from which we also get illuminate, and lumen, a unit by which light intensity is measured. None of the other words—(A) JAZZY, (C) ENERGETIC, or (D) IMPORTANT—have similar meanings.

6. **(C)** Malicious means SPITEFUL or full of ill-will or hatred. (A) CRIMINAL means disgraceful or relating to crime; (B) SUSPICIOUS means distrustful or arousing mistrust; (D) SELFISH means putting one's own interests ahead of others.

7. **(A)** The word closest in meaning to vicarious is SUBSTITUTE. When a father (for instance) places much more importance on his son's successes and failures in life than his own, he is said to be living vicariously through his son—his son's life is a substitute for his own. (B) LIVELY means full of vitality; (C) DANGEROUS is synonymous with

precarious; (D) IMAGINARY is related to vicarious, but in a secondary way; this word is the second-best choice.

8. **(B)** Lethargic means sluggish, INDIFFERENT, or apathetic. (A) ILL means in poor health; (C) ENERGETIC is the opposite of lethargic; (D) FRUSTRATED means discouraged, disappointed, or thwarted.

9. **(D)** Facet and ASPECT mean the same thing; one of several ways of looking at something (facets of a diamond, facets of a problem). (A) VISIBILITY is the degree to which something is able to be seen; (B) WIT is synonymous with facetiousness; (C) BRILLIANCE means brightness.

10. **(B)** Unwieldy means BULKY, not easily managed. An unwieldy object may also be (A) HEAVY or (C) LARGE, but weight and size aren't the measures of bulkiness. An unwieldy object is not easily managed, but an (D) IMMOVABLE object can't be managed at all, so this is an incorrect choice.

11. **(D)** Altruism and UNSELFISHNESS mean the same thing: putting the welfare of others ahead of one's own. (A) SELF-INDULGENCE, gratifying one's own desires, is the opposite of altruism; (B) WEAKNESS is a defect or the quality of not being strong; (C) CHARM is a demanding attractiveness.

12. **(B)** To wane is to dwindle, or decline; SUBSIDE is the closest synonym of the word choices. (A) FLUCTUATE is synonymous with the concept of wax and wane; (C) ALARM is synonymous with warn; (D) GROW can be synonymous with wax.

13. **(A)** Fleeting means quickly vanishing, or TEMPORARY. (B) CONTINUING (needing no renewal) and (C) ETERNAL (never ending) do not have the same meaning; (D) SIMULTANEOUS means occurring at the same time.

14. **(A)** Alleviate means to RELIEVE or lessen. (B) DETOUR is synonymous with deviate; (C) ANNOY means to pester; (D) DICTATE means to command.

15. **(D)** Defraud and CHEAT are synonymous. (A) CONFRONT and (B) THWART are synonymous with defy; (C) DISGRACE means to cause shame.

16. **(D)** The best synonym for facetious is WITTY. (A) EXACT, (B) SARCASTIC (nasty, bitter), and (C) FAKE do not have similar meanings.

17. **(B)** Effete can mean WEAK, infertile, exhausted, effeminate, or outdated. (A) BUBBLY is synonymous with effervescent; (C) DOUBT-FUL means full of misgivings or uncertainties; (D) INNOCENT means blameless (among other unrelated meanings).

18. **(C)** The best synonym for benevolent is CHARITABLE. (A) HARMLESS is synonymous with benign (which does share the Latin root *bene*, meaning well, with benevolent). (B) BLESSED means worshipped or favored; (D) COURTEOUS means polite and mannerly.

19. **(A)** Exotic can mean FOREIGN or unusual. An exotic dance may be (B) SUGGESTIVE, but since "suggestive" in this sense more closely means risque—and not exotic per se, suggestive is not as close a synonym as foreign. (C) STYLISH means fashionable; (D) WEIRD means odd or mysteriously strange; this word is too closely related to the supernatural to be considered a good synonym here.

20. **(B)** Hazardous means risky or chancy, possibly DANGEROUS. (A) SECURE is an antonym; (C) UNDECIDED (having not reached a decision) and (D) FICKLE (changeable, inconstant) are not related.

21. **(C)** Contrite means repentant (sorry); APOLOGETIC is the word choice closest in meaning. (A) DEMANDING means needing a great deal of time or effort; (B) AGAINST is synonymous with contrary; (D) DIS-AGREEABLE is synonymous with contradictory.

22. **(C)** Impetuous and IMPULSIVE mean the same thing; on the spur of the moment. (A) DISTANT is synonymous with imperious; (B) CRAZY has many meanings, none of which come close to the meaning of impetuous; (D) PLANNED is an antonym.

23. **(A)** Apathy means INDIFFERENCE or impassiveness (emotion-lessness). (B) STABILITY means firmness or resistance to change; (C) HOPE is expectancy or wishfulness; (D) INVOLVEMENT is the exact opposite of apathy.

24. **(B)** Volatile means able to fly, easily vaporized, explosive, light-hearted, fickle. Of the choices given, the best synonym is (B) UN-STABLE, which is similar in meaning to fickle. (A) PLEASANT means

agreeable; (C) ANGRY means feeling or showing displeasure, antagonism, and/or wrath; (D) QUARRELSOME means inclined to engage in petty arguments.

25. **(C)** Integrity can mean complete, incorruptible, displaying loyalty to a code of standards or ethics; HONESTY is the closest synonym. (A) DISDAIN means scorn or contempt; (B) SMARTNESS is synonymous with intelligence; (D) FRAUDULENCE is the state of being deceitful.

26. **(D)** Consent means to AGREE or permit; (A) REFUSE is an antonym; (B) PROVOKE is related to resent; (C) SUBDUE means to bring under control or tone down.

27. **(C)** Avid means EAGER, enthusiastic, or greedy. (A) HALF-HEARTED (lacking interest or enthusiasm) is the opposite of avid; (B) PREVENTABLE and (D) SUDDEN are not related.

28. **(D)** Gregarious means SOCIABLE. (A) INSANE means absurd or having a mental disorder; (B) BASHFUL (shy) is an antonym; (C) PUZZLING means bewildering, perplexing, or complicated.

29. **(A)** The best synonym for nostalgic is HOMESICK. Nostalgic may also mean sentimental, or having a longing for a period in the past. (B) SLOW is unrelated; (C) SYMPATHETIC means compassionate, sensitive, or approving, among other meanings. While nostalgia and sadness may occur simultaneously, (D) SAD is not a synonym for nostalgia.

30. **(C)** Opulence means wealth or abundance; AFFLUENCE is the word choice closest in meaning to either of these definitions. (A) TACKINESS is a lack of good taste, commonness; (B) OPTIMISM is the inclination to see things in a positive light; (D) HEAVINESS is not related.

31. **(B)** Awkward and UNGAINLY mean the same thing. (A) UNPLEASANT is synonymous with awful; (C) USELESS means good for nothing; (D) GRACEFUL is an antonym for awkward.

32. **(B)** Vivid can mean LIVELY, colorful, or intense. (A) EMPTY is synonymous with void; (C) LOUD can mean noisy or offensive; (D) BRIGHT has many meanings and can also mean lively, but is not as direct a synonym for vivid as the word "lively" itself is; bright would be the second-best choice of synonym for vivid.

33. **(A)** Preservation can mean PROTECTION, conservation, or maintenance. (B) INFORMATION can mean knowledge, intelligence, or facts; (C) GIFT is a synonym for presentation; (D) ENFORCEMENT is the act of carrying out, or strengthening.

34. **(B)** To opt for something is to choose or SELECT it. (A) WANTED, (C) NEEDED, and (D) REQUIRED do not have the same or related meaning.

35. **(B)** Appeal means to attract, accuse, request, or plead. Of the choices given, INTEREST is the best synonym for the meaning "to attract." (A) BE VISIBLE is synonymous with appear; (C) CALM is synonymous with appease; (D) REPEL is an antonym for appeal.

PARAGRAPH COMPREHENSION
TEST 3

ANSWER KEY

1. (B)	6. (B)	11. (B)
2. (D)	7. (B)	12. (C)
3. (A)	8. (C)	13. (D)
4. (D)	9. (C)	14. (C)
5. (B)	10. (D)	15. (B)

Add up your correct answers and put the number here. _____

Now record your score on pages 451-452.

DETAILED EXPLANATIONS OF ANSWERS

1.   **(B)**   "Academic" means part of or belonging to an academy or institution of learning. The reader can thus infer that academic background means college or university study. The writer contrasts this to all the other forms of information used for this study, so the other choices cannot be correct.

2.   **(D)**   Beta blockers ("these drugs") only "help test-takers who have low scores because of test fright, but not those who do not know the material."

3.   **(A)**   Since man-made causes such as "habitat alteration or destruction, pollution . . ." contribute to "many species . . . dying out," the reader can assume that (A) is the answer.

4.   **(D)**   The writer mentions no two other factors that act as shields in combination. Thus, "an extensive magnetic field which, *coupled* with the atmosphere, shields us . . ." The key word is "coupled," which means combined.

5.   **(B)**   The writer never specifically mentions this as an example of stress.

6.   **(B)**   Notice that the writer says "scattered . . . throughout the world," suggesting many such pieces (an abundance) of evidence exist in many places. The writer doesn't give evidence that supports the idea that prolific means confusing (A), bad smelling (D), or evil (C).

7.   **(B)**   "On the other hand" shows contrast. In this passage the only child is contrasted in learning with those who have brothers and sisters. The only child, the passage says, "may have to learn his lessons . . . on the playground or in the classroom," unlike those who can learn from brothers and sisters at home.

8.   **(C)**   The passage states that studies "have shown that the environmental impact of wind energy systems is small compared to . . . electric power systems."

9. **(C)** Don't be misguided by what *you* think a karat is. The writer states that a "karat" marking tells you "what proportion of gold is mixed with other metals."

10. **(D)** This is the only statement that reflects facts the writer uses. Apparently, using wood was down from 90 percent to one percent generally, based on the first sentence. But in 1976, in New England, over six percent were using wood. This is an *increase* of more than five percent.

11. **(B)** The writer states in the second sentence exactly what an audiologist is: "an expert in hearing".

12. **(C)** The writer clearly states that love should be constant, which means something that happens all the time. For example, the sun shines constantly (even though we can't see it when it's behind the clouds).

13. **(D)** AIDS is a disease caused by a virus. Pregnancy is not caused by a virus.

14. **(C)** The writer uses "hindering" and "interfering" in almost the same sense as "impair," in the same sentence. You can deduce that impair probably means something close to either or both of those words.

15. **(B)** The key here is the world "augmented," which means enriched by or added to. The Co-op program involves being both on and off campus. The writer states that a Co-op program will augment his education by up to two years. Only answer (B) states that "more years" (augmenting, or additional) will be added both on and off campus.

AUTO & SHOP
TEST 3

ANSWER KEY

1. (C)	8. (D)	15. (D)	22. (A)
2. (A)	9. (B)	16. (A)	23. (C)
3. (C)	10. (C)	17. (A)	24. (D)
4. (A)	11. (D)	18. (C)	25. (C)
5. (A)	12. (C)	19. (B)	
6. (C)	13. (B)	20. (A)	
7. (C)	14. (C)	21. (B)	

Add up your correct answers and put the number here. _____

Now record your score on pages 451-452.

DETAILED EXPLANATIONS
OF ANSWERS

1.   **(C)**   The clutch is the device which connects/disconnects the flow of power between engine and transmission. This allows the engine to run without driving the automobile (while the automobile is stationary, for example). The clutch also provides a smooth way to start an automobile moving and it facilitates the shifting of transmission gears.

2.   **(A)**   SI stands for "spark-ignition." In a spark-ignition internal combustion engine, combustion of the air-fuel mixture takes place due to ignition by a spark from a spark plug.

3.   **(C)**   The drive line is made up of usually two universal joints and a drive shaft. The universal joints, which are lubricated with grease, are designed to allow the drive shaft to keep spinning, yet move up and down without breaking in situations where the differential, rear axle, and wheels are pushed up by a bump in the road.

4.   **(A)**   If more air were used in a mixture than what is normally used (air-fuel ratio by weight of 20:1 versus more common ratio of 15:1), it would be called a lean ratio.

5.   **(A)**   The discharge tube is the part of the carburetor that connects the float bowl (which holds fuel) to the thin part of the venturi. When fuel enters the venturi, air and the fuel mix together and are pulled into the cylinder on its intake stroke. The exhaust port (C) is part of the cylinder head and the camshaft (B) is used to open and close valves; neither is part of the carburetor.

6.   **(C)**   Since brakes use friction to stop and since friction generates heat, brakes are designed to cool effectively by using vented (slotted) disc brakes. It is important to cool brakes because the heat generated from friction can adversely affect braking performance.

7.   **(C)**   Rpm is an abbreviation for revolutions per minute. An engine's speed of operation is measured in revolutions per minute of the crankshaft. Most modern day SI engines are designed to have their crankshaft rotate no faster than approximately 6,000 rpm.

8. **(D)** The fuel is pumped from the fuel tank to the float bowl by a fuel pump and is carried to the carburetor float bowl by a fuel line. The throttle (A) and choke (B) valves are part of the carburetor but have nothing to do with the float bowl; intake valves (C) are used in cylinder heads not carburetors.

9. **(B)** The radiator cools the coolant from the engine. When hot coolant enters the radiator, it flows down from the top through tiny copper tubes which have thin copper fins on them to transfer the heat from the coolant to the passing air from a fan. The coolant at the bottom of the radiator is now cool enough to be reused and once again flows back into the engine. A water (coolant) pump is what pumps the coolant.

10. **(C)** Oil is the fluid that circulates in the lubrication system and lubrication, the reduction of friction by the oil, is very important in an engine and in other systems of the automobile. When parts rub and scrape against each other, the friction between them creates heat, which can eventually melt or damage the parts. Oil, a slippery fluid, reduces friction between parts, cools engine parts, and makes movement of parts easier by being directly in contact with and between parts.

11. **(D)** Carbon monoxide, or CO, is produced when the gasoline does not burn completely to CO_2 due to rich air-fuel mixtures. Air injection injects compressed air through a nozzle into the engine's exhaust ports to create further burning of partially burned exhaust gases before they exit the exhaust system. Catalytic converters use pellets coated with, among other elements, platinum to act as a catalyst and promote chemical reactions, which essentially complete the combustion of CO into less harmful CO_2.

12. **(C)** Gear ratios are a way of measuring torque multiplication. The larger the first number in the ratio, the lower the gear ratio, and the greater the torque multiplication. Low ratios like 4:1 provide more torque for good acceleration and high ratios like 2:1 allow higher top speeds.

13. **(B)** An in-line six-cylinder engine, for example, may have an exhaust manifold made up of six pipes (one for each cylinder) leading into one exhaust pipe. This is called a six-into-one exhaust system.

14. **(C)** When the air-fuel mixture is ignited by a spark under the pressure of compression, it begins to burn and becomes very hot gases. Combustion temperatures range between approximately 2,000° and 5,000° F.

Therefore, of the choices given, the temperature can exceed at most 4,000° F.

15. **(D)** For any two gears attached to each other of different sizes, the larger gear will always spin slower, yet with more torque than the smaller gear.

16. **(A)** The tool pictured is an inside spring caliper. Inside spring calipers are a type of simple, noncalibrated caliper used, in conjunction with a scale, to measure inside diameters. Spring calipers have the legs joined by a strong spring hinge and linked together by a screw and adjusting nut. Inside spring calipers have straight legs with the feet turned outward.

17. **(A)** Hacksaws are used to cut metal that is too heavy for snips or boltcutters. Thus, metal bar stock can be cut readily with hacksaws. There are two parts to a hacksaw: the frame and the blade. Common hacksaws have either an adjustable or solid frame.

18. **(C)** There are times when, for engineering reasons, a definite force must be applied to a nut or bolt head. In such cases a torque wrench must be used. The three most commonly used torque wrenches are the Deflecting Beam, Dial Indicating, and Micrometer Setting types.

19. **(B)** Box wrenches are safer than open-end wrenches since there is less likelihood they will slip off the work. They completely surround or box a nut or bolt head.

20. **(A)** A socket has a square opening cut in one end to fit a square drive lug on a detachable handle. In the other end of the socket is a 6-point or 12-point opening very much like the opening in the box end wrench.

21. **(B)** The Bristol wrench is made from round stock. It is L-shaped, but one end is fluted to fit the flutes or little splines in the Bristol setscrew.

22. **(A)** Taps and dies are used to cut threads in metal, plastics, or hard rubber. The taps are used for cutting internal threads, and the dies are used to cut external threads. There are many different types of taps. However, the most common are the taper, plug, bottoming, and pipe taps.

23. **(C)** After a pin has been loosened or partially driven out, the drift punch may be too large to finish the job. The follow-up tool to use is the

pin punch. It is designed to follow through the hole without jamming. Both of these punches will have flat points, never edged or rounded.

24. **(D)** Vises are used for holding work when it is being planed, sawed, drilled, shaped, sharpened, or riveted, or when wood is being glued.

25. **(C)** Auger bits are used for boring holes for screws, dowels, and hardware, as an aid in mortising (cutting a cavity in wood for joining members), and in shaping curves and for many other purposes. Auger bits are screw-shaped tools consisting of six parts: the cutter, screw, spur, twist, shank, and tang.

MATHEMATICS KNOWLEDGE
TEST 3

ANSWER KEY

1. (C)	8. (C)	15. (C)	22. (A)
2. (A)	9. (A)	16. (B)	23. (D)
3. (B)	10. (C)	17. (B)	24. (C)
4. (C)	11. (A)	18. (C)	25. (A)
5. (A)	12. (B)	19. (C)	
6. (D)	13. (C)	20. (A)	
7. (B)	14. (C)	21. (C)	

Add up your correct answers and put the number here. _____

Now record your score on pages 451-452.

DETAILED EXPLANATIONS OF ANSWERS

1. **(C)** The answer is (C) because $(x + 3)(x - 3) = x^2 - 3x + 3x - 9 = x^2 - 9$.

2. **(A)** The answer is (A) because $25 \times 25 = 625$.

3. **(B)** The answer is (B) because an octagon has eight sides.

4. **(C)** The answer is (C) because dividing both sides by 12 gives $y > 7$.

5. **(A)** The answer is (A) because $11(-3) + 34 = 1$.

6. **(D)** The answer is (D) because $(y + 6)(y - 3) = y^2 - 3y + 6y - 18 = y^2 + 3y - 18$.

7. **(B)** The answer is (B) because the number of boys equals $66^2/3\%$ of 75 or $.66^2/3 \times 75 = 50$.

8. **(C)** The answer is (C) because factoring $w^2 + 3w - 10 = (w + 5)(w - 2)$.

9. **(A)** The answer is (A) because the area of the square equals s^2 and the area of the rectangle equals $6l$, but the area of the rectangle is one-half the area of the square. Therefore, the equation is $s^2 = 3l$.

10. **(C)** The answer is (C) because multiplying both sides by -4 (and reversing the direction of the inequality) gives $x > -8$.

11. **(A)** The answer is (A) because using the Pythagorean Theorem and letting l be the other leg, $12^2 + l^2 = 15^2$ (because one foot equals 12 inches). Then $144 + l^2 = 225$, or $l^2 = 81$. The other leg equals 9 inches.

12. **(B)** The answer is (B) because the coat cost 70% of the original price, or $.70 \times \$64 = \$44.80$.

13. **(C)** The answer is (C) because the sum of the angles in a triangle equals 180, and the sum of the angles in a square equals 360. The combined sum equals 540.

14. **(C)** The answer is (C) because $(x + 7)(x - 5) = x^2 - 5x + 7x - 35 = x^2 + 2x - 35$.

15. **(C)** The answer is (C) because $3(8) + 16 = 40$.

16. **(B)** The answer is (B) because $16 \times 16 = 256$.

17. **(B)** The answer is (B) because an isosceles triangle has two equal sides.

18. **(C)** The answer is (C) because factoring $y^2 + 5y + 6 = (y + 2)(y + 3)$.

19. **(C)** The answer is (C) because the area of the circle is equal to the circumference or $\pi r^2 = 2\pi r$, or $r^2 = 2r$. Since r cannot equal zero, $r = 2$.

20. **(A)** The answer is (A) because total number of seniors – number of boys equals the number of girls in the senior class or $90/.45 - 90 = 200 - 90 = 110$.

21. **(C)** The answer is (C) because a rectangle has two pairs of sides that are equal.

22. **(A)** The answer is (A) because the perimeter of the rectangle equals $2l + 8$ and the area of the rectangle equals $4l$ but the perimeter equals twice the area. Therefore, the equation to find l is $2l + 8 = 8l$.

23. **(D)** The answer is (D) because $5(5) - 39 = -14$.

24. **(C)** The answer is (C) because multiplying both sides by 5 gives $x \le -10$.

25. **(A)** The answer is (A) because the total amount of work – the 60% already finished equals the amount of work to finish the assignment or $(5 \times 6)/.60 - (5 \times 6) = 50 - 30 = 20$.

MECHANICAL COMPREHENSION TEST 3

ANSWER KEY

1. (B)	8. (B)	15. (C)	22. (D)
2. (A)	9. (D)	16. (A)	23. (A)
3. (D)	10. (A)	17. (D)	24. (B)
4. (B)	11. (B)	18. (D)	25. (A)
5. (C)	12. (D)	19. (C)	
6. (A)	13. (D)	20. (A)	
7. (D)	14. (D)	21. (D)	

Add up your correct answers and put the number here. _____

Now record your score on pages 451-452.

DETAILED EXPLANATIONS OF ANSWERS

1.   **(B)**   This is a second-class lever because the resistance (drill) is between the effort and the fulcrum. In a first-class lever (A), the fulcrum is between the resistance and the effort, and in a third-class lever (C) the effort is between the fulcrum and the weight. A runner (D) is a block-and-tackle type of machine.

2.   **(A)**   The effort is obtained from the formula:

$$\text{M.A.} = \frac{R}{E}$$

Therefore,

$$\frac{100}{E} = 4 \ \text{ and } \ E = \frac{100}{4} = 25 \text{ pounds.}$$

(B) is obtained by taking the wrong ratio:

$$\text{M.A.} = \frac{E}{R} = 4$$

while (C) is obtained from

$$\text{M.A.} = \frac{R}{E} = 2$$

and (D) is obtained from

$$\text{M.A.} = \frac{E}{R} = 2.$$

3.   **(D)**   The correct answer can be obtained from

$$\text{M.A.} = \frac{R}{E} = \frac{L}{l} = 4$$

where $l = 2$ ft $\Rightarrow L = 8$ ft. (A) is the length $l = 2$ ft, (B) is obtained from

$$\frac{l}{L} = 4,$$

(C) is $L + l = 8 + 2 = 10$ ft.

4. **(B)** The mechanical advantage in a block-and-tackle system is equal to the number of strands of rope supporting the movable block. In this case, the movable block is made up of the lower two pulleys and the load and is supported by 4 ropes, hence the M.A. is 4.

5. **(C)** The correct answer (C) is obtained by using the correct mechanical advantage (4) properly:

$$\frac{R}{E} = M.A. = 4 \Rightarrow E = \frac{R}{4} = \frac{400}{4} = 100 \text{ pounds.}$$

(A) is obtained by using a M.A. = 5, while (B) is obtained from M.A. = 2. (D) uses M.A. = 4 but

$$\frac{E}{R} = M.A. \text{ instead of } \frac{R}{E} = M.A.$$

6. **(A)** The correct answer is obtained by making use of the mechanical advantage:

$$M.A. = 4 = \frac{R}{E} = \frac{L}{l};$$

$l = 5$ ft, therefore, $L = 4 \times 5 = 20$ ft. (B) is obtained from

$$\frac{l}{L} = 4,$$

while (C) and (D) use a M.A. of 5 and 2, respectively.

7. **(D)** Choices (A), (B), and (C) are incorrect because both gears are of the same size, a pinion is always smaller than the gear it's connected to. The correct type is the spiral bevel gear (D).

8. **(B)** The efficiency is obtained from the ratio of the Actual Mechanical Advantage to the Theoretical (or Ideal) Mechanical Advantage:

$$\text{efficiency} = \frac{\text{Actual Mechanical Advantage}}{\text{Theoretical Mechanical Advantage}} = \frac{AMA}{TMA}$$

The AMA in this case is obtained as:

$$\text{AMA} = \frac{\text{Resistance}}{\text{Effort}} = \frac{400 \text{ kg}}{2 \text{ kg}} = 200.$$

$$\text{TMA} = \frac{2\pi r}{p} = \frac{2\pi \times 0.40 \text{ m}}{0.005 \text{ m}} = 500.$$

Note that for the jackscrew, the TMA is the ratio of the distance the jack handle is moved around one complete circle ($2\pi r$) to the distance the jack is lifted (pitch).

The efficiency is then

$$\text{efficiency} = \frac{200}{500} = 0.4 = 40\%.$$

9. **(D)** An object immersed in a fluid is subject to pressure in all directions, thus answer (D) is the correct answer.

10. **(A)** The pressure exerted on the fluid must balance:

$$\frac{10 \text{ lb}}{10 \text{ sq. in}} = \frac{1 \text{ lb}}{\text{surface}}$$

therefore, surface = 1 sq. in. Answer (B) was obtained by taking pressure to be force × area. Answers (C) and (D) have no basis.

11. **(B)** The mechanical advantage for the gear and pinion system can be found by:

$$\text{M.A.} = \frac{T_0}{T_a} = \frac{\text{Number of teeth on driven gear}}{\text{Number of teeth on driver gear}}$$

$$= \frac{60}{10} = 6$$

(A) is the inverse of this ratio; (C) and (D) were calculated using the length ratios of the crank arm and the drum radius.

12. **(D)** The mechanical advantage of this part is found by dividing the distance the effort moves ($2\pi R$) in making one complete turn, by the distance the cable is drawn up in one revolution of the drum: $2\pi r$

$$\mathrm{M.A.} = \frac{2\pi R}{2\pi r} = \frac{R}{r} = \frac{30}{15} = 2.$$

13. **(D)** The total, or overall, mechanical advantage of a compound machine is equal to the product of the mechanical advantages of the several simple machines that make it up. Therefore, the answer is

$6 \times 2 = 12.$

(A) is the sum, (B) is the difference, and (C) is the ratio of 6 and 2.

14. **(D)** It is obvious that one half turn corresponds to one stroke, and that the piston moves downwards for a $1/2$ clockwise turn. For two strokes, the crank has to turn a full turn.

15. **(C)** This gear system is known as a worm gear, made up of a worm (a screw) and a wheel. Bevel gears (A), (B) are made up of two gear wheels at an angle, and the rack gear (D) is made up of a pinion and a linear gear.

16. **(A)** To determine the number of turns necessary, divide the distance 9'5" by the circumference of the drum:

3.14×1 ft.

It is best to perform the calculation in inches:

$9'5" = 113"$

circumference $= 3.14 \times 12 = 37.68"$

So that the number of turns necessary is 3.

17. **(D)** The valve will be lifted to a maximum height equal to the difference between the maximum radius and the minimum radius of the cam: $R - r$.

18. **(D)** The upper block and wheel are attached to a fixture and make up the only part that remains stationary as the load is hoisted.

19. **(C)** This solution is arrived at by making use of the mechanical advantage. In this block-and-tackle system, the moving block consists of the lower two pulleys and the load. With four ropes attached to this moving block, it is clear that the mechanical advantage is 4, and therefore

$$\mathrm{M.A.} = 4 = \frac{R}{E}$$

hence

$$E = \frac{R}{4} = 25\ \mathrm{lb}.$$

20. **(A)** A fluid is in balance if the pressures balance. The pressure on the right column is kept constant in all three configurations. This constant pressure must equal the pressure on the left column, which is

$$\frac{F}{A}.$$

Therefore,

$$\frac{F}{A} = P \quad \text{and} \quad F = P \times A,$$

where A is the area of the column cross section. It is obvious that F is smallest for the column with the least diameter. Hence, the answer is (A).

21. **(D)** This is an antifrictional ball bearing that permits only rotational motion.

22. **(D)** A universal joint is a coupling device used to couple two shafts that are not rotating in the same plane.

23. **(A)** The correct answer is (A). The actual mechanical efficiency is obtained by taking the ratio of the resistance to the actual effort

$$\mathrm{AMA} = \frac{R}{E} = \frac{2,500}{6} = 417,$$

and the efficiency is the ratio of the actual mechanical advantage to the theoretical mechanical advantage:

$$\text{efficiency} = \frac{\mathrm{AMA}}{\mathrm{TMA}} = \frac{417}{1,257} = 0.33 \quad \text{or} \quad 33\%.$$

Answer (B) obtains AMA as

$$\frac{E}{R}$$

and thus is wrong. Answer (C) interchanges the values of the AMA and the efficiency and thus is wrong. Answer (D) ignores the data given in the second part of the problem statement. No machine can be 100% efficient.

24. **(B)** The amount of work done is force × distance, where force is

$3 \times 2,000 \text{ lb} = 6,000 \text{ lb}$

and the distance is 15 feet. Hence, the work is 90,000 ft-lb. (A) assumes a ton to be 1,000 lb; (C) and (D) have units of power and cannot be the answer.

25. **(A)** To obtain the power, divide the work in ft-lb by the time in minutes:

work = 90,000 ft-lb

time = 3 × 10 × 60 = 1,800 minutes

Thus:

$$\text{power} = \frac{90,000 \text{ ft-lb}}{1,800 \text{ min.}} = 50 \text{ ft-lb per min.}$$

To convert to hp, divide this by 33,000: 0.0015 hp.

ELECTRONICS INFORMATION
TEST 3

ANSWER KEY

1. (D)	6. (B)	11. (D)	16. (A)
2. (C)	7. (D)	12. (D)	17. (D)
3. (A)	8. (C)	13. (D)	18. (D)
4. (B)	9. (B)	14. (D)	19. (A)
5. (D)	10. (B)	15. (A)	20. (D)

Add up your correct answers and put the number here. _____

Now record your score on pages 451-452.

DETAILED EXPLANATIONS OF ANSWERS

1. **(D)** Since kilo is Greek for 1,000, a kilowatt is 1,000 Watts. A kilowatt hour is 1,000 Watts for one hour.

2. **(C)** Heat and current have a relationship of

$I^2 = H$, so $3^2 = 9$.

3. **(A)** A short circuit means that the resistance goes to zero. From Ohm's Law then

$V/R = I$,

this means that the current goes to infinity.

4. **(B)** A switch has a pole for every position.

5. **(D)** Electrical tape has a high insulation coefficient due to its rubber content. Masking tape does not provide any insulation so current will flow through.

6. **(B)** From Ohm's Law,

$R = V/I$,

the plot shows a constant V/I, which means it must be a resistor since the other three vary with a change in voltage.

7. **(D)** By definition the impedance load is the output resistance.

8. **(C)** Wire with shielding cable has a conductor with insulation wrapped around it. A metallic mesh is wrapped around the insulation. This metallic mesh acts to shield the conductor from electrical noise in the outside world. For this to be effective though, the shield must be grounded.

9. **(B)** Recalling that if resistors are in parallel, the amount of current that will flow through each leg is proportional to the resistance in each leg. Since each leg has the same resistance, the current must be split in

five equal parts.

If ten amps are being generated, then

$$\frac{10 \text{ amps}}{5 \text{ legs}} = 2 \text{ amps / leg.}$$

10. **(B)** This is a plug fuse. It is probably the most common in the U.S. Plug fuses are rated at 15, 20, 25, and 30 amps.

11. **(D)** By definition

Power = (Voltage) × (Current)

$\therefore P = VI$

12. **(D)** Electromagnetic radiation produces current flow in conducting surfaces. If current were to flow through a metal object in your food, there is a good chance some of the metal will react with your food.

13. **(D)** From the code standards, a #6 wire is needed. Recall that the greater the current, the greater the heat, so you need a larger wire.

14. **(D)** S-Fuses stand for safety fuses. It forces you to put the proper fuses in and not try to increase capacity for a system that can't handle it.

15. **(A)** The symbol for a current generating source is standard.

16. **(A)** Copper is the best conductor because it has the highest conductivity — in other words, very little resistance.

17. **(D)** This is, by definition, current to the number-of-turns in a transformer.

18. **(D)** Line drop is caused by excessive resistance in the line. The resistance drops much of the voltage across the line as opposed to the device.

From Ohm's Law,

$V = RI,$

we can see how if R increases, V increases.

19. **(A)**   Some motors can only run on AC or DC voltage. The universal motors can run on either.

20. **(D)**   Voltages in series add. Since the curves are mirror images of each other, their sum would be zero.

ASVAB
Armed Services Vocational Aptitude Battery

Scoring Your Tests

HOW DO YOUR SCORES STACK UP?

Whether you've taken only one complete test or all the tests in this book, you may be curious to know what your scores really mean. Since each test has a different amount of questions and a different format, there isn't one standard raw score for all nine subtests. The chart below will help you to evaluate your performance on each of the tests by comparing your number of correct answers to our ASVAB subtest scale. This scale is not the official ASVAB evaluation scale; it merely serves as an indicator to help you evaluate your own performance.

Compare Your Scores

Fill in your sample test scores for each subtest in the blank next to the subtest name. Then compare your scores to the scale to see how you did.

SELF-ASSESSMENT CHART

SUBTEST	NUMBER CORRECT			SCALE
	Diag. Test 1	Test 2	Test 3	
1. General Science 25 Questions				More than 23 correct = **Outstanding** 20–22 correct = **Satisfactory** Less than 20 correct = **Needs More Work**
2. Arithmetic Reasoning 30 Questions				More than 28 correct = **Outstanding** 25–27 correct = **Satisfactory** Less than 25 correct = **Needs More Work**
3. Word Knowledge 35 Questions				More than 33 correct = **Outstanding** 30–32 correct = **Satisfactory** Less than 30 correct = **Needs More Work**
4. Paragraph Comprehension 15 Questions				More than 14 correct = **Outstanding** 12–13 correct = **Satisfactory** Less than 12 correct = **Needs More Work**

SUBTEST	NUMBER CORRECT			SCALE
	Diag. Test 1	Test 2	Test 3	
5. Auto and Shop Information 25 Questions				More than 23 correct = **Outstanding** 20–22 correct = **Satisfactory** Less than 20 correct = **Needs More Work**
6. Mathematics Knowledge 25 Questions				More than 23 correct = **Outstanding** 20–22 correct = **Satisfactory** Less than 20 correct = **Needs More Work**
7. Mechanical Comprehension 25 Questions				More than 23 correct = **Outstanding** 20–22 correct = **Satisfactory** Less than 20 correct = **Needs More Work**
8. Electronics Information 20 Questions				More than 18 correct = **Outstanding** 16–17 correct = **Satisfactory** Less than 16 correct = **Needs More Work**
9. Assembling Objects 16 Questions				More than 14 correct = **Outstanding** 12–13 correct = **Satisfactory** Less than 12 correct = **Needs More Work**

After you have completed all of the tests in the book, evaluate your progress and potential. If you achieved a rating of "Outstanding" on **all** the sample tests in one subject area, consider that subtest to be one of your strong areas. Circle the name of that subtest on the chart above. (For example, if you got above 23 on **all** of the General Science subtests, you would circle the words "General Science" on the chart.)

Likewise, if your correct answers earn a rating of "Satisfactory" or better on two or more subtests, put a square around the name of that subtest. (For example, if you got between a 42 and a 45 on two or more of the Mechanical Comprehension subtests, you would put a square around the words "Mechanical Comprehension" on the chart above. At the end of this book, you will have an opportunity to match these strong areas to other interests you may have and discover the occupation fields that may be best for you.

ASVAB
Armed Services Vocational Aptitude Battery

Career Options

INTRODUCTION

Your potential for success is not the only factor to keep in mind when considering career goals. It is important to discover your interests and apply them to your search for a future occupation. The ASVAB is designed to measure your potential; it is up to you to decide what to do with it. It is often the case that the more interested you are in a specific area, the more you will enjoy learning and working in that field.

The following chapter will give you an idea of some of the positions available in the Armed Services. You may be pleasantly surprised by the new jobs you discover in the Career Options Chapter. For instance, did you know that there is a position in the Armed Services for Camera Operators? You could make movies! The spectrum is wide and varied, and this is the time to browse through your options and pursue your interests. The occupations are listed by group and explained in detail to allow you to learn more about each one. If any particular occupation or field interests you, discuss it with your school guidance counselor or your local Armed Forces recruiter.

Read through each occupation description to learn about the requirements, conditions, and responsibilities for that specific job. At the end of each description are a number of Interest Level Questions. These questions are designed to help you objectively evaluate your interest in a specific occupation. To respond to the questions, circle the number that corresponds with your interest: on a 1–5 scale, 1 would indicate no or very little interest, while a 5 would indicate extreme interest. For example, if the question reads: "Do you like working with people?" and you do enjoy working with people very much, you would circle the number 5. After you have answered all the questions, add the numbers you have circled for that occupation and place the result in the corresponding blank. (See the following example.) This is how Darryl responded to one set of Interest Level Questions:

Interest Level:

Do you enjoy doing physical work?   1 ②3 4 5

Do you like working with written instructions?   1 2 3 ④5

Do you enjoy working outdoors?   1 ②3 4 5

Darryl would add all the numbers he circled, and place the sum in the blank called "general interest quotient," as he has done below.

General Interest Quotient: _*8*_

At the end of this chapter, you will be instructed how to combine these interest level quotients with your subtest scores to pinpoint what occupations may be best for you.

MECHANICAL AND CRAFTS

AIRCRAFT MECHANICS

Mechanics inspect the engines, landing gear, instruments, valves, and other parts of the aircraft and handle the necessary maintenance. They may use precision instruments to measure engine parts for wear, and they use x-ray and magnetic inspection equipment to check for invisible cracks. Mechanics usually work in hangars or other indoor areas. However, if the hangars are full or repairs must be made quickly, they may work outdoors, sometimes in unpleasant weather. Frequently, mechanics must lift or pull as much as 50 pounds. They often stand, lie, and kneel in awkward positions and occasionally must work in precarious situations or on scaffolds or ladders. Some mechanics specialize in repairing electronic systems, such as computerized controls, while most usually inspect and repair different types of aircraft.

Interest Level Questions

Do you like to use hand and power tools?   1 2 3 4 5

Do you enjoy physical work?   1 2 3 4 5

Are you interested in engines and how they operate? 1 2 3 4 5

General Interest Quotient: _____

AUTOMOTIVE BODY REPAIRERS

Automotive body repairers remove dents and replace crumpled parts of vehicles that are usually beyond repair. Usually, they can fix all types of vehicles, but most body repairers work on small cars and trucks. They use special machines to restore damaged metal frames and body sections to their original shape and location. They chain or clamp the frames and sections to alignment machines that align the damaged metal. They work indoors in noisy body shops. Body repairers often work in awkward or cramped positions, and much of their work is strenuous and dirty. Body repair work has variety and challenge: each vehicle presents a different problem. Repairers must develop appropriate methods for each job, using their broad knowledge of automotive construction and repair techniques.

Interest Level Questions

Do you enjoy physical work?   1 2 3 4 5

Do you like to use hand and power tools?   1 2 3 4 5

Do you like working with cars and trucks?   1 2 3 4 5

General Interest Quotient: _____

AUTOMOTIVE MECHANICS

Anyone whose car or truck has broken down knows the importance of the mechanic's job. Automotive mechanics, often called automotive service technicians, repair and service automobiles and occasionally light trucks with gasoline engines. Mechanics frequently work with dirty and greasy parts, and in awkward positions, and they often must lift heavy parts and tools. They use power tools such as pneumatic wrenches to remove bolts quickly, machine tools such as lathes to rebuild brakes and other parts, and a growing variety of electronic service equipment, such as infrared engine analyzers. The ability to diagnose the source of the problem quickly and accurately, one of the mechanic's most valuable skills, requires good reasoning ability. In fact, many mechanics consider diagnosing "hard to find" troubles one of their most challenging and satisfying duties.

Interest Level Questions

Do you enjoy working with hand and power tools?   1 2 3 4 5

Do you have an interest in problem solving?   1 2 3 4 5

Are you interested in engines and how they work?   1 2 3 4 5

General Interest Quotient: _____

BOAT OPERATORS

Boat operators operate and maintain deep sea merchant ships, tugboats, tow boats, ferries, and other water craft on the oceans, Great Lakes, and other waterways. A boat operator directs the course and speed of boats by consulting maps, charts, weather reports, and navigation equipment. He or she also assists in search and rescue missions and maintains boats, deck equipment, and operation logs.

Interest Level Questions

Do you like to work outdoors?   1 2 3 4 5

Do you enjoy doing detailed work?   1 2 3 4 5

Would you enjoy being on the water for long
periods of time?   1 2 3 4 5

General Interest Quotient: _____

BOILER TECHNICIANS

Boiler technicians operate or tend low-pressure steam boilers and auxiliary steam equipment, such as pumps, compressors, and air-conditioning equipment. This equipment is quite heavy, and the technicians are often responsible for moving it. In addition to heavy lifting, boiler technicians may have to bend, kneel, and work in awkward positions. They operate the steam turbines that supply power to a ship, and maintain equipment by using hand and power tools. Their responsibilities may also include water testing, to ensure its quality and purity.

Interest Level Questions

Do you enjoy working with machines and heavy
equipment?   1 2 3 4 5

Do you like physical work?   1 2 3 4 5

Do you like working in confined areas?   1 2 3 4 5

General Interest Quotient: _____

BRICKLAYERS AND CONCRETE MASONS

Bricklayers and concrete masons usually work outdoors. They stand, kneel, and bend for long periods and may have to lift heavy materials. Their work involves building structures with brick or concrete block. They cut and shape the masonry with power saws, chisels, and hammers, as well as mix and pour concrete for foundations and floor slabs.

Interest Level Questions

Do you enjoy doing physical work?   1 2 3 4 5

Do you like working with written instructions?   1 2 3 4 5

Do you enjoy working outdoors?   1 2 3 4 5

General Interest Quotient: _____

CARPENTERS

Almost all building construction requires carpentry. As in other building trades, carpentry is active and sometimes strenuous. Prolonged standing, climbing, bending, and kneeling often are necessary. Working from blueprints or instructions from supervisors, carpenters first do the layout—measuring, marking, and arranging materials. They cut and shape materials, such as wood, plastic, and ceiling tile, with hand and power tools, such as chisels, planes, saws, and drills. Carpenters may also assist in moving or installing machinery.

Interest Level Questions

Do you enjoy physical work?   1 2 3 4 5

Are you interested in how structures are put
together?   1 2 3 4 5

Do you like to work with power tools and hand tools? 1 2 3 4 5

General Interest Quotient: _____

COMBAT ENGINEERS

This field involves combat operations and is not open to women. Combat engineers must meet demanding physical requirements, and they have to perform strenuous physical activities over a long period of time. Some specialties also require good swimming abilities. Combat engineers construct trails, roads, and temporary shelters, as well as floating and prefabricated bridges. They lay and clear mine fields and booby traps, along with erecting camouflage and constructing airfields. Their duties may also include moving supplies using planes, helicopters, and trucks.

Interest Level Questions

Do you like to work outdoors?   1 2 3 4 5

Do you like high pressure and fast-paced action?   1 2 3 4 5

Do you enjoy working with hand and power tools?   1 2 3 4 5

General Interest Quotient: _____

CONSTRUCTION EQUIPMENT OPERATORS

Material moving equipment operators use machinery to move construction materials and manufacturer goods, earth, logs, and other heavy materials. Many material moving operators work outdoors, in hot and cold weather and sometimes even in rain or snow. Operators control equipment by moving levers or foot pedals, operating switches, or turning dials. They set up and inspect equipment and make adjustments and minor repairs. They may also remove ice and snow from runways using equipment such as scrapers and snow blowers.

Interest Level Questions

Do you like to work outdoors?   1 2 3 4 5

Do you have an interest in operating heavy
equipment?   1 2 3 4 5

Would you be interested in working with the raw
materials of the construction process?   1 2 3 4 5

General Interest Quotient: _____

DISPATCHERS

Dispatchers act as a link between the public requesting assistance and the appropriate service provider. They see to it that each request for service is carried out quickly and accurately. They carefully question callers as to the nature of their request. They then decide on the number and kind of units needed, locate the closest and most suitable units, and send them to the scene of the emergency or service call. They prepare reports about the fuel used, miles driven, and the number of vehicles needing repair.

Interest Level Questions

Do you enjoy planning and scheduling the work
of others?   1 2 3 4 5

Do you enjoy working with figures?   1 2 3 4 5

Do you have the ability to speak clearly and
distinctly?   1 2 3 4 5

General Interest Quotient: _____

DIVERS

Divers work in the water and maintain marine equipment. They must
be good swimmers and physically strong. They patrol the waters below
ships at anchor, salvage sunken equipment, and assist in the underwater
construction of piers and bridges. Specialists in this area may also be
involved in underwater welding or the use of explosives to clear underwater obstacles.

Interest Level Questions

Do you like working in the water?   1 2 3 4 5

Do you like high-pressure environments?   1 2 3 4 5

Do you like working on your own?   1 2 3 4 5

General Interest Quotient: _____

FIRE FIGHTERS

Every year, fires take thousands of lives and destroy property worth
billions of dollars. Fire fighters help to protect the public against this
danger. The job of a fire fighter has become more complex in recent years
due to the increased use of sophisticated equipment. In addition, many fire
fighters have assumed additional responsibilities, for example, working
with ambulance services which provide emergency medical treatment, as-
sisting in the recovery from natural disasters, and becoming involved in
the cleanup of oil spills and other hazardous chemical incidents. Fire fighters also teach fire protection procedures and repair fire fighting equipment.

Interest Level Questions

Is it important for you to help others?   1 2 3 4 5

Would you like to work in a high-pressure,
sometimes dangerous situation?   1 2 3 4 5

Do you enjoy physical work?   1 2 3 4 5

General Interest Quotient: _____

HEATING AND COOLING MECHANICS

Heating and air-conditioning systems control the temperature and humidity and total air quality in buildings. Heating and air-conditioning mechanics install, maintain, and repair such systems. Mechanics work outside in cold or hot weather or in buildings that are uncomfortable because their heating or air-conditioning systems have broken. They work in awkward and cramped positions and sometimes are required to work in high places. Heating and cooling systems consist of many electric and mechanical components, including motors, compressors, fans, switches, ducts, and pipes. Mechanics must be able to diagnose and repair problems throughout the entire system, using special tools and equipment.

Interest Level Questions

Do you like working on machines?   1 2 3 4 5

Do you enjoy working with hand and power tools?   1 2 3 4 5

Are you interested in problem solving?   1 2 3 4 5

General Interest Quotient: _____

IRONWORKERS

Structural ironworkers fabricate, assemble, and install metal stairways, railings, fences, decorative ironwork, and other iron-reinforced structures. They usually work outside in all kinds of weather. Ironworkers must read blueprints to determine correct placement of structural steel, and then operate arc and gas welding rigs to cut and weld it. These workers also repair, renovate, and maintain older buildings and structures such as steel mills, highways, and bridges.

Interest Level Questions

Do you enjoy physical work?   1 2 3 4 5

Do you enjoy working outdoors?   1 2 3 4 5

Do you like working as a member of a team?   1 2 3 4 5

General Interest Quotient: _____

MACHINISTS

Precision metal parts are essential for the production of industrial machinery, aircraft, automobiles, and other durable and nondurable goods. Machinists are skilled workers who produce metal goods that are made in numbers too small to produce with automated machinery. This job requires stamina because machinists stand most of the day and may lift moderately heavy workpieces. Using their skill with machine tools and their knowledge of metals, machinists plan and carry out the operations needed to make products that meet precise specifications.

Interest Level Questions

Do you like to work with your hands?   1 2 3 4 5

Do you like making things and finding solutions to mechanical problems?   1 2 3 4 5

Do you like working with power tools?   1 2 3 4 5

General Interest Quotient: _____

MARINE ENGINE MECHANICS

Small engines, like large engines, require periodic servicing to minimize the possibility of breakdowns and keep them operating at peak efficiency. At routine intervals, mechanics adjust, clean, lubricate, and, when necessary, replace worn or defective parts such as spark plugs, ignition joints, valves, and carburetors. Motorboat mechanics may work outdoors in all weather when repairing inboard engines aboard boats; they may have to work in cramped or awkward positions to reach a boat's engine. Motorboat engine mechanics may also work on propellers, steering mechanisms, marine toilets, and other boat equipment.

Interest Level Questions

Do you like doing physical work?   1 2 3 4 5

Do you enjoy working on the water?   1 2 3 4 5

Do you enjoy working with hand and power tools?   1 2 3 4 5

General Interest Quotient: _____

NON-DESTRUCTIVE TESTERS

Non-destructive testers ensure that products meet quality standards and are in working order. They may compare products to samples or to specifications in graphs or blueprints to make sure they are free from defects or other problems. Many inspectors use gauges, tools, and test machinery such as x-ray machines to check for cracks and flaws in engine parts. They may operate ultrasonic, atomic absorption, and other kinds of test equipment. Machine testers usually perform tests to make sure parts fit and move correctly, and conduct oil analysis and heat damage tests in order to detect engine wear. Some jobs involve only a quick inspection; others require a much longer, more detailed one. The testers mark, tag, or note problems and prepare inspection reports. They also notify superiors of the problems and may even analyze or correct the problems they find.

Interest Level Questions

Are you interested in machines and how they
operate?   1 2 3 4 5

Do you enjoy working with intricate material?   1 2 3 4 5

Do you like to piece together and solve puzzles?   1 2 3 4 5

General Interest Quotient: _____

OFFICE MACHINE REPAIRERS

These repairers may install new machines, do preventive maintenance, or correct emergency problems. Installing a typewriter may not require the service of a field technician but more complex copiers and computers may need special cable and wiring to hook up electrical connections. Repairers work closely with electricians, who install wiring of the new system to ensure proper layout. Technicians thoroughly test the equipment before the customer uses the machine. Large computers take a few days to install before they are fully operational. A repairer answers service calls, during which he inspects the machine for unusual wear and replaces any worn or broken parts. Then all mechanical parts of the machine are cleaned, oiled, and adjusted to ensure peak operating efficiency and to prevent any future breakdowns. The repairer may also advise machine operators on how to use the equipment more efficiently and how to spot a problem in its early stages.

Interest Level Questions

Do you like working with machines?	1 2 3 4 5
Are you interested in solving problems?	1 2 3 4 5
Do you like to use hand tools?	1 2 3 4 5

General Interest Quotient: _____

PAVING EQUIPMENT OPERATORS

These specialists operate equipment used for applying concrete, asphalt, or other materials to roadbeds, parking lots, or airport runways. They may patch worn pavement or inspect existing pavement for cracks and wear. They are also responsible for maintaining quality standards by taking samples and testing the asphalt or concrete surfaces.

Interest Level Questions

Do you like to work outdoors?	1 2 3 4 5
Do you like working with machines and large equipment?	1 2 3 4 5
Do you enjoy physical work?	1 2 3 4 5

General Interest Quotient: _____

PETROLEUM SUPPLY SPECIALISTS

Petroleum supply specialists maintain the equipment needed for the storage and shipment of petroleum products. They connect hoses and valves and operate pumps to load petroleum into tanker trucks, airplanes, or ships. They also repair any of these lines if they break down. These specialists test oil and fuels for pollutants and check the volume and temperature of petroleum and gasses in barges, tankers, and storage tanks. They may prepare records to report their findings, or become involved in the actual storage or moving of packaged petroleum products.

Interest Level Questions

Are you interested in working with machines?   1 2 3 4 5

Are you comfortable with following oral instructions? 1 2 3 4 5

Do you like to do physical work?   1 2 3 4 5

General Interest Quotient: _____

PLUMBERS AND PIPE FITTERS

Plumbers and pipe fitters measure and mark areas where pipes will be installed and connected. They check for obstructions, such as electrical wiring, and, if necessary, plan the pipe installation around the problem. Physical stamina is required for plumbing and pipe fitting work because workers frequently lift heavy pipes, stand for long periods, and sometimes work in uncomfortable or cramped positions. They may also have to work outdoors in inclement weather. Plumbing work also includes the planning of pipe systems using blueprints and drawings, and the recording of materials used and tasks completed.

Interest Level Questions

Do you enjoy doing physical work?   1 2 3 4 5

Do you enjoy working with detailed written
instructions?   1 2 3 4 5

Do you like to work outdoors?   1 2 3 4 5

General Interest Quotient: _____

SURVIVAL EQUIPMENT SPECIALISTS

These specialists keep survival equipment in working order. Their job is very important, because lives depend on the equipment to be intact and operational. Survival equipment specialists test parachutes, life rafts, and fire extinguishers and other emergency gear. They are also responsible for training crews in the use of the equipment. They may repair life rafts or load them with emergency provisions, or stock aircraft with flares and other survival provisions.

Interest Level Questions

Do you have an interest in maintaining the safety of
others?   1 2 3 4 5

Do you like working with intricate material?   1 2 3 4 5

Do you enjoy following written plans and
instructions?   1 2 3 4 5

General Interest Quotient: _____

TRUCK DRIVERS

Nearly all goods are transported by trucks during some of their journey
from producers to consumers. Before leaving the terminal or warehouse,
truck drivers check their trucks for fuel and oil. They inspect the trucks
they will drive to make sure the brakes, windshield wipers, and lights are
working and to see that the fire extinguisher, flares, and other safety
equipment aboard are in working order. They also inspect cargo to make
sure that it is secured properly and will not shift during the trip. Drivers
report any equipment that does not work or is missing, or cargo that is not
loaded properly to the dispatcher. Once underway, drivers must be alert to
prevent accidents and to drive their trucks efficiently. They must read
travel instructions to determine routes and arrival dates, and keep records
of the mileage driven and fuel and oil used.

Interest Level Questions

Are you interested in mechanics?   1 2 3 4 5

Do you enjoy following written plans and
instructions?   1 2 3 4 5

Do you enjoy being alone for extended periods
of time?   1 2 3 4 5

General Interest Quotient: _____

WATER AND SEWAGE PLANT OPERATORS

Water is pumped from wells, rivers, and streams to water treatment
plants. Waste materials are carried by water through sewer pipes to water
treatment plants. Operators in both types of plants control the process and

equipment used to remove solid materials, chemicals, and micro-organisms from the water to render it harmless. By operating and maintaining the pumps, water pipes, valves, and processing equipment of the treatment facility, operators move the water or wastewater through the various treatment processes. They read and interpret gauges to make sure plant equipment and processes are working properly and adjust controls as needed. They operate chemical-feeding devices; take samples of the wastewater, and perform testing and laboratory analyses. Operators may also make minor repairs to valves, pumps, and other equipment. They use gauges, wrenches, pliers, and other common hand tools, as well as special tools.

Interest Level Questions

Are you interested in working with mechanical
equipment?   1 2 3 4 5

Are you interested in protecting natural resources?   1 2 3 4 5

Do you like working with hand tools?   1 2 3 4 5

General Interest Quotient: _____

WELDERS

Skilled welders use all types of welding equipment in a variety of positions, such as flat, vertical, horizontal, and overhead. They generally plan work from drawings or specifications or by analyzing damaged metal by using their knowledge of welding and metals. They select and set up welding equipment and may also examine welds to ensure they meet standards or specifications.

Interest Level Questions

Do you enjoy doing physical work?   1 2 3 4 5

Do you enjoy working with your hands?   1 2 3 4 5

Do you like working with power tools?   1 2 3 4 5

General Interest Quotient: _____

BUSINESS AND CLERICAL

ACCOUNTANTS

Accountants prepare, analyze, and verify financial reports that furnish information to managers in all business, industrial, and government organizations. Computers are increasingly being used in accounting and auditing. With the aid of special computer software systems, accountants summarize transactions in standard formats for financial records, put the data in standard formats that aid in financial or management analysis, and prepare income tax returns. A growing number of accountants and auditors have extensive computer skills, and specialize in correcting problems with software systems or developing special software programs to meet unique data needs.

Interest Level Questions

Do you have an interest in working with numbers?   1 2 3 4 5

Do you enjoy working with detailed material?   1 2 3 4 5

Do you like working with computers?   1 2 3 4 5

General Interest Quotient: _____

ADMINISTRATIVE SUPPORT SPECIALISTS

Administrative support specialists coordinate and direct supportive services such as secretarial and correspondence, conference planning and travel, information processing, personnel, and financial records processing. They are responsible for mail, materials scheduling and distribution, supply, disposal, and data processing. They work within the same managerial hierarchy as other managers, and coordinate training sessions and leave for unit personnel.

Interest Level Questions

Do you like working with people?   1 2 3 4 5

Do you like working in an office?   1 2 3 4 5

Are you interested in organizational work?   1 2 3 4 5

General Interest Quotient: _____

COURT REPORTERS

Court reporters take down all statements made at legal proceedings and present their record as an official transcript. Some reporters dictate notes on magnetic tapes that a typist can transcribe later. Others transcribe their notes with the help of note readers (persons skilled in reading back shorthand notes). A large and growing number of reporters use Computer-Aided Transcription, a system in which a computer directly translates the reporter's shorthand into English. Because the reporter's transcript is the official record of a legal proceeding, accuracy is vital.

Interest Level Questions

Do you feel comfortable retaining information?　　1 2 3 4 5

Do you like working with and listening to other people?　　1 2 3 4 5

Do you have an interest in the legal system?　　1 2 3 4 5

General Interest Quotient: _____

LEGAL TECHNICIANS

Legal technicians generally do background work for lawyers. They research court decisions, process legal claims, appeals, and summonses to appear in court. Sometimes they can prepare military punishment and discharge orders. Legal technicians also meet with clients and take statements, prepare trial requests, and type up legal documents.

Interest Level Questions

Do you like working in an office environment?　　1 2 3 4 5

Are you interested in the law and how it works?　　1 2 3 4 5

Do you like to do research?　　1 2 3 4 5

General Interest Quotient: _____

LODGING SPECIALISTS

Lodging specialists are in charge of issuing rooms to military personnel and seeing that their needs are accommodated. They issue courtesy items, such as alarm clocks, padlocks, and towels, along with assigning and keeping records on room occupancy. The specialist might find hotel accommodations when there is no room available on base, receive payments, and keep financial records. They also operate the switchboard and provide information to callers.

Interest Level Questions

Do you have an interest in meeting and serving
people?   1 2 3 4 5

Do you like working independently?   1 2 3 4 5

Are you interested in record-keeping and organizing? 1 2 3 4 5

General Interest Quotient: _____

PAYROLL SPECIALISTS

In the payroll department, payroll clerks screen the time cards for evaluating, coding, or other errors. Then they compute earnings, vacation days, and sick leave balances. They review computer reports listing time cards that cannot be processed because of errors, and contact employees or managers for further information. Payroll clerks maintain manual back-up files for research and reference. They also adjust mistakes in earnings, record changes in employee addresses, and advise employees on income tax withholding. They mail earnings and tax withholding statements in early January for employees' tax returns.

Interest Level Questions

Do you like working with numbers?   1 2 3 4 5

Do you like working in an office environment?   1 2 3 4 5

Do you like working with detailed material?   1 2 3 4 5

General Interest Quotient: _____

PERSONNEL SPECIALISTS

The personnel specialist helps management make effective use of employees' skills and also helps employees find satisfaction in their job and working conditions. These specialists provide career guidance, and assist personnel and their families who have special needs. They also provide information about personnel programs and procedures to servicemen and women. Although some jobs in this field require limited contact with people outside the office, most involve frequent contact. Dealing with people is an essential part of the job.

Interest Level Questions

Do you enjoy following written instructions? 1 2 3 4 5

Would you like to formulate plans and instructions? 1 2 3 4 5

Do you enjoy helping people work more effectively? 1 2 3 4 5

General Interest Quotient: _____

POSTAL SPECIALISTS

Postal specialists unload sacks of incoming mail; separate letters, parcel post, or newspapers and transport them to the appropriate processing center. They may perform canceling procedures or inspect packages to ensure they meet mailing standards. They prepare postal reports and claims for lost or damaged material, and accept payment for and issue money orders and stamps.

Interest Level Questions

Do you enjoy working in an office environment? 1 2 3 4 5

Do you like working with names and numbers? 1 2 3 4 5

Do you enjoy working with people? 1 2 3 4 5

General Interest Quotient: _____

RELIGIOUS PROGRAM SPECIALISTS

Religious program specialists assist chaplains by planning religious activities. They may conduct religious services, organize charitable volunteer programs, or maintain relations with religious community and public service organizations. Their responsibilities also include scheduling appointments, maintaining files, and handling the finances of the chaplain.

Interest Level Questions

Are you interested in religious activities?	1 2 3 4 5
Do you like doing organizational work?	1 2 3 4 5
Are you sensitive to the needs of others?	1 2 3 4 5

General Interest Quotient: _____

SALES AND STOCK SPECIALISTS

Sales and stock specialists are primarily involved with accepting payment, answering questions, and taking returns in a retail environment. In addition, they may do some selling and reordering, account for money received, and prepare bank deposits. Stock specialists are responsible for ordering and inspecting merchandise, stocking shelves, and counting the merchandise during inventories. Both sales and stock specialists check and maintain merchandise quality.

Interest Level Questions

Do you like working with people?	1 2 3 4 5
Do you have an interest in working in a sales environment?	1 2 3 4 5
Do you like using calculators, adding machines, and working with figures?	1 2 3 4 5

General Interest Quotient: _____

SECRETARIES

Secretaries perform a wide variety of administrative and clerical duties that are necessary to run and maintain organizations effectively. They schedule appointments, give information to callers, organize and maintain files, fill out forms, and take and transcribe dictation. Experienced and highly skilled stenographers take complicated dictation, and they may sit in on staff meetings and later give a word-for-word record of the proceedings. They are also responsible for greeting visitors and answering telephones.

Interest Level Questions

Do you have an interest in serving others?   1 2 3 4 5

Do you enjoy working with people?   1 2 3 4 5

Do you enjoy working in an office environment?   1 2 3 4 5

General Interest Quotient: _____

SHIPPING AND RECEIVING SPECIALISTS

Shipping and receiving specialists keep records of all goods shipped and received. Shipping clerks are responsible for all outgoing shipments. They make sure an order has been filled correctly, and sometimes fill it themselves. This involves obtaining merchandise from the storeroom and wrapping or packing it in shipping containers. They address and label packages, look up postal rates, and record the weight and cost of each shipment. Once a shipment is ready to go, shipping clerks may move it to the shipping dock and direct its loading. Receiving clerks perform similar tasks. They confirm that orders have been filled correctly, record incoming shipments, and the condition of the contents. They may route the shipments to the proper department, warehouse, or stockroom. They also arrange for adjustments when material has been damaged in shipment.

Interest Level Questions

Would you enjoy a combination of office and
physical work?   1 2 3 4 5

Do you like working with office equipment?   1 2 3 4 5

Do you have an interest in operating forklifts and
other heavy equipment?   1 2 3 4 5

General Interest Quotient: _____

STOCK AND INVENTORY SPECIALISTS

Stock and inventory specialists receive, unpack, check, store, and keep track of merchandise and materials. They keep records of items entering and leaving the stockroom and report damaged or spoiled goods. They organize and, when necessary, mark items with identifying codes and prices so they can be found quickly and easily. They also give special handling to medicine, ammunition, and other delicate supplies.

Interest Level Questions

Do you like doing physical work? 1 2 3 4 5

Do you have an interest in operating forklifts and other heavy equipment? 1 2 3 4 5

Do you like organizing material and keeping records? 1 2 3 4 5

General Interest Quotient: _____

TRANSPORTATION SPECIALISTS

Transportation specialists plan, organize, direct, control, or coordinate management activities related to transporting people or goods by air, highway, railway, water, or pipeline. They find the cheapest and most direct shipping route. They serve as military airplane flight attendants and check in passengers and baggage before military transport flights.

Interest Level Questions

Are you interested in serving people? 1 2 3 4 5

Do you have an interest in using adding machines and other office equipment? 1 2 3 4 5

Would you like to travel? 1 2 3 4 5

General Interest Quotient: _____

ELECTRONICS AND ELECTRICAL

AIRCRAFT ELECTRICIANS

Aircraft electricians keep airplanes in top operating condition by troubleshooting aircraft electrical systems. They repair or replace defective generators and motors, replace faulty wiring, and solder electrical connections using soldering equipment and electrical wiring diagrams. They work as fast as safety permits so that the aircraft can be put back into service quickly.

Interest Level Questions

Do you like to work with hand tools?   1 2 3 4 5

Do you like solving problems?   1 2 3 4 5

Rate your ability to follow written instructions: 1 2 3 4 5

General Interest Quotient: _____

BUILDING ELECTRICIANS

Building electricians work with blueprints when they install electrical systems in buildings. They connect wire to circuit breakers, transformers, and other components. Wires are joined by twisting ends together with pliers and covering ends with special plastic connectors. They may also use soldering guns to melt metal onto the twisted wire. When wiring is finished, they test circuits for the proper connections. Some electricians install telephone and computer wiring and equipment, or install electronic controls for industrial equipment.

Interest Level Questions

Do you like working with hand tools?   1 2 3 4 5

Do you like doing physical work?   1 2 3 4 5

Do you like working with detailed diagrams and
drawings?   1 2 3 4 5

General Interest Quotient: _____

ELECTRONIC INSTRUMENT REPAIRERS

Electronic instrument repairers install and repair electronic equipment used in industrial automated equipment control, missile control systems, radar systems, transmitters, and antennas. They read technical diagrams and manuals in order to locate, isolate, and repair equipment parts, and replace them as needed. Repairers also must keep a log on each piece of equipment to provide a history of performance problems and repairs.

Interest Level Questions

Do you like to solve problems?   1 2 3 4 5

Do you enjoy working with hand tools?   1 2 3 4 5

Do you have an interest in working with electrical equipment?   1 2 3 4 5

General Interest Quotient: _____

ELECTRONIC WEAPON SYSTEMS REPAIRERS

These specialists are responsible for installing, maintaining, and repairing electronic weapons systems. Since this job sometimes involves weapons firing, some specialties may only be open to men. Weapons firing is adjusted using electronic test equipment, while systems like launch mechanisms may be repaired using hand and power tools. These specialists may also be asked to do routine maintenance, such as cleaning and lubricating gyroscopes and sights, and prepare for inspections. These repairers are required to keep logs and repair reports in addition to their mechanical and technical duties.

Interest Level Questions

Do you like working with electronic equipment?   1 2 3 4 5

Do you enjoy working with intricate material?   1 2 3 4 5

Do you like working with hand and power tools?   1 2 3 4 5

General Interest Quotient: _____

FLIGHT ENGINEERS

Flight engineers are highly trained, skilled professionals who carry out a wide variety of tasks. Some specialties in this field are only open to men, although there are women who are flight engineers. These specialists ensure flight plans proceed smoothly by monitoring, inspecting, and preparing aircraft before, during, and after flight. They use calculators and charts to compute fuel consumption and inform the pilot of any problems. They monitor instruments and gauges and follow pilot's orders to adjust them. These specialists must be physically fit, alert, and quick to react if anything goes wrong.

Interest Level Questions

Would you like to fly?	1 2 3 4 5
Do you like to work with others as a team?	1 2 3 4 5
Are you interested in mechanical systems? (Do you enjoy working with diagrams and drawings?)	1 2 3 4 5

General Interest Quotient: _____

LINE INSTALLERS

To install new electric power or telephone lines, line installers install poles and terminals and place wires and cables either overhead between utility poles or underground in trenches. They usually use power-driven equipment to dig holes for the underground lines. They may add other equipment to existing poles and towers, such as circuit breakers and switches, or install airfield lighting systems. Line installers work on poles, aerial ladders, and platforms, in manholes or in the basements of large buildings.

Interest Level Questions

Do you like to work outdoors?	1 2 3 4 5
Do you enjoy working with others as part of a team?	1 2 3 4 5
Do you like working with hand and power tools?	1 2 3 4 5

General Interest Quotient: _____

ORDNANCE MECHANICS

Ordnance mechanics are responsible for keeping gun systems in working order. They load and repair weapons systems, and carry explosives. They check the accuracy of radar-sighting systems and correct any problems. Ordnance mechanics are also responsible for defusing unexploded bombs. The work is physically taxing and dangerous; it requires a high level of concentration and an ability to work under stress. This occupation is not open to women.

Interest Level Questions

Do you enjoy physical work? 1 2 3 4 5

Are you interested in working with guns? 1 2 3 4 5

Do you like working with highly detailed systems and system diagrams? 1 2 3 4 5

General Interest Quotient: _____

PHOTOGRAPHIC REPAIRERS

Photographic repairers are responsible for maintaining photographic and sound recording equipment, such as enlargers, printers, and motion picture cameras. They diagnose and repair problems in all types of cameras, such as those that are mounted on airplanes to detect foreign military activity. These specialists must pay close attention to detail, and use specialized tools and testing devices.

Interest Level Questions

Do you like working with hand tools? 1 2 3 4 5

Do you like putting together complicated puzzles with small pieces? 1 2 3 4 5

Are you interested in photography and movie-making? 1 2 3 4 5

General Interest Quotient: _____

POWER PLANT OPERATORS

Power plant operators control the machines that generate electricity in power ships and submarines. They operate switches to distribute power demands among generators and auxiliary equipment, such as fans and condensers. They also keep records of switching operations and inspect equipment to guard against malfunctions. Nuclear power plant specialties in the military are open only to men.

Interest Level Questions

Do you like working with large machinery?   1 2 3 4 5

Do you like working in noisy environments?   1 2 3 4 5

Are you interested in electricity and how it
is generated?   1 2 3 4 5

General Interest Quotient: _____

RADAR AND SONAR EQUIPMENT REPAIRERS

These specialists monitor radar control systems to make sure there are no problems. Some specialties in this field are not open to women, although there are women who are radar and sonar repairers. This job requires the use of hand tools to solder and install components, along with the ability to read and interpret diagrams. These technicians also use special test equipment to monitor the operation of air traffic control, air defense, and other radar systems.

Interest Level Questions

Do you enjoy working with hand tools?   1 2 3 4 5

Do you like working with detailed diagrams
and drawings?   1 2 3 4 5

Are you interested in working with electrical
equipment?   1 2 3 4 5

General Interest Quotient: _____

RADIO EQUIPMENT REPAIRERS

Radio equipment repairers install and repair stationary and mobile radio transmitting and receiving equipment. Some of these workers repair intercommunication equipment such as microwave and fiber optic installations. They adjust and tune satellite, ship, and aircraft radio systems, and locate and replace defective parts using diagrams and technical guides. Some specialties in this field are open only to men.

Interest Level Questions

Do you like solving puzzles?   1 2 3 4 5

Do you like working with hand tools?   1 2 3 4 5

Do you like working with electrical systems?   1 2 3 4 5

General Interest Quotient: _____

RADIO INTELLIGENCE OPERATORS

These specialists are involved in the coding and decoding of messages. They tune radios to certain frequencies and study incoming signals to understand tactics used by foreign military forces. They may also be responsible for translating messages into Morse code and typing them for review by superiors. Radio intelligence operators are required to keep logs of all signals intercepted.

Interest Level Questions

Do you like finding clues and solving mysteries?   1 2 3 4 5

Do you enjoy working with radios and electrical
equipment?   1 2 3 4 5

Would you like remaining still and quiet for long
periods of time?   1 2 3 4 5

General Interest Quotient: _____

SPACE SYSTEMS SPECIALISTS

Operation of a spacecraft involves more than just astronauts. People are needed on the ground to monitor computers, handle incoming data, and transmit and verify commands to the spacecraft. It is the space system specialist's job to help space missions meet their objectives. They prepare the spacecraft for flight and maintain communication equipment. They also do repairs and collect the data that helps track the spacecraft when it is operational.

Interest Level Questions

Do you like to work with others as part of a team?   1 2 3 4 5

Do you like working with electronic systems?   1 2 3 4 5

Are you interested in space exploration?   1 2 3 4 5

General Interest Quotient: _____

TELEPHONE TECHNICIANS

Telephone technicians install, service, and repair telephones and other communications equipment. They connect telephones to outside service wires and sometimes must climb poles and ladders to make these connections. Before making any installations or repairs, they read and interpret service orders, technical manuals, and circuit wiring diagrams. Then they test, clean, fix, or replace faulty equipment or wiring. They also keep detailed and accurate records of all work activity.

Interest Level Questions

Do you like working with hand tools?   1 2 3 4 5

Do you like problem solving?   1 2 3 4 5

Do you enjoy climbing and working from unstable
heights?   1 2 3 4 5

General Interest Quotient: _____

TELETYPE OPERATORS

Teletype operators help to code and decipher military messages. They follow, translate, and interpret messages following distinct military procedures. They also classify incoming material with the appropriate security classification: "Top Secret," "Secret," etc. These operators may also be involved in the installation and maintenance of teletype equipment.

Interest Level Questions

Do you like working in an office environment?　　1 2 3 4 5

Are you interested in working with codes and coded materials?　　1 2 3 4 5

Do you like working with business machines?　　1 2 3 4 5

General Interest Quotient: _____

HEALTH, SOCIAL, AND TECHNOLOGY

AIR CREW MEMBERS

There are many jobs to be done on military aircraft, although some of the specialty jobs are restricted only to men. Air crew members operate the gunnery systems on aircraft, along with the communication and radar equipment. They maintain in-flight refueling systems and operate helicopter hoists to lift cargo and personnel from land and sea. An air crew member must be in top physical condition, and be able to work well under stress.

Interest Level Questions

Do you like to work with others as a team?　　1 2 3 4 5

Are you interested in flying?　　1 2 3 4 5

Do you like to do physical work?　　1 2 3 4 5

General Interest Quotient: _____

AIR TRAFFIC CONTROLLERS

Air traffic controllers are the guardians of the airways. They keep track of planes flying within their assigned area and make certain that they are safe distances apart. Their main concern is safety, but some controllers must also manage planes effectively to minimize delays. Some regulate airplane traffic; others regulate flights between airports. Relying on radar, charts, maps, and visual observation, they closely observe planes to maintain a safe distance between aircraft and to guide pilots between the hangar or ramp and the end of the airport's airspace.

Interest Level Questions

Do you like working in a high-pressure environment? 1 2 3 4 5

Are you interested in using mathematical formulas? 1 2 3 4 5

Do you like solving problems and making decisions? 1 2 3 4 5

General Interest Quotient: _____

ARTILLERY CREW MEMBERS

Artillery crew members set-up, maintain, and fire artillery weapons. Since this occupation involves the preparation of ammunition, fuses and firing powder, and loading artillery systems, it is not open to women. Crew members must calculate target locations and fire according to the instructions of artillery officers. This occupation requires stamina and peak physical capabilities.

Interest Level Questions

Do you enjoy working with others as a team?   1 2 3 4 5

Do you have an interest in weapons systems?   1 2 3 4 5

Do you like challenge and danger?   1 2 3 4 5

General Interest Quotient: _____

AUDIOVISUAL PRODUCTION SPECIALISTS

This occupation is both creative and technical. Specialists must often invent and revise imaginative programming and then operate the equipment to help make the scripts and plans a reality. They may manage audiovisual production crews, or operate the equipment themselves. They design production scenery, graphics, and special effects as well as work with directors to help them decide the best way to convey their message clearly and effectively.

Interest Level Questions

Are you interested in creative and artistic work?   1 2 3 4 5

Do you enjoy working with others as a team?   1 2 3 4 5

Do you have an interest in working with audiovisual equipment?   1 2 3 4 5

General Interest Quotient: _____

BARBERS

Barbers cut, trim, shampoo, and style hair. Most barbers offer hair and scalp treatments and shaves. As part of their responsibilities, barbers keep their scissors, combs, and other instruments sterilized, sharpened, and in good condition.

Interest Level Questions

Do you like working closely with people?   1 2 3 4 5

Do you like following other people's directions?   1 2 3 4 5

Are you interested in hair styling?   1 2 3 4 5

General Interest Quotient: _____

BROADCAST TECHNICIANS

Broadcast technicians install, test, repair, and operate the electronic equipment used to record and transmit radio and television programs. They work with television cameras, microphones, tape recorders, light and sound effects, transmitter antennas, and other equipment. They operate the control board that selects the source of the material being broadcast and may also set up and operate public address systems.

Interest Level Questions

Do you like working with others as a member of
a team?   1 2 3 4 5

Do you enjoy working with audiovisual equipment?   1 2 3 4 5

Are you interested in doing creative work?   1 2 3 4 5

General Interest Quotient: _____

CARDIOPULMONARY AND EKG TECHNICIANS

The EKG is a basic diagnostic tool used for measuring and monitoring activity in the heart. These technicians administer and record the findings of these tests, along with adjusting the settings of the individual machines. Their careful monitoring of graphs and screens during tests may help to discover treatments and alert doctors when read-outs suggest a change in a patient's condition.

Interest Level Questions

Is it important for you to help others?   1 2 3 4 5

Are you interested in how the heart, lungs, and
blood work together?   1 2 3 4 5

Do you like working with machines?   1 2 3 4 5

General Interest Quotient: _____

CASEWORKERS AND COUNSELORS

Caseworkers help personnel and their families to cope with problems of every type. They interview personnel who request help and are recommended for help by their supervisors. Their responsibilities also include administering and scoring psychological tests and teaching classes on human relations. Caseworkers and counselors keep records on counseling sessions and make reports to supervisors that cite any further need for professional help.

Interest Level Questions

Do you enjoy working with people?   1 2 3 4 5

Are you interested in helping other people solve
their problems?   1 2 3 4 5

Are you interested in working on projects that take a
long period of time to finish?   1 2 3 4 5

General Interest Quotient: _____

COMPUTER OPERATORS

Computer operators oversee the operation of computer hardware systems. They must ensure that these expensive machines are used as efficiently as possible. This includes anticipating problems before they occur and taking preventive action, as well as solving problems that do occur. Working from operating instructions prepared by programmers or operations managers, computer operators set controls on the computer and peripheral devices required to run a particular job. Computer operators load the computer with disks and tapes as needed. While the computer is running, operators monitor the computer console, and respond to operating and computer messages. If an error message occurs, operators must locate the problem and solve it or terminate the program.

Interest Level Questions

Do you enjoy working with computers?   1 2 3 4 5

Do you like doing work that is repetitive and routine? 1 2 3 4 5

Are you interested in machines and how they work? 1 2 3 4 5

General Interest Quotient: _____

COMPUTER PROGRAMMERS

Computer programmers write the detailed instructions that list the logical order the machine must follow. Programmers work from descriptions prepared by systems analysts who have carefully studied the task that the computer system is going to perform. Programmers then code the instructions the computer will execute in a program language, such as *COBOL* or *FORTRAN*. Next, programmers test or "debug" the operation of the program to be sure the instructions are correct and will produce the desired information. Finally, programmers prepare an instruction sheet for the computer operator who will run the program. They may also assist in writing the user's manual for a software package.

Interest Level Questions

Are you interested in working with computers?   1 2 3 4 5

Do you like solving problems?   1 2 3 4 5

Do you enjoy projects that are detailed and logical?   1 2 3 4 5

General Interest Quotient: _____

COMPUTER SYSTEMS ANALYSTS

Systems analysts plan and develop new computer systems or devise ways to apply existing systems to processes that are still completely manual or that use a less efficient method. They may design whole new systems, including the hardware and software for each, or add a single new software application to harness more of the computer's power. Systems analysts prepare charts and diagrams that describe it in terms that managers and other users can understand and they develop cost benefit analysis to help determine if the project will be cost efficient. Military analysts also make systems secure from unofficial access.

Interest Level Questions

Do you like working with computers?   1 2 3 4 5

Do you enjoy coordinating many activities at once?   1 2 3 4 5

Do you enjoy working with detailed charts and
diagrams?   1 2 3 4 5

General Interest Quotient: _____

CORRECTIONS SPECIALISTS

Corrections officers are charged with the safety and security of persons who have been arrested, are awaiting trial, or have been tried and convicted of a crime and have been sentenced to serve time in a correctional institution. They maintain order within the institution, enforce rules, and often supplement the counseling inmates receive from psychologists or social workers. Sometimes it is necessary to search inmates and their living quarters for contraband, such as drugs or weapons, settle disputes between inmates, and enforce discipline. To prevent escapes, officers staff security towers and gates. They are also expected to perform fire and riot control duties.

Interest Level Questions

Do you enjoy working in high-pressure situations?   1 2 3 4 5

Do you have an interest in safeguarding or caring for others?   1 2 3 4 5

Do you like to maintain order and follow strict guidelines?   1 2 3 4 5

General Interest Quotient: _____

DENTAL HYGIENISTS

In addition to carrying out clinical responsibilities, such as cleaning and scaling teeth, specialists keep records, and help personnel develop and maintain good oral health. They remove stain and plaque from above and below the gumline, apply fluoride treatments, take x-rays, and they may even administer anesthesia. Specialists having advanced training may teach or conduct research.

Interest Level Questions

Do you enjoy working closely with people?   1 2 3 4 5

Do you enjoy working with precision tools and machines?   1 2 3 4 5

Do you have an interest in health and medicine?   1 2 3 4 5

General Interest Quotient: _____

DENTAL LABORATORY TECHNICIANS

Although dentures, bridges, crowns, and other prosthetic devices are fitted by dentists, they are actually made by skilled craftworkers known as dental laboratory technicians. All work is performed at the request of a dentist, who sends the technician the specification for the item to be produced along with an impression (mold) of the patient's mouth or teeth. The technician molds or shapes a wax tooth or teeth using hand instruments called wax instruments or wax carvers. This wax model is used to cast the metal base of the prosthetic device. This work is extremely delicate and quite time consuming. Moreover, precision is of ultimate importance. Every tooth must fit perfectly, and technicians must be patient and meticulous in their craft.

Interest Level Questions

Do you enjoy working with precision tools?   1 2 3 4 5

Do you like working in a laboratory environment?   1 2 3 4 5

Do you enjoy working with detailed material?   1 2 3 4 5

General Interest Quotient: _____

DETECTIVES

Detectives help maintain the safety of our nation by investigating crimes against country and government property. These investigations may require interviewing suspects, and help with ballistic or forensic studies for clues. Detectives are often required to testify at a trial after a case has been solved.

Interest Level Questions

Do you like challenge and danger?   1 2 3 4 5

Do you like solving puzzles?   1 2 3 4 5

Do you have an interest in crime prevention?   1 2 3 4 5

General Interest Quotient: _____

DRAFTERS

Drafters prepare technical drawings used by workers who build spacecraft, industrial machinery and other manufactured products, office buildings, bridges, roads, and other structures. Their drawings show the technical details of the project from all sides, with exact details, and specify dimensions, materials to be used, cost, and the procedures to follow. For this, they may also use technical handbooks, tables, and calculators. Drafters also work with engineers and construction supervisors to change drawings when needed.

Interest Level Questions

Do you like to draw?   1 2 3 4 5

Are you interested in construction?   1 2 3 4 5

Do you like to work independently for long periods
of time?   1 2 3 4 5

General Interest Quotient: _____

EMERGENCY MANAGEMENT SPECIALISTS

It is important to have emergency equipment and procedures functional in case of a disaster. An emergency management specialist maintains nuclear, biological, and chemical detection and decontamination equipment on hand and keeps it operational should the need arise. He or she ensures that military and civilian personnel are ready for such situations, training people what to do in a disaster, and administering surveys to determine needs. He or she also assists in preparing disaster operations plans.

Interest Level Questions

Do you like working in high-pressure situations?   1 2 3 4 5

Do you like to plan and organize?   1 2 3 4 5

Do you like managing and maintaining resources?
(Do you like to help people?)   1 2 3 4 5

General Interest Quotient: _____

ENVIRONMENTAL HEALTH SPECIALISTS

These specialists work with engineers, chemists, microbiologists, health workers, and lawyers to ensure compliance with public safety regulations governing food, drugs, and other products. They administer regulations that govern the quarantine of persons and products entering the United States from foreign countries. They also plan the disposal of radioactive waste and inspect water and wastewater systems. Additionally, they may be involved in the administering of hearing exams and noise-level reduction at job sites.

Interest Level Questions

Do you have an interest in gathering information?   1 2 3 4 5

Do you have an interest in protecting the
environment?   1 2 3 4 5

Do you like working with detailed material?   1 2 3 4 5

General Interest Quotient: _____

FOOD SERVICE SPECIALISTS

Smooth operation of food service facilities requires that specialists efficiently use food and other supplies, achieve consistent quality in food preparation and service, keep utensils clean and functional, and attend to any administrative aspects of the job. Duties may include preparing cuts of meat, baking breads, preparing gravies and sauces, and the ordering, receiving, and inspection of fruits, vegetables, and other foodstuffs.

Interest Level Questions

Do you like working with your hands?   1 2 3 4 5

Do you have an interest in cooking?   1 2 3 4 5

Do you enjoy working independently?   1 2 3 4 5

General Interest Quotient: _____

GRAPHIC DESIGNERS AND ILLUSTRATORS

Visual artists use an almost limitless variety of methods and materials to communicate ideas, thoughts, and feelings. They use a variety of media, including computers, to develop artwork that will help communicate and represent a given quantity of information. Graphic designers draw graphs and charts to represent numbers of troops, supply levels, and office organization. They design artwork for training programs, and develop drawings used in military training. They may also work on films, by drawing cartoons or designing backdrops and props for film sets.

Interest Level Questions

Do you like to draw?   1 2 3 4 5

Do you like working with abstract ideas?   1 2 3 4 5

Do you enjoy highly detailed work?   1 2 3 4 5

General Interest Quotient: _____

INFANTRYMEN

This is a combat occupation and therefore is not open to women. Infantrymen clean, store, position, and transport firearms. They may parachute from planes, go on scouting missions, or operate two-way radios to help pinpoint enemy troop locations. They dig foxholes and trenches and perform hand-to-hand combat techniques. This job has very demanding physical requirements, and infantrymen must perform strenuous physical activities.

Interest Level Questions

Do you enjoy challenge and danger?   1 2 3 4 5

Do you like working with others as a member of a
team?   1 2 3 4 5

Do you enjoy physical work?   1 2 3 4 5

General Interest Quotient: _____

INTELLIGENCE SPECIALISTS

Intelligence specialists collect and analyze the information necessary to plan and implement military strategy. Intelligence experts collect information from maps, photographs, and foreign military codes. They also analyze troop movements and study land and sea areas that could become battlegrounds in time of war. They compile this information with computers, and develop reports, maps, and charts to convey the material to the appropriate military personnel.

Interest Level Questions

Do you like information-gathering?   1 2 3 4 5

Do you enjoy writing?   1 2 3 4 5

Are you interested in working with maps and photos
and piecing together clues and patterns?   1 2 3 4 5

General Interest Quotient: _____

INTERPRETERS AND TRANSLATORS

Since armed forces work involves people and cultures from all over
the world, there is a need for personnel qualified in translating and inter-
preting. These specialists may question prisoners of war, translate foreign
documents, books, or radio transmissions. They translate both to and from
English, and must pay special attention to preserve the original meaning.
Additionally, translators must prepare written reports of their findings.

Interest Level Questions

Do you enjoy working with people?   1 2 3 4 5

Do you enjoy reading?   1 2 3 4 5

Do you have an interest in foreign languages?   1 2 3 4 5

General Interest Quotient: _____

MAPPING TECHNICIANS

Mapping technicians measure, map, and chart the earth's surface but
generally cover large areas. These specialists mainly work in offices and
seldom visit the sites they are mapping. Along with drawing geographic
regions, they may develop scale models of land areas from wood or clay.
Mapping technicians also record troop movement for intelligence purposes.

Interest Level Questions

Do you like working with abstract ideas?   1 2 3 4 5

Do you like to draw?   1 2 3 4 5

Do you have an interest in maps and how they
are made?   1 2 3 4 5

General Interest Quotient: _____

MEDICAL LABORATORY TECHNICIANS

Because changes in body fluids, tissues, and cells are often a sign that something is wrong, clinical laboratory testing plays a crucial role in the detection, diagnosis, and treatment of disease. Test results may be used to establish values against which future measurements can be compared or to monitor treatment. Although physicians depend heavily on laboratory results, they do not perform the tests themselves. That is the job of the medical lab personnel. Many labs are highly automated, and the jobs reflect this. Using microscopes, cell counters, and other laboratory equipment, these workers perform tests, interpret the results, and relay them to the physician.

Interest Level Questions

Do you enjoy working in a laboratory environment?   1 2 3 4 5

Do you like following instructions and procedures?   1 2 3 4 5

Do you have an interest in scientific work?   1 2 3 4 5

General Interest Quotient: _____

MILITARY POLICE

The military police are in charge of maintaining order within the armed forces. They patrol areas, guard entrances, and direct traffic. They also interview witnesses and arrest and charge criminal suspects. Often they are required to testify in court to supply information or eyewitness accounts. The work of the military police ensures running efficiency within the armed forces, as well as protecting the rights and interests of military personnel.

Interest Level Questions

Do you like to work in high-pressure situations?   1 2 3 4 5

Are you interested in law enforcement and crime prevention?   1 2 3 4 5

Do you like working closely with people?   1 2 3 4 5

General Interest Quotient: _____

MOTION PICTURE CAMERA OPERATORS

Taking quality pictures and movies is a technical as well as a creative process. Photographers and camera operators must be familiar with all the possible combinations of light, film, and cameras, and how they are combined to make pictures of professional quality. Camera operators must be able to follow the instructions of the director and also to set up and operate the motion picture equipment including sound recorders and lighting.

Interest Level Questions

Do you like working with cameras and movie equipment?	1 2 3 4 5
Do you like following detailed instructions?	1 2 3 4 5
Do you like to work with people?	1 2 3 4 5

General Interest Quotient: _____

MUSICIANS

Musicians may play musical instruments, sing, write musical compositions, or conduct instrumental or vocal performances. They spend many hours in rehearsal when not performing, so that they may improve and expand their repertoire. Military musicians perform at banquets, festivals, ceremonies, and dances.

Interest Level Questions

Do you like working with others as a member of a team?	1 2 3 4 5
Do you enjoy being in the public eye?	1 2 3 4 5
Are you interested in music?	1 2 3 4 5

General Interest Quotient: _____

NURSING TECHNICIANS

Nursing technicians work under the supervision of registered and licensed practical nurses. Typical duties include answering patients' call bells, delivering messages, serving meals, making beds, and dressing and bathing patients. Aides may give massages, take temperatures, obtain pulse and blood pressure readings, and assist patients in getting out of bed and walking. They may escort patients to operating and examining rooms or store and move supplies in hospital pharmacies and supply rooms.

Interest Level Questions

Do you have an interest in helping others?   1 2 3 4 5

Are you interested in the health field?   1 2 3 4 5

Do you enjoy working with detailed directions and
procedures?   1 2 3 4 5

General Interest Quotient: _____

OCCUPATIONAL THERAPY SPECIALISTS

Occupational therapists help mentally, physically, developmentally, or emotionally disabled individuals develop, recover, or maintain daily living and work skills. They help patients improve their basic motor functions and reasoning abilities, as well as help them learn to dress, bathe, cook, or operate machinery. Occupational therapists also help permanently disabled patients cope with the physical and emotional effects of being disabled. With support and direction, personnel learn (or re-learn) many of the day-to-day tasks necessary to establish an independent, productive, satisfying lifestyle.

Interest Level Questions

Do you enjoy helping people?   1 2 3 4 5

Do you enjoy working in relaxed environments?   1 2 3 4 5

Do you like long-term projects?   1 2 3 4 5

General Interest Quotient: _____

OPERATING ROOM TECHNICIANS

Operating room technicians work with and under the supervision of surgeons or registered nurses. They help set up the operating room with surgical instruments, equipment, sterile linens, and fluids such as saline solution or glucose. Operating room technicians may also prepare patients for surgery by washing, shaving, and disinfecting body areas where the surgeon will operate. They may transport patients to the operating room and help drape them and position them on the operating table.

Interest Level Questions

Do you like helping others?   1 2 3 4 5

Do you like working in high-pressure
environments?   1 2 3 4 5

Are you comfortable following verbal
instructions from others?   1 2 3 4 5

General Interest Quotient: _____

OPTICIANS

After a checkup at an ophthalmologist or an optometrist, people generally go to opticians to have their prescriptions filled. Opticians may grind the lens to the appropriate thickness, dye the lenses, and apply the necessary solutions. After the ophthalmic work is done, they help the customer select the appropriate frames and adjust the finished eyeglasses.

Interest Level Questions

Do you like working with your hands?   1 2 3 4 5

Do you like doing intricate work and following
detailed instructions?   1 2 3 4 5

Do you like to work in a relaxed environment?   1 2 3 4 5

General Interest Quotient: _____

ORTHOTIC SPECIALISTS

Physicians need the help of orthotic specialists to design and make orthotic devices such as braces and supports. Orthotic specialists can also make plaster or fiberglass casts for patients, or adjust existing devices. Their main jobs are to draw up blueprints to the physician's specifications and operate the lathes and grinders necessary to make parts from plastic and steel.

Interest Level Questions

Do you like to use hand and power tools?   1 2 3 4 5

Do you like working on detailed projects and
seeing them through to completion?   1 2 3 4 5

Do you like helping others?   1 2 3 4 5

General Interest Quotient: _____

PHARMACY TECHNICIANS

In addition to providing information, pharmacists dispense drugs and medicines prescribed by health practitioners, such as physicians and dentists. Pharmacists must understand the use, composition, and effects of drugs, and how they are tested for purity and strength. Compounding (the actual mixing of ingredients to form a powder, syrup, or paste) is now only a small part of the pharmacist's practice, because most medicines are made by large companies in the dosage and form used by the patient. Pharmacists must also keep track of all the materials ordered and used, and store and dispense of them in the proper manner.

Interest Level Questions

Do you like mixing and combining ingredients?   1 2 3 4 5

Do you enjoy working with detailed procedures and
instructions?   1 2 3 4 5

Do you like organizing and keeping records?   1 2 3 4 5

General Interest Quotient: _____

PRINTING SPECIALISTS

Printing specialists prepare and operate the printing presses in a pressroom. They are responsible for the preparation, operation, and maintenance of the press. Printers must make sure that ink and paper meet specifications and then adjust and mix the necessary solution. Some printers may be involved in the layout of the text, along with the process of transferring it to lithographic plates. Finally, printers bind the printed material into hardback or paperback books using binding machines.

Interest Level Questions

Do you like physical work?   1 2 3 4 5

Are you interested in how books are put together?   1 2 3 4 5

Do you enjoy working with large machines?   1 2 3 4 5

General Interest Quotient: _____

QUARTERMASTERS

Quartermasters are integral members of a ship's crew. They are responsible for collecting navigational data, such as compass readings, radar bearings, and depth soundings. The data they collect help them to steer ships and boats. The quartermaster announces the charted course to the helmsman and then records all the data in ships logs.

Interest Level Questions

Are you interested in sailing and navigation?   1 2 3 4 5

Do you like working with charts and graphs?   1 2 3 4 5

Do you enjoy working with mathematical equations,
charts, and graphs?   1 2 3 4 5

General Interest Quotient: _____

RADIO AND TELEVISION ANNOUNCERS

Announcers and newscasters are well-known personalities to radio and television audiences. Radio announcers, often called *disc-jockeys,* select and introduce recorded music; present news, sports, weather, and commercials; introduce guests, and report on other matters of interest to their audience. They may also operate a control board and maintain record, tape, and film libraries.

Interest Level Questions

Do you like working in the public eye?   1 2 3 4 5

Do you have an interest in music, sports, or current
events?   1 2 3 4 5

Do you have an interest in writing?   1 2 3 4 5

General Interest Quotient: _____

RADIOLOGIC TECHNOLOGISTS

Radiologists take x-ray film of all parts of the human body for use in diagnosing medical problems. They prepare patients for radiologic examinations and position patients so that the proper parts of their body can be photographed. The radiologic technician may also prepare solutions for patients to drink for other tests to examine their internal organs. Finally, these specialists process and keep records of patient treatment.

Interest Level Questions

Are you interested in helping others?   1 2 3 4 5

Do you like following detailed instructions and procedures?   1 2 3 4 5

Do you have an interest in the health field?   1 2 3 4 5

General Interest Quotient: _____

RECREATIONAL SPECIALISTS

Recreational specialists plan programs for personnel and their families such as softball games, crafts, and other leisure activities. They clean and repair equipment and schedule the use of sport facilities. It is also their job to publicize events as they are planned, and train all the referees and personnel needed for the event.

Interest Level Questions

Do you enjoy working with people?   1 2 3 4 5

Do you enjoy sports and leisure time activities?   1 2 3 4 5

Do you like planning events?   1 2 3 4 5

General Interest Quotient: _____

RECRUITING SPECIALISTS

Recruiting specialists help people undergo a process similar to the one you are going through now. They attend job fairs and career day programs to help high school students and other civilians who are interested in military careers. By describing military programs to high school groups and explaining the purpose of the ASVAB, they help civilians to decide which military occupation would best suit their talents and interests.

Interest Level Questions

Do you enjoy working with young people?	1 2 3 4 5
Do you like working independently?	1 2 3 4 5
Do you like speaking in front of large groups?	1 2 3 4 5

General Interest Quotient: _____

REPORTERS AND NEWSWRITERS

Reporters and newswriters gather and prepare stories that inform personnel about local, state, and international events. They present points of view and monitor the actions of public officials, special interest groups, and others who hold power. They investigate leads, tips, and documents, observe on the scene, and interview people. At their office, they organize material, determine their focus or emphasis, and write their stories.

Interest Level Questions

Do you like to write?	1 2 3 4 5
Are you curious about what is going on behind public figures and issues?	1 2 3 4 5
Do you like working with detailed material?	1 2 3 4 5

General Interest Quotient: _____

SPECIAL OPERATIONS FORCES

This is a combat occupation that may require going behind enemy lines; it is not open to women. These forces carry out demolition raids against enemy military targets, such as bridges or tunnels. They may conduct offensive raids, or try to recruit, aid, and equip friendly forces for guerilla raids. They work on both land and sea, sometimes destroying underwater mines and enemy ships in coastal waters.

Interest Level Questions

Do you like working as the member of a team?   1 2 3 4 5

Do you like challenge and danger?   1 2 3 4 5

Do you enjoy physical work?   1 2 3 4 5

General Interest Quotient: _____

TRAINERS

Trainers work closely with military students. They prepare course outlines and course materials, such as textbooks and films. They may teach classes or give lectures either in person or on videotape. They are also responsible for monitoring student's progress with written and oral evaluations.

Interest Level Questions

Do you like working with young people?   1 2 3 4 5

Do you like helping people?   1 2 3 4 5

Are you patient and understanding?   1 2 3 4 5

General Interest Quotient: _____

WEATHER OBSERVERS

Updated weather information is crucial to the efficiency of the armed services. It is the job of weather observers to monitor weather conditions, and make clear and accurate reports. They study information on temperature, air pressure, humidity, and wind velocity using weather satellites, radar, and other remote sensors from all parts of the world. They record the information on charts and maps in order to make long-term, short-term, and local area forecasts.

Interest Level Questions

Do you like working with formulas, tables,
and graphs?   1 2 3 4 5

Are you interested in the weather and why it
changes?   1 2 3 4 5

Do you like gathering information and discovering
patterns?   1 2 3 4 5

General Interest Quotient: _____

So many occupations from which to choose, your head must be spinning! What should you do if you are interested in several occupations you feel as though you can't possibly choose? This is where your self-evaluation comes in. If you combine your performance on the ASVAB subtests with the areas in which you indicated a high interest level, your search can become more directed. Keep in mind that you don't have to make lifetime plans at this moment; this exercise will simply help to get an idea of possible career options.

Your individual subtest scores on the ASVAB are evaluated in groups called *composites*. Composites are used to evaluate your potential future performance in academics or specific vocational fields. The following charts will help you to build your own composites similar to those used with the ASVAB. By using the following charts together with the Self-Assessment Chart on pages 451–452, you will be able to discover the areas for which you have the most potential.

Turn to the Self-Assessment Chart on pages 451–452. For all the tests you circled, put a "*" in the corresponding blank in all the composites on pages 508 and 509. For all the tests you squared, put a "+" in the corresponding blank in all the composites.

Here's an example of one student's subtest scores. It may help you to see exactly how they were put into one of the composites.

Darryl earned the following scores:

1.	General Science	25
2.	Arithmetic	26
3.	Word Knowledge	33
4.	Paragraph Comprehension	15
5.	Auto and Shop	22
6.	Mathematics Knowledge	21
7.	Mechanical Comprehension	22

According to the Self-Assessment Chart on pages 451–452, Darryl earned a rating of "Outstanding" in General Science, Word Knowledge, and Paragraph Comprehension, so he has circled the names of these subtests. His scores on the Auto & Shop and Mechanical Comprehension subtests were both "satisfactory," so the name of each of these tests has a square around it.

Mechanics and Crafts is the first Vocational Composite, and Darryl would fill it out in this way:

Arithmetic Reasoning   _____
(gets no mark because his rating was below satisfactory)

Mechanical Comprehension   __+__
(because his rating was satisfactory)

Auto and Shop Information   __+__
(because his rating was satisfactory)

Electronics Information   _____
(gets no mark because his rating was below satisfactory)

Darryl filled in this composite chart according to his scaled score. Only two marks were made in this composite, and they were both "+." Therefore, this is not one of Darryl's strongest composite areas. Complete each of the composite charts with your own score results.

Be aware that the following charts are not ASVAB procedure. This section is designed to help you apply the results of your practice testing, and also to help you to explore possible career decisions. When you receive your actual ASVAB results, you can work more with your guidance counselor to determine your possible career options.

The **Academic Composites** project your potential success in an academic career beyond high school.

The **Vocational Composites** project your potential success in specific occupations. The names of the composites match occupation groupings in the career options chapter.

ACADEMIC COMPOSITES

Verbal
      Word Knowledge   _____

      Paragraph Comprehension   _____

      General Science   _____

Math
      Mathematical Knowledge   _____

      Arithmetic Reasoning   _____

Academic Ability
      Word Knowledge   _____

      Paragraph Comprehension   _____

      Arithmetic Reasoning   _____

OCCUPATIONAL COMPOSITES

Mechanical and Crafts
      Arithmetic Reasoning   _____

      Mechanical Comprehension   _____

      Auto and Shop Information   _____

      Electronics Information   _____

Business and Clerical
      Word Knowledge   _____

      Paragraph Comprehension   _____

      Mathematics Knowledge   _____

Electronics and Electrical
      Arithmetic Reasoning   _____

      Mathematics Knowledge   _____

      Electronics Information   _____

      General Science   _____

Health and Social Technology
    Word Knowledge   _____
    Paragraph Comprehension   _____
    Arithmetic Reasoning   _____
    Mechanical Comprehension   _____

The ASVAB composites are evaluated separately in order to indicate your strength in each occupational area. Look at each composite individually to decide whether or not you performed well in that area. Remember, the stars indicate superior work while pluses indicate a job well done. The more pluses and stars you have on that composite, the better you did.

Many stars and pluses in one composite show that you have a high potential for succeeding in the jobs associated with that composite. It may be a good idea to highlight your best composites in some way, so that you can remember which areas are the strongest for you. Where your composites are strong and your General Interest Quotient is high, those are the areas to which you should probably pay the closest attention. For example, if your performance were strong in the Mechanical and Crafts Composite, and your General Interest Quotient for Aircraft Mechanics is high, the occupation of Aircraft Mechanic might be worth further investigation.

ASVAB

Armed Services Vocational Aptitude Battery

Answer Sheets

ASVAB – DIAGNOSTIC TEST 1

General Science

1. (A) (B) (C) (D)
2. (A) (B) (C) (D)
3. (A) (B) (C) (D)
4. (A) (B) (C) (D)
5. (A) (B) (C) (D)
6. (A) (B) (C) (D)
7. (A) (B) (C) (D)
8. (A) (B) (C) (D)
9. (A) (B) (C) (D)
10. (A) (B) (C) (D)
11. (A) (B) (C) (D)
12. (A) (B) (C) (D)
13. (A) (B) (C) (D)
14. (A) (B) (C) (D)
15. (A) (B) (C) (D)
16. (A) (B) (C) (D)
17. (A) (B) (C) (D)
18. (A) (B) (C) (D)
19. (A) (B) (C) (D)
20. (A) (B) (C) (D)
21. (A) (B) (C) (D)
22. (A) (B) (C) (D)
23. (A) (B) (C) (D)
24. (A) (B) (C) (D)
25. (A) (B) (C) (D)

Arithmetic Reasoning

1. (A) (B) (C) (D)
2. (A) (B) (C) (D)
3. (A) (B) (C) (D)
4. (A) (B) (C) (D)
5. (A) (B) (C) (D)
6. (A) (B) (C) (D)
7. (A) (B) (C) (D)

8. (A) (B) (C) (D)
9. (A) (B) (C) (D)
10. (A) (B) (C) (D)
11. (A) (B) (C) (D)
12. (A) (B) (C) (D)
13. (A) (B) (C) (D)
14. (A) (B) (C) (D)
15. (A) (B) (C) (D)
16. (A) (B) (C) (D)
17. (A) (B) (C) (D)
18. (A) (B) (C) (D)
19. (A) (B) (C) (D)
20. (A) (B) (C) (D)
21. (A) (B) (C) (D)
22. (A) (B) (C) (D)
23. (A) (B) (C) (D)
24. (A) (B) (C) (D)
25. (A) (B) (C) (D)
26. (A) (B) (C) (D)
27. (A) (B) (C) (D)
28. (A) (B) (C) (D)
29. (A) (B) (C) (D)
30. (A) (B) (C) (D)

Word Knowledge

1. (A) (B) (C) (D)
2. (A) (B) (C) (D)
3. (A) (B) (C) (D)
4. (A) (B) (C) (D)
5. (A) (B) (C) (D)
6. (A) (B) (C) (D)
7. (A) (B) (C) (D)
8. (A) (B) (C) (D)
9. (A) (B) (C) (D)
10. (A) (B) (C) (D)
11. (A) (B) (C) (D)

12. (A) (B) (C) (D)
13. (A) (B) (C) (D)
14. (A) (B) (C) (D)
15. (A) (B) (C) (D)
16. (A) (B) (C) (D)
17. (A) (B) (C) (D)
18. (A) (B) (C) (D)
19. (A) (B) (C) (D)
20. (A) (B) (C) (D)
21. (A) (B) (C) (D)
22. (A) (B) (C) (D)
23. (A) (B) (C) (D)
24. (A) (B) (C) (D)
25. (A) (B) (C) (D)
26. (A) (B) (C) (D)
27. (A) (B) (C) (D)
28. (A) (B) (C) (D)
29. (A) (B) (C) (D)
30. (A) (B) (C) (D)
31. (A) (B) (C) (D)
32. (A) (B) (C) (D)
33. (A) (B) (C) (D)
34. (A) (B) (C) (D)
35. (A) (B) (C) (D)

Paragraph Comprehension

1. (A) (B) (C) (D)
2. (A) (B) (C) (D)
3. (A) (B) (C) (D)
4. (A) (B) (C) (D)
5. (A) (B) (C) (D)
6. (A) (B) (C) (D)
7. (A) (B) (C) (D)
8. (A) (B) (C) (D)
9. (A) (B) (C) (D)
10. (A) (B) (C) (D)

11. Ⓐ Ⓑ Ⓒ Ⓓ
12. Ⓐ Ⓑ Ⓒ Ⓓ
13. Ⓐ Ⓑ Ⓒ Ⓓ
14. Ⓐ Ⓑ Ⓒ Ⓓ
15. Ⓐ Ⓑ Ⓒ Ⓓ

Auto & Shop

1. Ⓐ Ⓑ Ⓒ Ⓓ
2. Ⓐ Ⓑ Ⓒ Ⓓ
3. Ⓐ Ⓑ Ⓒ Ⓓ
4. Ⓐ Ⓑ Ⓒ Ⓓ
5. Ⓐ Ⓑ Ⓒ Ⓓ
6. Ⓐ Ⓑ Ⓒ Ⓓ
7. Ⓐ Ⓑ Ⓒ Ⓓ
8. Ⓐ Ⓑ Ⓒ Ⓓ
9. Ⓐ Ⓑ Ⓒ Ⓓ
10. Ⓐ Ⓑ Ⓒ Ⓓ
11. Ⓐ Ⓑ Ⓒ Ⓓ
12. Ⓐ Ⓑ Ⓒ Ⓓ
13. Ⓐ Ⓑ Ⓒ Ⓓ
14. Ⓐ Ⓑ Ⓒ Ⓓ
15. Ⓐ Ⓑ Ⓒ Ⓓ
16. Ⓐ Ⓑ Ⓒ Ⓓ
17. Ⓐ Ⓑ Ⓒ Ⓓ
18. Ⓐ Ⓑ Ⓒ Ⓓ
19. Ⓐ Ⓑ Ⓒ Ⓓ
20. Ⓐ Ⓑ Ⓒ Ⓓ
21. Ⓐ Ⓑ Ⓒ Ⓓ
22. Ⓐ Ⓑ Ⓒ Ⓓ
23. Ⓐ Ⓑ Ⓒ Ⓓ
24. Ⓐ Ⓑ Ⓒ Ⓓ
25. Ⓐ Ⓑ Ⓒ Ⓓ

Mathematics Knowledge

1. Ⓐ Ⓑ Ⓒ Ⓓ
2. Ⓐ Ⓑ Ⓒ Ⓓ
3. Ⓐ Ⓑ Ⓒ Ⓓ
4. Ⓐ Ⓑ Ⓒ Ⓓ

5. Ⓐ Ⓑ Ⓒ Ⓓ
6. Ⓐ Ⓑ Ⓒ Ⓓ
7. Ⓐ Ⓑ Ⓒ Ⓓ
8. Ⓐ Ⓑ Ⓒ Ⓓ
9. Ⓐ Ⓑ Ⓒ Ⓓ
10. Ⓐ Ⓑ Ⓒ Ⓓ
11. Ⓐ Ⓑ Ⓒ Ⓓ
12. Ⓐ Ⓑ Ⓒ Ⓓ
13. Ⓐ Ⓑ Ⓒ Ⓓ
14. Ⓐ Ⓑ Ⓒ Ⓓ
15. Ⓐ Ⓑ Ⓒ Ⓓ
16. Ⓐ Ⓑ Ⓒ Ⓓ
17. Ⓐ Ⓑ Ⓒ Ⓓ
18. Ⓐ Ⓑ Ⓒ Ⓓ
19. Ⓐ Ⓑ Ⓒ Ⓓ
20. Ⓐ Ⓑ Ⓒ Ⓓ
21. Ⓐ Ⓑ Ⓒ Ⓓ
22. Ⓐ Ⓑ Ⓒ Ⓓ
23. Ⓐ Ⓑ Ⓒ Ⓓ
24. Ⓐ Ⓑ Ⓒ Ⓓ
25. Ⓐ Ⓑ Ⓒ Ⓓ

Mechanical Comprehension

1. Ⓐ Ⓑ Ⓒ Ⓓ
2. Ⓐ Ⓑ Ⓒ Ⓓ
3. Ⓐ Ⓑ Ⓒ Ⓓ
4. Ⓐ Ⓑ Ⓒ Ⓓ
5. Ⓐ Ⓑ Ⓒ Ⓓ
6. Ⓐ Ⓑ Ⓒ Ⓓ
7. Ⓐ Ⓑ Ⓒ Ⓓ
8. Ⓐ Ⓑ Ⓒ Ⓓ
9. Ⓐ Ⓑ Ⓒ Ⓓ
10. Ⓐ Ⓑ Ⓒ Ⓓ
11. Ⓐ Ⓑ Ⓒ Ⓓ
12. Ⓐ Ⓑ Ⓒ Ⓓ
13. Ⓐ Ⓑ Ⓒ Ⓓ
14. Ⓐ Ⓑ Ⓒ Ⓓ
15. Ⓐ Ⓑ Ⓒ Ⓓ

16. Ⓐ Ⓑ Ⓒ Ⓓ
17. Ⓐ Ⓑ Ⓒ Ⓓ
18. Ⓐ Ⓑ Ⓒ Ⓓ
19. Ⓐ Ⓑ Ⓒ Ⓓ
20. Ⓐ Ⓑ Ⓒ Ⓓ
21. Ⓐ Ⓑ Ⓒ Ⓓ
22. Ⓐ Ⓑ Ⓒ Ⓓ
23. Ⓐ Ⓑ Ⓒ Ⓓ
24. Ⓐ Ⓑ Ⓒ Ⓓ
25. Ⓐ Ⓑ Ⓒ Ⓓ

Electronics Information

1. Ⓐ Ⓑ Ⓒ Ⓓ
2. Ⓐ Ⓑ Ⓒ Ⓓ
3. Ⓐ Ⓑ Ⓒ Ⓓ
4. Ⓐ Ⓑ Ⓒ Ⓓ
5. Ⓐ Ⓑ Ⓒ Ⓓ
6. Ⓐ Ⓑ Ⓒ Ⓓ
7. Ⓐ Ⓑ Ⓒ Ⓓ
8. Ⓐ Ⓑ Ⓒ Ⓓ
9. Ⓐ Ⓑ Ⓒ Ⓓ
10. Ⓐ Ⓑ Ⓒ Ⓓ
11. Ⓐ Ⓑ Ⓒ Ⓓ
12. Ⓐ Ⓑ Ⓒ Ⓓ
13. Ⓐ Ⓑ Ⓒ Ⓓ
14. Ⓐ Ⓑ Ⓒ Ⓓ
15. Ⓐ Ⓑ Ⓒ Ⓓ
16. Ⓐ Ⓑ Ⓒ Ⓓ
17. Ⓐ Ⓑ Ⓒ Ⓓ
18. Ⓐ Ⓑ Ⓒ Ⓓ
19. Ⓐ Ⓑ Ⓒ Ⓓ
20. Ⓐ Ⓑ Ⓒ Ⓓ

Assembling
Objects

1. Ⓐ Ⓑ Ⓒ Ⓓ
2. Ⓐ Ⓑ Ⓒ Ⓓ
3. Ⓐ Ⓑ Ⓒ Ⓓ
4. Ⓐ Ⓑ Ⓒ Ⓓ
5. Ⓐ Ⓑ Ⓒ Ⓓ
6. Ⓐ Ⓑ Ⓒ Ⓓ
7. Ⓐ Ⓑ Ⓒ Ⓓ
8. Ⓐ Ⓑ Ⓒ Ⓓ
9. Ⓐ Ⓑ Ⓒ Ⓓ
10. Ⓐ Ⓑ Ⓒ Ⓓ
11. Ⓐ Ⓑ Ⓒ Ⓓ
12. Ⓐ Ⓑ Ⓒ Ⓓ
13. Ⓐ Ⓑ Ⓒ Ⓓ
14. Ⓐ Ⓑ Ⓒ Ⓓ
15. Ⓐ Ⓑ Ⓒ Ⓓ
16. Ⓐ Ⓑ Ⓒ Ⓓ

ASVAB – TEST 2

General Science

1. (A) (B) (C) (D)
2. (A) (B) (C) (D)
3. (A) (B) (C) (D)
4. (A) (B) (C) (D)
5. (A) (B) (C) (D)
6. (A) (B) (C) (D)
7. (A) (B) (C) (D)
8. (A) (B) (C) (D)
9. (A) (B) (C) (D)
10. (A) (B) (C) (D)
11. (A) (B) (C) (D)
12. (A) (B) (C) (D)
13. (A) (B) (C) (D)
14. (A) (B) (C) (D)
15. (A) (B) (C) (D)
16. (A) (B) (C) (D)
17. (A) (B) (C) (D)
18. (A) (B) (C) (D)
19. (A) (B) (C) (D)
20. (A) (B) (C) (D)
21. (A) (B) (C) (D)
22. (A) (B) (C) (D)
23. (A) (B) (C) (D)
24. (A) (B) (C) (D)
25. (A) (B) (C) (D)

Arithmetic Reasoning

1. (A) (B) (C) (D)
2. (A) (B) (C) (D)
3. (A) (B) (C) (D)
4. (A) (B) (C) (D)
5. (A) (B) (C) (D)
6. (A) (B) (C) (D)
7. (A) (B) (C) (D)

8. (A) (B) (C) (D)
9. (A) (B) (C) (D)
10. (A) (B) (C) (D)
11. (A) (B) (C) (D)
12. (A) (B) (C) (D)
13. (A) (B) (C) (D)
14. (A) (B) (C) (D)
15. (A) (B) (C) (D)
16. (A) (B) (C) (D)
17. (A) (B) (C) (D)
18. (A) (B) (C) (D)
19. (A) (B) (C) (D)
20. (A) (B) (C) (D)
21. (A) (B) (C) (D)
22. (A) (B) (C) (D)
23. (A) (B) (C) (D)
24. (A) (B) (C) (D)
25. (A) (B) (C) (D)
26. (A) (B) (C) (D)
27. (A) (B) (C) (D)
28. (A) (B) (C) (D)
29. (A) (B) (C) (D)
30. (A) (B) (C) (D)

Word Knowledge

1. (A) (B) (C) (D)
2. (A) (B) (C) (D)
3. (A) (B) (C) (D)
4. (A) (B) (C) (D)
5. (A) (B) (C) (D)
6. (A) (B) (C) (D)
7. (A) (B) (C) (D)
8. (A) (B) (C) (D)
9. (A) (B) (C) (D)
10. (A) (B) (C) (D)
11. (A) (B) (C) (D)

12. (A) (B) (C) (D)
13. (A) (B) (C) (D)
14. (A) (B) (C) (D)
15. (A) (B) (C) (D)
16. (A) (B) (C) (D)
17. (A) (B) (C) (D)
18. (A) (B) (C) (D)
19. (A) (B) (C) (D)
20. (A) (B) (C) (D)
21. (A) (B) (C) (D)
22. (A) (B) (C) (D)
23. (A) (B) (C) (D)
24. (A) (B) (C) (D)
25. (A) (B) (C) (D)
26. (A) (B) (C) (D)
27. (A) (B) (C) (D)
28. (A) (B) (C) (D)
29. (A) (B) (C) (D)
30. (A) (B) (C) (D)
31. (A) (B) (C) (D)
32. (A) (B) (C) (D)
33. (A) (B) (C) (D)
34. (A) (B) (C) (D)
35. (A) (B) (C) (D)

Paragraph Comprehension

1. (A) (B) (C) (D)
2. (A) (B) (C) (D)
3. (A) (B) (C) (D)
4. (A) (B) (C) (D)
5. (A) (B) (C) (D)
6. (A) (B) (C) (D)
7. (A) (B) (C) (D)
8. (A) (B) (C) (D)
9. (A) (B) (C) (D)
10. (A) (B) (C) (D)

11. Ⓐ Ⓑ Ⓒ Ⓓ
12. Ⓐ Ⓑ Ⓒ Ⓓ
13. Ⓐ Ⓑ Ⓒ Ⓓ
14. Ⓐ Ⓑ Ⓒ Ⓓ
15. Ⓐ Ⓑ Ⓒ Ⓓ

Auto & Shop

1. Ⓐ Ⓑ Ⓒ Ⓓ
2. Ⓐ Ⓑ Ⓒ Ⓓ
3. Ⓐ Ⓑ Ⓒ Ⓓ
4. Ⓐ Ⓑ Ⓒ Ⓓ
5. Ⓐ Ⓑ Ⓒ Ⓓ
6. Ⓐ Ⓑ Ⓒ Ⓓ
7. Ⓐ Ⓑ Ⓒ Ⓓ
8. Ⓐ Ⓑ Ⓒ Ⓓ
9. Ⓐ Ⓑ Ⓒ Ⓓ
10. Ⓐ Ⓑ Ⓒ Ⓓ
11. Ⓐ Ⓑ Ⓒ Ⓓ
12. Ⓐ Ⓑ Ⓒ Ⓓ
13. Ⓐ Ⓑ Ⓒ Ⓓ
14. Ⓐ Ⓑ Ⓒ Ⓓ
15. Ⓐ Ⓑ Ⓒ Ⓓ
16. Ⓐ Ⓑ Ⓒ Ⓓ
17. Ⓐ Ⓑ Ⓒ Ⓓ
18. Ⓐ Ⓑ Ⓒ Ⓓ
19. Ⓐ Ⓑ Ⓒ Ⓓ
20. Ⓐ Ⓑ Ⓒ Ⓓ
21. Ⓐ Ⓑ Ⓒ Ⓓ
22. Ⓐ Ⓑ Ⓒ Ⓓ
23. Ⓐ Ⓑ Ⓒ Ⓓ
24. Ⓐ Ⓑ Ⓒ Ⓓ
25. Ⓐ Ⓑ Ⓒ Ⓓ

Mathematics Knowledge

1. Ⓐ Ⓑ Ⓒ Ⓓ
2. Ⓐ Ⓑ Ⓒ Ⓓ
3. Ⓐ Ⓑ Ⓒ Ⓓ
4. Ⓐ Ⓑ Ⓒ Ⓓ

5. Ⓐ Ⓑ Ⓒ Ⓓ
6. Ⓐ Ⓑ Ⓒ Ⓓ
7. Ⓐ Ⓑ Ⓒ Ⓓ
8. Ⓐ Ⓑ Ⓒ Ⓓ
9. Ⓐ Ⓑ Ⓒ Ⓓ
10. Ⓐ Ⓑ Ⓒ Ⓓ
11. Ⓐ Ⓑ Ⓒ Ⓓ
12. Ⓐ Ⓑ Ⓒ Ⓓ
13. Ⓐ Ⓑ Ⓒ Ⓓ
14. Ⓐ Ⓑ Ⓒ Ⓓ
15. Ⓐ Ⓑ Ⓒ Ⓓ
16. Ⓐ Ⓑ Ⓒ Ⓓ
17. Ⓐ Ⓑ Ⓒ Ⓓ
18. Ⓐ Ⓑ Ⓒ Ⓓ
19. Ⓐ Ⓑ Ⓒ Ⓓ
20. Ⓐ Ⓑ Ⓒ Ⓓ
21. Ⓐ Ⓑ Ⓒ Ⓓ
22. Ⓐ Ⓑ Ⓒ Ⓓ
23. Ⓐ Ⓑ Ⓒ Ⓓ
24. Ⓐ Ⓑ Ⓒ Ⓓ
25. Ⓐ Ⓑ Ⓒ Ⓓ

Mechanical Comprehension

1. Ⓐ Ⓑ Ⓒ Ⓓ
2. Ⓐ Ⓑ Ⓒ Ⓓ
3. Ⓐ Ⓑ Ⓒ Ⓓ
4. Ⓐ Ⓑ Ⓒ Ⓓ
5. Ⓐ Ⓑ Ⓒ Ⓓ
6. Ⓐ Ⓑ Ⓒ Ⓓ
7. Ⓐ Ⓑ Ⓒ Ⓓ
8. Ⓐ Ⓑ Ⓒ Ⓓ
9. Ⓐ Ⓑ Ⓒ Ⓓ
10. Ⓐ Ⓑ Ⓒ Ⓓ
11. Ⓐ Ⓑ Ⓒ Ⓓ
12. Ⓐ Ⓑ Ⓒ Ⓓ
13. Ⓐ Ⓑ Ⓒ Ⓓ
14. Ⓐ Ⓑ Ⓒ Ⓓ
15. Ⓐ Ⓑ Ⓒ Ⓓ

16. Ⓐ Ⓑ Ⓒ Ⓓ
17. Ⓐ Ⓑ Ⓒ Ⓓ
18. Ⓐ Ⓑ Ⓒ Ⓓ
19. Ⓐ Ⓑ Ⓒ Ⓓ
20. Ⓐ Ⓑ Ⓒ Ⓓ
21. Ⓐ Ⓑ Ⓒ Ⓓ
22. Ⓐ Ⓑ Ⓒ Ⓓ
23. Ⓐ Ⓑ Ⓒ Ⓓ
24. Ⓐ Ⓑ Ⓒ Ⓓ
25. Ⓐ Ⓑ Ⓒ Ⓓ

Electronics Information

1. Ⓐ Ⓑ Ⓒ Ⓓ
2. Ⓐ Ⓑ Ⓒ Ⓓ
3. Ⓐ Ⓑ Ⓒ Ⓓ
4. Ⓐ Ⓑ Ⓒ Ⓓ
5. Ⓐ Ⓑ Ⓒ Ⓓ
6. Ⓐ Ⓑ Ⓒ Ⓓ
7. Ⓐ Ⓑ Ⓒ Ⓓ
8. Ⓐ Ⓑ Ⓒ Ⓓ
9. Ⓐ Ⓑ Ⓒ Ⓓ
10. Ⓐ Ⓑ Ⓒ Ⓓ
11. Ⓐ Ⓑ Ⓒ Ⓓ
12. Ⓐ Ⓑ Ⓒ Ⓓ
13. Ⓐ Ⓑ Ⓒ Ⓓ
14. Ⓐ Ⓑ Ⓒ Ⓓ
15. Ⓐ Ⓑ Ⓒ Ⓓ
16. Ⓐ Ⓑ Ⓒ Ⓓ
17. Ⓐ Ⓑ Ⓒ Ⓓ
18. Ⓐ Ⓑ Ⓒ Ⓓ
19. Ⓐ Ⓑ Ⓒ Ⓓ
20. Ⓐ Ⓑ Ⓒ Ⓓ

ASVAB – TEST 3

General Science

1. Ⓐ Ⓑ Ⓒ Ⓓ
2. Ⓐ Ⓑ Ⓒ Ⓓ
3. Ⓐ Ⓑ Ⓒ Ⓓ
4. Ⓐ Ⓑ Ⓒ Ⓓ
5. Ⓐ Ⓑ Ⓒ Ⓓ
6. Ⓐ Ⓑ Ⓒ Ⓓ
7. Ⓐ Ⓑ Ⓒ Ⓓ
8. Ⓐ Ⓑ Ⓒ Ⓓ
9. Ⓐ Ⓑ Ⓒ Ⓓ
10. Ⓐ Ⓑ Ⓒ Ⓓ
11. Ⓐ Ⓑ Ⓒ Ⓓ
12. Ⓐ Ⓑ Ⓒ Ⓓ
13. Ⓐ Ⓑ Ⓒ Ⓓ
14. Ⓐ Ⓑ Ⓒ Ⓓ
15. Ⓐ Ⓑ Ⓒ Ⓓ
16. Ⓐ Ⓑ Ⓒ Ⓓ
17. Ⓐ Ⓑ Ⓒ Ⓓ
18. Ⓐ Ⓑ Ⓒ Ⓓ
19. Ⓐ Ⓑ Ⓒ Ⓓ
20. Ⓐ Ⓑ Ⓒ Ⓓ
21. Ⓐ Ⓑ Ⓒ Ⓓ
22. Ⓐ Ⓑ Ⓒ Ⓓ
23. Ⓐ Ⓑ Ⓒ Ⓓ
24. Ⓐ Ⓑ Ⓒ Ⓓ
25. Ⓐ Ⓑ Ⓒ Ⓓ

Arithmetic Reasoning

1. Ⓐ Ⓑ Ⓒ Ⓓ
2. Ⓐ Ⓑ Ⓒ Ⓓ
3. Ⓐ Ⓑ Ⓒ Ⓓ
4. Ⓐ Ⓑ Ⓒ Ⓓ
5. Ⓐ Ⓑ Ⓒ Ⓓ
6. Ⓐ Ⓑ Ⓒ Ⓓ
7. Ⓐ Ⓑ Ⓒ Ⓓ

(General Science continued)

8. Ⓐ Ⓑ Ⓒ Ⓓ
9. Ⓐ Ⓑ Ⓒ Ⓓ
10. Ⓐ Ⓑ Ⓒ Ⓓ
11. Ⓐ Ⓑ Ⓒ Ⓓ
12. Ⓐ Ⓑ Ⓒ Ⓓ
13. Ⓐ Ⓑ Ⓒ Ⓓ
14. Ⓐ Ⓑ Ⓒ Ⓓ
15. Ⓐ Ⓑ Ⓒ Ⓓ
16. Ⓐ Ⓑ Ⓒ Ⓓ
17. Ⓐ Ⓑ Ⓒ Ⓓ
18. Ⓐ Ⓑ Ⓒ Ⓓ
19. Ⓐ Ⓑ Ⓒ Ⓓ
20. Ⓐ Ⓑ Ⓒ Ⓓ
21. Ⓐ Ⓑ Ⓒ Ⓓ
22. Ⓐ Ⓑ Ⓒ Ⓓ
23. Ⓐ Ⓑ Ⓒ Ⓓ
24. Ⓐ Ⓑ Ⓒ Ⓓ
25. Ⓐ Ⓑ Ⓒ Ⓓ
26. Ⓐ Ⓑ Ⓒ Ⓓ
27. Ⓐ Ⓑ Ⓒ Ⓓ
28. Ⓐ Ⓑ Ⓒ Ⓓ
29. Ⓐ Ⓑ Ⓒ Ⓓ
30. Ⓐ Ⓑ Ⓒ Ⓓ

Word Knowledge

1. Ⓐ Ⓑ Ⓒ Ⓓ
2. Ⓐ Ⓑ Ⓒ Ⓓ
3. Ⓐ Ⓑ Ⓒ Ⓓ
4. Ⓐ Ⓑ Ⓒ Ⓓ
5. Ⓐ Ⓑ Ⓒ Ⓓ
6. Ⓐ Ⓑ Ⓒ Ⓓ
7. Ⓐ Ⓑ Ⓒ Ⓓ
8. Ⓐ Ⓑ Ⓒ Ⓓ
9. Ⓐ Ⓑ Ⓒ Ⓓ
10. Ⓐ Ⓑ Ⓒ Ⓓ
11. Ⓐ Ⓑ Ⓒ Ⓓ

12. Ⓐ Ⓑ Ⓒ Ⓓ
13. Ⓐ Ⓑ Ⓒ Ⓓ
14. Ⓐ Ⓑ Ⓒ Ⓓ
15. Ⓐ Ⓑ Ⓒ Ⓓ
16. Ⓐ Ⓑ Ⓒ Ⓓ
17. Ⓐ Ⓑ Ⓒ Ⓓ
18. Ⓐ Ⓑ Ⓒ Ⓓ
19. Ⓐ Ⓑ Ⓒ Ⓓ
20. Ⓐ Ⓑ Ⓒ Ⓓ
21. Ⓐ Ⓑ Ⓒ Ⓓ
22. Ⓐ Ⓑ Ⓒ Ⓓ
23. Ⓐ Ⓑ Ⓒ Ⓓ
24. Ⓐ Ⓑ Ⓒ Ⓓ
25. Ⓐ Ⓑ Ⓒ Ⓓ
26. Ⓐ Ⓑ Ⓒ Ⓓ
27. Ⓐ Ⓑ Ⓒ Ⓓ
28. Ⓐ Ⓑ Ⓒ Ⓓ
29. Ⓐ Ⓑ Ⓒ Ⓓ
30. Ⓐ Ⓑ Ⓒ Ⓓ
31. Ⓐ Ⓑ Ⓒ Ⓓ
32. Ⓐ Ⓑ Ⓒ Ⓓ
33. Ⓐ Ⓑ Ⓒ Ⓓ
34. Ⓐ Ⓑ Ⓒ Ⓓ
35. Ⓐ Ⓑ Ⓒ Ⓓ

Paragraph Comprehension

1. Ⓐ Ⓑ Ⓒ Ⓓ
2. Ⓐ Ⓑ Ⓒ Ⓓ
3. Ⓐ Ⓑ Ⓒ Ⓓ
4. Ⓐ Ⓑ Ⓒ Ⓓ
5. Ⓐ Ⓑ Ⓒ Ⓓ
6. Ⓐ Ⓑ Ⓒ Ⓓ
7. Ⓐ Ⓑ Ⓒ Ⓓ
8. Ⓐ Ⓑ Ⓒ Ⓓ
9. Ⓐ Ⓑ Ⓒ Ⓓ
10. Ⓐ Ⓑ Ⓒ Ⓓ

11. Ⓐ Ⓑ Ⓒ Ⓓ
12. Ⓐ Ⓑ Ⓒ Ⓓ
13. Ⓐ Ⓑ Ⓒ Ⓓ
14. Ⓐ Ⓑ Ⓒ Ⓓ
15. Ⓐ Ⓑ Ⓒ Ⓓ

Auto & Shop

1. Ⓐ Ⓑ Ⓒ Ⓓ
2. Ⓐ Ⓑ Ⓒ Ⓓ
3. Ⓐ Ⓑ Ⓒ Ⓓ
4. Ⓐ Ⓑ Ⓒ Ⓓ
5. Ⓐ Ⓑ Ⓒ Ⓓ
6. Ⓐ Ⓑ Ⓒ Ⓓ
7. Ⓐ Ⓑ Ⓒ Ⓓ
8. Ⓐ Ⓑ Ⓒ Ⓓ
9. Ⓐ Ⓑ Ⓒ Ⓓ
10. Ⓐ Ⓑ Ⓒ Ⓓ
11. Ⓐ Ⓑ Ⓒ Ⓓ
12. Ⓐ Ⓑ Ⓒ Ⓓ
13. Ⓐ Ⓑ Ⓒ Ⓓ
14. Ⓐ Ⓑ Ⓒ Ⓓ
15. Ⓐ Ⓑ Ⓒ Ⓓ
16. Ⓐ Ⓑ Ⓒ Ⓓ
17. Ⓐ Ⓑ Ⓒ Ⓓ
18. Ⓐ Ⓑ Ⓒ Ⓓ
19. Ⓐ Ⓑ Ⓒ Ⓓ
20. Ⓐ Ⓑ Ⓒ Ⓓ
21. Ⓐ Ⓑ Ⓒ Ⓓ
22. Ⓐ Ⓑ Ⓒ Ⓓ
23. Ⓐ Ⓑ Ⓒ Ⓓ
24. Ⓐ Ⓑ Ⓒ Ⓓ
25. Ⓐ Ⓑ Ⓒ Ⓓ

Mathematics Knowledge

1. Ⓐ Ⓑ Ⓒ Ⓓ
2. Ⓐ Ⓑ Ⓒ Ⓓ
3. Ⓐ Ⓑ Ⓒ Ⓓ
4. Ⓐ Ⓑ Ⓒ Ⓓ

5. Ⓐ Ⓑ Ⓒ Ⓓ
6. Ⓐ Ⓑ Ⓒ Ⓓ
7. Ⓐ Ⓑ Ⓒ Ⓓ
8. Ⓐ Ⓑ Ⓒ Ⓓ
9. Ⓐ Ⓑ Ⓒ Ⓓ
10. Ⓐ Ⓑ Ⓒ Ⓓ
11. Ⓐ Ⓑ Ⓒ Ⓓ
12. Ⓐ Ⓑ Ⓒ Ⓓ
13. Ⓐ Ⓑ Ⓒ Ⓓ
14. Ⓐ Ⓑ Ⓒ Ⓓ
15. Ⓐ Ⓑ Ⓒ Ⓓ
16. Ⓐ Ⓑ Ⓒ Ⓓ
17. Ⓐ Ⓑ Ⓒ Ⓓ
18. Ⓐ Ⓑ Ⓒ Ⓓ
19. Ⓐ Ⓑ Ⓒ Ⓓ
20. Ⓐ Ⓑ Ⓒ Ⓓ
21. Ⓐ Ⓑ Ⓒ Ⓓ
22. Ⓐ Ⓑ Ⓒ Ⓓ
23. Ⓐ Ⓑ Ⓒ Ⓓ
24. Ⓐ Ⓑ Ⓒ Ⓓ
25. Ⓐ Ⓑ Ⓒ Ⓓ

Mechanical Comprehension

1. Ⓐ Ⓑ Ⓒ Ⓓ
2. Ⓐ Ⓑ Ⓒ Ⓓ
3. Ⓐ Ⓑ Ⓒ Ⓓ
4. Ⓐ Ⓑ Ⓒ Ⓓ
5. Ⓐ Ⓑ Ⓒ Ⓓ
6. Ⓐ Ⓑ Ⓒ Ⓓ
7. Ⓐ Ⓑ Ⓒ Ⓓ
8. Ⓐ Ⓑ Ⓒ Ⓓ
9. Ⓐ Ⓑ Ⓒ Ⓓ
10. Ⓐ Ⓑ Ⓒ Ⓓ
11. Ⓐ Ⓑ Ⓒ Ⓓ
12. Ⓐ Ⓑ Ⓒ Ⓓ
13. Ⓐ Ⓑ Ⓒ Ⓓ
14. Ⓐ Ⓑ Ⓒ Ⓓ
15. Ⓐ Ⓑ Ⓒ Ⓓ

16. Ⓐ Ⓑ Ⓒ Ⓓ
17. Ⓐ Ⓑ Ⓒ Ⓓ
18. Ⓐ Ⓑ Ⓒ Ⓓ
19. Ⓐ Ⓑ Ⓒ Ⓓ
20. Ⓐ Ⓑ Ⓒ Ⓓ
21. Ⓐ Ⓑ Ⓒ Ⓓ
22. Ⓐ Ⓑ Ⓒ Ⓓ
23. Ⓐ Ⓑ Ⓒ Ⓓ
24. Ⓐ Ⓑ Ⓒ Ⓓ
25. Ⓐ Ⓑ Ⓒ Ⓓ

Electronics Information

1. Ⓐ Ⓑ Ⓒ Ⓓ
2. Ⓐ Ⓑ Ⓒ Ⓓ
3. Ⓐ Ⓑ Ⓒ Ⓓ
4. Ⓐ Ⓑ Ⓒ Ⓓ
5. Ⓐ Ⓑ Ⓒ Ⓓ
6. Ⓐ Ⓑ Ⓒ Ⓓ
7. Ⓐ Ⓑ Ⓒ Ⓓ
8. Ⓐ Ⓑ Ⓒ Ⓓ
9. Ⓐ Ⓑ Ⓒ Ⓓ
10. Ⓐ Ⓑ Ⓒ Ⓓ
11. Ⓐ Ⓑ Ⓒ Ⓓ
12. Ⓐ Ⓑ Ⓒ Ⓓ
13. Ⓐ Ⓑ Ⓒ Ⓓ
14. Ⓐ Ⓑ Ⓒ Ⓓ
15. Ⓐ Ⓑ Ⓒ Ⓓ
16. Ⓐ Ⓑ Ⓒ Ⓓ
17. Ⓐ Ⓑ Ⓒ Ⓓ
18. Ⓐ Ⓑ Ⓒ Ⓓ
19. Ⓐ Ⓑ Ⓒ Ⓓ
20. Ⓐ Ⓑ Ⓒ Ⓓ

ASVAB

*Armed Services Vocational
Aptitude Battery*

Index

NOTES

NOTES

NOTES

NOTES

Do you know that the U.S. Armed Services provides CLEP exams *free of charge* for eligible military and civilian personnel? The CLEP program offers you college credits without the classes.

Want to learn more about the college credit CLEP program and exciting options available to you?

Visit us—your source for the best CLEP preparation!

www.rea.com/clep